The Army and Society
1815-1914

Themes in British Social History

edited by Dr J. Stevenson

The Englishman's Health: Disease and Nutrition 1500–1700
Poverty and Society 1500–1660
*Popular Disturbances in England 1700–1870
*Religion and Society in Industrial England 1740–1940
Religion and Society in Tudor England
Sex, Politics and Social Change 1875–1975
*A Social History of Medicine
*Leisure and Society 1830–1950
*The Army and Society 1815–1914
*Before the Welfare State: Social Administration in Early Industrial Britain 1780–1850
A History of Education in Britain 1500–1800
*The Gentry: the Rise and Fall of a Ruling Class
*The Press and Society from Caxton to Northcliffe
Crime in Early Modern England 1550–1750
The English Family 1450–1700

*already published

The Army and Society
1815–1914

Edward M. Spiers

Longman
London and New York

Longman Group Limited London

Associated companies, branches and representatives throughout the world

Published in the United States of America by Longman Inc., New York

First published 1980

British Library Cataloguing in Publication Data

Spiers, Edward M
The army and society, 1815-1914. -

(Themes in British social history).
1. Great Britain. Army - History
2. Sociology, Military - Great Britain
I. Title II. Series
301.5'93'0941 UA649 79-40042

ISBN 0 582 48565 7
ISBN 0 582 48566 5 Pbk

Set in Compugraphic Baskerville 10 on 11pt
Printed in Hong Kong by
Wilture Enterprises (International) Ltd.

Contents

Acknowledgements

I should like to acknowledge my indebtedness to Her Majesty the Queen for her gracious permission to use materials from the Royal Archives at Windsor Castle and to consult the royal correspondence in the Palmerston (Broadlands) Mss. For access to the Palmerston Mss, I am also grateful to the Trustees of the Broadlands Archives Trust and to the Royal Commission on Historical Manuscripts. I must further thank Sir Robin Mackworth-Young, the Royal Librarian, and his staff for their efforts on my behalf. The following individuals and institutions have kindly given me access to unpublished manuscripts for which they own the copyright: Mr Bonham Carter, the Centre for Military Archives, King's College, London; His Grace, the Earl of Dalhousie; Mr P. C. Metcalfe; Mrs J. Spencer Ellison; the Earl of Esher; the Earl of Haig; and the Earl of Pembroke.

I am obliged to several librarians for their assistance and co-operation, namely Mr C. A. Potts (Ministry of Defence Library), Mr J. K. Bates (Scottish Record Office), Mr B. Mollo (National Army Museum), Mr J. S. G. Simmons (Codrington Library, All Souls, Oxford); the curators and directors of the British Library, the Public Record Office, and the staff of the National Library of Scotland. Finally, I am indebted to Mrs E. McClea for her careful and accurate typing, and to Fiona, my wife, for her advice, encouragement, and constructive criticism.

Cover illustrations: Radio Times Hulton Picture Library (Horseguards); Mary Evans Picture Library (Ceremonial); Reproduced by Gracious Permission of Her Majesty the Queen (Wounded soldier).

1 The officer corps

Throughout the nineteenth century the British army perpetuated an officer gentleman tradition. It attracted officers who were prepared to serve the State in a manner which accorded with the customs and values of the English ruling class. An officer had either to be born and bred and educated as a gentleman, or be prepared to act and behave like a 'natural' gentleman within the confines of regimental society. Embodied in the norms of gentlemanly behaviour were requirements of dress and deportment, an emphasis on honour and integrity, and a conformity with the manners and etiquette of polite society. Upholding these standards of behaviour was deemed necessary for maintaining the harmony and concord of the officers' mess; it was considered a prerequisite in earning the respect and obedience of the rank and file. Although the adequacy of these assumptions would be increasingly questioned in the late nineteenth century, as the profession confronted the impact of social and technological change, the officer gentleman tradition remained a pervasive influence.

The military was not the sole profession which relied upon the services of gentlemen. The Established Church, the Bar, the highest ranks of the Civil Service (especially the Diplomatic Service) and the magistracy were all dependent upon the public spirit, probity and education of those whom contemporaries described as gentlefolk. The qualities which set these pillars of society apart from the rest, though never precisely specified, were not confined to the aristocracy and the landed gentry. The qualities included, as W. L. Burn has stated, 'gentle birth, the ownership of land and if possible of money also, some degree of education, courage and a high sense of honour, generosity and unselfishness'.[1]

A gentleman could be defined as such without possessing all these attributes, indeed different groups of society would select and emphasize certain criteria while neglecting or excluding others. Nevertheless gentlemen, however broadly or ambiguously defined, were expected to serve the State because they had the qualifications in an unspecialized age to do so. These public servants were not motivated by a sense of duty alone; the State might not pay for their services but it 'guarded their privileges and possessions and, if only for this reason, they owed it loyalty'.[2] The problem which confronted all branches of the public service was to recruit men who possessed not only gentlemanly credentials, but also the aptitude and ability to become professionally competent.

Apart from the early months of the Crimean and South African Wars, the army rarely encountered sustained criticism of its professional competence. There were critics in the press and in politics who periodically campaigned in favour of army reform. So, too, did individual officers like Major-General John Mitchell, General Sir Charles Napier and Major-General Sir Patrick MacDougall. Yet the army had seemingly proved itself in many encounters; it had stood firm at Waterloo, had displayed exemplary heroism in the Crimea, had crushed the Mutiny in India, and had preserved and expanded the Empire. As Sir Garnet Wolseley prophesied in March 1878, 'great reforms are seldom effected in an army except after great reverses'.[3]

Lacking the salutary experience of 'great reverses' (the periodic colonial defeats were rarely decisive in themselves), the army continued to value its heroic, chivalrous concept of warfare. Emphasis was placed on qualities of character and morale, not intellect and application. Honour, courage and gallantry were rated above the acquisition of professional skills. Preserving the *esprit de corps* of the regimental system was deemed the essence of military efficiency. Since war was an uncertain business, what had succeeded in the past was considered the only touchstone for success in the future.

To sustain this code of values and the cohesive force of regimental *esprit de corps*, officers had to be gentlemen. Even Sir Garnet Wolseley, one of the few professional officers who emerged in the Victorian period, accepted this premise. Wolseley, though disparaged as 'no gentleman' and 'so very ambitious' by his critics,[4] always considered himself a gentleman. Admittedly, in *The Soldier's Pocket Book*, published in 1869, he had preferred to describe officers as soldiers and not gentlemen, but, unlike some historians, Wolseley regarded this iconoclastic work as a less than serious publication: he viewed its success as 'a never failing source of amusement'.[5] He never doubted that the army was a career only fit for gentlemen, albeit diligent and capable gentlemen. Ever contemptuous of his political masters, Wolseley delighted in contrasting their profession with his own. As he informed the Queen, 'The foolish public prefer believing the tradesman who has become a politician to the gentleman who wears Your Majesty's uniform'.[6]

So intense was the feeling about the officer gentleman tradition that promotions from the rank and file were never greatly encouraged. Almost every year some non-commissioned officers (NCOs) were promoted. During a major war the number of promotions was usually increased: 252 were promoted during the Crimean War. Once promoted, these former rankers could, like Major-General Cureton, attain high military rank, but the purchase system, by which officers could purchase their own promotion, reduced the vacancies available for officers without private means. After the abolition of the purchase system in 1871, promoted rankers could in theory rise more easily through the officer corps: Sir Hector Macdonald and Sir William Robertson even reached the ranks of general and field marshal respectively. These were rare exceptions, however. Few promoted non-commissioned officers rose beyond the rank of captain; many accepted the posts of quartermaster or riding master without any prospects of promotion. Officers commissioned from the ranks always remained a small proportion of the officer corps. Whereas the French army, by the 1870s, was obtaining one-third or more of its officers from the ranks,[7] the British army could not find more than 5 per cent of its combat officers from the rank and file (Table 1.1).

A reasonable case could be made for promoting officers from the ranks. As early as 1836 Lieutenant Thomas Blood, a promoted ranker, suggested that one-third of all commissions should be reserved for officers raised from the ranks. He reckoned that commissioned rankers were assiduous and attentive in their duties, and too familiar with the habits of the private soldier to be deceived by any malingering.[8] Equally important, argued ex-Sergeant Horace Wyndham, the former NCO, if previously a colour-sergeant, could understand the intricacies of regimental accounting. The promoted colour-sergeant, in other words, could supervise effectively such details as the pay of his men, the recovery of stoppages for 'necessaries and kit', fines for drunkenness, and the keeping of his company's savings-bank ledgers.[9] Nor was it the case that all non-commissioned officers lacked the breeding and manners of gentlemen. Occasionally gentlemen entered the ranks in the hope of gaining a commission by promotion, having already failed to attain one by the normal methods. Some, like H. D. Acland-Troyte, succeeded, but many more, as Sergeant Mole observed, 'found the game different to what they expected, and purchased their discharges'.[10]

Non-commissioned officers who sought promotion required a special recommendation from their commanding officer. Generally they received little encouragement, although there were some noble exceptions. Lieutenant-Colonel Lord Loughborough, 9th Lancers, doubted neither the competence of promoted rankers nor their ability to live comfortably in the mess.[11] Commissioned rankers, too, were not shunned on entering the mess. John Shipp, who had been raised in a poorhouse and who had been commissioned as an ensign in 1815, was apprehensive about entering the officers' mess. Aware of the prejudice against officers promoted from the ranks, he was startled by the cordiality of his reception: 'All the officers of the corps flocked round me, and greeted me in the most handsome and friendly manner. . . . Had I been the son of a duke my reception could not have been more flattering or friendly'.[12] Courtesy and hospitality, however, were the hallmarks of a good mess and gentlemanly behaviour; they did not mean that the reservations and prejudices about the values of promoted rankers were any less real or substantial.

Table 1.1 **Officers commissioned from the ranks**

	Promoted NCOs including quartermasters and riding masters	All commissions without purchase	Percentage of the total commissioned without purchase from the ranks
1830-39	182	795	22.9
1840-47	264	1,390	18.99
1850-59	570	4,001	14.2
	Promoted NCOs excluding quartermasters and riding masters in the Cavalry and Infantry	**All commissions in Cavalry and Infantry**	
1871-75	25	1,257	1.98
1875-80	35	2,026	1.7
1880-85	63	2,052	3.1
	Promoted NCOs in all arms excluding quartermasters and riding masters	**All commissions in the Cavalry, Infantry, Artillery, Engineers and Army Service Corps**	
1886-90	154	3,222	4.8
1891-95	118	3,593	3.3
1896-1900	111	5,427	2.0
1901-05	117	3,664	3.2
1906-10	64	2,944	2.2

Notes: The total number of officers commissioned in 1906-10 is an approximate figure calculated from the Parliamentary answer of Haldane that the 64 rankers promoted represented 1 in 46 of all officers commissioned.

The larger percentage of NCOs promoted in the earlier years reflects:

1. The inclusion of quartermasters and riding masters in the number of NCOs promoted;
2. The exclusion of the number of commissions purchased from the official returns.

The percentages recorded in the later years are more accurate.

Sources: *P.P.* No. 120 (1849), XXXII; C. 2,762 (1861), XV, p. 358; No. 189 (1893-94), LII; No. 224 (1914), LI; *Parl. Deb.*, Fifth Ser., Vol. 21, 15 Mar. 1911, col. 2,382.

The Duke of Wellington, for example, could never discount the lowly origins of officers raised from the ranks. These men, he informed the Royal Commission on Military Punishments:

> do not make good officers; it does not answer. They are brought into society to the manners of which they are not accustomed; they cannot bear being at all heated in wine or liquor . . . they are quarrelsome, they are addicted to quarrel a little in their cups, and they are not persons that can be borne in the society of the officers of the Army; they are men of different manners altogether.[13]

The Duke, apparently, did not confine himself to verbal abuse. When colonel-in-chief of the Rifle Brigade, he refused to exchange an officer into the regiment because he had risen from the ranks. Recording this incident with obvious relish, General Charles Philip de Ainslie argued that promotion from the ranks would 'never answer in the British service'. He believed that former NCOs, though able to perform the duties of an officer, would always lack the necessary instincts: 'although it is certain that the mere fact of being an officer does, in a sense, make a man a gentleman, it is the individual born, educated, and possessing the innate feelings of one that is required . . .'.[14]

Promotion from the ranks was not merely disliked, it was effectively discouraged. The financial impediments were neither removed nor substantially alleviated. When Sir William Robertson was commissioned, a cavalry officer could not live in the regiment without a private income of £300 a year.[15] A promoted ranker received a mere £100 as an outfit allowance; he had to meet all other expenses either by extreme economy or by transfer to the Indian service where the expenses were less. More intangible but no less serious were the social discomforts which attended promotion. A cordial reception and correct behaviour in the mess could not conceal the gulf between a promoted ranker and his fellow subalterns. As the biographer of Robertson notes: 'A true ranker could never disguise his origin. He was continually being given away by his accent, tastes, habits, jokes, relations, friends (or the lack of them), enforced parsimony, or whatever'.[16]

Even more galling was the view, so often expressed, that promoted rankers could never become 'good officers', since the ranks would always dislike them. Underpinning this view were two inter-related assumptions - that the ranks preferred to be led by their social superiors, and that they retained a healthy dislike of those who had ambitions above their station. So deeply ingrained were these assumptions that they were still being voiced in Edwardian years, even in the innermost sanctums of the Army Council.[17]

Though impossible to substantiate, these assumptions were not entirely implausible. Should promoted NCOs, aware of the artfulness and trickery of the rank and file, prove to be stricter disciplinarians than officers fresh from Sandhurst, then the dislike of the other ranks would be probable. Deferential habits and feelings had also persisted among sections of the working-class. A. F. Corbett would describe the officers under whom he served during the Boer War as 'gentlemen a soldier could look up to with respect and admiration'.[18] Yet deference did not wholly pervade the rank and file, some rankers looked to their officers for ability and professional competence. When facing an enemy, argued Horace Wyndham, 'the average private would much rather follow an intelligent lance-corporal than somebody who is all blue blood but no brains'.[19] Officers, however, were not interested in canvassing rank and file opinion. Accepting that the ranks were deferential and that they disliked promoted NCOs suited the preferences and the self-interest of the bulk of the officer corps. These views helped to insure that the officer gentleman tradition was not diluted by an infusion of promoted rankers.

To sustain its own values and corporate self-interest the officer corps relied upon recruitment from a fairly limited spectrum of society. Several scholars have analysed this recruitment; their results, though broadly similar, have reflected important differences in their methodologies and approaches. P. E. Razzell, who studied the backgrounds of generals, lieutenant-generals and major-generals of the home army, tabulated his results under the headings of 'aristocracy', 'landed gentry' and 'middle class'. Since he derived his status groups from *Burke's Peerage, Landed Gentry, etc.*, his findings are undoubtedly plausible for the aristocracy and landed gentry. He records their proportions as 21 per cent and 32 per cent respectively in 1830. However, he leaves the 'middle class' as simply a 'residual category' which rises from 47 per cent in 1830 to 50 per cent in 1875 and 59 per cent in 1912.[20] So large a proportion warrants further examination.

Dr C. B. Otley has produced a more detailed analysis. By using the admission registers of the Royal Military College, Sandhurst, and the Royal Military Academy, Woolwich, he has constructed a profile of the social origins of the officer corps in the late nineteenth and early twentieth centuries.[21] But Sandhurst and Woolwich were not the only sources of officer supply, and so their registers are not entirely adequate as sources for the study of the officer corps. To maintain a sufficient number of officers, especially in wartime, the army commissioned officers from the Militia and to a lesser extent from the ranks. The army even nominated officers to replenish the shortages which occurred in the cavalry and in the Guards after the South African War. During the period 1885–1906, Sandhurst and Woolwich furnished 9,021 officers out of 16,472 officers commissioned, approximately 55 per cent of the intake.[22] This proportion, too, may have been slightly distorted in social composition. As Sandhurst and Woolwich provided free places for orphans from military families and for the sons of impecunious officers who were unable to pay the full fees, the institutions may have attracted a disproportionately large number of sons

Table 1.2 Officer wastage

Number of officers commissioned in 1891	605
Number of the intake still serving in 1898	513 (85%)
Number of the intake still serving in 1910	313 (52%)
Number of officers commissioned from R.M.C., Sandhurst, and R.M.A., Woolwich, in 1891	407
Number of the cadet intake still serving in 1898	347 (85%)
Number of the cadet intake still serving in 1910	221 (54%)

Sources: *P.P.* No. 111 (1907), XLIX, pp. 3-5 and the Army Lists for 1891, 1898 and 1910.

from service families. Finally, former cadets were as likely as other subalterns to serve on a short commission and then leave the service (Table 1.2), hence a sample of the cadet intake in one year will not necessarily provide accurate information about the middle-ranking and senior officers of future years. Only by studying the officers who were serving on the active list in particular years can the officer corps be examined.

The approach adopted seeks to compare the social groups within the officer corps in 1854, 1899 and 1914, that is, on the eve of each major war in which the army was involved. The approach neither presumes a statistical precision nor the existence of wholly separate and cohesive groups within the officer corps. It merely recognizes that there may have been differences of status and prestige within the regimental mess, and that these differences may have been perceived at the time. It emphasizes, too, that the paramount concern of the officer gentleman tradition was the maintenance of social standards - not simply the possession of a private income, but the disposal of that income in a manner satisfactory to brother officers and in keeping with the customs of the regiment. Hence a perception of the different social types of officer who were especially, if not exclusively, identified with this tradition may form the basis of comparison between the officers in the chosen years. Of the types chosen, the possession of a title, prestige and sometimes greater wealth divided the peerage and baronetage from the landed gentry. Where officers in other categories had close connections with the titled aristocracy or the gentry, they have been judged members of the landed classes. The third type covers self-recruitment within the regular army, those who entered the service as the sons of serving or retired officers. The fourth and fifth types also comprise traditionally recognized sources of gentility, namely the Church of England and the professions (that is, doctors, barristers, surgeons and civil servants - home, diplomatic or ICS). The final category includes parents who were merchants, teachers, engineers, small farmers, estate managers, and in the case of Major-General J. B. Richardson, an 'Arctic traveller'. For the purposes of classification, they were either too few or too obscure or too wanting in detail to

Table 1.3 The social composition of the military leadership in 1854, 1899 and 1914, expressed in percentage terms

	Colonels			Generals		
	1854	1899	1914	1854	1899	1914
Peerage and baronetage	13	12	7	17	12	10
Gentry	25	26	26	29	39	32
Armed services	22	23	23	18	19	25
Clergy	10	12	14	4	9	6
Professional	5	9	12	4	7	6
Others	15	13	15	13	18	18
'Don't know'	10	5	3	15	8	3
Total (%)	100	100	100	100	100	100
Total number	122	129	118	144	113	116

Notes: The names of officers, excluding those who had retired or were placed on half-pay, were obtained from the relevant Army Lists. For 1899 and 1914, the 'military leadership' includes all field marshals, generals, lieutenant-generals and major-generals, and a random sample of one-third of each list of active colonels. Since the numbers were much larger in 1854, random samples of one-half of the field marshals, generals, lieutenant-generals and major-generals and of one-quarter of the active colonels and lieutenant-colonels were examined. For a methodological note on the sources consulted in the process of compiling Tables 1.3 and 1.4 see Appendix 1.

warrant a separate category. In each instance the aim was not statistical exactness but some idea of the relative proportions involved (Table 1.3).

The tables reveal little change in the social composition of the military leadership between 1854, 1899 and 1914. Evident throughout the period are the preponderant degree of self-recruitment and the substantial contribution of the landed aristocracy. Relying upon the landed classes for officers, however, did not mean that the army remained a static or caste-like body, unable to reflect the changes in the rest of society. The landed interest was a relatively open group; while old-established families lost their fortunes and vacated their estates, newcomers having made their money in industry, commerce and speculation moved on to the land. Such movement had occurred during the first half of the nineteenth century, when the value of land had not yet declined as an economic and political asset. These new landowners were usually seeking a more elusive commodity than mere profits and power; they were often in search of respectability or some entrée into the activities and gatherings of county society. Military service, as Harries-Jenkins has indicated, was one method by which an aspirant or his descendants might seek the approval of local society.[23]

Military service could 'confirm' social status because it had already become a traditional and highly regarded career for many landed families. Army officers, in their memoirs, frequently cited the influence of family tradition as a source of their career motivation. These memoirs must be treated with caution inasmuch as they are few in number, restricted largely to successful soldiers, and perforce impressionistic about childhood and adolescent experiences. Nevertheless they not only underline the importance of family tradition, but emphasize that it was sustained in different ways by different families. In many instances it appears to have been a wholly positive influence, with both parents and children willing to perpetuate a military connection often stretching back over several generations. Officers like Sir Hubert Gough, Sir Ian Hamilton, Sir Horace Smith-Dorrien and Viscount Wolseley appear to have followed gladly in the distinguished military traditions of their respective families.[24] Even allowing for an idealistic impression of childhood, this positive appeal seems to have been widespread within families with a service background. On the other hand, family traditions were sometimes preserved by filial determination in spite of parental discouragement. Fearful lest his son incur financial hardship, General Abraham Roberts hoped that 'Freddy [later Field Marshal Lord Roberts] will remain at home', and that 'if Freddy is clever, I hope he will not think of the Army'.[25] Where there were conflicting family traditions (for example, naval on the father's side and army on the mother's) reasons of estate management occasionally prevailed. Both parents dissuaded the Earl of Dundonald from following in the footsteps of his father since the family had suffered losses of property by being so much at sea, and hence that the earldom would be better preserved by a military head of the family.[26] Family tradition, finally, may have been maintained (in more cases than some would like to remember) by the meek acquiescence of the son concerned. Only a writer as candid as Lord Wavell would recollect

> I never felt any special inclination to a military career, but it would have taken more independence of character than I possessed at the time, to avoid it. Nearly all my relations were military. I had been brought up amongst soldiers; and my father, while professing to give me complete liberty of choice, was determined that I should be a soldier. I had no particular bent towards any other profession, and I took the line of least resistance.[27]

Contrasting patterns of career motivation also characterized those officers who emerged from non-service families. Some pursued a military career in spite of their parents, overcoming a bias either in favour of a civilian profession or against a military career. Aware that their parents regarded an army commission as bereft of prospects, Havelock, Wilson and Carton de Wiart had to defy their parents in choosing to enter the army.[28] Lord Ismay recalled that 'my father was particularly upset at the idea of my joining the Indian Cavalry and never tired of telling the story about the cavalry officer who was so stupid that even his brother officers noticed it'.[29] Some officers, conversely, had attempted to fulfil the career expectations of their parents but had found them too demanding. For Baden-Powell, Allenby and McMahon, failure in University or Indian Civil Service examinations had left the army as the only profession within reach of their academic attainments.[30] Occasionally officers came from non-service families which were neither vehemently opposed to the army nor merely tolerant of it as a substitute career: on the contrary they received every encouragement for their military predilections. Within this category came the father of Sir Noel Mason-Macfarlane, who had abandoned his medical practice in 1896 and had begun to devote all his energies to Volunteer soldiering. He insisted that his sons should convert this amateur passion, developed rather late in life, into a professional vocation.[31]

Reflected in these patterns of career motivation is not the salience of parental influence (no doubt there were other factors as important, if not more so, in particular cases), but the relative lack of career opportunities for the sons of self-assigned gentlemen. For younger sons, in particular, the opportunities could be extremely restricted. Should participation in county life, the professions, Church or civil service be neither desired nor obtainable then the army was one of the few careers which a gentleman might consider. As Wavell recollects, 'it was quite natural that some of those who failed for the Indian Civil Service should turn to the Army for a career; in fact, other openings were limited, for commercial business was not those days considered a suitable occupation for a gentleman'.[32] When coupled with the element of family tradition, this artificial restriction preserved the relative homogeneity of the social intake, and thereby the standards and pretensions of the officer gentleman tradition.

Another factor making for homogeneity was the connection between the army and the land (see Table 1.4 and Appendix 2). The county communities remained a primary source of officer recruitment throughout the nineteenth and early twentieth centuries. Within their confines, an uncomplicated patriotism and sense of duty could flourish - motives which were reinforced in depressed rural areas by the lack of other occupations for younger sons. Equally important was the enthusiasm for hunting and shooting in county society. Apart from the relevance of these pursuits for the military activities of a pre-technological army, these recreations were zealously pursued by the peacetime service. By offering abundant opportunities for sporting and social enjoyment, the army enhanced its appeal and attraction for the sons of county families.

Of even more importance in buttressing the officer gentleman tradition were the methods of officer recruitment. Until 1871 the army retained the practice of purchasing commissions in the Guards and in the regiments of cavalry and infantry. Potential officers who had reached their sixteenth birthday had to be nominated or approved as

Table 1.4 The rural/urban background of the military leadership in 1854, 1899 and 1914, expressed in percentage terms

	Colonels			Generals		
	1854	1899	1914	1854	1899	1914
Estates, farms, villages under 1,000 pop.	62	38	46	60	40	43
Villages and towns 1,000–5,000 pop.	15	25	19	16	22	22
Total rural (%)	77	63	65	76	62	65
Towns in excess of 5,000 pop.	20	29	26	17	30	27
Abroad	3	8	9	7	8	8
Total (%)	100	100	100	100	100	100
Total number	95	107	87	121	91	91

eligible for commissioning. They had to seek nomination either from the Commander-in-Chief at the Horse Guards or, should they wish to enter the Guards, from the colonel of their chosen regiment. If approved, their names would be added to the list of eligible candidates. Thereafter they would lobby supporters to keep their claims to the fore and await a vacancy in their selected regiment. The commissions of successful candidates were gazetted and the new officers paid the appropriate purchase price which, as set by the Warrant of 1821, was £450 in the infantry, £840 in the Dragoon Guards and Dragoons, £1,200 in the Horse and Foot Guards and £1,260 in the Life Guards.

It was possible to enter the army without purchasing a commission. Officers in the artillery and engineers did not purchase their commissions; they entered the army after a course of training at the Royal Military Academy, Woolwich. In the pre-Crimean army, however, the proportion of 'scientific' officers in the officer corps was always small, usually less than 15 per cent.[33] In the other branches of the service a small number of non-purchase commissions were regularly awarded by the Commander-in-Chief. After 1842, cadets from the Royal Military College, Sandhurst, could enter the army without purchasing commissions. Many of these free commissions were granted to the sons of impecunious officers or to orphans from military families, so buttressing the pattern of self-recruitment within the Victorian army. During the Crimean War there was a twelvefold increase in the number of free commissions awarded (Table 1.5), but the traditional pattern of recruitment was restored in the post-war years.

Approximately three out of every four officers purchased their commissions, so sustaining a mode of entry into the army which aroused considerable criticism from reformers in the House of Commons. Sir Charles Trevelyan, for example, condemned purchase as a means by

Table 1.5 Commissions awarded with and without purchase 1849–55, excluding the Artillery and Engineers

	By purchase	Without purchase	To cadets from Sandhurst	To NCOs	Total
1849	338	74	25	24	461
1850	370	3	23	10	406
1851	299	56	26	30	411
1852	325	63	30	19	437
1853	339	58	32	21	450
1854	372	319	50	121	862
1855	338	1,271	17	110	1,736

Source: *Report of the Commissioners appointed to inquire into the system of purchase and sale of Commissions in the army, with evidence and appendix*, C.2,267 (1857), XVIII, p. 389.

which the middle class, particularly the sons of farmers and shop-keepers, were excluded from the officer corps. He believed that purchase was incompatible with an army organized upon the basis of professional instruction and qualification. The system, he averred, by artificially restricting the number of candidates, lowered the quality of the officer intake; it also undermined the value of professional qualifications by attracting men who could afford to purchase their initial commissions and then their subsequent promotions to rank of lieutenant-colonel.[34] Military spokesmen, however, stubbornly defended the system before a succession of Select Committees and Royal Commissions. The Duke of Wellington argued that 'Promotion by purchase [had brought] into the Service men of fortune and education; men who have some con-nexion with the interests and fortunes of the Country, besides the Commissions which they hold from His Majesty'.[35] The British army, as a consequence, was not a mercenary army, but one identified with the interests of the State and hence, as Wellington put it, a 'safe and beneficial' force. Purchase rendered the army 'safe', or loyal to the civil power, in two respects, one largely theoretical, the other much more practical. The purchase system discouraged misconduct since an officer could be cashiered and so lose the price which he had paid for his commission. Normally, officers were not dismissed from the Service, but were invited to retire, and so were allowed to sell their commis-sions. More fundamentally, purchase buttressed the State by attracting officers from families whose status, privileges and possessions were already protected by the State itself: if only for this reason, these officers owed the State their allegiance.

Purchase was also a financial asset for successive governments. It enabled the authorities to avoid the expense of educating, remunerating and pensioning the officer corps. The Royal Military College, Sand-hurst, languished under severe financial restrictions throughout the pre-Crimean period, losing its Parliamentary grant altogether in 1832. The College never enrolled its established quota of 400 cadets. Having reached a maximum of 330 cadets in 1818, the numbers slumped below 200 in 1824 and remained below that total thereafter. The College reduced its free cadetships for the orphans of officers from 100 to 10 in 1820, and gradually, by about 1832, abandoned the practice completely. Forced to operate upon strict economic lines, the College reduced its establishment to 180 and attracted even fewer cadets.[36] In the decade prior to 1848, 650 cadets entered the College of whom 350 gained free commissions while another 200 failed to pass out and purchased their commissions.[37] With so few officers coming from Sandhurst, there was little inclination to improve the educational standards of the College. Until the post-Crimean reforms, when Queen's cadetships were introduced for the sons of poor officers, the junior department of Sandhurst enrolled boys of thirteen to fifteen years and concentrated upon remedying the defects of their general education. The department did not provide for the studying of practical subjects such as military law, administration, transport, logistics and communications. Nor did the Sandhurst course include the study of military theory in strategy and tactics; the candidates had to pass examinations in mathematics, fortification and military surveying and in three optional subjects chosen from French, German, Latin, siege operation, landscape drawing, military drawing, general history and geography. Little more than another, somewhat inferior, public school, the College did not establish itself as a centre of professional instruction. It failed to overcome those reservations which some officers still retained about the value of specialist training in a military academy.

Leading the reaction against the concept of a specifically military education was the Duke of Wellington. Although the Duke professed confidence in the men who had founded and had supervised the Military College since 1802, he still preferred 'the education usually given to English gentlemen . . .'.[38] He would affirm repeatedly that prospective officers should be educated in the established public schools. He would condemn the training of the French officers in their military academies, training which, in his opinion, had simply produced 'pedants and coxcombs'. He claimed that 'an officer in the British army was not a mere fighting machine', but a man required to serve the State in a host of civil capacities at home and abroad, for which a general education in the liberal classical tradition was essential.[39] He firmly believed that the development of military academies, and even of staff colleges, would be detrimental to the Service: that it would lower the 'tone' of the army, and would impair the cohesion of the officer corps. The only good officers, argued Wellington, were men who learned their military duties by service and practical experience within their regiments; gentlemen, fitted for command by their breeding and education, who could purchase their commissions and were willing to serve the Crown for honour and not material reward.

This ideal chimed neatly with the reluctance of Parliament to pay army officers in a satisfactory manner. Army rates of pay, as established in 1806, varied from £95 16*s* 3*d* per annum for an ensign to £365 for a lieutenant-colonel. These rates represented less than half the remuneration paid to clerks of equivalent grades in the War Office. Officers could receive additional payments; a lieutenant after seven years in that rank received an extra shilling a day, a captain with a company might make about £12 a year from his contingent allowance, officers in command of service or reserve companies of a regiment received 3*s* a day command money, and the senior effective lieutenant-colonel and major in a regiment drew £20 annually as a 'non-effective allowance'. Even if an officer qualified for these payments and possibly earned a little extra for civilian duties when stationed abroad, or for still-hunting or smuggling duties when stationed at home, he was still abysmally paid. The regimental officer had to wait until 1 January 1914 before his basic rate of pay was even marginally altered. If promoted above the ranks of lieutenant-colonel, the officer, under the purchase system, could no longer sell his commission and was almost bound to lose money. Unless appointed a colonial governor or a colonel of a regiment, from which he gained a monopoly for clothing his men and could make a profit of about £1,000 a year, the senior officer relied upon 'unattached pay' or the pay he received by remaining on the muster roll of his regiment as a nominal officer.

'Unattached pay', first introduced in 1814, provided a small annual salary for general officers, but the House of Commons, in 1818, restricted the list of unattached generals to 120 and standardized the pay at £456 per annum. As Harries-Jenkins has rightly concluded 'There was certainly no class of a comparable social status, with the possible exceptions of the naval officer and the country clergyman, who had to work for so little'.[40]

Officers could leave the service before attaining senior rank. Only a fortunate few could qualify for a pension, since officers were not entitled to a pension as 'a right'. Severely wounded officers or officers who performed meritoriously on the field of battle could qualify, but the numbers allowed a pension were always small. Consequently the vast majority of officers either sold their commissions, recouping their capital investment and severing all ties with the Service, or went on to half-pay. Many chose the latter course and received a 'retaining fee', which in theory, if not necessarily in practice, indicated that they were available for future service. Whereas half-pay was taken by some officers merely to mark time until they could return to active service, usually at a higher rank, it was viewed more commonly as the first step towards retirement. Once in receipt of half-pay, officers were entitled to promotion, but were only paid on the basis of the rank which they held when they left the active list. Unless they had private means, officers could not support themselves on half-pay. Many supplemented their income by acquiring posts in Civil Offices as barrack-masters, chief constables of police, superintendents of military departments, comptrollers of customs and excise, local postmasters and in a variety of foreign and colonial appointments.

The size and cost of the half-pay list was a source of recurrent concern to the Treasury. In 1822 there were 8,676 officers on half-pay, more than were actively serving at home and abroad. Nor were these officers all Peninsular veterans; over 1,000 were ensigns or second lieutenants, many of whom as Sir Henry Hardinge recognized, had no intention of returning to active service.[41] Hence the government tried periodically to shorten the half-pay list by bringing officers back on to full pay. Thereupon these officers could only retire by selling their commissions as they could not return to a half-pay status. The government managed thereby to reduce the cost of half-pay from nearly £3 million in the late 1820s to about £2¼ million in 1848.[42] The system nevertheless remained an immense asset to successive governments; it enabled them to avoid paying an appropriate pension to the superannuated officer, a dereliction of duty which persisted for many years after the abolition of purchase. When Viscount Wolseley retired as Commander-in-Chief in December 1900, he wrote to his wife 'I left the W[ar] O[ffice] with a pension some £200 or more less than the Session Clerk did who leaves as Permanent Under Sec[retary]'.[43]

Officers rarely expressed anguish publicly over their rates of pay and pensions since material reward was not normally their main interest in seeking an army commission. John George Champion, later lieutenant-colonel of the 95th Regiment, was an unusual exception. At the age of thirteen he forsook his clerical ambitions, which would have proved even less remunerative than a military career, entered Sandhurst, and thereafter embarked on an army career from which he endeavoured to support his widowed and dependent mother.[44] Officers who purchased their commissions, however, could not reckon upon the prospect of immediate financial gain. Like entrants into other nineteenth century professions, especially the law, they paid a considerable sum for the privilege of entering their chosen profession, and then lived for several years in the manner and style of a gentleman, largely upon the basis of private means or parental support. Where the army differed from other professions was in the continued operation of the purchase system throughout the regimental career structure. Outside the artillery and the engineers, officers could purchase their promotions to the ranks of lieutenant, captain, major and lieutenant-colonel respectively.

For the rich, ambitious and competent officer, there were few problems in the path of his promotion. He could pass directly from an ensign to a lieutenancy, if a vacancy was available, complete two years as a subaltern before becoming a captain, accumulate a total of six years' service before becoming a major, and then purchase a lieutenant-colonelcy, if one was available, without any further delay. The officer had to be certified as 'fit and qualified' by the commanding officer of his regiment. He could neither secure a promotion without purchase over the head of a senior officer, nor could he purchase a promotion over the head of a senior officer, should the latter be prepared to purchase the commission on sale. Notwithstanding these caveats, promotion could be extremely rapid for an immensely rich officer: he had merely to wait for the first suitable vacancy, either in his own or another regiment, and pay the price demanded for it. Hence Lord Brudenell (later Earl of Cardigan) became a cornet in May 1824, a lieutenant in January 1825, a captain in June 1826 (one month over the statutory two years), a major in August 1830 (three months over the six years) and a lieutenant-colonel in December 1830. Each step in promotion cost the officer concerned the difference in value between his commission and that of the next higher commission, along with any over-regulation payment which had been agreed upon. Although the prices of commissions were regulated by Royal Warrant in 1821 (Table 1.6), it was common practice to demand and to receive much more than the official price. Occasionally the over-regulation payments were extremely high; Lord Brudenell, for example, should have paid £6,175 for the lieutenant-colonelcy of the 15th Hussars, but he paid between £35,000 and £40,000.[45] More commonly, cavalry officers paid about double the regulation price, and infantry officers about one-third over the prescribed amount,[46] an abuse so common and flagrant that it generated vehement criticism of the purchase system. As Colonel Lord West informed the Purchase Commission of 1857, the abuse led 'to a sordid and degrading traffic in commissions in the higher grade . . . '.[47]

The trafficking in over-regulation payments probably derived from the predicament of officers at the vertex of the regimental system. After three years' service a lieutenant-colonel was guaranteed promotion to the army rank of colonel, from which he would be promoted through the operation of the seniority rule to the rank of major-general. As a major-general, however, he could not sell his commission, a rule intended to encourage retirement from the Service. The individual faced the dilemma of either selling out and losing promotion, or of accepting promotion and losing a substantial capital investment. He could only secure his promotion and avoid losing his entire capital investment by exchanging with another lieutenant-colonel on half-pay. In the 1850s the War Office restricted this option by insisting that officers could not exchange unless medically unfit or until they had completed twenty-one years' service. Should a lieutenant-colonel be able to exchange, he could then approach the senior purchase officer in the next lower rank and request an over-regulation payment to ensure that he would exchange with a half-pay officer who wanted to sell rather than one who wanted to serve. Each officer who would gain promotion would pay a share of the over-regulation sum and would

Table 1.6 Regulation prices (£) of commissions established by the Royal Warrant of 1821 (difference in price between the commissions is shown in parentheses)

Rank	Line regiments of Foot		Cavalry		Life Guards		Royal Horse Guards		Foot Guards	
Cornet	450	(–)	840	(–)	1,260	(–)	1,200	(–)	1,200	(–)
Lieutenant	700	(250)	1,190	(350)	1,785	(525)	1,600	(400)	2,050	(850)
Captain	1,800	(1,100)	3,225	(2,035)	3,500	(1,715)	3,500	(1,900)	4,800	(2,750)
Major	3,200	(1,400)	4,575	(1,350)	5,350	(1,850)	5,350	(1,850)	8,300	(3,500)
Lieutenant-colonel	4,500	(1,300)	6,175	(1,600)	7,250	(1,900)	7,250	(1,900)	9,000	(700)

Note: In 1860 the prices of Cavalry commissions were reduced and made equal with the prices in the infantry. As commissions in the Guards carried higher social prestige and a concurrent and higher army rank, their prices remained higher.

gain from the promotion vacancies throughout the regiment. The lieutenant-colonel, meanwhile, preserved his promotion, while recovering at least part of the cost of his commission.[48] The former half-pay officer, in spite of surrendering his half-pay, would also benefit; he could probably make a substantial profit by selling his new commission, especially if he had already been promoted on the half-pay list but was still being paid on the basis of his former rank on the active list.

Should an officer refuse to pay the over-regulation price, then his position in the regiment became scarcely tolerable. Legally he was within his rights and would receive support from the Commander-in-Chief, but the lieutenant-colonel could exchange with the lieutenant-colonel in another regiment and seek an arrangement with the officers of his new regiment. Unable to frustrate his lieutenant-colonel, the recalcitrant officer would merely block promotion in his own regiment and incur considerable opprobrium as a consequence. As General Sir John Macdonald, when Adjutant-General, conceded, 'there is no member of a regimental society so unpopular as he who proclaims his determination not to exceed the regulated price, thereby standing as an obstacle to promotion by purchase in the regiment to which he belongs'.[49] Officers rarely adopted this course; having entered a purchase corps, they felt under an honourable, though tacit, engagement to conform to the customs of the regiment. When an officer found himself unable to pay an over-regulation price, he could either withdraw his name from the purchase list and allow a junior officer to pass over his head, or borrow the money at a ruinous rate of interest. Taking either of these choices could prove painful and embarrassing for the officer concerned.

Compounding the severity with which the purchase system and its abuses bore upon the less wealthy officer were the privileges accorded to officers in the Foot Guards. An officer in the Guards possessed not only a rank in the Guards but also a concurrent and a higher army rank. An ensign in the Guards was styled as an 'ensign and lieutenant', a lieutenant as a 'lieutenant and captain', and a captain as a 'captain and lieutenant-colonel'. A Foot Guards officer could exchange into a Line regiment at the higher rank. A captain in the Guards could exchange with a lieutenant-colonel of a cavalry or infantry regiment and gain command of an army regiment. As subsequent promotion to the rank of major-general was normally based upon seniority, the Foot Guards captain who held the army rank of lieutenant-colonel could attain senior rank much quicker than the captain in the cavalry or infantry. For Line officers, the consequences could be galling. After the fall of Sebastopol, Sir William Codrington, who had begun the war with the rank of captain and lieutenant-colonel, Coldstream Guards, was appointed General Commanding-in-Chief in the Crimea. Sir Colin Campbell, who began the war as a brigadier-general, left the Crimea disgusted, only returning at the Queen's request. On his arrival he reportedly quipped: 'I have come out to serve under a man who, at the beginning of the war, commanded a company in the division in which I commanded a brigade'.[50]

Impecunious officers, who usually served in the Line regiments and could neither afford to sell out nor pay the over-regulation payments, had to wait upon promotion without purchase. Opportunities for promotion without purchase occurred most frequently in regiments which either fought in costly campaigns or languished in unhealthy tropical stations. As soon as an officer died through wounds or disease he forfeited his commission to the Crown, enabling the senior officer of the lower rank to be promoted without purchase. Vacancies caused by deaths, or by full-pay retirements, or by promotions to major-general in a non-purchase regiment, were not particularly common in peacetime: from 1849–53 a mere 30 per cent of all promotions were filled without purchase (none in the Guards and a bare 8 per cent in the cavalry).[51] Nevertheless an ambitious officer could transfer between regiments and seek promotion by serving in as many campaigns as possible. Distinguished service could be rewarded by brevet promotion to the rank of major and above. A brevet promotion conferred an army rank on its recipient, but not a regimental rank; hence an officer who was a major within his regiment, could rank as a brevet lieutenant-colonel and hold the rank of lieutenant-colonel when away from his regiment. Traditionally brevets had been distributed on special occasions such as a royal birth or a royal accession, but they were awarded on a more frequent and selective basis after 1854.[52] For Garnet Wolseley, who served in three wars within his first six years' service (the second Burma War, Crimean War and Indian Mutiny), brevet promotions were invaluable. By the time he was twenty-five he held the rank of brevet lieutenant-colonel: seven years later he was promoted to full colonel.

Possibly the main virtue of the purchase system was that it enabled some officers to attain field rank at an early age, even if the majority did so by buying their own advancement. Whether these newly-promoted officers were competent to perform their duties was a moot point, often raised in Parliament in the 1840s. Confronted by demands for an educational test of military competence, the Duke of Wellington eventually vouchsafed to issue new regulations 'in conformity with public opinion'. In 1849 he required that any candidate should be examined before being commissioned, and that an officer seeking promotion to lieutenant or captain should have to prove his knowledge of the duties required of officers commanding battalions and of matters pertaining to 'military skill and science'.[53] Neither regulation was particularly effective. When the examination was found to be too difficult the qualifying standard was adjusted to suit the candidates from the older public schools. The assessment of prospective lieutenants and captains was so vaguely worded that it was seldom enforced.[54] The purchase system provided little incentive for professional study; it simply facilitated the retirement of elderly officers and the promotion of their younger subordinates.

As an alternative to promotion by purchase, Parliamentary critics often advocated a system of promotion based upon selection and professional qualification.[55] Serving officers, in their evidence before Select Committees and Royal Commissions, repeatedly opposed the idea. They expressed doubts about the criteria of selection and, more especially, about the manner in which the selections would be made. They voiced fears that jobbery and influence would be used to distort selective appointments.[56] From a military perspective, the sole guarantee of fairness and impartiality was promotion by strict seniority, the practice followed by the artillery and engineers. Within these corps the rates of promotion were agonizingly slow compared to the rates attained in the purchase regiments. In 1838 the average length of service for the juniors of each rank in the artillery was nearly twenty years for a second captain, thirty years for a first captain, 34¼ years for a lieutenant-colonel, and nearly forty-two years for a colonel.[57] Fortescue recalls that a captain who served at that rank in every battle of the Peninsular War was still a captain in 1836; and Sir George Wood, who commanded the artillery at Waterloo, was only a major twenty-one years after the battle.[58]

Given this bleak alternative it was not surprising that officers in the 'non-scientific' corps resigned themselves to the lottery of promotion by purchase. Even officers who had to rely upon non-purchase promotions found that the system could be financially remunerative. Once promoted without purchase, the recipient could realize a substantial capital sum when he sold out, as the full price was never refused an officer who had completed twenty years' service unless he had committed misconduct. On the other hand, the hopes of an officer could be dashed in a multitude of ways. The chances of promotion varied considerably from regiment to regiment. Non-purchase vacancies did not automatically result in a series of non-purchase promotions. These vacancies could be used to absorb supernumerary officers within a particular regiment; they might even be sold for the benefit of the Reserve Fund, which the Secretary of State for War retained to buy half-pay commissions and to ameliorate some of the financial difficulties of the purchase system.[59] The financial investment of an officer could be lost entirely should he die in service. The family of a deceased officer gained nothing from his commission as it reverted to the Crown whenever the officer died. An officer, too, would lose financially should his regiment be reduced or amalgamated with another. In 1849, for example, Major Dunsmore bought a lieutenant-colonelcy from Colonel MacDougall for £7,000 – £2,500 above the regulation price. A year later, when the Reserve Battalion of the 42nd was amalgamated with the 1st Battalion, Dunsmore was placed on half-pay and his property became worthless.[60] Notwithstanding these vagaries of fortune and individual cases of hardship, it has been argued that the purchase system was not a source of unrest within the officer corps, that officers generally accepted the system as a traditional aspect of army life, dating back to the reign of Charles II, and that the critics of the system were often those who had attained their own high rank by operating the system itself.[61]

This conclusion, though broadly correct, should be qualified in certain particulars. Admittedly those who suffered from the purchase system neither protested too openly nor campaigned in favour of reforming or abolishing the system. Such behaviour would have been considered improper within the regimental mess, or at least imprudent since it would have drawn attention to the personal predicaments of the officers concerned. Nevertheless the rancour and resentment of the bypassed officer was often deeply felt. Sir Henry Havelock used to describe himself as 'the neglected Lieutenant' who had been 'purchased over by two fools and three sots'.[62] Sir William Butler ruefully recalled, after twelve years' service, that he 'had been five or six times purchased over by officers, most of whom were many years junior to me'.[63] Even more distraught were the officers who suffered in time of war. Sir George Bell, the Peninsular veteran, recalled that 'Many brave men were driven out of the service by tyrannical injustice. They could not break the system of being passed by and purchased over by boys from the nursery, who stayed at home and never smelt powder.'[64] Major, later Lieutenant-General, Ewart, would express similar feelings during the Crimean War. In September 1855, he experienced 'a great and bitter disappointment' when the senior major of the 93rd Highlanders, and Ewart himself, who held the brevet rank of lieutenant-colonel, were purchased over by the Hon. Adrian Hope, who was serving at home with the 60th Rifles. As Hope had been a captain until five months previously, Ewart was so distraught that he protested to the Commander-in-Chief in the Crimea and to Sir Colin Campbell. He even allowed a cousin who was a Member of Parliament to intercede on his behalf at the Horse Guards. All protest was futile as the military authorities would not alter the system, however baleful its consequences, in war or peace.[65]

Within the officer corps unrest was occasioned by the purchase system, but the unrest was largely personal in character. Individuals were bitter at being purchased over; their feelings were accentuated when the other officer was younger or less competent or had stayed at home while an overseas campaign was waged. Even worse, the officer who had been thwarted had little hope of redressing his grievance. Since protest was likely to prove abortive and half-pay retirement seemed a miserable and depressing prospect, the bypassed officer generally acquiesced: he resigned himself to his fate, saving his fulminations for close friends and for post-service memoirs. Very few officers, even among the disadvantaged, endorsed the desire of Trevelyan to abolish the purchase system as a means of altering the social composition of the officer corps. By abolishing purchase and by increasing the pay of junior officers, Trevelyan hoped to attract a larger proportion of officers from the middle classes, as represented 'by farmers in the country and shopkeepers in town', and to enable one-third and one-fourth of all commissions in each regiment to be set aside for promoted rankers.[66] Had this proposal ever been implemented, it would have transformed the character and 'tone' of the officers' mess, a prospect which had little appeal for the serving officer. With or without purchase, officers still wished to be viewed as gentlemen and to live in the manner and style befitting a gentleman.

In the nineteenth-century army the social life, customs and extra-military life-style of the officer corps were considered an essential ingredient of regimental *esprit de corps*. Peacetime officers, when based at home and not on leave, spent a great deal of time in each other's company. Social contacts assumed a considerable importance as the junior officer had relatively little to do apart from attending some parades of his regiment. Normally the commanding officer supported by his adjutant, quartermaster and sergeant-major, and aided by a phalanx of sergeant-majors and colour-sergeants, discharged almost all the duties connected with the drill, discipline, feeding and well-being of the men. Except in the artillery, where the battery organization required more direct officer involvement, the command of the various officers was virtually 'nominal', limited largely to financial responsibilities. Captains were held responsible for the loss of government articles of clothing and equipment from their companies and for any faulty accounting by their pay sergeants. The other ranks were instructed by specialists. In the mounted corps riding was taught by the riding master, often a promoted non-commissioned officer. Drill was taught by the adjutant, assisted by the sergeant-major. Rifle-shooting was supervised by a musketry instructor, whose prime concern was the firing of the regulation number of rounds as authorized by the School of Musketry. Apart from the occasional inspection or field day, the regimental training had little focal point or purpose. Although manoeuvres were held in 1872 and in 1898, they never became a regular part of the training programme until the Edwardian years. For the young officer who joined the Victorian army, the sheer lack of work could have debilitating or deleterious effects. It was 'often hard' as Sir Charles Fortescue-Brickdale recalls, for the young subaltern who 'had little or no work to do, not to get into loafing, idle, if not disreputable ways'.[67]

The social life of regimental officers differed little from that enjoyed by their counterparts in civilian society. Officers based in or near London, especially the Guards, were expected to lead the life of a man-about-town. They were members of several clubs, where they could indulge in dining, drinking and gambling. They were welcome at the great hunts of the shires and at the fashionable gatherings of country-house society. They seldom wore uniform except on duty, but appeared in their splendid attire at the dinners and balls of the London season. As Sir George Higginson recalls of his life as a Guards officer in the 1840s, 'balls, theatres and country visits relieved the not over arduous duties even of a subaltern . . .'.[68] The social scene was less hectic and less expensive in the more remote stations of Ireland and Scotland. Officers still amused themselves, however. In the afternoons they rode, hunted, shot, fished, attended race meetings, or possibly, in summer, played cricket. In the evenings the unmarried officers dined in the mess, which was often situated some distance from the barracks of the rank and file. As many barracks were constructed in the early nineteenth century for peace-keeping purposes, either in the less salubrious centres of large industrial towns or in small villages scattered across Ireland, officers sought more congenial quarters for their mess, occasionally in hotels in nearby towns. Within the mess, officers dined extremely well, at a modest charge, and those who had developed a taste for champagne and claret during the course of the Napoleonic wars could indulge their preferences and set an example for the younger officer. Remembering the guest nights at his mess in Dublin in 1853, Jervis-Waldy notes, somewhat ruefully, that the 'champagne and other expensive wines made an awful Mess bill, and a great hole in the pockets of the young lieutenants'.[69]

Officers were expected to participate in the activities and social life of the mess. In the more fashionable regiments these expectations could prove extremely expensive: cavalry officers were expected not only to hunt but to provide themselves with horses and hounds for the purpose. Sir Hope Grant, who was gazetted into the 9th Lancers in 1826, squandered 'the greater part' of £5,000 within his first nine years of service. He recalls that 'My brother officers were a gentleman-like set. Many were wealthy - a disadvantage, no doubt, as they led others less well off into extravagant habits. Several had teams turned out in first rate form, and never started to stay at a country-house without their chariot and four post horses'.[70] Coping with the expenses of regimental life and the scale of mess hospitality was a formidable problem for officers from less wealthy or only marginally wealthy backgrounds. These officers usually sought service in India, where they could enjoy the sport and social life of the home officer at much less cost. There was a distinct gulf between the home and Indian armies as Wolseley, succinctly but snobbishly, observed:

> The great bulk of the young men who then usually went to India were socially not of a high order. Of course, though very poor, many were sons of old officers of good families, whose poverty compelled their sons to serve in India, if serve they would in the Army. But the great bulk of those I met at Chatham, and afterwards in India and Burmah, at that time [the 1850s], struck me, I remember, as wanting in good breeding and all seemed badly educated.[71]

India acted as a syphon; it removed a large pool of potential discontent from the regimental messes in Britain.

The exclusive and expensive life-style enjoyed by officers who were stationed in Britain was not undermined by the abolition of purchase in 1871. To preserve the officer gentleman tradition, regiments continued to restrict the area of officer recruitment; they sought fresh blood from the products of particular schools, usually public schools, and from those aspirants who possessed the necessary degree of financial independence. Previous schooling or old school contacts could be used, like family ties, to enable military aspirants to enter the regiments of their choice. A public school education, though valued primarily as character forming, was regarded as likely to ensure that potential officers possessed the requisite manners and social attributes. Academic attainment was much less important; indeed, many candidates had to attend crammers after leaving school before they could pass the entry examinations for the army. By the end of the century the ties of the public schools with the army were well established. A. H. H. MacLean has calculated that 62 per cent of the regular officers who served in the South African War came from public schools, with 41 per cent from the ten great public schools and 11 per cent from Eton alone.[72]

It cannot be inferred from MacLean's statistics that the public schools exercised a decisive influence in predisposing their pupils towards a military career. Admittedly some schools possessed army classes and cadet corps; most preserved an ethos and life-style which harmonized with military values, instilling such concepts as 'honour' and '*esprit de corps*'. Nevertheless the proportion of pupils from these schools who subsequently entered the army was relatively small. Over the period 1880–99, the only schools from which more than one-fifth of their leavers served in the South African War were Eton, Harrow and Wellington.[73] Even participation in the school cadet corps was not an invariable sign of incipient militarism; it frequently reflected the bleak alternative of compulsory school drill on military lines in the winter months, or the marginally more interesting drill of the cadet corps. While the military flavour of public school life may have attracted or predisposed some pupils towards the army, it may also have deterred or disenchanted others. As the commentators on Winchester remark: 'All that one can say, at a minimum, is that the military flavour of Winchester life and the tendency of Wykehamists to choose military careers in large numbers are both legacies of the same gentry tradition.'[74]

A suitable family background or public school education would not ensure an entry into the late Victorian army. For those who wished to serve in a home-based regiment, private means were virtually essential as officers could not expect to live on their pay. Each subaltern, on joining his regiment, had to provide his own uniform, cases, furniture, mufti, servant's outfit and incoming mess contribution. Whereas these items would cost about £200 for an infantry officer, the more expensive uniform, saddlery, mufti and the purchase of two 'chargers' would require an expenditure of £600 or even £1,000 from a cavalry officer, depending on the customs of his regiment. Thereafter the annual expenses of dining and entertaining in the mess, sport, social entertainment, and the constant moving of army life presumed a private income of £100 to £150 for an infantry officer, and of £600 to £700 for a cavalry officer.[75] These calculations were included in the findings of a Select Committee, chaired by Lord Stanley, which reported in 1902. The Committee concluded that the dependence of an officer upon a private income could be reduced. It recommended that the government should provide chargers, some items of kit, and officers' furniture (at a small rent), and proposed that many aspects of mess and regimental expenditure should be curtailed and subjected to close surveillance by commanding officers. The Committee, however, did not propose that an officer should be able to live on his pay, a conclusion with which the government concurred. It refused to contemplate any increase in pay, which was still fixed at the rates determined in 1806. By simply endorsing the recommendations of the Stanley Committee, as qualified by Lord Roberts and the cavalry colonels,[76] the government confirmed that the possession of private means would remain a principal requirement for an army commission.

All officers were expected to comply with the standards and customs of their regimental mess. For some like Sir William Robertson, who was promoted from the ranks in a cavalry regiment, bearing a due share of regimental expenses was a constant struggle and worry; others, like Lord Gleichen, happily went into debt: 'it never worried me for a subaltern's views on the subject of cash are always pleasantly buoyant'.[77] Those who failed to match the spending of their brother officers, or offended the social code and customs of the mess in other respects, risked the possibility of social ostracism and in some cases of flagrant bullying. Occasionally the ragging was so vicious that Parliament was involved, as in the case of Ensigns Bruce and Hodge. They were both gazetted into the 4th Hussars in the 1890s; they had private incomes of £500 and £300 respectively. They were informed by their brother officers that these incomes were quite inadequate. They were then bullied for over two months, subjected to a remorseless boycott, and forced to leave the regiment, with Hodge requiring medical treatment thereafter for a period of three months.[78] Ragging, often fairly brutal in character, was a fairly prevalent pastime in Victorian public schools. More significant than its mere recurrence in the army was the implicit connivance of some senior officers. Viscount Wolseley, for example, who was Commander-in-Chief at the time of the ragging in the 4th Hussars, would openly condone such behaviour in his memoirs. He recalls his own participation, as a subaltern, in the bullying of four ensigns who had joined his regiment from the Militia in the 1850s. These ensigns, he writes, 'had practically no pretensions to the rank of gentlemen'; they would have been 'absolutely useless as officers, and we soon got rid of them'.[79]

Although the army continued to restrict the area of officer recruitment, it did not preserve an officer gentleman tradition that was entirely static. Officers who wrote their memoirs towards the end of the century frequently commented upon the changes which had occurred in the dress, manners and social life of an English gentleman. Some approved the decline of rakish behaviour, ostentatious dress and licentious living, particularly the vast consumption of port and spirits, which had blossomed during the Regency years and which had persisted within some regiments throughout the pre-Crimean period.[80] Others, like General de Ainslie, bemoaned the passing of that age; he feared that the suppression of the duel in particular had precipitated a deterioration in the manners, language and habits of society, and above all in 'that high and delicate sense of honour' which had characterized the English gentleman of his youth.[81] The practice of duelling, under proper circumstances, had been obligatory upon an English gentleman: it had enshrined a code of heroic, feudal and honorific virtues. Once that practice ceased, so the concept of gentlemanly conduct altered. As W. L. Burn observes, many of the old qualities of a gentleman were preserved, especially the manly attributes of loyalty and courage, bravery and patriotism, but Christian virtues became more pronounced - the unselfishness, thoughtfulness and sense of *noblesse oblige*, intrinsic aspects of Matthew Arnold's ideal of a Christian gentleman.[82] Within the army this change of behaviour would find reflection in the increasingly paternalistic concern of officers for the welfare of the other ranks.

The attitudes of officers towards their men were not strikingly and suddenly transformed during the nineteenth century. On the one hand complaints were regularly voiced that some officers knew nothing of their men, rarely came in contact with them, and were indifferent towards their wants. The protestations of Sergeant Wheatley recorded in his diary in 1819, that officers ignored their men and rarely visited a barrack room would be echoed eighty years later by Sergeant Wyndham.[83] Officer neglect, indeed, was all too likely, since officers did not mix with their men other than on special or festive occasions, while officers also enjoyed lengthy periods of leave, as much as four months annually for captains, five for majors, and six or more for colonels in the Brigade of Guards. On the other hand some officers, even in the early nineteenth century, were extremely concerned about the welfare and conditions of their men. The regimental inspection reports contain numerous references to subscriptions raised by officers for benevolent, widows' charity, and library funds. In 1837, for example, the officers of the 36th Foot raised a small monthly subscription 'to clothe the female Children of the Soldiers'; in 1844, the officers of the 5th Dragoon Guards, 8th Hussars, 34th and 37th Regiments raised similar subscriptions for the purpose of clothing children of their other ranks.[84] These acts represented not only the kindness and consideration of particular commanding officers, but also important initiatives and innovations by them. Libraries and savings banks were but two reforms which were initially instituted by the regimental officers, only to receive a somewhat tardy approval and endorsement from the Horse Guards.

The scale and range of welfare activities undertaken by Victorian officers would expand considerably in the later years of the nineteenth century. Benevolent ventures would no longer be confined to the regiments. More ambitious projects were launched, including the National Association for the Employment of Ex-Soldiers (1885) and the Army Temperance Association (1893). The National Association, organized by retired officers, was conspicuously successful; by 1914 it had become the largest employment-finding agency in the country, with 110 branches, securing jobs for nearly half of the ex-soldiers who found employment.[85] Distinguished officers supported these endeavours; indeed the sustained interest of some senior officers in the welfare of the ranks characterized the late Victorian army. Viscount Wolseley, Lord Roberts and Sir Redvers Buller, among others, consistently advocated improvements in the conditions of service at home and abroad. They evinced concern about the food, clothing and living conditions of the ranks not merely before a succession of Select Committees and Royal Commissions, but also when they were leading campaigns overseas or were holding senior commands in the United Kingdom and in India. The attitudes of these senior officers towards the rank and file contrasted sharply with the attitudes adopted by those officers who held field commands during the Peninsular War and who dominated the Horse Guards over the next forty years.

To an extent the contrast between the attitudes of officers of different generations was merely a matter of degree. In the first half of the nineteenth century some senior officers, notably the Duke of York, Commander-in-Chief (1798–1809 and 1811–27) and Major-General Sir Charles Napier, had cared deeply about their men. The Duke, in particular, was revered by the rank and file.[86] A change, nonetheless, occurred in the relations between the officers and the men, prompted by both the pragmatism and paternalism of the officer corps. More and more officers adopted an enlightened approach towards man-management, partly because they had to do so after flogging was abolished, partly because they wished to do so. Wolseley was unashamedly pragmatic; he believed that the army could not attract the necessary recruits without an increase in pay and improved conditions of service.[87] Lord Roberts also believed that a voluntary army could not compete for recruits in the labour market unless the men were dealt with fairly and honestly, with due attention to their wants and grievances.[88] Paternalism, however, was as evident a characteristic as pragmatism: officers would express concern about both the material lot and the spiritual welfare of the other ranks. From the late 1850s onwards, there was a resurgence of the Christian mission within the army.

Prior to the Crimean War, neither evangelism nor the revival of

Methodism had made much of an impact upon the soldier. Horse Guards had let the number of military chaplains steadily decline until there were a mere seven chaplains for the whole army in 1854. Officers like Henry Havelock and Hedley Vicars, who sought to fill the breach by leading their men in Bible study and in prayer meetings, were criticized severely within their respective messes. By consorting with their men and by preaching doctrines other than those of the Established Church, these officers incurred scorn and derision. Even worse, they were suspected of having acted in an improper and unseemly fashion which could subvert the discipline of the troops. Havelock persevered with his Baptist preaching 'in the very teeth of ridicule and opposition', while Vicars, the born-again Protestant, had 'hard work . . . to stand his ground'.[89] Ultimately their examples of Christian and military service reaped a considerable reward. Both died gallantly in battle; both gained enduring fame through quickly written and widely read biographies. Catherine Marsh vividly described the ministrations of Vicars in the Crimea - his care of the sick and wounded, his reading of Scripture at Sunday services, and his funeral orations warning the troops 'to flee from the wrath to come . . .'.[90] The Reverend Brock wrote a hagiography of Havelock in which he not only praised the heroism of the man identified with the relief of Lucknow (1857), but also extolled his exertions in advancing the evangelical cause in India.[91] Lord Panmure, Secretary for War (1855–58), capitalized upon this upsurge of interest in the role of religion within the army. Hoping to curb the incidence of crime and dissolute behaviour within the ranks, he appointed twenty-two more chaplains and thirty-five assistants, all of the Church of England, in 1858. Later in the same year, Presbyterian and Roman Catholic chaplains were engaged in due proportion to the men of each religion in the forces. Chaplains were commissioned in 1858, paid at a common rate in 1859, and uniformed in 1860. By the mid-1860s, the State had made more provision for the spiritual welfare of the army than for either the town or country population.[92]

Catering for the spiritual welfare of the ranks was undertaken at several levels. In the first place there were compulsory church parades every Sunday, involving the smart turnout of the ranks, followed by a collective act of worship. These parades, which were detested by many rankers,[93] ensured that Sunday became the focal point of the regimental week. Secondly there was a profusion of Soldiers' Homes, established by civilian evangelists at various army bases from the 1860s onwards. These Homes, as Chapter 2 will show, greatly expanded the recreational activities available to the rank and file; their objectives, however, were to wean the soldier from the demon drink and to give scope for the proselytizing enthusiasms of their civilian founders. Religion, finally, was promoted by the recurring emergence of extremely devout officers - Sir Hope Grant, Charles (Chinese) Gordon and Sir Douglas Haig, among others. For these officers, deeply-held religious convictions underpinned their sense of responsibility towards the men in their charge. Admittedly many, but not all, of the more pious officers were of a Presbyterian or a Nonconformist persuasion in an officer corps which was overwhelmingly Anglican.[94] Outward displays of religious zeal might still be considered eccentric, but that eccentricity was more readily accepted and its value more appreciated than in former years. Continuing the traditions of Havelock and Vicars, Sir Hope Grant would convene meetings of soldiers in the 1870s intended to inculcate notions of temperance, thrift and a few biblical precepts.[95]

Over the course of the nineteenth century, in sum, the officer gentleman code underwent a change in values. Officers were still attracted from roughly the same groups in society. Aspirants from the ranks and from other unwelcome sources were discouraged from seeking a commission. The criteria of a public school education and the possession of private means acted, like the purchase system, to ensure a largely restrictive pattern of recruitment. The customs, traditions and social life within the mess were preserved partly by recruitment, and partly by pressures upon those who entered the mess to conform to its mores and conventions. Even so, officers were not entirely oblivious of changes within society; as the concept of a gentleman changed within society, so it changed within the army too. By accepting the values implicit in the idea of *noblesse oblige*, officers recognized, more conspicuously than in former years, their paternalistic responsibility for the other ranks. The significance of this development will be underlined by examining the conditions of service endured by the rank and file and the relative indifference of the State towards them.

Notes and references

1. **W. L. Burn**, *The Age of Equipoise*, Allen & Unwin, London, 1964, p. 257.
2. *Ibid.*, p. 263.
3. **Sir G. Wolseley**, 'England as a Military Power in 1854 and in 1878', *Nineteenth Century*, Vol. III, No. xii, Mar. 1878, p. 441.
4. **G. R. St. Aubyn**, *The Royal George, The Life of H.R.H. Prince George Duke of Cambridge, 1819-1904*, Constable, London, 1963, p. 200, and the **Duke of Cambridge** to Queen Victoria, 12 Oct. 1882, quoted in *The Letters of Queen Victoria*, ed. G. Buckle, 1928, 2nd Ser., Vol. III, p. 347.
5. **Sir G. Wolseley** to Lady Wolseley, 11 Sept. 1879, Wolseley Mss., Hove public library, W/P, 3/24a.
6. **Lord Wolseley** to Queen Victoria, 22 Mar. 1885, *The Letters of Queen Victoria*, ed. G. Buckle, 1928, 2nd Ser., Vol. III, p. 632. See also **Viscount Wolseley**, 'The Standing Army of Great Britain', *Harpers New Monthly Magazine*, European edition, **LXXX**, Feb. 1890, p. 346.
7. *Accounts of the System of Military Education in France, Prussia, Austria, Bavaria, and the U.S.*, C.47, 1836, XXII.

8. Evidence (Q.5,077) before *His Majesty's Commissioners for inquiring into the System of Military Punishments in the Army* (hereafter referred to as the Military Punishments Commission), C.59, 1836, XXII.
9. **H. Wyndham,** *The Queen's Service,* Heinemann, London, 1899, pp. 252–3.
10. **E. Mole,** *A King's Hussar,* Cassell, London, 1893, p. 353.
11. Evidence (Qs.4,279, 4,284) before the Military Punishments Commission, *op. cit.*
12. **J. Shipp,** *Memoirs of the Extraordinary Military Career of John Shipp, late a Lieut. in His Majesty's 87th Regiment,* Fisher Unwin, London, 1894, p. 165.
13. Evidence (Q.5,853) before the Military Punishments Commission, *op. cit.*
14. **General C. P. de Ainslie,** *Life as I have found it,* Blackwood, London, 1883, pp. 488–9.
15. **Field Marshal Sir W. Robertson,** *From Private to Field Marshal,* Constable, London, 1921, p. 30.
16. **V. Bonham Carter,** *Soldier True: The Life and Times of Field Marshal Sir William Robertson, 1860–1933,* Muller, London, 1963, p. 30.
17. See the views of Sir W. G. Nicholson at the 122nd meeting of the Army Council on 21 Mar. 1910. Although Sir Ian Hamilton championed the claims of the NCO, the majority of the Council supported Nicholson. P.R.O. W.O.163/15.
18. **A. F. Corbett,** *Service through Six Reigns,* Norwich, 1953, p. 47.
19. **H. Wyndham,** *Following the Drum,* Melrose, London, 1914, p. 63.
20. **P. E. Razzell,** 'Social origins of officers in the Indian and British Home Army: 1758–1962', *British Journal of Sociology,* **14**, 1963, pp. 249–53.
21. **C. B. Otley,** 'The social origins of British army officers', *Sociological Review,* **18**, No. 2, July 1970, pp. 213–39.
22. *P.P.*, No. 111, 1907, XLIX, pp. 3–5.
23. **G. Harries-Jenkins,** *The Army in Victorian Society,* Routledge & Kegan Paul, London, 1977, pp. 24–5.
24. **General Sir H. Gough,** *Soldiering On,* Morrison & Gibb, Edinburgh, 1932, p. 27; **Sir H. Smith-Dorrien,** *Memories of Forty-Eight Years Service,* John Murray, London, 1925, p. 2; **I. Hamilton,** *A Life of General Sir Ian Hamilton,* Cassell, London, 1966, p. 11; **Field Marshal Viscount Wolseley,** *The Story of a Soldier's Life,* 2 vols, Constable, London, 1903, Vol. 1, p. 5.
25. **Field Marshal Earl Roberts,** *Letters written during the Indian Mutiny,* Macmillan, London, 1924, p. xvii.
26. **Earl of Dundonald,** *My Army Life,* E. Arnold, London, 1926, p. 4.

27. **J. Connell,** *Wavell, Scholar and Soldier,* Collins, London, 1964, p. 34.
28. **J. C. Pollock,** *Way to Glory: The Life of Havelock of Lucknow,* J. Murray, London, 1957, p. 8; **Sir C. M. Watson,** *The Life of Major-General Sir Charles William Wilson,* J. Murray, London, 1909, p. 6; **A. Carton de Wiart,** *Happy Odyssey: The memoirs of Lieutenant-General Sir Adrian Carton de Wiart,* Jonathan Cape, London, 1950, p. 16.
29. **Lord Ismay,** *The Memoirs of General the Lord Ismay,* Heinemann, London, 1960, p. 4.
30. **W. Hillcourt,** *Baden-Powell,* Heinemann, London, 1964, pp. 33–4; **Field Marshal Wavell,** *Allenby Soldier and Statesman,* Harrap, London, 1964, p. 25.
31. **E. Butler,** *Mason-Mac: The Life of Lieutenant-General Sir Noel Mason-Macfarlane,* Macmillan, London, 1972, p. 4.
32. Field Marshal Wavell, *op. cit.*, p. 25.
33. *P.P.*, No. 88, 1859, 2nd Session, XVII, pp. 8–37.
34. Evidence (Qs.4,605–6, 4,638–43) before the *Commission appointed to inquire into the system of purchase and sale of Commissions in the Army; with evidence and appendix* (hereafter referred to as the Purchase Commission 1857), C.2,267, 1857 Sess. 2, XVIII.
35. **Duke of Wellington** to Lord Hill, 7 Mar. 1833, Appendix 1 attached to the *Report from the Select Committee on Army and Navy Appointments: with minutes of evidence and appendix,* No. 650, 1833, VII.
36. *P.P.*, No. 426, 1830, XVIII and **Brigadier Sir John Smyth**, *Sandhurst*, Weidenfeld and Nicolson, London, 1961. pp. 56–7.
37. **H. Thomas**, *The Story of Sandhurst*, Hutchinson, London, 1961, p. 97.
38. *Supplementary Despatches, Correspondence and memoranda of Field Marshal Arthur Duke of Wellington, K.G.*, ed. by his son The Duke of Wellington, Vol. XI, John Murray, London, 1864, p. 687.
39. **G. R. Gleig**, *The Life of Arthur First Duke of Wellington*, Longman, London, 1862, p. 552.
40. G. Harries-Jenkins, *op. cit.*, p. 86.
41. *P.P.*, No. 456, 1822, XIX, p. 456. **Sir H. Hardinge** to Lord Fitzroy Somerset, 26 Nov. 1828, Hardinge Mss., McGill University Montreal.
42. *P.P.*, No. 295, 1849, XXXII, p. 91.
43. **Viscount Wolseley** to his wife, 1 Dec. 1900, Wolseley Mss., W/P, 24/80.
44. **Lieutenant-Colonel J. G. Champion**, *A Sketch of the Life of the Late Lieut.-Colonel Champion of the 95th Regiment*, private, London, n.d., p. 3.

45. **C. Woodham-Smith**, *The Reason Why*, Constable, London, 1956, p. 30.
46. *Report of the Commissioners appointed to Inquire into Over-Regulation Payments on Promotion in the Army; with minutes of evidence and appendix* (hereafter referred to as the Over-Regulation Commission), C.201, 1870, XII, p. xii.
47. Evidence (Q.2,628) before the Purchase Commission 1857, *op. cit.*
48. **Sir R. Biddulph,** *Lord Cardwell at the War Office*, John Murray, London, 1904, pp. 90–1.
49. Evidence (Q.1,912) before the *Commission for inquiring into Naval and Military Promotion and Retirement with Appendices* (hereafter referred to as the Commission on Naval and Military Promotion), C.235, 1840, XXII.
50. Sir R. Biddulph, *op cit.*, p. 186.
51. Calculated from Appendix XII of the Report of the Purchase Commission 1857, *op. cit.*, p. 389.
52. For a detailed analysis of brevet promotions and indeed of the purchase system as a whole, see **N. H. Moses**, *Edward Cardwell's abolition of the purchase system in the British army, 1868–1874: A study in administrative and legislative processes*, unpublished Ph.D. thesis, University of London, 1969, ch. II.
53. *Parl. Deb.*, Third Series, Vol. 103, 19 Mar. 1849, col. 963.
54. G. Harries-Jenkins, *op. cit.*, pp. 124–5.
55. Evidence (Q.4,623) before the Purchase Commission 1857, *op. cit.*
56. Report of the Purchase Commission 1857, *op. cit.*, p. xxx.
57. Report of the Commission on Naval and Military Promotion, *op. cit.*, p. xiv.
58. **J. W. Fortescue**, *A History of the British Army*, 13 vols., Macmillan, London, 1923, Vol. XI, p. 39.
59. N. A. Moses, *op. cit.*, pp. 29, 43.
60. **E.** and **A. Linklater**, *The Black Watch*, Barrie & Jenkins, London, 1977, p. 94.
61. G. Harries-Jenkins, *op cit.*, p. 72.
62. **L. Cooper**, *Havelock*, The Bodley Head, London, 1957, pp. 12–13.
63. **Lieutenant-General the Rt. Hon. Sir W. F. Butler,** *Sir William Butler: An Autobiography*, Constable, London, 1911, p. 123.
64. **G. Bell,** *Rough Notes by an old soldier*, 2 vols., Day & Son, London, 1867, Vol. 1, p. 115.
65. **Lieutenant-General J. A. Ewart, C. B.,** *The Story of a Soldier's Life*, 2 vols., Sampson Law & Co., London, 1881, Vol. 1, pp. 416–19.
66. Evidence (Qs.4,624–7) before the Purchase Commission 1857, *op. cit.*
67. *Major-General Sir Henry Hallam Parr, Recollections and Corres-*

pondence, ed. Sir Charles Fortescue-Brickdale, T. Fisher Unwin, London, 1917, p. 66.

68. **General Sir G. Higginson**, *Seventy-One Years of a Guardsman's Life*, Smith & Elder, London, 1916, p. 33.
69. **W. T. Jervis-Waldy**, *From Eight to Eighty*, Harrison, London, 1914, p. 28.
70. *Life of General Sir Hope Grant*, ed. H. Knollys, 2 vols., Blackwoods, London, 1894, Vol. 1, pp. 3, 11.
71. **Field Marshal Viscount Wolseley**, *The Story of a Soldier's Life*, 2 vols, Constable, London, 1903, Vol. 1, p. 10.
72. **A. H. H. MacLean**, *Public Schools and the War in South Africa*, Simpson and Marshall, London, 1902, p. 12.
73. *Ibid.*, p. 19.
74. **T. J. H. Bishop** and **R. Wilkinson**, *Winchester and the Public School Élite*, Faber and Faber, London, 1967, p. 73.
75. *Report of the Committee appointed by the Secretary of State to enquire into the nature of the expenses incurred by officers of the army* (hereafter referred to as the Stanley Report), Cd. 1,421, 1903, X, pp. 7-8.
76. They refused to impose a ban on polo and to implement other proposals, so preserving the private income for a cavalry officer at £300 per annum instead of the £120 per annum advocated by the Committee. **Lord Roberts** to Brodrick, 21 February 1903, Roberts Mss., NAM, R/124/3/707.
77. **Lord E. Gleichen**, *A Guardsman's memories*, Blackwoods, London, 1921, p. 47. Field Marshal Sir W. Robertson, *op. cit.*, p. 30.
78. *Parl. Deb.*, Fourth Ser., Vol. 38, 19 June 1896, cols. 1,481-4.
79. Field Marshal Viscount Wolseley, *op. cit.*, Vol. 1, p. 226.
80. On the decline of drinking in particular, see W. T. Jervis-Waldy, *op. cit.*, pp. 27-8; Lieutenant-General J. A. Ewart, *op. cit.*, Vol. II, p. 321.
81. General C. P. de Ainslie, *op. cit.*, p. 71.
82. W. L. Burn, *op. cit.*, pp. 259-60.
83. E. and A. Linklater, *op. cit.*, p. 85 and H. Wyndham, *op. cit.*, p. 152.
84. Inspection Reports, PRO, WO27/267, 332, 333.
85. **E. M. Spiers**, *The reform of the front-line forces of the regular army in the United Kingdom, 1815-1914*, unpublished Ph.D. thesis, University of Edinburgh, 1974, Appendix XI.
86. **J. Donaldson**, *Recollections of the Eventful Life of a Soldier*, R. Martin, Edinburgh, 1854, pp. 233-4.
87. Evidence (Q.4,480) before the *Committee appointed by the Secretary of State for War to consider the terms and conditions of service in the Army* (hereafter referred to as the Wantage Committee), C.6,582, 1892, XIX.
88. **Lieutenant-General Sir F. S. Roberts**, 'Free trade in the Army',

Nineteenth Century, **XV**, No. lxxxviii, June 1884, pp. 1,055-74.
89. J. C. Pollock, *op. cit.*, p. 41 and **C. M. Marsh**, *Memorials of Captain Hedley Vicars, 97th Regiment*, Nisbet, London, 1856, pp. 32-3.
90. C. M. Marsh, *op. cit.*, p. 168; see also pp. 169-269.
91. **Rev. W. Brock,** *A Biographical Sketch of Sir Henry Havelock*, Nisbet, London, 1858, pp. 2-3.
92. **O. Anderson**, 'The growth of Christian militarism', *The English Historical Review*, **LXXXVI**, 1971, pp. 61-3.
93. Field Marshal Sir W. Robertson, *op. cit.*, p. 9; H. Wyndham, *op. cit.*, p. 66.
94. Appendix 3.
95. *Op. cit.*, ed. H. Knollys, Vol. 2, p. 317.

2 The rank and file

Few social questions bedevilled the British army as persistently as those which attended the annual intake of recruits to the rank and file. Attracting men in sufficient numbers to offset the wastage caused by deaths, discharges and desertion was a perennial problem. It had ramifications throughout the service, and impinged directly upon the strength and effectiveness of the home-based units. To sustain the flow of recruits was a fundamental objective for a voluntary service army; it became a prerequisite in the schemes of army reform. Improvements in pay and changes in the terms and conditions of service were advocated not merely as intrinsically worthwhile objectives, but also as inducements which might enhance the appeal and the attraction of service life. Shortfalls in recruiting, however, would constantly recur; they would underline the intractability of the problem, the inherent difficulty of persuading men to join the army.

The size of the army increased relatively slowly over the period from 1815 to 1914. After the battle of Waterloo and the occupation of France (1815–18), the army was steadily reduced until it was virtually halved in size. Nearly forty years would elapse before the ranks would again number 200,000 men, that is in 1856 during the Crimean War. Sustained throughout the Indian Mutiny and the invasion crisis of 1859, this total was reduced in the 1860s and 1870s until the colonial expansion in the later years of the nineteenth century required larger military establishments. Nevertheless, the proportion of men under arms in the regular army remained within fairly confined parameters. Even including the army reserve of the late nineteenth and early twentieth centuries, the proportion of men under arms merely oscillated between 1 and 2 per cent of the male population (Table 2.1).

Maintaining the effective strength of the army involved the replacement of the vacancies caused by the annual wastage. Henry Marshall, a former deputy inspector-general of hospitals and a medical statistician who specialized in the statistics of recruiting, reckoned that the army of the 1840s required approximately 11,000 to 12,000 men to replace the annual wastage.[1] That army was a long-service force in which soldiers served nominally for life but in practice for approxi-

Table 2.1 Proportion of men under arms

	Male population in the United Kingdom	Effective strength of non-commissioned officers and men	1st class Army Reserve	Total	Proportion under arms (%)
1815	9,375,000	233,952	—	233,952	2.5
1820	10,117,000	114,513	—	114,513	1.1
1825	10,891,000	99,718	—	99,718	0.9
1830	11,622,000	104,066	—	104,066	0.9
1835	12,275,000	102,051	—	102,051	0.8
1840	12,937,000	124,659	—	124,659	1.0
1845	13,583,000	131,832	—	131,832	1.0
1850	13,436,000	136,932	—	136,932	1.0
1855	13,575,000	168,552	—	168,552	1.2
1860	13,997,000	219,631	—	219,631	1.6
1865	14,553,000	203,171	—	203,171	1.4
1870	15,189,000	174,198	—	174,198	1.1
1875	15,957,000	178,276	7,676	185,952	1.2
1880	16,844,000	183,942	16,651	200,593	1.2
1885	17,505,000	181,008	39,286	220,294	1.3
1890	18,197,000	201,848	54,136	255,984	1.4
1895	19,027,000	213,555	82,804	296,359	1.6
1900	19,957,000	291,145	5,251	296,396	1.5
1905	20,854,000	260,035	94,770	354,805	1.7
1910	21,797,000	252,686	135,712	388,398	1.8

Sources: B. R. Mitchell, *Abstract of British Historical Statistics*, University Press, Cambridge, 1962, pp. 8–10; *P.P.* No. 88 (1859), 2 Sess., XVII; No. 412 (1867-68), XLII; C.1,323 (1875), XLIII; C.6,196 (1890), XLIII; C.9,426 (1899), LIII; Cd. 5,016 (1910), LX; Cd. 7,252 (1914), LII.

mately twenty-one years. When Edward Cardwell, the Secretary of State for War, shortened the terms of enlistment in 1870 to six years in the Colours, followed by six years in the Reserve, he accelerated the turnover of men and set new targets for the recruiting process. To replace the wastage and produce an Army Reserve of 178,000 men by 1883, he required an annual intake of 32,000 recruits.[2] Although the Reserve numbered a mere 78,859 men by 1898, the overseas commitments of the army had so expanded in the 1880s and 1890s that the demand for manpower had never slackened. During the Edwardian period, War Office actuaries forecast that the army needed an annual intake of 34,000 to 35,000 recruits to sustain its establishments.[3]

Recruiting rarely met its annual targets. Even the pre-Crimean army appears to have found the recruiting of relatively small numbers of men extremely difficult. Over the twenty-five years from 1815 to 1839, the effective strength of the rank and file sank below its establishment on sixteen occasions.[4] From the sample of later years recorded in Table 2.2, the effective strength of the army only reached its establishment in eleven of the twenty-six years. When the abnormal enlistments and discharges during and immediately after the South African War (1898–1902) are excluded, it would appear that the annual decrease from the rank and file was replenished by the intake of recruits on a mere eight occasions. Only when coupled with returning deserters and extraordinary intakes from the East India Company or the Army and Militia Reserve, did the volume of recruits prove entirely adequate. When these factors were added together they ensured a larger increase than decrease in fourteen out of the twenty-four years.

Wastage remained substantial throughout the years from 1862 to 1912. Even in the 1860s and 1870s, when the establishments were being gradually reduced, the wastage remained remarkably constant. After 1876 the effects of short-service enlistment began to compound this problem; by 1912 the number of men annually discharged had practically doubled. As the short-service men who left the Colours entered the Army Reserve, they were still available for military service; indeed the Army Reserve proved its worth during the South African War and then later in the First World War. But the loss of trained soldiers placed an additional strain on the home-based battalions, many of which were largely composed of raw recruits. Recruitment was unable to ease this strain; its failure was reflected in the expedients adopted by the authorities, on various occasions, to bolster the yearly intake.

The main expedients were threefold. In the first place the War Office would occasionally offer bounties to tempt soldiers into extending their service with the Colours. Bounties of up to £12 were offered to soldiers in 1883, initially to those soldiers who were due to return from India and later to all soldiers in the Line. Less expensive was the second expedient of lowering the minimum physical standards required

Table 2.2 Manpower requirements 1862–1912

	Effective strength	Estab-lishments	Increase				Decrease			
			Recruits	From desertion	Other sources	Total increase	Dead	Discharges including reserves	Desertion and other causes	Total decrease
1862	189,968	194,271	8,814	1,215	14,211*	24,240	3,450	12,231	2,895	18.576
1864	188,025	192,153	16,323	947	—	17,270	3,373	13,118	3,622	20,113
1866	176,731	182,468	15,277	1,039	—	16,316	2,730	14,323	4,144	21,197
1868	172,014	172,633	17,060	1,221	—	18,281	2,685	16,419	3,431	22,535
1870	157,017	161,150	24,594	1,088	—	25,682	2,508	15,720	3,332	21,560
1872	166,985	170,029	17,791	1,855	20	19,666	2,546	11,570	6,602	20,718
1874	162,079	161,031	20,640	2,052	27	22,719	2,011	13,999	6,770	22,780
1876	159,640	160,537	29,370	2,063	21	31,454	1,998	16,921	6,516	25,435
1878	166,366	164,877	28,325	2,751	34,855 †	65,931	2,171	54,532 ‡	7,493	64,196
1880	167,909	164,115	25,622	1,557	3	27,182	3,186	20,802	5,903	29,891
1882	165,655	163,401	23,802	1,297	10,840 §	35,939	2,140	24,657	5,366	32,163
1884	158,029	165,386	35,653	1,568	1,415 §	38,636	1,521	24,874	4,762	31,157
1886	176,865	180,130	39,409	1,864	31	41,304	2,721	25,108	5,897	33,726
1888	186,839	186,180	25,153	1,737	29	26,919	1,852	20,882	4,484	27,218
1890	185,432	189,426	31,407	1,565	24	32,996	1,738	26,579	4,411	32,728
1892	186,447	191,348	41,659	1,944	61	43,664	1,859	30,261	5,424	37,544

Table 2.2 — *continued*

	Effective strength	Establish-ments	Increase				Decrease			
			Recruits	From desertion	Other sources	Total increase	Dead	Discharges including Reserves	Desertion and other causes	Total decrease
1894	193,896	190,690	33,698	1,833	340	35,871	1,792	27,353	4,034	33,179
1896	195,980	192,054	28,532	1,533	57	30,127	1,769	26,021	3,637	31,427
1898	194,705	195,304	40,729	1,789	4,578 §	47,096	2,578	29,892	4,646	37,116
1900	291,145 ‖	239,137 ‖	73,709 ¶	2,438	76,651	152,798	10,153	19,435	7,681	37,269
1902	383,547	272,231	62,250	2,851	5,041	70,142	3,896	124,654	13,668	142,218
1904	279,303	269,013	35,824	2,189	6,540	44,553	1,432	46,674	11,186	59,292
1906	260,035	255,862	35,506	1,647	1,745	38,898	1,186	46,864	5,418	53,468
1908	239,292	242,862	34,274	1,642	1,338	37,254	967	30,096	4,061	35,124
1910	240,712	242,427	30,036	1,355	5,447	36,838	744	26,084	8,331	35,159
1912	241,709	244,743	28,759	1,382	1,148	31,289	669	32,732	4,348	37,749

Notes: * The transfer of East India Company troops to the regular army.
† Transferred from Army and Militia Reserve.
‡ Includes 21,637 transferred to Militia Reserve.
§ From Army Reserve.
‖ Effective strength and establishments for 1900–12 include non-commissioned officers and men.
¶ Includes 10,242 from Imperial Yeomanry and 1,664 from City of London Imperial Volunteers.

of new recruits. Altering physical standards was a traditional ploy; whenever the authorities needed fewer recruits they raised the standards, when they sought more recruits they lowered the standards. Expanding or contracting the field of search, though occasionally productive if timed to coincide with the outbreak of war or the threat of war, was not a panacea. The height regulations for infantry recruits were changed repeatedly; there were sixteen alterations between 1820 and 1859, before the requirements spiralled into a decline from 5 feet 8 inches in 1861 to 5 feet 3 inches in 1900, a testimony to the desperation of the recruiting service. As shortages of recruits recurred, the War Office had recourse to another palliative, namely 'special enlistments'. In the late nineteenth century, boys were enlisted who were thought likely to make efficient soldiers in spite of failing to meet one of the minimum standards of physique or age (eighteen years was the minimum age requirement after 1871). By the early 1890s, 32 per cent of recruits were classified as 'special enlistments', either underage or under-developed adolescents.[5] None of these expedients proved entirely satisfactory as the army, throughout this period, persistently failed to attain its manpower objectives.

Numbers were not the sole concern. The traditional methods by which the Wellingtonian army had sought recruits were another source of controversy. Critics who appeared before two Royal Commissions on recruiting in the 1860s feared that the system itself had contributed to the poor results. Lieutenant-Colonel George Thomson, the commander of the Cork recruiting district, feared that reliance upon inexperienced officers and the use of dishonest and disreputable methods in recruiting ensured enlistment from 'the lowest portion of the population'. Even worse, it rendered the recruiting service and the army targets for abuse by the civilian populace, so lowering the appeal of military service and deterring recruitment from the more respectable sections of the population.[6] The recruiting service was rated as a factor which had compounded the recruiting problem and which had exacerbated relations between the army and society.

In the early nineteenth century the army had found its recruits by a variety of methods. Several large recruiting districts were established throughout the United Kingdom. In 1830 there were 9 such districts, 1 in Scotland, 3 in Ireland, and 5 in England. Centred upon major towns and manned by a full-time staff, they provided facilities where men could be attested and medically examined. Within the districts men were found by recruiting parties of non-commissioned officers and men under the command of regimental officers on two-year secondments. Other recruits were brought in by pensioners and/or by the permanent staff of Militia units. Recruits were also enlisted by the individual regiments at their own headquarters. Unrestricted by centralized supervision, the regimental colonels sent out parties wherever they thought that men might be found. Lieutenant-Colonel C. O. J. Arbuthnot, who commanded the 90th Foot (Perthshire

Volunteers), preferred to send his parties 'almost wholly' to London where they found ' excellent recruits, north countrymen, generally . . . from Scotland, from Yorkshire, and Northumberland . . . They are men who come up for employment to London, but fail in finding it; and I desire my people to take as good characters as they can get, and to be on the watch for these men'.[7]

Sergeants and their recruiting parties, who received a 'bringing-in' fee of 15*s* for every man produced, did not normally trouble themselves about anything other than the physique of the potential recruit. Although some colonels evinced concern about the character of their recruits, they were under no compunction to do so. Not until 1903 did the War Office require character references from the men who offered themselves for enlistment. Unconcerned about factors like sobriety, honesty and respectability, the recruiting parties made straight for the public houses and fair-grounds. Robert Macdonald, a former sergeant, who recruited men for the Rifle Brigade in the 1830s, recalls 'that it was only in the haunts of dissipation or inebriation, and among the very lowest dregs of society, that I met with anything like success. I could seldom prevail on even the uneducated to enlist, when they were sober-living and industriously inclined'.[8] Recruiting sergeants would engage prospective recruits in conversation, ply them with drinks, portray the advantages of a soldier's life as vividly as possible, and press the sovereign's shilling upon them. Until 1870 the recruiters could also tempt their clients with the promise of cash bounties, usually of £2 to £3, should they accept the shilling. Before 1856 such promises were largely bogus; the bounty, paid in intervals as the recruit passed through the stages of attestation and medical inspection, was merely an allowance to pay for the necessary articles of kit. Final payment was made in clothes and cash, with the cash element so small that it could not cover the cost of the remaining kit. New recruits frequently entered the army in debt. Alexander Somerville received a mere 2*d* per day during his first year's service in the Scots Greys, the bulk of his pay being debited at source to pay off an outfit debt of £3 10*s*.[9] Even when the government accepted responsibility for the supply of a soldier's kit, and the bounties were paid in a lump sum, so many recruits either squandered the money in drinking or absconded with the bounty intact that the payments were utterly discredited. The whole system of recruitment, in other words, was pervaded by drink and deception, a disreputable exercise which encouraged drunkenness, desertion and fraudulent enlistment.

Once a man had taken the sovereign's shilling, he had formally enlisted. Of the men who took the shilling, barely half of them ever joined the ranks. Medical inspections, though liable to vary in thoroughness from district to district, were never a simple formality. However desperate the manpower shortage, the army was not prepared to accept grossly undernourished or malformed or disease-ridden men. Over the years from 1837 to 1840 some 2,718 men were rejected out of the 7,829 inspected by the Glasgow district. Rejection rates were higher in urban than in rural districts; the 34.7 per cent recorded in Glasgow contrasted with 17.6 per cent in Cork.[10] The effects of this contrast would become more pronounced during the latter half of the nineteenth century. As the army became increasingly dependent upon urban areas for recruits, it rejected between a quarter and a third of those who offered themselves for enlistment. By Edwardian years nearly half of those who took the King's shilling were subsequently rejected for physical, medical or other reasons (Table 2.3).

The service could also reject men during the process of attestation. To be confirmed as an eligible soldier, the recruit had to be brought before a justice of the peace between twenty-four and ninety-six hours after he had accepted the shilling. Thereupon particulars of the man's background were recorded (they were rarely checked) and, if satisfactory, the magistrate would administer the oath of allegiance. In theory men could be rejected as ineligible should they admit being married, or an apprentice, or a member of certain trades, for example a sailor; in practice every few were rejected as the recruits could fill in any details without fear of scrutiny. Should the recruit have second thoughts about entering the army, he had several avenues of escape. He might abscond with his shilling before seeing the magistrate, providing that he could elude the watch of his recruiting party. Legally he could pay £1 'smart money' before the process of attestation, and so avoid the obligation to military service. More deviously, he could await payment of his bounty and then desert with the money. All three avenues were used as men repented of the evenings with the recruiting sergeant (Table 2.3).

Efforts would be made to reform the recruiting system and to remove the worst abuses. The office of Inspector-General of Recruiting was established in 1867 to enforce uniformity in the methods adopted. Sweeping changes were introduced in 1870. The number of pensioners employed in recruiting was greatly reduced. Recruiting parties were instructed to remove their offices from public houses. Advertisements were required to be clear and honest in their presentations. Enlistment bounties were prohibited. Free discharges were instituted for any recruit who could prove that he had been deceived during the process of enlistment, and the responsible recruiters were required to bear the cost of the expenses incurred. Subsequently more importance would be attached to publicity and to advertisements in the local and national press. Traditional recruiting marches would be supplemented by public displays, like the Royal Naval and Military Tournament, held annually after 1893, and even by a recruiting film in 1914.[11] Not until the Edwardian years, however, was there any noticeable decline in the proportion of losses from desertion, payment of 'smart money' and other causes (Table 2.3). The recruiting sergeants, indeed, may have been less ready to change their time-honoured methods than the authorities in the War Office. As late as October 1890 Horace Wyndham

Table 2.3 Wastage rate in recruiting 1862–1910

	Number of men enlisted	Rejected by the authorities	Absconded	Paid smart	Deserted	Losses from other causes	Number who joined units
1862	12,516	4,565 (36.5%)	294	756	133	40	6, 728 (53.8%)
1866	23,410	7,075 (30.2%)	472	1,870	264	89	13,640 (58.3%)
1870	34,547	8,278 (24.0%)	501	2,370	248	133	23,031 (66.7%)
1874	30,356	6,208 (20.5%)	677	2,588	323	248	20,312 (73.9%)
1878	42,734	9,556 (22.4%)	903	3,248	525	393	28,109 (65.8%)
	Number of men served with notice papers			**Failed to come up for attestation**			
1882	45,385	12,487 (27.5%)		8,841	279	234	23,555 (51.9%)
1886	71,786	22,593 (31.5%)		9,725	370	127	38,953 (54.3%)
1890	61,434	20,518 (33.4%)		9,628	245	107	30,918 (50.3%)
1894	70,999	28,349 (39.9%)		8,618	424	167	33,441 (47.1%)
1898	84,626	32,330 (38.2%)		12,732	593	81	38,890 (46.0%)
							Finally approved
1902	n.a.	39,354		n.a.	782	n.a.	52,897
							Number who joined units
1906	83,155	40,976 (49.3%)		4,665	406	769	36,339 (43.7%)
1910	63,751	35,165 (55.2%)		2,074	107	19	26,386 (41.4%)

Sources: *P.P.* C.1,323 (1875), XLIII, p. 22; C.6,196 (1890), XLIII, p. 28; C.9,426 (1899), LIII, p. 30; Cd. 5,016 (1910), LX, p. 45; Cd. 7,252 (1914), LII, p. 49.

Notes: Where statistics were not collected, i.e. during and immediately after the Boer War, 'n.a.'='not available' has been inserted in the appropriate columns. In these years, too, only the number of men finally approved were recorded. Usually there were a few casualties and desertions after the stage of final approval, and hence the number who joined their units can be assumed to be slightly smaller in those particular years.

It should be noted that these tables reproduce official published statistics including the small arithmetical errors which occur in various returns up to 1890. As the source of these errors cannot be pin-pointed with any accuracy, the raw data have not been altered.

enlisted in the army, having consummated his decision over a couple of whisky and sodas with a recruiting sergeant in a nearby hostelry.[12] Dubious methods, in other words, probably persisted in some localities, although the more glaring abuses were undoubtedly removed.

Of those who entered the army, the first Royal Commission on Recruiting concluded 'that but few enlist from any real inclination for military life, and that Enlistment is, for the most part, occasioned by want of work - by pecuniary embarrassment - by family quarrels - or by any other difficulties of a private nature'.[13] Unemployment was always reckoned to be the motive which prompted the majority of recruits to enlist. It was a commonplace assumption, voiced before numerous Select Committees and Royal Commissions, that recruiting flourished whenever unemployment was high, and that recruiting slumped whenever the terms of trade improved. Statistical evidence to support this assumption was lacking, however. The army never tabulated its dependence upon the unemployed. During the process of enlistment, prospective recruits were required to state their previous trade, but not whether they were actually employed in it.

In 1890 the War Office tried to substantiate the correlation between recruiting and unemployment. It prepared a graph comparing the trends of imports and exports, pauperism, and army and militia recruitment over the years from 1859 to 1888. The graph was clearly intended to show a close correlation between the trend of recruiting and the fluctuations of civil unemployment, as indicated by the number of paupers receiving outdoor relief.[14] But this conclusion, as Dr Skelley has argued, rests on fairly tenuous foundations. Pauperism and recruiting varied from region to region, and these local variations were left unexplained. The graph, too, could not allow for other factors which might affect recruitment, like alterations in the terms and conditions of service, the excitement caused by war or the threat of war, and the size of the establishments voted annually by Parliament (battalions had to cease recruiting should they reach their prescribed limits). As a consequence, the graph could only reveal a simplified correlation which, in any case, was less than conclusive. When pauperism fell to its lowest total of nearly three-quarters of a million in 1877-78, recruitment, instead of falling too, remained relatively high, in excess of 28,000 men.[15]

Enlistment motivation was a complicated and many-sided phenomenon. It cannot be understood by isolating one factor, however important, and by comparing that factor with the national returns. In the first place, market forces never operated in conditions of perfect freedom; there was never a free flow of men from the unemployed into the ranks, as the War Office regulated the intake by altering age and physical standards, while Parliament limited the numbers by imposing rigid establishments on an annual basis. Secondly the vast majority of the unemployed preferred the condition of unemployment to enlistment in the regular army. Whereas the largest number of recruits recorded in any year from 1859 to 1888 was 39,552 men, there was never less than 745,453 paupers in any particular year in the same period.[16] Many of the latter would have been too old or too unfit for military service, yet there was a vast reservoir of eligible unemployed men which the army, though perennially short of recruits, failed to attract. Unemployment, in sum, was never a panacea for the recruiting problems of the regular army.

Nevertheless unemployment prompted many men to offer themselves for enlistment. Various rankers testified before Royal Commissions that unemployment alone had driven them into the army.[17] Others confirmed in their memoirs that lack of work or lack of money had precipitated their decision to enlist. Alexander Somerville recalled that he enlisted in 1831 while moneyless and in a 'black prison of despair'.[18] Sergeant John Menzies recalled that he had met his recruiting sergeant when 'going home one night with a heavy heart and a light purse . . .'.[19] Sergeant J. MacMullen, writing in 1846, estimated that two-thirds of those who enlisted felt compelled to do so by want of employment.[20] Sergeant Robert Edmondson reckoned that, by the 1890s, 70 to 80 per cent of the army was recruited from the unemployed.[21] The Health Report of 1909 confirmed that 'well over 90 per cent' of those inspected were out of work.[22] Although only a small number of the nation's unemployed entered the army each year, that number probably represented the majority of each recruiting intake.

Hunger and poverty were not the sole motives for enlistment. Traditionally, the regular army served as a refuge for men escaping from their domestic circumstances, particularly from their amatory indiscretions. Once enlisted, the soldier could not be arrested for leaving a wife and a child as a charge on the parish, or for incurring a debt of under £30.[23] Some men enlisted on impulse; they admitted leaving their civilian occupations on a mere whim or fancy, either to travel abroad, or to join family and friends in the ranks, or to embark on a life more glamorous and exciting than the one which they had currently endured.[24] Gentlemen joined the ranks in small but conspicuous numbers. Mainly students or professional men who had encountered a setback in their former careers, they entered the ranks in the hope of promotion to an officer's commission.[25] More attracted by the delights of soldiering were those recruits who came from the auxiliary forces or who were the sons of soldiers. Included in the latter group were the boy soldiers of fourteen years from the Royal Military Asylum at Chelsea and from the Royal Hibernian School at Dublin. From 1801 to 1830 the Military Asylum furnished 1,500 boy soldiers, while the Hibernian School provided another 550 boys from 1815 to 1830. By 1889–92, these institutions were each supplying about 100 recruits per annum, a large contribution by their own standards but still minute as a proportion of the annual enlistments.[26] The Wellingtonian army augmented its numbers of boy soldiers by accepting pauper children from union houses. In 1843–44, 271 boys

Table 2.4 **Previous civilian occupations of recruits expressed in percentage terms**

	Labourers	Artisans	Mechanics	Shopmen/ clerks	Profes- sions	Boys
1861	48.4	15.1	24.3	9.6	0.6	2.0
1864	59.2	14.2	17.4	6.5	0.7	2.1
1867	59.1	15.8	16.4	6.4	0.7	1.6
1870	64.7	7.5	19.5	6.5	0.7	1.2
1873	58.9	10.1	21.4	7.4	0.6	1.6
1876	61.0	12.0	17.5	6.8	0.8	1.9
1879	59.4	10.1	19.5	8.1	0.9	2.0
1882	59.5	13.8	15.9	6.7	1.3	2.8
1885	64.1	14.5	13.4	5.4	0.8	1.8
1888	61.6	15.7	12.0	6.6	1.2	2.9
1891	64.0	15.8	10.8	5.7	1.0	2.7
1894	65.1	14.7	9.9	6.4	1.2	2.7
1897	64.0	14.8	10.2	7.3	1.0	2.7
1900	61.6	14.2	13.3	7.0	1.0	2.9
1903	67.9	11.4	11.2	4.9	0.7	3.9

Notes: The classifications of the Medical Department, cited above, were defined as follows:

1. Labourers includes servants and husbandmen;
2. Artisans includes cloth-makers, lace-makers and weavers;
3. Mechanics includes trades favourable to physical development like smiths, carpenters and masons;
4. Boys were under seventeen years of age.

were removed from unions in England, of which 132 went into the army, while the remainder joined the navy.[27]

Regardless of motive, those who joined the army came primarily from the least skilled sections of the working-class. Casual labourers comprised the bulk of the recruits from rural areas and the largest single group from the towns. Revealed in the recruiting returns from Cork and Glasgow in the 1840s,[28] this trend became more and more pronounced throughout the late nineteenth century (Table 2.4). Evidence from these returns must be treated with caution as the occupations recorded were either notional in some cases, or classified in categories too all-embracing to be meaningful. Yet the dependence of the army upon unskilled labour, especially town casuals, remains abundantly clear. Even in the later Edwardian years, when more precise returns were published, the army appears to have found nearly half of its recruits from this occupational group (Table 2.5).

Officers claimed that better recruits were found from some trades than from others. Colonel T. W. Brotherton affirmed that 'the worst description of soldier is a decayed gentleman, or a man born to a better sphere of life'.[29] Many officers shared this opinion, viewing the gentleman ranker as a disruptive and a discontented

Table 2.5 Trades of men offering themselves for enlistment who were medically examined 1907–13 expressed in percentage.terms

	Year ending 30.9.07	Year ending 30.9.08	Year ending 30.9.09	Year ending 30.9.10	Year ending 30.9.11	Year ending 30.9.12	Year ending 30.9.13
Town casuals	19	20	19	21	20	16	16
Agricultural unskilled labour	11	11	11	11	12	12	11
Other unskilled labour	17	17	17	14	16	18	18
All unskilled labour	47	48	47	46	48	46	45
Skilled labour	22	23	24	23	22	24	24
Other occupations	26	24	24	26	25	25	26
Professions, students	1	1	1	1	1	1	1
Boys under 17 years	4	4	4	4	4	4	4
Total (%)	100	100	100	100	100	100	100
Total number	58,764	61,182	56,327	45,085	47,421	47,008	42,977

Notes: These tables were collated and percentaged from the General Annual Returns for the years in question. The classifications differ from those recorded in Table 2.5:

1. Unskilled labour – agricultural and other outdoor labourers, factory and indoor labourers, town and country casuals;
2. Skilled labour – most of the trades classified under 'artisans' and 'mechanics' in Table 2.5, including coal-miners, smiths, farriers, carpenters, butchers, textile workers;
3. Other occupations – clerks/tradesmen's assistants along with the servants, porters and carters which were included in 'labourers' in Table 2.5.

element within the ranks. They considered that gentlemen did not mix well in the barracks, were often self-opinionated and litigious, and were frequently impertinent towards non-commissioned officers.[30] Occasionally individuals, like H. D. Acland-Troyte, would be encouraged to enter the ranks in the hope of promotion to an officer's commission, but his case was highly unusual. Officers doubted that there was anything in the duties of a private soldier which qualified him for a commission. As Captain G. T. Younghusband observed, 'most men lose more than they gain during their term of service in the ranks: in self-reliance, in manner, in polish - even in speech. We have known for instance, a born gentleman, who after three years in the ranks had utterly lost the proper use of the letter "h"'.[31]

Unlike gentlemen rankers, agricultural labourers were regarded as possessing all the qualities required of the Victorian soldier. Officers and non-commissioned officers alike praised the fitness and the docility of the rural recruit. Not only were agricultural labourers viewed as stronger and healthier than their slum-bred counterparts, but they were also regarded as more malleable, more obedient, and more contented with their lot.[32] These impressions, repeatedly voiced before Select Committees and Royal Commissions, would be increasingly emphasized as the army witnessed a rapid decline in rural recruitment. Although national statistics are lacking, the extent of the decline was evident by Edwardian years, when a mere 11 per cent of recruits were agricultural labourers (Table 2.5). During the nineteenth century, those regiments which had traditionally recruited in rural areas had had to seek additional recruits from other localities. Whereas the 42nd Foot (the Black Watch) had found 51 per cent of its recruits in the Highlands in 1798, it secured only 9 per cent from that region in 1830-34, and a bare 5 per cent in 1854. Like other Highland regiments, it had to seek an increasing proportion of its men from the Lothians and Glasgow.[33]

The urbanization of the Victorian army mirrored a massive transformation in its national composition. In 1830 and 1840, over half of the non-commissioned officers and men came from Scotland and Ireland. By 1912, 79.6 per cent of the non-commissioned officers and men were either English or Welsh. In the early Victorian army, both Scotland and Ireland were over-represented in the rank and file. Massive unemployment had produced the bulk of the 42,897 soldiers from Ireland in 1830, a contribution which amounted to 42.2 per cent of the British army. Overwhelmingly rural in composition, the Irish enlistments would decline sharply after the famine of 1846. As large scale emigration from Ireland would continue over the next sixty years, taking away 5½ million people by 1911, so many young men who might otherwise have enlisted sailed for the United States. The Irish proportion of the army dropped to 27.9 per cent in 1870, 15.6 per cent in 1888, and 9.1 per cent in 1912. By the end of the period the military contribution from Ireland corresponded to her proportion of the population of the United Kingdom. Scotland, by contrast, never provided as many soldiers as Ireland. In 1830 she supplied 13,800 troops, or 13.6 per cent of the army. By 1879, 7.7 per cent of the army was Scots, a proportion which remained remarkably steady over the next generation: by 1912, 7.8 per cent of the army came from Scotland (Table 2.6). As Scotland contained about 10.5 per cent of the population of the United Kingdom, her recruiting had simply failed to keep pace with the growth in population.[34]

Although recruiting from the cities of England would compensate for the declining numbers of Scots and Irish soldiers, only some Englishmen were attracted to the Colours. The army remained 'un-English', as Professor Hanham has noted, inasmuch as it grossly under-represented the nonconformist religions.[35] Until the 1860s the army only recognized the Church of England, the Roman Catholic Church, and the Presbyterians. The religions of new recruits were classified in brusque and summary fashion. Those who could not profess any religious adherence were allocated a religion, usually 'C. of E.'. Those who affirmed belief in a Dissenting creed were given the option of joining any of the three prescribed religions. After 1863, 'Other Protestants' were registered and soon constituted about 3 per cent of the army. Once Wesleyans were allowed to register, their numbers gradually expanded until they constituted about 5 per cent of the army by the 1890s. From 1903 onwards, Baptists and Congregationalists were also permitted to register separately, but the proportion of avowed nonconformists in the ranks never exceeded 7 per cent (Table 2.7). This proportion merely underscored the class basis of both the army and the nonconformist creeds. As the rank and file of the army was drawn overwhelmingly from the working class, and usually from the least respectable sections of the working class, it held little attraction for religious groups which, excluding the Methodists, were preponderantly middle-class in composition.

The army, in sum, never broadened the base of its social composition. Despite altering methods of recruitment, reducing physical standards, and accepting, albeit reluctantly, an ever-increasing proportion of recruits from the urban industrial centres of England, the army failed to alleviate its recruiting problem. All initiatives to improve the quality and quantity of the recruiting intake foundered upon the profound contempt with which the military career was viewed. The army never eroded the stigma of enlistment. The reaction of the father of John Fraser, when told of his son's enlistment in 1876, was typical:

> Never have I seen a man so infuriated. To him my step was a blow from which he thought he would never recover, for it meant disgrace of the worst type. His son a soldier! . . . Rather would he have had me out of work for the rest of my life than earning my living in such a manner. More than that, he would

Table 2.6 Nationalities of non-commissioned officers and men

	England and Wales		Scotland		Ireland		Others and those not reported
	% of UK pop.	% of Army	% of UK pop.	% of Army	% of UK pop.	% of Army	% of Army
1830	58.2	43.7	9.5	13.6	32.2	42.2	—
1840	59.4	46.5	9.5	13.7	31.0	37.2	2.6
1870	72.1	60.3	10.5	9.6	17.4	27.9	2.2
1873	72.9	67.0	10.5	8.5	16.6	23.6	0.9
1876	73.5	68.3	10.6	7.9	15.9	22.7	1.1
1879	74.0	66.8	10.6	7.7	15.4	20.3	5.2
1882	74.8	69.3	10.6	7.6	14.6	20.6	2.5
1885	75.5	71.6	10.6	7.7	13.8	17.4	3.3
1888	76.2	74.3	10.6	8.5	13.2	15.6	1.6
1891	76.8	76.2	10.6	8.3	12.6	13.9	1.6
1894	77.3	77.5	10.7	8.1	12.0	12.6	1.8
1897	77.7	77.0	10.7	7.8	11.5	12.4	2.8
1900	78.1	n.a.	10.8	n.a.	11.0	n.a.	n.a.
1903	78.6	75.8	10.8	8.4	10.7	11.8	4.0
1906	78.9	77.8	10.7	8.0	10.4	10.3	3.8
1909	79.2	78.8	10.6	7.8	10.1	9.7	3.7
1912	79.6	79.6	10.4	7.8	9.9	9.1	3.5

Notes: These statistics are for 1 January of each year to January 1900, then from 1 October. The 'others' category includes British subjects who were born abroad, those born in the Empire and foreigners.

Sources: *P.P.* No. 307 (1841), XIV; C.3,083 (1881), LVIII; C.9,426 (1899), LIII; Cd. 3,798 (1908), XI; Cd. 7,252 (1914), LII.

Table 2.7 **Religious denominations of non-commissioned officers and men expressed in percentage terms**

	Church of England	Presbyterians	Roman Catholics	Wesleyans	Other Protestants	Baptists and Congrega-tionalists	Others and those not reported
1862	60.0	10.5	28.2	n.a.	n.a.	n.a.	1.3
1868	58.2	9.6	28.4	n.a.	3.1	n.a.	0.7
1873	64.5	8.8	22.8	n.a.	3.3	n.a.	0.6
1878	64.5	7.8	23.0	n.a.	3.9	n.a.	0.8
1883	64.3	7.6	22.9	3.7	0.6	n.a.	0.9
1888	66.7	7.8	19.7	5.0	0.6	n.a.	0.2
1893	68.2	7.3	17.9	5.2	0.7	n.a.	0.7
1898	68.0	7.2	17.5	5.2	0.9	n.a.	1.1
1903	68.4	7.5	16.5	5.0	1.2	n.a.	1.3
1908	70.2	7.4	14.7	4.6	0.7	1.4	1.0
1913	70.6	7.0	14.7	4.3	0.7	1.7	1.0

Sources: *General Annual Returns of the British Army . . . P.P.* C.3,083 (1881), LVIII; C.9,426 (1899), LIII; Cd. 3,798 (1908), XI; Cd. 7,252 (1914), LII.

> rather see me in my grave, and he would certainly never have me in his house again in any circumstances.[36]

When a soldier enlisted with a blessing from his family, it was usually where there was already a service connection. The army never eroded the deeply-held reservations about the character and life-style of the serving soldier, and his prospects once he had returned to civilian life. As Lord Wavell recalled, 'There was in the minds of the ordinary God-fearing citizen no such thing as a good soldier; to have a member who had gone for a soldier was for many families a crowning disgrace'.[37]

The terms and conditions of service

To explain the failure of the army to attract a 'better class' of recruit, the Duke of Wellington declared that: 'The objection to entering into the army, in my opinion, is the severity and regularity of the discipline, and the life which the soldier is obliged to lead, and which you must oblige him to lead - the climates to which he is exposed, and the constancy of the service in those climates'.[38] In other words, the terms and conditions of service warrant analysis in any attempt to explain the disdain which was felt for service in the rank and file. The low status of an army career reflected the terms of enlistment, pay and living conditions of the ordinary soldier, his life-style and recreational habits, the discipline and punishments which he endured, and the fate which awaited him when discharged from the service.

Until 1829 men enlisted either for life (in practice twenty-one years in the infantry, artillery and engineers or twenty-four years in the cavalry), or for a limited period of seven years, with an option of extending their service for the same period. The limited service option, first introduced in 1806, had little appeal. Over the twelve years from 1817 to 1829, the proportion of recruits who chose limited service varied from less than 2 per cent in Cork, Dublin and London to a maximum of 14.5 per cent in Glasgow. So poor a response underlined the disparity of the bounties offered for the alternative terms of service; the larger bounty for unlimited service was always the more attractive.[39] From 1829 till 1847 the army was allowed to recruit for unlimited service only, which incensed reformers like Henry Marshall and ensured regular attempts in Parliament to amend the terms of service. Captain Layard, MP, believed that unlimited service had led to the high rate of crime, desertion and suicide in ranks. He thought, too, that it had contributed to the feelings of those parents who had maimed their sons to prevent them from entering the army.[40] When the government, in the search for more recruits, conceded reform, it did so grudgingly. In 1847, it allowed soldiers to enlist initially for ten years in the infantry, or twelve years in the cavalry, artillery and engineers, with the opportunity of re-enlisting for another eleven years in the infantry and twelve in the rest of the army. As Earl Grey explained, the reform was intended to make the army more popular and to enhance its appeal, but only 'for the better classes of the labouring population'.[41] It was not intended that the army should discard the old soldier, so highly regarded by the Duke of Wellington. Soldiers, under the Act of 1847, would not be entitled to a pension unless they completed a period of re-enlistment. Long service, in effect, was preserved as the normal term of enlistment; it carried less opprobrium than service for life but was hardly an attractive feature of army life. Not until the Army Enlistment Act of 1870 was short service introduced - six years in the Colours followed by six years in the regular Reserve, with only a minority being allowed to extend their service to twenty-one years.

Soldiers received the same rate of basic pay throughout the first half of the nineteenth century; it ranged from 1*s* 3*d* per day in the cavalry to 1*s* per day in the infantry, plus an allowance for beer of 1*d* per day. Compared with wages of unskilled labourers, these rates were low but competitive in some regions of the country. J. H. Clapham estimated that average weekly wages in 1847 varied from 11*s* 6*d* in the ten northern counties of England to 9*s* 6*d* in southern Scotland, and 8*s* 5*d* in the eighteen southern counties of England. The extremes ranged from 14*s* in the West Riding to 7*s* in Gloucester, south Wiltshire and Suffolk.[42] Recruits, however, were probably attracted as much by the promise of regular payment as by the rates of pay - a clear one shilling a day was implied by the recruiting sergeants. In fact the soldier never received one shilling, as 6*d* a day was deducted for messing, more than 2*d* for laundry and the 'maintenance of necessaries', various amounts for hair-cutting and barrack damages, and as much as 10*d* a day should he enter hospital (or 9*d* if hospitalized abroad). The new recruit in the Wellingtonian army, burdened by additional stoppages to pay for his kit, would be lucky if he received one penny a day for his first six months in the service. Indeed, Horse Guards had to issue a regulation affirming that a soldier should not receive less than 1*d* a day.

Few soldiers depended entirely upon their regimental pay. Carpenters, shoemakers, tailors, and men with similar skills could easily supplement their wages. Wives could augment the pay of their husbands by as much as 4*s* or 5*s* a week by washing for the regiment. In all units men could earn extra pay through employment as officers' servants and mess waiters. Extra duty pay was available for artillerymen and engineers: up to 2*s* per day could be paid for work in road and bridge building, surveying and telegraphy. Gratuities, too, were awarded in limited number for distinguished service. Cavalrymen could draw additional pay as grooms for the horses of sergeants, farriers and bandsmen. Rankers, finally, could benefit from the receipt of good conduct pay, which was first introduced in 1836. Men of unblemished conduct were awarded an additional penny a day for every five years they remained in service. Nevertheless these extra payments hardly compensated the majority of rankers, especially those in the infantry, for the loss of money through stoppages. Nor were these payments of any assistance in recruiting. The offer of 1*s* a day would prove to be increasingly less competitive as a wage in the labour market.

A substantial increase in pay was repeatedly demanded by reformers inside and outside the army. As late as 1892, Viscount Wolseley would protest, before a Select Committee appointed to consider the terms and conditions of military service, that 'unless we can give a very high rate of pay, we shall always be obliged to take in "the waifs and strays"'.[43] Until the reverses of the Boer War, these protestations fell on deaf ears. Fears of incurring a large increment in public expenditure, fuelled by the pessimistic reports of senior civil and military advisers, ensured opposition from successive Secretaries of State for War. Arthur Haliburton, Permanent Under-Secretary of State at the War Office (1895–97), doubted whether any increase in pay, other than an extremely large one, would affect recruitment.[44] Sir Redvers Buller, Adjutant-General (1890–97), opposed any attempt to raise a highly-paid army; he recommended that soldiers be given free groceries rather than increased pay.[45] By taking this advice Sir Henry Campbell-Bannerman, like his predecessors as Secretary of State for War, could ignore the claim that a pay-rise was overdue and nécessary. He would argue subsequently that the inducement to enlist was not pay but 'the military life, the adventurous life and the change'.[46]

Yet the net pay of the soldier was more than doubled in the latter half of the nineteenth century. Governments, though reluctant to increase the basic rate of pay, would prove more amenable to the suggestion that stoppages should be reduced; from 9½*d* per day in 1866, stoppages were gradually reduced to 4½*d* per day in 1892. Improvements were also conceded in those additional payments awarded to soldiers who behaved well, or acquired special skills, or undertook long-service engagements. The qualifying periods for good conduct pay were revised and shortened on several occasions between 1860 and 1899; from 1870 onwards more than 40 per cent of the rank and file possessed at least one good conduct badge.[47] Another benefit, introduced in 1876, was deferred pay, by which additional payments of 2*d* a day were credited over a maximum period of twelve years' service, but were held back and paid in a lump sum on discharge. As a means of deterring desertion the scheme was not a success; indeed it was soon criticized for discouraging men from re-engaging for a further period of service, and for tempting soldiers into a reckless spending spree when discharged from the ranks. In 1898 deferred pay was replaced by a messing allowance and a gratuity of £1 per year of service, which brought the basic pay of an infantry private to 1*s* 3*d*.

As stoppages were still deducted, soldiers were not receiving a clear one shilling as their basic daily pay.

Only in 1902 was army pay radically improved. Implemented during the South African War, the reforms included the provision of a clear one shilling a day for 'efficient' soldiers (that is, for those over nineteen years of age), and the introduction of service pay, an additional 6*d* a day for soldiers who had completed two years' service, subject to character suitability and a second-class standard of shooting (third-class or lower received an extra 4*d* a day). The war itself had not occasioned these reforms, although the defeats and humiliations in battle had shattered the complacency with which the government viewed its military arm. As late as 8 March 1901, William St John Brodrick, the Secretary of State for War, expressed 'the gravest reservations whether any increased pay we could give, unless we give something like double, would really bring in a different stamp of recruit'.[48] Brodrick did not take any initiative on army pay until he perceived that his own scheme of army reform, which had been launched during the war, was liable to be vitiated by a manpower crisis: only then did he accede to the demands of Lord Roberts, the Commander-in-Chief, for an increase in pay.[49] A concession so limited and so tardy could not be sufficient. After two years' service an infantry private, if awarded the extra 6*d* service pay, would earn 1*s* 11*d* daily less 3½*d* stoppages - a net 'weekly' pay of 11*s* 4½*d*. This was not merely an abysmal wage by contemporary urban standards, but it was also over 2*s* lower than the average weekly wage of an agricultural labourer in Caithness, the poorest paid agricultural labourer in mainland Britain.[50] Unable to compete with the wages of the labour market, the army was doomed to rely upon the destitute and the unemployed for its potential recruits.

Soldiers were not only poorly paid, they were also indifferently housed. When serving in the United Kingdom, they were quartered almost entirely in barracks, although Guardsmen were still being billeted on innkeepers as late as 1837. Barracks had always been an object of controversy, a symbol of the standing army separating soldiers from the rest of society. Indeed barracks were not extensively constructed until the outbreak of the French and Napoleonic Wars. Whereas the Board of Ordnance could accommodate only 20,487 men in 1792, it quartered 97,269 in 1816. The barrack department defended this mode of accommodation. Barracks, it claimed, kept 'the Young Soldier from the contaminating influence of the very lowest and most disorderly part of Society'.[51]

The barracks varied enormously in size and in amenities. Some were old forts and castles, like Edinburgh Castle and the Tower of London; others had been hastily erected during the Napoleonic Wars. A few, as in Dublin, Weedon and Woolwich appear to have been reasonably spacious and well-appointed. The majority, however, were extremely small and incapable of housing a whole regiment. Barracks in the south of England were better than those in the north, where troops were often quartered in the centre of manufacturing towns, and lacked either adequate accommodation or training facilities. Conspicuously absent were proper washing and cooking facilities. Of 146 barracks in Britain, 89 lacked any washing accommodation for men while 77 were bereft of washing accommodation for clothes. In the smaller, overcrowded barracks of Ireland conditions were considerably worse; in the 139 barracks separate accommodation for washing clothes was missing in 105 barracks, and for washing men in 130. Where separate accommodation was lacking, men drew water from a pump in the barrack-square or sometimes from a nearby stream, and washed in a wooden tub which also served as a urinal overnight.[52]

Spartan and severe in appearance, the sleeping chambers in which the men ate, drank, and slept were cramped and poorly ventilated. In 1816 men were still huddled together by fours in wooden cribs. Even when beds for each man were provided, the minimum amount of space permitted a soldier was 450 cubic feet, 30 cubic feet less than a pauper was afforded in a Scottish workhouse. While the regulations were rigorously upheld within the workhouses of Scotland, they more commonly went by default within the army. The majority of barracks fell below requirements; some provided only 300 cubic feet, others less than 225 cubic feet.[53] The men compounded the effects of overcrowding by blocking up ventilation so that the air became foetid and unwholesome. By morning, as Sergeant Brown recalled, 'The air was offensive from the men's breath and from the urine tube in the room; and, of course, some soldiers do not keep their feet very clean especially in summer time'.[54] Insanitary surroundings aggravated the effects of overcrowding and inadequate ventilation. Nauseating odours pervaded the barrack-rooms; they emanated from the urine tubes left overnight in the sleeping chambers, from the open cesspools which adjoined the buildings, and from the soil soaked with sewage. Arguably the worst barracks were located in London, where Guardsmen were crowded into cramped and inadequate quarters or languished in the lowest part of the Tower. As the quarters in the Tower were situated close to a ditch kept wet for purposes of defence, which was used as a sewage receptacle by local residents, the Guards were swept periodically by bouts of typhus. Improvements were made before the revelations of the Crimean War Commissions: the ditch near the Tower was drained, and in 1845 the Hyde Park barracks were re-designed so that the space for each man was quadrupled. Yet the Barrack Committee would report in 1855 that 'the accommodation hitherto provided in barracks, notwithstanding an improvement in those built of late years, has been generally inadequate both for the comfort and convenience of the soldiers, and for the creation of a higher tone of social habits amongst them . . .'.[55]

Sharing these confined quarters were usually the wives and

children of the soldiers who had married with the permission of their regimental colonels. As the army always frowned on marriage, a mere six soldiers in every 100 were allowed to marry 'on the strength'. Wives who were 'on the strength' lived inside the barracks, fed free on army rations, and could enrol their children in the regimental schools. Separate married quarters were only provided in twenty of the 251 stations which sent returns to the Sanitary Commission in 1857.[56] Marriages were consummated and babies were born in communal barrack-rooms, in the presence of other soldiers, screened by a flimsy curtain. These conditions, though nauseating, involved less heart-break and suffering than those endured by the couples who married 'off the strength'. The wives of these marriages were neither allowed in barracks, nor granted separation allowances, nor entitled to accompany their husbands abroad (although this rule was sometimes evaded). Undoubtedly these women suffered considerably from the regulations imposed by the army. They were destined to eke out a living as seamstresses or servants; some perforce had to live off the parish or off the streets.[57]

Living conditions would improve in the latter half of the nineteenth century. Several Select Committees and a Royal Commission reported during and after the Crimean War; they were overwhelmingly critical about the standards of barrack accommodation and the sanitary provisions. They recommended the creation of separate quarters for married soldiers as well as separate dining facilities, day-rooms, ablution rooms and baths, laundry and drying rooms. They favoured a thorough ventilation of barracks, more space for each soldier (not less than 600 cubic feet per man and at least 3 feet between each bed). They proposed the removal of urine tubes from the barracks, the erection of proper urinals outside the rooms, with a water supply, the replacement of cesspools by a drainage and sewerage system, and the provision of an abundant water supply.[58] The government endorsed these recommendations; it appointed sub-commissions to supervise the implementation of the proposals, and it increased expenditure upon the repair, construction and enlargement of barracks from £233,876 in 1854 to £756,841 in 1859. Improvements were made in the heating, lighting and ventilation of barracks. Water supplies were extended, drainage systems supplied, and kitchens re-designed. Above all, separate married quarters were built, providing some privacy for soldiers and their families.

Yet the standard of accommodation was not quickly transformed. The magnitude of the task, which, in 1860, involved over 250 barracks accommodating 97,832 men, limited the rate of progress. The costs of repairing and renovating barracks were not only formidable but were apparently never-ending. Advances in the minimum requirements of public health, hygiene and sanitation set new, and usually more costly, standards of barrack accommodation. Conditions which the Royal Commission had accepted in the 1850s, like the quartering of cavalrymen above their horses, would be condemned less than ten years later.[59] Once the initial furore over barrack reform had subsided, governments would prove increasingly reluctant to meet the large expenditure required. Only the occasional scandal, like the revelation in the late 1880s of insanitary and fever-ridden conditions within the Royal Barracks, Dublin, would shame the government into facing its responsibilities. Under immense Parliamentary pressure, the Unionist government prepared a new plan of barrack renovation which it would fund by raising loans outside the army estimates. Within the next sixteen years, over £12,000,000 was spent on building and repairing barracks until Haldane curtailed the programme in 1906 by abolishing the use of loans.[60]

Increased expenditure, however essential as a prerequisite for reform, could not ensure that the living conditions of the rank and file would actually improve. In the first place, many barracks were incapable of modernization because of their age and structure, while others were badly sited, far from exercise, recreation and manoeuvring areas. The poor situations reflected the tendency of barracks to outlive their original purpose: at the turn of the century troops were still quartered in the centre of large cities (to control riots in the early nineteenth century), and in forts along the coastline (to thwart the anticipated French invasion of 1859). Any policy of modernization required not merely repairs and renovation, but a scale of reconstruction which no Edwardian government would contemplate. Secondly, if the barracks building programme was to aid recruiting, it required a measure of civilian supervision, since improvements by military standards would not necessarily comply with civilian expectations. As this supervision was not provided before 1905, the new barracks at Colchester and Tidworth, despite their separate dining facilities and recreation rooms, were basically a reproduction of the old-style barracks. The Royal Engineers who designed, built, and maintained the buildings were less enthusiastic about innovations (like sleeping cubicles) than either the Commander-in-Chief or the Secretary of State for War. Somewhat mournfully, Arnold-Forster concluded that 'Rule and precedent have evidently controlled design to an extent which has gone far to exclude originality, and to stereotype that which was never satisfactory, and which is in no way in accordance with modern views and requirements'.[61] When, in June 1906, Haldane established new criteria for further building (that is, where existing barracks were insanitary and dangerous or where a barracks was lacking for a part of the military organization), he limited the rebuilding programme and refrained from examining the cases of mere discomfort and lack of privacy.[62]

The rations of the ordinary soldier were another aspect of his daily life which attracted the criticism of Victorian reformers. The standard daily diet, fixed in 1813, was 1 lb of bread and ¾ lb of meat (weighed with fat, bone and gristle). An extra ½ lb of bread was allowed by a Warrant issued in February 1833. The barracks lacked any cooking utensils other than two copper boilers, one for meat and one for potatoes. As the men were unable to bake, roast, stew or fry their meat, they lived on an unchanging diet of beef broth and boiled beef for the duration of their military service. Even worse, they enjoyed but two meals a day, breakfast at 7.30 in summer or 8.00 in winter and dinner at 1.30. Although some regiments provided an evening meal of tea or coffee and bread, they were not required to do so until the 1840s. Messing in the pre-Crimean army was undoubtedly monotonous, but the prospect of a daily meal, including a portion of meat, was not enjoyed by every member of the civilian community. The soldier, too, did not always eat in barracks. Apart from the Guards, army units were frequently moved from barracks to barracks. While en route the soldiers were freed from stoppages and allowed 10*d* per day for dinner (except in Scotland), for which they could buy sumptuous dinners by comparison with army fare. Not until he entered the army did Alexander Somerville taste delicacies like roast goose and Yorkshire puddings.[63]

Catering reforms were implemented in accordance with the findings of the Sanitary Commission which reported in 1858. Kitchens and cooking facilities were installed in many barracks. Although the basic meat and bread ration remained unchanged, the regiments were allowed to contract for and supply vegetables, spices and condiments. In 1870 a School of Cooking was instituted at Aldershot, from which trained cooks would emerge within a few years of opening. After the report of Sir Stafford Northcote's Committee in 1889, even more care would be taken in the preparation of army food. Special classes were convened in London to instruct regimental officers in the inspection of meat; three officers were assigned to supervise the quality of army cooking; the contract system was revised to deter, by threat of heavy fines, any tampering with the carcasses of meat; and the army agreed to bake its bread in 2-lb instead of 4-lb loaves.[64] Yet soldiers would continue to bemoan the quality and quantity of army cooking. A. F. Corbett, who enlisted in the 1890s, vividly remembered the pangs of hunger he experienced at night: 'Fortunately the heavy drinkers were light eaters, and many times I have felt along the barrack shelves and found a dry crust for my supper'.[65] When regular meals were coupled with physical exercise and an open-air life, the benefits were quickly revealed. In 1907, 15,351 infantrymen were re-measured six months after enlistment; their average gain was ¾ in. in height, 1 in. in chest measurement, and nearly ten pounds in weight.[66]

Although improvements in rations and living conditions hardly enhanced the appeal of military service, they proved an unmitigated blessing for the health of the rank and file. The mortality rate of the pre-Crimean army was considerably higher than the rate recorded for men of the same age in civilian life. Whereas the civilian death rate was 11.9 per cent in twenty-four large English towns over the years from 1837 to 1846, the mortality rate in the army over the corresponding period was 17.1 per cent.[67] Respiratory diseases, so prevalent within society, were even more evident within the army, especially the Foot Guards, where the consequences of regular night duty compounded the ill-effects of overcrowding in appalling barracks. As Table 2.8 indicates, however, the mortality rate rapidly declined and the health of the army markedly improved in the latter half of the nineteenth century. Undoubtedly this trend reflected improvements in public health within society itself. Civilian mortality rates had been declining since the late eighteenth century, deriving from the success of attempts to control the spread of infectious diseases like smallpox and cholera. The army, nonetheless, was recruiting primarily from the ranks of the urban poor, and was forced repeatedly to lower its minimum physical standards. It was not recruiting from a stratum of society whose health was deteriorating, as some alarmists at the turn of the century believed,[68] but it was accepting an increasing proportion of lighter and smaller adolescents from environments which were appallingly unhealthy. Even so the conditions of service had improved to such an extent that the army could absorb these recruits and still maintain a healthier rank and file.

Notwithstanding the benefits of more wholesome rations and more sanitary surroundings, the life-style or daily routine of the ordinary soldier changed remarkably little. After reveille at 6.00 a.m., the ranks paraded, and then breakfasted at 7.30 a.m. Thereafter they completed various fatigues (like polishing their kit, peeling potatoes, cleaning barrack-rooms and latrines), paraded again before dinner at 12.45 p.m., possibly drilled in the afternoon, had tea at 4.30 p.m., and then a period of free time until 9.30 p.m., when a roll call was taken of each company, followed either by guard duty or 'lights out' at 10.15 p.m. Additional drills were completed by all recruits, while cavalrymen generally endured a more exhausting schedule, being responsible for their horses, saddlery and stables. This monotonous routine was rarely interrupted by formal military training. As units were frequently scattered over the country in various out-stations, the pre-Crimean regiments mustered very infrequently. Even in the later nineteenth century, regimental training was restricted to occasional field days or to camps when the regiment was based at larger stations like the Curragh. Not until the Edwardian years were annual manoeuvres held on a divisional scale. Fatigue duties always loomed larger in the consciousness of the peacetime soldier than military training; the routine was dull and tedious, the underemployment enervating. 'Idleness', remarked Sergeant Menzies, 'is the bane of the soldier, and the hardest foes to overcome are not always to be found on the field of battle'.[69]

Underemployed and lacking organized recreation, soldiers sought solace and comfort in drink. Drunkenness was a recurrent problem within the Victorian army, as it was within the class of society from

Table 2.8 Health of the army

	Mortality rate per 1,000 men					
	Household Cavalry	Foot Guards	Cavalry	Infantry	NCOs and men of Home Army	Number of hospital admissions per 100 men in Home Army
1837	18.9	22.7	13.3	19.1	n.a.	n.a.
1846	9.1	16.9	13.9	19.8	n.a.	n.a.
1857	11.0	20.4	13.3	18.7	17.5	n.a.
1861	5.8	7.8	6.5	7.4	9.2	102.5
1867	8.2	6.9	6.4	8.7	9.4	87.0
1873	1.2	8.3	7.4	8.1	7.9	75.9
1879	1.7	7.6	5.5	6.9	7.6	82.2
1885	2.4	10.0	5.5	5.8	6.7	87.7
1891	3.2	4.3	4.0	4.5	4.9	77.2
1897	2.5	4.2	4.0	2.8	3.4	64.1
1903	3.0	2.5	4.5	3.4	3.4	58.7
1909	3.1	3.1	2.7	2.9	2.9	37.8

Sources: *P.P.* C.1,639 (1852–53), LIX, C.2,318 (1857–58), XVIII; C.3,233 (1863), XXIV; C.4,185 (1868–69), XXXVII; C.1,374 (1875), XLIV; C.2,960 (1881), LIX; C.5,128 (1887), LI; C.7,047 (1893), LII; C.8,936 (1898), LIV; Cd. 2,434 (1905), XLVI; Cd. 5,477 (1911), XLVII.

Notes: It should be noted that the column which records the mortality rate of NCOs and men of the Home Army includes all branches of the service.

An arithmetical error in the official returns for the Household Cavalry in 1873 has been corrected as it merely involved a misplaced decimal point.

which the army took the bulk of its recruits. Drunkenness in the army, however, was not only a crime, but was also a factor which contributed to other military crimes like the high rate of desertion, and to the spread of venereal disease. Pay-days, the first, eighth, fifteenth, and twenty-second of each month, frequently occasioned bouts of excessive drinking, followed by rowdy barrack-room scenes, and almost inevitably a rash of crimes - insubordination, absence without leave (AWOL), violence towards superior officers, and drunkenness itself. The Inspector-General of Military Prisons reported that soldiers often deserted to avoid the consequences of a drinking spree which had resulted in an involuntary absence without leave (AWOL).[70] Undoubtedly, too, the drinking of the rank and file correlated with the high incidence of venereal disease. Although soldiers could obtain beer and spirits in their barrack canteens, the canteen prices were high, the surroundings dreary, and the liquor all too commonly watered.[71] Where possible, rankers sought more congenial drinking haunts, in which female companions could procure drinks for them. In 1861 Captain Pilkington Jackson surveyed the twenty-five public houses and forty-seven beer houses near the Aldershot garrison. He found widespread prostitution within these premises, describing the beer houses as 'almost without exception, public brothels of the worst description'. The Aldershot garrison, he added, boasted the highest number of hospital admissions in the United Kingdom 'for diseases incident to lust'.[72]

Traditionally the army relied upon retributive punishments to deter crime and curb the excesses of drunken behaviour. Capital punishment, inflicted by hanging or by firing-squad, was retained for those offences, which would be similarly punished under civilian criminal law, as well as for offences committed on active service, such as mutiny, desertion and violence towards a superior officer. The death penalty, however, was used sparingly and often commuted. Whereas 76 sentences of death were issued in the ten years between 1826 and 1835, 35 of these were commuted to transportation. In the thirty-four years between 1865 and 1898, 44 sentences were passed of which 33 were carried out.[73] Less drastic and more common was the recourse to corporal punishment. Serious miscreants were liable to be branded ('BC' for Bad Character or 'D' for Deserter) upon their arm, hand or chest. Retained until 1871, the practice was justified as a means of identifying deserters and of preventing fraudulent enlistments.[74]

For offences which ranged from serious crimes not involving the death penalty to relatively trivial misdemeanours, a flogging was the main response of the early Victorian army. Awarded for almost any breach of discipline during the Napoleonic Wars, flogging remained a military punishment until 1881. Although corporal punishment was dispensed within the public schools and prisons of nineteenth-century Britain, the scale and severity of military flogging was exceptional. Over fifty sentences of 1,000 lashes were issued during the Peninsular

War; as late as 1825 a soldier was sentenced to 1,900 lashes, of which 1,200 were actually inflicted. Lesser sentences, varying from 25 to 500 lashes, were relatively common. Returns from foreign stations in 1818 indicated that 2,273 men, or about 1 in 12 of the total complement, were hospitalized after the receipt of corporal punishment. During the last half of the 1820s, the army was flogging about 1 in every 50 soldiers every year.[75] Almost as nauseating as the severity and the frequency of military flogging was the manner in which the flogging was delivered. Intent upon deterring similar crimes, the army required that the punishment be delivered before the whole regiment assembled at a punishment parade. Soldiers, unused to the spectacle, were known to reel and faint. Occasionally, too, the culprit would not survive the punishment - Private Slim died after fifty lashes in 1867.

Flogging, though preferred by some soldiers to the alternative of working a treadmill in a civilian prison,[76] was the least tolerable aspect of army discipline. It outraged spokesmen for liberal and humanitarian opinion, ensuring that the army would be repeatedly censured in the press and Parliament. The Horse Guards would bow, albeit reluctantly, before these criticisms. In 1812 regimental courts martial were restricted to punishments of 300 lashes. In 1829 district and general courts martial were also limited to 300 lashes, while three years later the maximum sentence of regimental courts martial was reduced to 200 lashes. In 1833 a Horse Guards circular required that corporal punishment should only be administered for certain offences, namely mutiny, insubordination and violence towards superior officers, drunkenness on duty, and theft or 'making away with necessaries'. By the Mutiny Act of 1836 a general court martial was limited to the award of 200 lashes, a district to 150 and a regimental to 100. A common maximum of 50 lashes was set in 1847, reduced to 25 lashes in 1879. Coupled with the progressive reduction in the scale of punishments was a steady diminution in the number of sentences. By 1833 the 1,007 rankers who were flogged represented less than 1 per cent of the effective strength, by 1846 that proportion had halved, and by 1852 the number punished was only 45.[77] Nevertheless, the obloquy which the army incurred by virtue of retaining the lash tarnished its image and reduced the appeal of service life.

As the army reduced its reliance upon corporal punishment, it began, though belatedly, to take an interest in the leisure-hour activities of the rank and file. Enterprising officers and non-commissioned officers encouraged sports within their regiments. Football, only played by the Guards in 1815,[78] became increasingly popular in the regiments of the line. Several barracks possessed fives and rackets courts by the Crimean War, while more and more regiments formed cricket clubs for their private soldiers. By the last decades of the nineteenth century regimental sports were firmly established; they institutionalized the enthusiasm for football and boxing, adding the competitive spice of inter-regimental rivalry. More difficult to generate was interest in indoor pastimes, since the barrack canteens, in spite of their drawbacks, always attracted a regular clientele. To curb these spending habits, some regiments established savings banks for their men in the 1830s. They encountered a mixed reponse (the number of depositors and the level of savings were usually higher in the regiments stationed abroad). The Horse Guards did not lend their approval until 1843, when they required all regiments to establish savings banks, but by 31 March 1852 the savings of 11,144 depositers totalled £137,355 7*s* 8½*d*.[79]

Another pre-Crimean reform was the formation of regimental libraries. Once again the initiative was left to the regimental colonels like Sir Charles Gordon of the Black Watch. Concerned about the drinking of his regiment, he curtailed the hours of the 'wet' canteen and started a regimental library in 1830.[80] At least a dozen regiments had followed suit by 1838, despite the lukewarm reaction of the Horse Guards. Although Lord Hill, the Commander-in-Chief, had feared the consequences of 'men collecting in societies of that sort',[81] he would eventually approve the formation of regimental libraries in 1841. By 1876 there were 150 libraries in the United Kingdom and the Colonies, containing nearly 230,000 volumes. When coupled with the day-rooms and games-rooms of the post-Crimean barracks, the libraries were offering an alternative haven for the private soldier.[82]

The appeal of this haven was perforce limited. Only those soldiers who were literate and who were prepared to eschew the dissipated habits of their barrack-room comrades were disposed to read. But literate soldiers comprised a fairly small fraction of the rank and file. The precise size of that fraction cannot be determined exactly as the army tested educational attainments in a highly cursory manner. Throughout the 1860s, 1870s and 1880s, a startling improvement in army literacy was regularly recorded by the annual returns. By 1889 less than 2 per cent of the rank and file were described as illiterate, while 85.4 per cent were rated as possessing a 'superior education'. As these returns contradicted the report of the Director-General of Military Education, which recorded the failure of over 60 per cent of the ranks to attain even the lowest army education certificate in 1888,[83] the returns were re-classified in the 1890s. During the next decade the army disclosed that every year over 60 per cent of the ranks failed to obtain a certificate.[84] In other words, thirty years after the passage of Forster's Education Act (1870), and after a decade in which school attendance was compulsory for new recruits, the ranks still contained 60 per cent who were either illiterate or were barely literate. Colonel Delavoye feared that even this impression was too optimistic. Writing to Lord Roberts in December 1902, he revealed that recruits were being passed as literate if they could scrawl their signatures and read a few words of print (but not a word of cursive writing).[85] Not until 1907, when the War Office correlated its educational standards with civilian criteria, was a clear impression of recruiting literacy produced.

Table 2.9 The educational attainments of Edwardian recruits 1907–1913 expressed in percentage terms

	Year ending 30.9.07	Year ending 30.9.08	Year ending 30.9.09	Year ending 30.9.10	Year ending 30.9.11	Year ending 30.9.12	Year ending 30.9.13
Class A	8	5	6	6	6	5	6
Class B	22	20	23	25	25	24	25
Class C	32	31	30	31	30	30	30
Class D	27	30	29	28	29	30	28
Class E	11	14	11	10	10	11	11
Total (%)	100	100	100	100	100	100	100
Total number	8,644	34,731	32,065	25,365	28,195	29,019	27,093

Class A: 'Men of good education', i.e. read Standard VII Reader, write a composition, work compound rules of arithmetic, vulgar fractions and measure rectangles and rectangular solids.

Class B: 'Men of fair education', i.e. read Standard V Reader (for eleven-year-olds), write from dictation and work compound rules of arithmetic.

Class C: 'Men of moderate education', i.e. read Standard III Reader (for nine-year-olds), write dictation from Reader and work simple rules of money.

Class D: 'Men of inferior education', i.e. read Standard II Reader, write dictation from Reader and work problems with small numbers on simple rules of arithmetic.

Class E: 'Illiterate', i.e. men who fail to reach Class D.

Sources: *The General Annual Return on the British Army for the year ending 30 September 1913*, Cd. 7,252 (1914), LII, p. 96 and *House of Lords*, Fourth Ser., Vol. 196 (16 Nov. 1908), cols. 820-1.

Thereafter the army revealed throughout the period 1907–1913 that 11 per cent of its annual intake was illiterate, and that some 70 per cent could not pass the educational standards set for eleven-year-old children (Table 2.9).

These returns were not too surprising as less than 20 per cent of children in England and Wales extended their education beyond the age of twelve years.[86] By using both compulsion and monetary inducements, the War Office sought to improve the basic literacy of the rank and file. All soldiers were required to attend army schools until they had obtained a third-class certificate of army education. Possession of this certificate was made a condition for the award of proficiency pay, first introduced in 1906. The proportion of the strength who possessed the certificate rose steadily from 52.3 per cent in 1906 to 75.8 per cent in 1913.[87] Yet the increase was only possible because of the minimal nature of the standards required. A third-class certificate corresponded to the standard set for nine-year-old children in elementary schools; as over 60 per cent of the annual intake were accorded a class C or better rating, they entered the army with an educational attainment equal to, or in excess of, the minimal military standards. A relatively modest improvement had occurred, but hardly enough to suggest that recreational habits would radically change through the provision of day-rooms and regimental libraries.

Fearing that the efforts of the army authorities would prove inadequate, concerned citizens sought to alter the life-style of the private soldier by establishing social centres within the garrisons, which would serve as an alternative to the regimental canteens. At Chatham in 1861, the Weslyan Charles Henry Kelly founded the first Soldiers' Home, a small club-house located in a basement, with a reading-room, chapel and minimal sleeping quarters.[88] Another house was established in the following year at Aldershot by Mrs Louisa Daniell, an army officer's widow. Supported by evangelical philanthropists like Lord Shaftesbury, Lord Kinnaird and Robert Baxter, she was able to expand and develop the home. Her temporary mission-hall was soon replaced by a 'Mission Hall and Soldiers' Home and Institute', which seated 500 in a lecture-hall and possessed a tea- and coffee-bar, a smoking- and games-room, a reading-room, baths, sleeping quarters and an annex for soldiers' wives. She founded branch homes in other English garrisons, while in 1877 Elsie Sandes opened the first soldiers' home in Ireland.[89] The churches followed these examples. A Wesleyan Soldiers' Home was built in 1869, a Church of England Soldiers' Institute was founded in 1883, and modest homes were opened by the Salvation Army and the Primitive Methodists in the 1890s.

Those who sponsored the soldiers' homes were largely concerned with their missionary impact. Saving souls was the driving purpose of Mrs Daniell and her lady helpers. Hence they distributed religious tracts within the homes, prohibited the consumption of liquor, and held Bible classes nightly. In spite of this proselytizing, the homes served a genuine social purpose. They provided a range of facilities in comfortable surroundings which were generally lacking for the common soldier. They offered classes in which basic educational deficiencies could be remedied. They enabled the more respectable soldier to centre his social life upon premises other than the regimental canteen. Undoubtedly the missions contributed to a raising of standards of behaviour in the army, although the extent of their impact was never entirely clear. By the 1890s the churches were actively engaged in countering the drunkenness of the rank and file. In 1893 they joined forces to form a non-denominational Army Temperance Association. By 1895 it claimed 8,641 members, a number which would increase to 20,000 a few years later.[90]

Drunkenness, indeed all crimes, diminished considerably in the late Victorian army. Although fines for drunkenness were imposed more readily in Edwardian years, the decline steadily continued: whereas 51,501 fines were levied in 1872, 9,230 were levied in 1912-13.[91] When coupled with the threat of less severe punishments under military law, the decline of recidivism might have been expected to improve the status and appeal of military life. This did not occur, or at least not sufficiently to broaden the social composition of the rank and file. The prejudice against military service, so keenly felt within respectable working-class families, was too deeply rooted to be allayed by mere statistics or by recruiting publicity. That prejudice, whether based on material or emotional considerations, was understandable. Army rates of pay became less and less competitive with civilian wages. The army provided few opportunities for a soldier to learn a trade or skill while serving on a short-service engagement. One in four soldiers left the Edwardian army to become an unemployed or unemployable vagrant.[92] For those who sought either a remunerative or a secure career, the army held little attraction.

More important, perhaps, were the emotional feelings still evoked by the army as a social institution. Ever separate and distinct from the rest of society, the army maintained its cohesiveness by enforced discipline, communal living, and a sacrifice of individual liberty. These requirements were likely to have but limited appeal; some might deplore the purpose of military training, many more would fear that a boy once enlisted was lost to family and friends, if not necessarily corrupted, then at least changed beyond recognition by the experience of service life. For families with respectable or genteel aspirations, these fears contained a substance of truth. As Horace Wyndham, a gentleman ranker of the 1890s, recalled, 'Those who have not actively experienced what a barrack-room, crowded with noisy, foul-mouthed, and more or less drunken, men, means at night cannot conceive what a man who is in the slightest degree sensitive feels at such times'.[93] Service in the ranks, in short, remained a career of lowly status and of little esteem.

Notes and references

1. **H. Marshall,** *Military Miscellany,* John Murray, London, 1846, p. 78.
2. *Parl. Deb.*, Third Series, Vol. 205, 16 Mar. 1871, col. 129.
3. Meeting of the Army Council and Precis No. 815, 22 May 1914, PRO, WO163/20.
4. H. Marshall, *op. cit.*, pp. 350-1.
5. *Report of The Inspector General of Recruiting*, *P.P.*, C.6,597, 1892, XX, p. 5. For a detailed analysis of the subterfuges of late Victorian recruiting see **A. R. Skelley,** *The terms and conditions of service and recruitment of the rank and file of the British Regular Home Army 1856-1899*, unpublished Ph.D. thesis, University of Edinburgh, 1974, pp. 358-61.
6. Evidence (Q.1,161) included in the *Report of the Commissioners Appointed to Inquire into the Present System of Recruiting in the Army*, C.2,762, 1861, XV.
7. Evidence (Qs.3,367-9) before the Military Punishments Commission, *op. cit*.
8. **R. Macdonald,** *Personal Narrative of Military Travel and Adventure in Turkey and Persia,* A. & C. Black, Edinburgh, 1859, p. 296.
9. **A. Somerville,** *The Autobiography of a Working Man*, ed. by J. Carswell, Turnstile Press, London, 1951, pp. 128-9.
10. 'Recruiting Service' and 'General Correspondence', *United Service Magazine,* Part III, Oct. and Nov. 1841, pp. 271-4, 389-90.
11. A.R. Skelley, *op. cit.*, pp. 369-70.
12. H. Wyndham, *op. cit.*, p. 1.
13. Report of the Commission on Recruiting, *op. cit.*, p. xvii.
14. *Report of the Committee on Questions (Recruiting, etc.) with respect to Militia; with evidence and appendices,* C.5,992, 1890, XIX, Appendix 2 and **B. J. Bond**, 'Recruiting the Victorian army 1870-1892', *Victorian Studies,* V, No. 1, Sept. 1961, p. 331.
15. A. R. Skelley, *op. cit.*, pp. 381-2.
16. Report of the Committee on the Militia, *op. cit.*, Appendix 2.
17. Evidence of a corporal in the Coldstream Guards (Q.2,093), and privates from the 50th Ft and Royal Artillery (Qs.2,688. 3,740) before the Military Punishments Commission, *op. cit.*
18. A. Somerville, *op. cit.*, p. 114.
19. **Sergeant J. Menzies,** *Reminiscences of an Old Soldier,* Crawford & McCabe, Edinburgh, 1883, pp. 5-6.
20. **J. MacMullen,** *Camp and Barrack-Room; or the British Army as it is,* Chapman Hall, London, 1846, p. 311.
21. **R. Edmondson,** *Is a Soldier's Life Worth Living?*, Twentieth Century Press, London, 1902, p. 5.

22. *Report of the Health of the Army for the year 1909*, Cd. 5,477, 1911, XLVII, p. 2.
23. **M. F. Cunliffe,** *The army 1815–54 as an institution,* unpublished B.Litt. thesis, University of Oxford, 1947, p. 78.
24. Evidence (Qs.2,187, 2,607, 2,740, 3,616, 3,661) before the Military Punishments Commission, *op. cit.*
25. **H. D. Acland-Troyte,** *Through the Ranks to a Commission,* Macmillan, London, 1881, pp. 1-5.
26. M. F. Cunliffe, *op. cit.*, p. 93 and A. R. Skelley, *op. cit.*, p. 164.
27. H. Marshall, *op. cit.*, p. 93.
28. *United Service Magazine, op. cit.*, pp. 273, 390.
29. Evidence (Q.4,060) before the Military Punishments Commission, *op. cit.*
30. Evidence (Qs.4,063, 3,375-9) *ibid.*
31. **Capt. G. T. Younghusband,** *The Queen's Commission: How to prepare for it, How to obtain it and How to use it,* John Murray, London, 1891, p. 52.
32. Evidence (Qs.1,551, 3,473-5, 3,553, 3,622, 4,061, 4,385-7) before the Military Punishments Commission, *op. cit.*
33. E. and A. Linklater, *op. cit.*, p. 227.
34. **H. J. Hanham,** 'Religion and nationality in the mid-Victorian army', *War and Society*, ed. M. R. D. Foot, P. Elek, London, 1973, pp. 162-3.
35. *Ibid.*, pp. 163-4.
36. **J. Fraser,** *Sixty Years in Uniform*, Stanley Paul, London, 1939, p. 42.
37. **Field Marshal Sir A. Wavell,** *Soldiers and Soldiering,* J. Cape, London, 1953, p. 125.
38. Evidence (Q.5,806) before the Military Punishments Commission, *op. cit.*
39. H. Marshall, *op. cit.*, pp. 74-5.
40. *Parl. Deb.*, Third Series, Vol. 88, 3 March 1846, cols. 289-93.
41. *Parl. Deb.*, Third Series, Vol. 90, 26 Apr. 1847, col. 1,324.
42. **J. H. Clapham,** *An Economic History of Modern Britain,* 3 Vols., Cambridge University Press, London, 1926, Vol. II, pp. 466-7.
43. Evidence (Q.4,480) before the Wantage Committee, *op. cit.*, C.6,582, 1892, XIX.
44. A. L. Haliburton, 'Dissent', the Wantage Report, *op. cit.*, pp. 35, 40.
45. Evidence (Qs.324, 162) before the Wantage Committee, *op. cit.*
46. *Parl. Deb.*, Fourth Ser., Vol. 98, 13 May 1901, col. 1,501, and Vol. 10, 17 March 1893, col. 409.
47. A. R. Skelley, *op. cit.*, p. 275.
48. *Parl. Deb.*, Fourth Ser., Vol. 90, 8 Mar. 1901, col. 1,080.
49. E. M. Spiers, *op. cit.*, ch. 5, p. 17.
50. J. H. Clapham, *op. cit.*, Vol. III, pp. 98-9.

51. 'Memorandum upon the Barrack Department of Great Britain', 31 December 1823, PRO, HO 50/443; A. R. Skelley, *op. cit.*, p. 27; and **Lieutenant-Colonel Ross of Bladensburg,** *A History of the Coldstream Guards from 1815 to 1895*, Innes, London, 1896, p. 77.
52. M. F. Cunliffe, *op. cit.*, pp. 171–3 and J. W. Fortescue, *op. cit.*, Vol. XI, p. 10.
53. *Report of the Commissioners appointed to inquire into the Regulations affecting the Sanitary condition of the Army, the organization of military hospitals, and the treatment of the sick and wounded,* hereafter referred to as the Sanitary Commission, C.2,318, 1857–58, XVIII, p. xvii.
54. Evidence (Q.1,566) included in the *Report from an Official Committee on Barrack Accommodation for the Army*, hereafter referred to as the Barrack Committee, C.405, 1854–55, XXXII.
55. *Ibid.*, p. 111.
56. Report of the Sanitary Commission, *op. cit.*, p. xviii.
57. *Report of an Enquiry by Mrs. Tennant regarding the conditions of Marriage off the Strength,* Cd. 7,441, 1914, LI.
58. Reports of the Barrack Committee, *op. cit.*, pp. iv–xii and the Sanitary Commission, *op. cit.*, pp. lxxvi–lxxvii.
59. Compare the Report of the Barrack Committee, *op. cit.*, p. xii with the *Report of the Committee on the Ventilation of Cavalry Stables,* C.3,290, 1864, XVI, p. 5.
60. E. M. Spiers, *op. cit.*, Appendix X and **A. R. Skelley,** *The Victorian Army at Home,* Croom Helm, London, 1977, pp. 38–40.
61. **H. O. Arnold-Forster,** *The Army in 1906: A Policy and a Vindication,* John Murray, London, 1906, p. 282.
62. *Parl. Deb.*, Fourth Ser., Vol. 168, 7 June 1906, cols. 566–7.
63. A. Somerville, *op. cit.*, p. 131.
64. *Report of the Committee on the Soldiers' Dietary,* C.5,742, 1889, XVII.
65. A. F. Corbett, *op. cit.*, p. 10.
66. *The National Service Journal,* Vol. II, No. 15, July 1907, p. 175.
67. *Statistical Reports on the Sickness, Mortality and Invaliding among the troops in the United Kingdom, the Mediterranean and British North America,* C.1,639, 1852–53, LIX.
68. Compare Major-General Sir F. Maurice, 'National Health, A Soldier's Study', *The Contemporary Review,* Vol. LXXXIII, 1903, pp. 41–57 with the *Report of the Inter-departmental Committee on Physical Deterioration,* Cd. 2,175, 1904, XXXII.
69. Sergeant J. Menzies, *op. cit.*, p. 3.
70. *Report on the Discipline and Management of Military Prisons,* C.4,209, 1868–69, XXX, p. 4.
71. Until 1863 canteens were run by civilian contractors for a profit. Thereafter they were run by the regiments, but dishonest practices remained all too prevalent: **J. Fortescue,** *A Short Account*

of Canteens in the British Army, University Press, Cambridge, 1928, pp. 29–30.

72. *Army (Soldiers' Institutes), and Army (Soldiers' Libraries)*, No. 126, 1862, XXXII, p. 2.
73. *Parl. Deb.*, Third Ser., Vol. 91, 26 April 1847, col. 1,325 and *General Annual Returns of the British Army . . .*, C.1,323, 1875, XLIII, p. 40; C.6,196, 1890, XLIII, p. 56; and C.9,426, 1899, LIII, p. 58.
74. **R. L. Blanco,** 'Attempts to abolish branding and flogging in the army of Victorian England before 1881', *Journal of the Society for Army Historical Research,* **46**, Part 187, Autumn 1968, pp. 137–8.
75. *Parl. Deb.*, Third Ser., Vol. 91, 26 April 1847, col. 1,324. For Peninsular War statistics see **Sir C. W. C. Oman,** *Wellington's Army 1809–1814,* Arnold, London, 1912, p. 238.
76. Evidence (Qs.2,215, 2,702) before the Military Punishments Commission, *op. cit.*
77. Appendix to the Military Punishments Commission, *op. cit.*, p. 197 and *Return of the Number of Persons flogged in the Army of Great Britain and Ireland in each of the years 1847–1852 inclusive,* No. 936, 1852–53, LIX.
78. **J. W. Fortescue,** *History of the British Army,* Vol. XI, p. 45.
79. *Account of the amount due by the Public to Depositors in Military Savings Banks . . .*, No. 554, 1852–53, LIX.
80. E. and A. Linklater, *op. cit.*, p. 89.
81. Evidence (Q.5,790) before the Military Punishments Commission, *op. cit.* and M. F. Cunliffe, *op. cit.*, pp. 142–4.
82. *Report of the Director-General of Military Education,* C.1,885, 1877, XXX, p. xxiv.
83. Compare *General Annual Return of the British Army . . .*, C.6,196, 1890, XLIII, p. 85 with *Report of the Director-General of Military Education,* C.5,805, 1889, XVII, p. 21.
84. *General Annual Return of the British Army . . .*, C.9,426, 1899, LIII, p. 96.
85. **Colonel Delavoye,** 'Memorandum' enclosed in Lord Roberts to Brodrick, 8 December 1902, Roberts Mss., NAM, R/122/4/370.
86. *Statistics of Public Education in England and Wales 1913–14,* Cd. 8,097, 1914–16, LI, p. 18.
87. *General Annual Return of the British Army for the year ending 30 September 1913,* Cd. 7,252, 1914, LII, p. 96.
88. H. J. Hanham, *op. cit.*, p. 169.
89. O. Anderson, *op. cit.*, pp. 59–60.
90. H. J. Hanham, *op. cit.*, pp. 170–1.
91. *General Annual Returns of the British Army . . .*, C.1,323, 1875, XLIII, p. 40 and Cd. 7,252, 1914, LII, p. 77.
92. E. M. Spiers, *op. cit.*, Appendix XI.
93. H. Wyndham, *op. cit.*, p. 84.

3 Wellington's army

After the battle of Waterloo (18 June 1815), Britain enjoyed nearly forty years of freedom from war in Europe. Once the occupation of France was terminated in 1818, the government of Lord Liverpool reduced the strength of the army to approximately 100,000 men and assigned three-quarters of the infantry battalions to garrison duty in overseas stations. The army would become primarily a colonial force, required to protect the frontiers of the Empire and to quell any incidence of native unrest. Retained at home were the Guards battalions, nearly all the cavalry regiments and the remaining infantry battalions, the bulk of which would be deployed in Ireland. During the years from 1815 to 1854, the home-based force would decay and stagnate; in the view of several historians, it suffered from a widespread fear of militarism, from the passion of successive governments for the cause of national economy, and from the neglect and indifference of Parliament.[1] Other scholars have added that the army languished under the control of the Crown and the domination of the Duke of Wellington, whose attitudes and ideas blighted the prospects of reform until his death in 1852.[2] As these factors interacted with each other throughout the pre-Crimean period, they warrant examination.

Fears of militarism were evident in nineteenth-century Britain. The constitutional distrust of standing armies, a cornerstone of the English libertarian tradition, still existed. Lord Liverpool deferred to this feeling in 1816, when he opposed the building of the United Service Club in Pall Mall. He considered that this was a 'most ill-considered measure', which would engender prejudice against the military establishment and would evoke controversy in Parliament.[3] Four years later a similar incident occurred. The prospect of a barracks being built in Regent's Park, London, excited considerable opposition, not least from the radical paper *The Black Dwarf*. Quoting from Blackstone's *Commentaries on the Laws of England* (1765–69), *The Black Dwarf* declaimed against the separation of the soldiery from the rest of the community in camps, barracks or inland fortresses.[4] The paper feared that isolating the soldier would divorce him from the habits and feelings of the ordinary citizen, and would enable the formation of a standing army, which it viewed as little more than an instrument of State oppression. A standing army, declared Henry ('Orator') Hunt, was 'inimical to the liberties of the country'.[5] Many radicals, too, despaired of the consequences of military service for the individual soldier; in their own terminology, training to kill one's fellow man was inherently degrading. Soldiers, argued *The Poor Man's Guardian*, 'to be fit instruments of our slavery, . . . must be the most degraded of slaves themselves'.[6] Anti-militarists, in short, denounced the standing army as unconstitutional in its role and as brutalizing in its effects.

Dislike of the military was not confined entirely to radical spokesmen and writers. Major Edward Macready recalled that the reception accorded to the 30th Foot on its return from Waterloo was anything but cordial: 'We were barbarously treated at Ramsgate, overcharged by the innkeeper at Margate, misled by our guide, and wrongly directed by a ploughman on our road to Sandwich; drenched to the skin every day, and looked crossly on by everyone but the waiters at the inns. As to the peasantry a civil word could not be extracted from them'.[7] To feel unease at the approach of a redcoat was understandable. Reports of rakish and riotous behaviour by both officers and men recurred throughout this period, often circulating in the provincial and radical press. Some regiments, particularly some cavalry regiments, earned reputations for running amok; occasionally they would ride around the streets of a nearby town with swords drawn, damaging property, frightening the citizens, even assaulting policemen and bystanders. 'Military outrages' were all too prevalent in the pre-Crimean army.[8]

Yet fears of the military were not omnipresent; adulation of recent military achievements, particularly the victories of the Napoleonic wars, was apparently widespread. George Bell was feted and feasted and flattered on his return from the Peninsular War. Rated as 'a great hero' by his friends and family in Dublin, he was 'talked to death almost day and night' and never lacked for 'a fair partner' in the evening dances.[9] Nor was the rejoicing restricted to the immediate aftermath of the wars. Waterloo Day became an annual celebration; it was commemorated with fever and enthusiasm until the death of Wellington in 1852. The Iron Duke himself was lauded as a national hero, as the 'saviour of Europe' and as an oracle in military matters. Admittedly the Duke of Wellington would become a highly controversial figure in domestic politics and would incur considerable opprobrium over his opposition to the Reform Bill, but he still retained enormous reverence and respect from many sections of the community. Radical criticism of the Duke only incensed his own supporters, sometimes provoking them into raucous displays of cheering and emotion whenever they caught sight of him.[10]

Feelings about the army, whether for or against, paled by comparison with the passions aroused by the Corn Laws, the Test and Conformity Acts, the abolition of slavery and the reform of Parliament. The army was too small and too widely scattered to arouse sustained controversy. Only 64,426 officers and men were stationed in the United Kingdom in 1820, and a mere 44,731 by 1825. Nor were the troops concentrated in brigades, divisions and corps, able to train and manoeuvre as a large-scale military force. Other than the Guards regiments, which largely remained in London, the regiments were scattered across the country and were constantly on the move. The 1st Royal Dragoons, for example, experienced forty-four changes of station between 1816 and 1852, moving from Lancashire in 1820 to Dorset in 1821 and then, on yearly or half-yearly rotas, to Kent, London, York, Edinburgh, Dundalk, Dublin, Newbridge, Cork and Ballincollig, before returning to Lancashire in May 1829.[11] That the army was both so small and so itinerant reflected two concerns of successive governments - the cost of the army and its utility in the maintenance of public order.

After the conclusion of the Napoleonic Wars, in which the country had amassed an immense national debt, economic retrenchment was a principal objective of the post-war government. As the army and navy were the main items of public expenditure, their estimates were targets for immediate reduction. Expenditure on the army and ordnance fell from £43,256,260 in 1815 to £10,699,865 in 1820: thereafter it slipped below £10 million, plummeting to just under £8 million in 1836, before rising in the wake of the Chartist disturbances and various war scares to reach £9,635,709 in 1853. Of the money expended, moreover, approximately one-quarter and sometimes nearly one-third was disbursed on half-pay and pensions. Although efforts were repeatedly made to curtail the burden of 'non-effective' expenditure (by reducing the length of the half-pay list), the outlay remained considerable - over £2¼ million in 1853.[12] The size of the 'non-effective' expenditure only compounded the financial restrictions upon the army as a whole.

Retrenchment was not the policy of any particular party or government in the 1820s and 1830s. Although radical Members of Parliament such as Joseph Hume might press for ever greater reductions of military expenditure, governments were not reticent about cutting the army vote. Even the government of the Duke of Wellington (1828-30) did not arrest the slide in military expenditure. Governments sought retrenchment for several reasons. In the first place, the foreign policy of the country, originated by Castlereagh and developed by Canning, depended upon the maintenance of a balance of power in Europe. Although the various Foreign Secretaries would interpret this concept differently, none, not even Lord Palmerston, believed that it should be pursued by military force. Whereas Palmerston upheld a policy of 'intermeddling, and intermeddling in every way and to every extent short of actual military force', Lord Aberdeen, Foreign Secretary (1828-30 and 1841-46), claimed that 'the influence of England was really diminished by such a course'; indeed he would insist that 'morality forbade interference at all where we were not prepared to face its legitimate results'.[13] British foreign policy, in other words, did not rest primarily, or even implicitly, upon the threat of armed intervention on the continent of Europe.

Secondly the main support of Britain's foreign policy was the navy. The Senior Service provided the power which buttressed the diplomatic moves of Canning and Palmerston. By Peel's ministry of 1841-46, annual expenditure on the navy began to exceed annual expenditure on the army (with the exception of 1844). The navy ensured Britain's status as a leading maritime and commercial nation by preserving her command of world ocean routes. Naval patrols also enabled successive Foreign Secretaries to try to implement the abolition of the slave trade. The navy provided the means by which Palmerston could demonstrate his support for liberal causes in Portugal and Greece, and for his protection of British trade in the Far East. Unlike the army, the navy could be used as an adjunct to diplomacy; by threatening naval intervention, or by authorizing limited naval intervention, British Foreign Secretaries, especially Palmerston, could protect British trade and investments, enhance British prestige, and occasionally promote a moral or ideological cause. Much less useful in peacetime, the army would receive a progressively smaller share of defence expenditure.

Thirdly, the army hardly fostered the impression that it required additional funding. Admittedly, the Duke of Wellington stoutly opposed reductions in military establishments. He believed that the policy of thinning the ranks merely imposed additional strain on the remaining forces, especially those stationed overseas, for whom a sufficient number of reliefs could not be found. Reducing establishments, argued the Duke, was a short term and improvident policy as, within a few years, reasons would be found for augmenting the ranks 'at a large expense' to the Exchequer.[14] Even so he accepted that cuts in expenditure should be made: military expenditure continued to fall under his own ministry. Indeed Horse Guards, under the sway if not the command of Wellington, seldom sought the introduction of new and expensive items of military equipment (with the exception of the Minié rifle). It was reluctant to change the uniforms, weaponry, and training of the army, since those factors had contributed to the triumph of 1815. Moreover British arms continued to conquer all before them. From 1815 to 1854, British troops were engaged in at least fifteen small colonial wars, and were required to suppress a rebellion in Canada. Occasionally a defeat or a reverse occurred - notably the retreat of Major-General Elphinstone's forces from Kabul (January 1842) - but triumphs regularly followed. The arms, discipline and fire-power of British soldiers proved victorious in battlefields as far apart as West Africa and New Zealand, Afghanistan and Ceylon: these successes undermined the case for army reform.

Nevertheless, expenditure on the army would rise, albeit

gradually, during the course of the 1840s. Although this increase is sometimes overlooked by military historians who fail to distinguish between the several decades of the pre-Crimean period,[15] it was only too clear to contemporary radicals. Prominent radical spokesmen such as Richard Cobden, John Bright and Joseph Sturge repeatedly voiced their concern about the mounting volume of military armaments as an economic burden and as a threat to peace. The economic burden might not appear large in retrospect; military expenditure in the 1840s and early 1850s never returned to the levels of spending in the Regency years, and, when allowance is made for inflation, the gap between these levels of spending is even more considerable. Yet military expenditure, the main item of public expenditure, always seemed a burden to contemporary radicals. When spending on the army, navy and ordnance exceeded the estimates for 1847 by about £1½ million, Cobden ruefully noted that the increased charge 'is more than all our poor rates'.[16] Radical protestations, however, could not thwart the trend in military expenditure. As the Duke of Wellington had presciently observed, 'reasons' would be found for augmenting the army estimates. The main reasons would be the increasing dependence of the government upon the army to maintain public order, compounded in the early 1850s by a war scare and invasion panic.

Providing aid to the civil power was a traditional military function. The army had always carried out a variety of constabularly duties. Even during the Peninsular War, in 1812, more than 12,000 soldiers were deployed in the districts between Leicester and York to suppress the Luddite disturbances.[17] Indeed, the army was bound to fulfil these duties so long as Britain remained, in whole or in part, an unpoliced society. Dependence upon the army was not removed by the ratification of the Metropolitan Police Act (1829) and the Municipal Corporations Act (1835). Although the Act of 1835 required the reformed corporations to establish Watch Committees, which would then appoint a sufficient number of constables to be paid at the expense of the ratepayers, many of the corporations were not eager to comply. As Mrs J. M. Hart has observed, there were still in 1849 at least twenty-one corporate towns (12 per cent of the whole) who had not established a police force.[18] Even more boroughs in England and Wales were reluctant to incur the expense of a large police force. Complying with the letter but not the spirit of the 1835 Act, they established police forces which were woefully under strength. Whereas the Metropolitan Force had established a ratio of constables to citizens of 1:443 as early as 1840, only 1 in 20 boroughs maintained a ratio of about 1:600 or better from 1839 to 1848. Barely one-quarter of the provincial boroughs maintained a police ratio of 1:1,100 throughout the period of the Chartist disturbances.[19] In these circumstances, where the old system of petty constables, assisted by part-time special constables during emergencies, stood discredited but where the new full-time police forces were not fully established, the army continued to provide a wide range of assistance.

In coastal communities, particularly in Cornwall, the military assisted customs and excise officers in the seizure of contraband and in the countering of smugglers. In Ireland, military units accompanied excise officers in their periodic attempts to curtail illicit whiskey distilling. In Ireland, too, troops provided escorts, guards for food wagons, and protection for tithe collectors. Above all the army assisted in the maintenance of public order during elections and during outbreaks of civil commotion. Commanding officers did not relish the duties required of their men during elections; they disliked having to disperse their troops and to billet them throughout widespread constituencies.[20] On this issue the military and the radicals were in complete agreement, but for very different reasons. William Cobbett, deplored the calling forth of the army as merely a crude attempt to stifle 'the voice of the people'. *The Black Dwarf* was even more vitriolic; it likened any civil authority who enforced its laws by the use of military force to an incipient 'military despotism'.[21] Army officers were worried too, but about the effects of intervention upon Service discipline. They voiced fears about the loyalty of the rank and file. After a mutiny over living conditions, insufficient pay and excessive duty in a battalion of the 3rd Regiment of Guards in June 1820, Wellington warned Lord Liverpool immediately. He exhorted him to form either a police force in London or a military corps which differed from the regular military force. By these means alone, he averred, could the government ensure 'that the mutiny of the regular force, if it should ever occur, would be of little or no importance'.[22]

The Duke of Wellington retained a dim view of the rank and file. Having described his men at Waterloo as 'the scum of the earth', he never modified his opinions. New recruits he characterized as among the 'most drunken' and 'worst' specimens of humanity. 'In ninety-nine instances out of one hundred', he claimed, 'soldiers enlisted on account of some idle or irregular, or even vicious motive'. Only iron discipline, affirmed the Duke, could 'remove those irregular or vicious habits or propensities . . .'.[23] He feared the repercussions of letting these men associate with the discontented populace. Radicals perceived these fears and sought to exploit them. While their newspapers focused upon military issues such as flogging, their activists disseminated seditious literature amongst the troops. *The Poor Man's Guardian* even believed that a 'major part of a battalion of Grenadier Guards' had been 'republicanized' by reading its pronouncements. The paper viewed this development as 'the harbinger of the new "holy alliance" between the military and the people . . .'.[24] Neither the fears of senior officers nor the hopes of the radical press were realized. Although there were signs of dissent, disaffection was rare. Economic distress in town and country areas hardly induced men to leave the army. Any evidence of indiscipline was severely punished. On 27 May

1832, *The Weekly Dispatch* published a letter from Alexander Somerville which claimed that the Scots Greys would not become 'the tools of a tyrant' in the repression of liberty. Somerville was given 200 lashes and dismissed from the army.[25] Fearing further indiscipline, the Horse Guards disliked the duties involved in the maintenance of public order.

Horse Guards was especially concerned about the reliability of Irish Catholic troops on service in Ireland. It was alarmed by two incidents which occurred when the 87th Foot was stationed in Armagh and Newry in October 1830. An overwhelmingly Catholic regiment, the 87th was the only regiment whose men marched to the Roman Catholic chapel on Sundays with the band playing traditional Irish airs. When the regiment was sent to Ulster, the playing of music was forbidden as provocative. Partisan feelings appear to have erupted within the regiment, incited undoubtedly by the local townsfolk. Soldiers from the four companies quartered in Armagh brawled with local Orangemen on 4 October 1830. Six days later, the Catholic detachment of the six companies based at Newry repeatedly refused to obey orders and march to chapel without their music. Having refused to obey both their company captain and their Commanding Officer, discipline was only restored by the instigation of a drumhead court martial and the threat of instantaneous punishment for any further disobedience.

Although these incidents are dismissed by the regiment's historian as merely 'a little unrest',[26] they caused consternation in Dublin and in Whitehall. Colonel D'Aguilar, the Adjutant-General, hurried north to Newry where he harangued the men, reminding them of their rights under the Emancipation Act, 'the Boon of a Patriotic Sovereign and a beneficient Legislature . . .'.[27] Sir Henry Hardinge, the Secretary to Ireland, dispatched several frantic letters to London calling for the immediate removal of the 87th. To retain the regiment in Ireland, he argued, would be worse than not having it at all. Other regiments would have to be detailed to watch its conduct, its example could be contagious, and it could defect during a crisis. Even the prospect of a possible defection could encourage the mass to 'rush into insurrection'. Hardinge recommended consigning the regiment to a West Indian colony.[28] Sir Robert Peel, the Home Secretary, deplored the overreaction of Colonel D'Aguilar but endorsed the feelings of Hardinge. He was appalled at the 'shameful' conduct and 'defective' discipline of the 87th. Acting on the advice of the Duke of Wellington, he recommended a full inquiry and an immediate removal of the regiment to Dublin. He repeated the Duke's admonition that the regiment should not be sent to the West Indies in case service in the West Indies became considered a disgrace and a punishment.[29] These wise words of counsel prevailed. Within a month, the regiment had returned to England to be quartered in Plymouth.

Misgivings about the loyalty of the rank and file persisted. More than a dozen years after the incident at Newry, Hardinge would still cite the 'insubordination' of the 87th as evidence of what could happen to troops in Ireland. He urged Sir James Graham, Home Secretary during Peel's ministry (1841-46), to refrain from deploying soldiers within earshot of demogogues and priests at political meetings in Ireland.[30] Major-General Sir Charles Napier, the Commanding Officer of the northern district of England from 1839 to 1841, feared that Chartist ideas might infect the rank and file. Although he sympathized with many of the Chartist aims, he deplored that section of the movement which was prepared to use physical force. Napier, nonetheless, could not record more than a few instances of disaffection, in spite of his suspicion that there were 'many Chartists among the Rifles'. He was reluctant to use troops too often against the Chartists, and exhorted the civil authorities to employ Yeomanry more frequently as a first recourse in cases of civil disorder.[31] His proposal was endorsed by the Duke of Wellington, who never concealed his doubts about the value of using infantry to quell civil disturbances. Believing that the mounted Yeomanry would be much more useful, he advocated the arming and training of these part-time volunteers, including the Protestant Yeomanry of the North of Ireland.[32]

Both Tory and Whig Home Secretaries became increasingly reluctant to depend on the Yeomanry. In the first place, employing the Yeomanry instead of regular troops involved additional expense. Unlike soldiers, who were paid at the same rates whether they remained in barracks or were used to counter civil disorders, Yeomanry were purely volunteers. Composed of tenant farmers and small landowners, and officered by local gentry and aristocracy, they had to be reimbursed for their services, their costs being born on the Home Office vote. As the responsible department, the Home Office determined the annual strength of the Yeomanry, which fell from 17,818 in 1817 to nearly 14,000 in 1838, a reflection of the retrenchment policies of successive governments. Apart from a shortage of numbers, the main weakness of the Yeomanry was its mal-distribution. Originally raised in 1794 to resist a possible invasion, the Yeomanry remained strong in the maritime counties of the south-west, and it had also developed viable corps in the Midlands. In the more populous northern counties, where many of the Chartist disturbances would occur, the Yeomanry were much less numerous: in 1839, there were only 171 Yeomanry in Lancashire while there were none in Durham. Lord Palmerston, when Secretary at War, had raised this issue with the Home Office as early as February 1824. He had proposed a complete reorganization of the force, with the formation of Yeomanry corps in each county and the requirement that each corps undertake a fixed number of days duty every year.[33]

The Home Office did not act upon this advice; it did not wish to rely upon the Yeomanry in the maintenance of public order. The events of 16 August 1819 at St Peter's Field, Manchester, which became popularly known as the Peterloo Massacre, damaged the reputation of the Yeomanry beyond repair. On that day some 60,000 people had assembled to listen to Orator Hunt and other radical speakers discuss Parliamentary reform. Determined to arrest these speakers, the Manchester magistrates authorized the Manchester and Salford Yeomanry to assist the 300 special constables in their duty. In the resulting *mêlée*, the chairman of the magistrates gave the order to disperse the crowd, whereupon the Yeomanry moved into the crowd, found themselves trapped, and were rescued by the Hussars, who beat back the crowd with the flats of their swords and sometimes with their edges also. Within ten minutes the square from Mount Street to Deansgate was cleared, eleven were dead, and nearly 400 were injured (though more by crushing than by sabring).[34] In spite of a test case in 1822 which absolved several officers of the Manchester Yeomanry from any unlawful acts, confidence in the Yeomanry had been fatally eroded.

Governments, however, were unwilling to reform the force; indeed they began to restrict the use of the Yeomanry in the suppression of public disorder. 'For his own part', admitted Lord John Russell, 'he would rather that any force should be employed in case of local disturbance than the local corps of yeomanry'.[35] When disturbances erupted over the introduction of the New Poor Law, Lord Russell, the Whig Home Secretary, called upon regular troops and Metropolitan policemen in preference to the Yeomanry corps. Sir James Graham pursued a similar policy. He discouraged those Lords-Lieutenant and military commanders who desired a too protracted use of the Yeomanry. He deplored the suggestion of the Duke of Wellington that the Yeomanry should be armed and trained in the north of Ireland: it would be 'the signal of insurrection in the South'.[36] He felt, in other words, that the local connections of the county forces gave them the appearance of parties to local disputes. But whenever the regular forces seemed likely to become too stretched during the Chartist disorders, the Yeomanry corps would be called upon to assist the civil power. The response of these corps was more moderate and restrained than in 1819, in spite of ferocious assaults by the mob. Having earned the plaudits of Sir Robert Peel, the force was slightly expanded in the centres prone to civil discord.[37] Even so, the army remained the main instrument used by the civil power to suppress popular disturbances.

Quelling public disorder in the United Kingdom was a delicate and difficult operation. Officers and men were not specially trained to undertake it. Only the prevalence of disorder in these years, coupled with the experience acquired in countering the riots, disorders and turmoil of the period 1789-1815, enabled the army to become increasingly proficient in tackling the problems posed by civil unrest. Senior officers, as already stated, disliked the duties involved; but not even the radical generals, like Sir Charles Napier, doubted the rightness of their task and the importance of avoiding a military defeat.

In preserving public order some problems would occur which defied a 'military solution'. Wellington and Hardinge reckoned that the Irish press, along with the priesthood, were malevolent influences in Ireland, liable to inflame passions and to incite sedition, protest and disorder. Writing from Dublin in October 1830, Hardinge informed Peel that the press was a constant 'source of mischief' which should be 'stopped' immediately. Hardinge did not believe that the press would arouse 'the mass of the people' to insurrection, since the peasantry lacked the arms and leadership, but he was concerned about the news of successful revolts elsewhere. He assured Peel that 'The successful example of Belgium has of course excited a restless expectation throughout the lower classes, that they can by similar means overpower the military and dissolve the Union'.[38] Peel was aware that the events in Paris and Brussels could prove contagious, and that they could excite rebellious feelings not only in Ireland but also in the manufacturing districts of the north of England. Nonetheless he would not attempt to stifle the press. Instead he resolved to reinforce military garrisons so that the first sign of violence could be 'signally put down'.[39]

However prudent as a precaution, reinforcing garrisons merely exposed a serious military problem, namely a grave shortage of men. This shortage was never remedied completely. During the disturbances of 1819, the Duke of Wellington doubted that the army could counter a general and simultaneous uprising in different parts of the country. Unable to rebut such a rising, he instructed Major-General Sir John Byng to ensure that the radicals, at least, had 'no success against any body of the trooops'. To avoid defeat, the Duke required that all garrisons, castles, and magazines should be made secure. He advised that troops should not be deployed in bodies of less than 200 or 300 men and that small detachments should not be exposed in populous towns. The men, he proposed, should not be billeted on the townsfolk, but quartered in 'large barns or warehouses . . . removed from the temptations held out to them in the large towns'.[40] Given lack of numbers, the first concern of the Horse Guards and of the officers in command was to avoid defeat. The military would seek temporary accommodation from the local authorities. The thought of small detachments being cut off and then overpowered, disarmed and possibly destroyed was too terrible to contemplate.

Some twenty years later, during the Chartist disturbances, Sir Charles Napier would encounter the same problem of limited numbers, and would emphasize the same objective of concentrating and not dispersing the troops. He had witnessed two rebellions in Ireland in 1798 and in 1803. During both rebellions he had witnessed small detachments endangered. In 1798 he had known of an instance at Prosperous, Co. Kildare, where Captain Swayne and 100 men had been burned in a barracks by a force which could never have met them in the open. 'The great great evil of small detachments', he shrewdly observed, 'is not that they cannot *resist* but that they cannot *keep watch*'.[41] Once isolated and overcome by fatigue, the troops would become much more vulnerable. Indeed the limitations of troops had been clearly exposed during the Reform Bill riots of 1831. At the height of the Bristol riots (29–31 October 1831), Lieutenant-Colonel Brereton moved his squadron of the 14th Light Dragoons out of the city, pleading that they were too tired and would be needlessly sacrificed by remaining on duty.[42] In the worst riots of the year, Bristol city-centre was sacked.

Normally governments tried to obviate the shortage of troops by moving batallions from England to Ireland, or from Ireland to England as the circumstances required. By the late 1830s and 1840s, governments could use the railways to move troops more quickly and less expensively across the country. Large concentrations of troops in any one area, however, could only be provided at the expense of another. In September 1828, every available soldier, excluding those in the capital, was placed at the disposal of the Lord-Lieutenant of Ireland. Of the six battalions of infantry, three regiments of cavalry and one battalion of Guards, Lord Anglesey immediately requested two battalions of infantry, leaving a tiny residual force in England. During the urban riots of 1831–32, approximately 11,000 troops were stationed in England, the majority of whom were based in the London area. Had an organized insurrection occurred, instead of uncoordinated spasmodic rioting, the military would have found themselves completely outnumbered.

Where army units were deployed, another problem was their relationship with the local magistracy. On home service army units received their instructions through the Horse Guards, but effectively from the Home Office. At local level their presence was requested and their operations were directed and supervised by the local magistrates. Indeed, the magistrates were obliged to accompany soldiers to the scene of a disturbance, and if necessary to read the Riot Act and authorize the officer to order his men to fire. Serving under the magistracy would, in many cases, prove extremely tiresome and vexatious for commanding officers. Officers would repeatedly complain to the Home Secretary, and to each other, about the timidity of the magistrates, their vacillation, their local enmities and, at times, their gross neglect of duty. In 1819 Captain Harry Smith, having ordered his Hussars to repress a Glaswegian mob with the flats of their swords, found that the magistrates were 'horridly timid and frightened lest I should order the troops to fire'.[43] Sir John Byng, serving in the manufacturing districts of Lancashire in 1827, described the magistrates as 'far from good and little respected'. He ascribed the lack of an adequate civil force to the preoccupation of the magistrates with money-making ventures, a preoccupation for which the officer gentleman had little admiration.[44] During the Chartist disorders, complaints poured forth, not least from the pen of Sir Charles Napier. When appointed commander of the Northern District, he was appalled by the tergiversation of the town magistrates, and, even worse, by the overriding concern of some county magistrates for the protection of their own homes and property. 'Funk', he claimed, 'is the order of the day'.[45]

As F. C. Mather has indicated in his admirable study, *Public Order in the Age of the Chartists*, these sweeping condemnations cannot be taken too literally. Personal and political animosities coloured the impressions and the reports of some officers. Although many justices of the peace warranted the criticisms of them, others displayed exemplary bravery and competence in carrying out their duties. The individual qualities of the magistracy were of less importance, as Mather argues, than three more general characteristics. In the first place there was a lack of local self-reliance: a reluctance to spend the money on a large permanent police establishment, and a preference for the cheaper expedient of calling upon the troops whenever disorder erupted or threatened to erupt. Sir James Graham would appeal to local magnates like Lord Londonderry to persuade his county authorities of the wisdom of establishing a large permanent civil force.[46] Secondly many magistrates were blinkered by an entirely parochial perspective. The 'small interests and personal fears' of magistrates merited attention in Napier's eyes, but only as part of a more national concern. He recalled that the Bristol riots, though the worst conflagration of recent years, represented no more than a local loss. 'A military mishap', he feared, 'would be a national misfortune', while a 'civil defeat', would be 'only a trifling private loss'.[47] Thirdly, the county bench were prone to over-react in dealing with local disturbances. Justices tended to request soldiers where none were needed, to use force excessively in dispersing crowds or in arresting seditious speakers at public meetings. Over-reaction was not invariable; sometimes magistrates were criticized for being too apprehensive in the face of incipient disorder. In August 1842, Colonel Thorn would lay this charge against the magistrates of Birmingham, complaining that they should have arrested the local Chartist leaders more quickly.[48] Whether their reaction was too vigorous or too supine the magistrates, unlike the soldiery, had to live with the consequences of their decisions. They were responsible for preserving the peace; should they fail, arson, looting and perhaps loss of life could ensue. Concerned about the repercussions within their own locality, magistrates often differed in outlook and approach from their assigned military officers.

In spite of these difficulties, the army would prove to be reasonably effective in countering civil disorders. Unlike the rioters, the soldiery were well armed and disciplined. Although ingenious ideas about street fighting - the use of hand-made pikes, moveable barricades, and burning acids - were reproduced in the radical press, only rarely did the soldiers encounter effective resistance. Even when the demonstrators, including many Peninsular veterans, were organized, as they were in Glasgow in 1819, into street battalions and regiments with a central committee of delegates, they proved no match for the Hussars. Exhaustive precautions were taken to protect military arsenals and to prevent arms from falling into radical hands. The military were prepared to use their whole array of weapons. The Duke of Wellington even recommended moving 5½-inch howitzers, with 24-pound shot, into Chester Castle, from whence they could be rapidly moved to Manchester should their assistance be requested.[49]

Of more importance than force of arms was the discipline and restraint of the rank and file. Mounted charges and orders to open fire were relatively rare occurrences. More often soldiers simply patrolled the streets, or mounted guard at public meetings, or assisted in the arrest of radical speakers. Often their appearance, embodying as it did the authority of the State, would occasion insults, abuse, and sometimes volleys of stones and mud. Maintaining discipline was of the essence. The army wished to avoid another Peterloo and the stigma which had bedevilled the Yeomanry in subsequent years. It did not suffer the delusion that spilling blood was an effective method of crowd control. Napier, in particular, who sympathized with the plight, if not with the tactics, of the Chartists, had no wish to shed their blood and compound their misery. It was more prudent to overawe the Chartists by a display of arms than by force of arms.

Preserving the peace, however, required more than a show of force. Like the Home Office, police, and magistracy, the army tried to gather intelligence. At a time when spies and *agents provocateurs* were active within radical groups, some officers relied upon simpler and cheaper methods of obtaining information. During the disturbances of 1817, 1819 and 1820, many old soldiers joined the protests and some of them happily talked to their former comrades or officers. Captain Harry Smith ascertained how the striking weavers in Glasgow were organized from an old Rifleman whom he had served with in Spain and France.[50] As old soldiers were not so numerous twenty years later, Sir Charles Napier had to rely upon information gleaned by privates and pensioners as they sat drinking in public houses. He accepted that such information would be 'less copious' than that obtained by the magistrates. On the other hand, he believed that it would be less tainted 'by any party, personal or political bias'. While some officers relied upon information from spies and informers, Napier affirmed that his system might supply impartial and useful intelligence, at no expense.[51]

To supplement the peace-keeping activities of the army, retired soldiers were enrolled by the civil and military authorities. Chelsea out-pensioners were employed extensively during the early years of the Chartist disturbances. Initially they were used in a civil capacity as special constables for street patrols and for dispersing meetings. In this role, without uniform and the steadying influence of martial discipline, the pensioners were not always impressive. They were once withdrawn from patrol duty during the Plug-plot disturbances in Manchester having purportedly fled at the approach of a mob.[52] Seeking a more effective use of the pensioners, the War Office devised a scheme, embodied in the Enrolled Pensioners Act of 1843, by which the pensioners were transformed from a civil into an auxiliary military force. Under the Act, pensioners would be compulsorily enrolled in local uniformed corps. Armed and required to attend eight days' inspection in each year, they would be liable to deductions from their pensions if they lost their arms or equipment. The authorities found difficulty in enrolling the full establishment of 10,000 pensioners. Even after an amending Act of 1846, by which Greenwich (naval) pensioners became liable for enrolment also, only 8,720 veterans were mustered in Great Britain by 1847-48. Nevertheless these pensioners assisted both the police and military in countering the last flourishes of Chartism in 1848. By taking over guard duties they freed regular troops for other employments; by aiding the police and soldiers at the vast public meetings they contributed to the final demoralization of the Chartist movement.

In the maintenance of public order the army generally coped with the many and various demands which were placed upon it. Although a popular desire for revolution was probably lacking,[53] the military commanders still faced a formidable array of problems. Cautious tactics and a disciplined control of the ranks served them well. Officers were usually sanguine about their ability to defy 'the mob'. Captain Gronow, whose company of Life Guards occupied the Cold Bath prison at Spa Fields during the tempestuous riots of December 1816, recalled that 'the mob' were neither 'well drilled' nor 'accustomed to the use of arms'.[54] Sir Henry Hardinge expressed similar views about the Irish peasantry in 1830, as did Napier in his reports on Chartists in 1839. Nevertheless there were occasions when 'the mob' seemed particularly menacing, even moving the Duke of Wellington to prepare the defence of Apsley House, his London home, during Reform Bill riots in November 1830. The coercive power of the State barely contained the Reform Bill protests, and in Bristol it failed to do so. Only political concessions or, in the Chartist years, the temporary relief of economic distress could assuage the feelings of popular discontent.

Though closely involved with the State in preserving public order, the army remained in many respects distinct from the rest of society. Both a cause and a reflection of this schism was the division of power between the Crown and Parliament over responsibility for army administration. Whereas Parliament retained control over the finances and the disciplinary code of the army, the Crown, by creating the Horse Guards in 1798, maintained its control over the command and organization of the army. Several different departments, each independent of the other, administered the army. While the Secretary of State for War and the Colonies was responsible for the overall size of the army, the Secretary at War was responsible for army finances and for introducing the annual Mutiny Act in the House of Commons. The Treasury, apart from controlling army finances, managed the Commissariat department, from which the army abroad and in Ireland obtained its fuel and provisions. The Home Secretary was responsible for military questions in Great Britain; he also controlled the Militia and Yeomanry so long as those forces remained disembodied. The Commander-in-Chief, based in the Horse Guards, was responsible for the discipline and efficiency of the infantry and cavalry. Empowered, as the Sovereign's deputy, to command the forces at home, the Commander-in-Chief had no control over the supply of their arms, stores, accoutrements, ammunition, nor over their fortifications and barracks. Responsibility for these matters was vested in the Master-General of the Ordnance, who was also responsible for the discipline, pay and allowances of the Royal Artillery and Royal Engineers. Completely lacking in this organization was any overall co-ordination of the deliberations of the different departments.

In these circumstances, Horse Guards remained a bastion of royal authority, contemptuous of Parliamentary interference, and jealous of its own prerogatives. A senescent high command held office. The Duke of York was Commander-in-Chief from 1811 until his death in 1827. The Duke of Wellington then held the post on an interim basis, to be succeeded by Lord Hill, his Peninsular colleague, in 1828. Lord Hill retired, shortly before his death, after fourteen years in office. Wellington returned to be Commander-in-Chief until his death in 1852. Viscount Hardinge, another Peninsular veteran, succeeded him and held the post at the outbreak of the Crimean War. These officers had rendered invaluable service during their younger and more active days, not least the Duke of York, who had established the office of Commander-in-Chief and had staved off encroachments upon his authority. But the fealty of these officers and their staffs was first and foremost to the Crown, a belief undiminished by the Parliamentary control of finance. Horse Guards felt that its *raison d'être* transcended the vagaries of party politics, and carried a superior constitutional status. The very real dependence of the army upon Parliament not only galled but intensified these emotional feelings. Horse Guards could not admit that the army required reform since this would have implied an inability to fulfil onerous and prized responsibilities, while conceding a weakness liable to exploitation by unsympathetic and ignorant politicians.[55]

Undoubtedly an entrenched Horse Guards bureaucracy, reluctant to tamper with the army which had triumphed at Waterloo, impeded the cause of army reform. Yet it is not the case that the army quietly stultified in these years, with its shortcomings unknown and unpublicized until the Crimean War. The conditions of the rank and file periodically engaged the attention of writers and politicians. The temperance press reacted vehemently to the drunkenness so prevalent within the rank and file. It condemned the canteen system, the living quarters and the lack of recreational facilities in the army, while recording joyously the formation of any teetotal society within particular regiments.[56] Complaints about the squalid accommodation, the rates of pay, the degree of supervision, and the plight of married soldiers were raised occasionally, albeit largely in the military journals. Nevertheless these issues were examined in the civilian papers and periodicals. Extensive articles were written about 'The Moral Discipline of the Army' and 'The Army and the People'. Various reforms were proposed, including the abolition of purchase, limited enlistment, curbs upon mess expenditure, an increase in the number of clergymen, and a 'diffusion of education' throughout the army.[57]

No issue, however, aroused more controversy than flogging in the army and navy. Floggings were frequently reported in the local and national press. Lurid accounts of the punishments and, when the victims died, exhaustive reports of the coroner's inquests kindled abolitionist sentiment. Campaigns were frequently mounted to abolish the lash. Large protest meetings were convened, usually in the wake of a particularly horrendous flogging. Pressure groups were formed, including a Society for the Abolition of Flogging in the Army and Navy. Occasionally the protests became so vehement that regiments moved away from their local billets.[58] Sir Francis Burdett, Joseph Hume and William Cobbett championed the abolitionist cause in Parliament; they protested over individual floggings and regularly moved abolitionist motions during the debates on the annual Mutiny Bills.

Abolitionists condemned flogging as a brutal and degrading form of punishment. They contrasted the severity of the punishment with the nature of the crimes committed, many of which were infractions of Service discipline as distinct from criminal offences. As some military offences, like insubordination, were imprecise, they were interpreted differently by the various regimental colonels. The dispositions of these officers mattered because many courts martial sentenced offenders to a certain number of lashes to be inflicted 'in such a manner as the commanding officer shall think fit'. Retaining the power of mercy, these officers could pardon and admonish culprits; some did, and in their corps floggings were a relatively rare occurrence, but others did not - preferring to enforce obedience by the lash. 'Where rigid flogging is practised', wrote John Shipp, formerly a lieutenant in the 87th Foot, 'discontent, disorder, and a great deal of bad feeling towards the officers, are sure to prevail'.[59] Critics feared that flogging a soldier in full view of the regiment drawn up at attention in the barrack square was more likely to degrade and harden the offender than to reform his character. So sickening a spectacle, they claimed, would disgust the comrades of the victim and produce sympathy for him instead of serving as an example and deterring crime.[60]

Arguing about the effects of flogging was rarely conclusive, however. The proponents of flogging merely countered, with equal conviction, that the lash was a deterrent, and that some men who had been flogged were not turned into hardened criminals but rose through the ranks to become efficient non-commissioned officers. Napier, one of the few officers who favoured abolition, prepared a more persuasive case. He objected to flogging because it was a form of torture, a torture of 'very unequal infliction'. The punishment varied considerably; some victims suffered more than others, some drummers lashed more vigorously than others, some commanding officers and drum-majors enforced a more severe or a slighter punishment, according to their influence over the drummers. The torture could lead to unintended results; it could produce fatalities. Whatever the effects of the flogging upon the victim, it left him branded and thereby an object of suspicion.[61] Military critics of flogging accepted that the punishment might have to be retained for active service. Nevertheless they believed that other punishments - solitary confinement, extra drills, forfeiture of pay - could be substituted in peacetime. By abolishing the lash and rewarding good behaviour, argued Lieutenant-Colonel, later Lieutenant-General, De Lacy Evans, MP, the army would induce 'a better class of youth' to enter military service.[62]

Fundamentally, abolitionists regarded flogging as an offence to civilized values. It was a barbarity which should not be perpetuated in the armed services. Many abolitionists had already agitated in favour of abolishing slavery within the British Empire, and had seen their efforts rewarded by the Emancipation Act of 1833. Henceforth they focused, even more vehemently, upon 'white slavery' in the British army. The British soldier, thundered *The North Devon Journal*, was denied 'the privileges accorded to the African'; he had become 'a debased slave' whose 'loathsome mark' of bondage could only be obliterated by death.[63] Campaigners for the abolition of slavery in the United States were welcomed at the protest meetings on flogging. Frederick Douglass, the escaped slave from Maryland who toured Britain raising support for the abolitionist cause in the United States, and Henry C. Wright, the radical pacifist from Philadelphia, attended the inaugural meeting of the Flogging Abolition Society in August 1846. Wright even proposed the motion constituting the Society, in the hope of ensuring that 'iron dukes, or brazen dukes, or wooden dukes, could never treat their opinions with indifference'.[64]

Senior officers opposed concessions over corporal punishment. In March 1826, Sir Henry Hardinge catalogued his objections to the proposal of Lord Palmerston that the maximum punishment imposed by regimental courts martial should be reduced from 300 to 200 lashes. This proposal, he feared, would undermine the authority of commanding officers. He doubted that an alternative could be found for flogging as a wartime punishment. He rejected the compromise of two codes of discipline, one for peace and the other for war, believing that this would inhibit recruiting in wartime. Any concession, he affirmed, would weaken the deterrent effect of corporal punishment and would not conciliate those who objected to the practice itself.[65] Hardinge would compromise these sentiments when, as Secretary at War (1828–30), he encountered pressure 'on all sides to abolish the flogging system'. In a memorandum addressed to Lord Hill, he repeated that he still preferred the British system, but was prepared to sponsor a modified form of Prussian discipline whereby corporal punishment would be restricted to extraordinary offences only – 'mutiny, insubordination, felonies and disgraceful crimes'.[66] The Duke of Wellington intervened immediately. Having relied upon the lash to enforce discipline throughout the Peninsular Wars, the Duke maintained that flogging was an essential prerequisite for military success in the future. Trifling with the system of military discipline he regarded as 'one of the morbid symptoms of the times'. The abolitionists, he averred, 'forget what the army is, and what it may become, if not kept in order'. Brutal punishments were necessary because the soldiery were brutal. Only 'the terror' of corporal punishment could establish subordination among the soldiers, and ensure discipline.[67]

In their evidence before the Royal Commission on Military Punishments, other generals and regimental officers generally endorsed the use of the lash. A small minority favoured abolition, at least in the peacetime army, but the vast majority believed that flogging was essential to curb the excesses of the rank and file. So long as the army retained the services of 'incorrigible villains', or men whose pleasures were 'entirely sensual', corporal punishment alone, they claimed, could maintain military discipline. Should corporal punishment be abolished, declared Major-General Thornton, the army would become 'the most formidable enemy the country could have'.[68] The majority of officers agreed that flogging was a deterrent, that it did not degrade the victim, and that any options were impractical on active service. Several non-commissioned officers and even some private soldiers concurred. Other rankers disputed these views, claiming that corporal punishment not only degraded the offender but caused bitter resentment within the ranks. Inevitably the seven commissioners, who included three generals and an ex-judge advocate general, adjudicated in favour of the cat-o'-nine-tails: corporal punishment, however regrettable, was deemed indispensable.

Horse Guards, nonetheless, could not ignore the persistent pressure from the House of Commons and from successive governments. In spite of ill-concealed misgivings, concessions were announced. The maximum punishment which general and district courts martial could award was limited to 300 lashes in 1829. The maximum punishment of a regimental court martial was reduced from 300 to 200 lashes in 1832. Five years later these punishment rates were again revised: a general court martial was reduced to 200 lashes, a district to 150, and a regimental to 100. As Hardinge had predicted, these reductions would not appease the abolitionist conscience. Indeed the abolitionists would continue the crusade, with their protests reaching crescendo over the death of Private White in July 1846. White had received 150 lashes for 'insubordination with threats and violence' and had died twenty-six days after the punishment. The jury at the coroner's inquest delivered its verdict on 4 August. Rejecting the view of the military post-mortem that White's death was 'in no way connected with the corporal punishment he received', the jury attributed the death to the effects of 'a severe and cruel flogging'. It also expressed the view that petitions should be forwarded to the Legislature pressing for the abolition of 'the disgraceful practice of flogging'. The radical press rejoiced. Four days after the verdict the House of Commons began to debate another abolition motion. The Whig government of Lord John Russell consulted the Duke of Wellington. Unwilling to abolish the lash, the Duke offered another concession, and Parliament responded by crushing the abolition motion by 90 votes to 37. On 11 August 1846, the Duke announced the reduction of the maximum punishment of all courts martial to 50 lashes 'in consequence of the feeling of the Government, of the Parliament, and of the Public on this subject'.[69] The Duke had prevailed again. Abetted by a pusillanimous Whig government, he had out-manoeuvred his critics: the lash would continue to be used in the British army, with a steadily decreasing frequency, for another thirty-five years.

However reluctantly, the Duke of Wellington was prepared to make concessions to preserve the essential features of the army he had led to victory at Waterloo. In 1847, when faced with an Army Service Bill, proposing a limited period of enlistment, he insisted that it should only apply to new recruits. Although willing to endorse the amended Bill in the Upper House, the Duke disassociated himself from the Whig reformers. He doubted that the new terms of service would attract 'a superior description of men'. Those who enlisted for ten years, he argued, would re-enlist after the completion of their first engagement, so thwarting the creation of an army reserve. The army would still rely upon 'old soldiers' whom the Duke rated as vital to its 'very existence'.[70] Three years later he made another concession to Parliamentary pressure; he issued an order requiring ensigns and lieutenants to undergo an examination before promotion, a largely ineffectual concession for some time at least, since both books and instructors had to be provided from England for troops serving in India and the Colonies.

Whenever possible, the Duke of Wellington stood firm and defied the reformers. In 1837 and 1849, he resisted attempts to centralize military administration and place the various departments under a Secretary at War, with a seat in the cabinet. He feared incursions upon the prerogative and patronage of the Commander-in-Chief. He feared that placing the army under the absolute control of a civilian minister who was responsible to the reformed House of Commons would undermine the discipline and efficiency of the Service. Preserving the army from the clutches of the Commons became a primary concern of the Duke: his care 'was less to improve the Army than to save it from destruction'.[71] The Duke's suspicions, though understandable, were coloured by the personal and mutual enmity which the Duke and the radical spokesmen felt towards each other. During the Reform Bill debates the Duke had never concealed his dislike of Reform and his disdain for the apostles of Reform. As he informed Lord Cowley in July 1831, reform would lead to 'the total extinction of the power and of the property of this country': only 'the mob, the Radicals, the Dissenters from the Church', would benefit, they would 'hail the measure as the commencement of a new era of destruction and plunder'.[72] The radicals were equally vehement. Their detestation of the Duke persisted long after the passage of the Reform Bill. Even at the death of the Duke, John Bright could neither forgive nor forget, nor understand the widespread remorse throughout the country. In a letter to Cobden, Bright gave vent to his frustrations: 'The people owe him little. His sentiments were never liberal, he gave them nothing he could retain, he treated them generally with something like contempt. He served the Aristocracy, and they only should be his mourners'.[73]

This seething animus reflected more than mere hatred of the Duke and his reactionary outlook. It underlined that the radicals were becoming increasingly frustrated by the trend of government policies in the late 1840s and early 1850s. Not only had successive governments allowed the Duke to preserve his control over the patronage and discipline of the army, but they had also increased military expenditure and had passed a Militia Bill in 1852. Governments had become concerned about the defences of the country after several invasion scares, or 'panics' as the radicals described them. On 7 November 1846, Sir John Burgoyne, a veteran Engineer who had served in the Peninsular Wars, sent a memorandum to the Duke of Wellington about the lack of defences on the south coast of England. He noted that a mere 5,000 to 10,000 regular troops were available to resist invasion, that the field artillery could not equip an army of more than 20,000 men, and that fortresses were conspicuous by their absence. The Duke concurred with this estimate of the available manpower and equipment. He feared that an invasion force of 40,000 French troops could not possibly be resisted. The only solution, he argued, was 'to raise, embody, organize and discipline the militia'.[74]

The Duke's letter, written on 9 January 1847, found its way into *The Times* of 1 December 1847 via the indiscreet hands of Sir John's wife and daughters. Publication provoked an 'invasion scare' in the press and periodicals. Editorials and articles were written quoting the letter as unanswerable proof that the country was in danger. When Parliament reassembled, Lord John Russell responded to the controversy by including radically new proposals in his financial statement. He recommended that income tax should be raised by 5*d* in the pound, from 7*d* to 1*s*, to pay for a reorganization of the Militia.

Almost immediately a reaction set in; petitions poured into the House of Commons protesting about the additional taxation. Reports of a revolution in France and the overthrow of Louis Philippe doused the fears of an imminent invasion. Although the budget was promptly withdrawn for amendment, a mere ten days after its introduction, expenditure upon the regular army continued to rise. During 1848, the last year of Chartist disorders and the year of the attempted 'Young Ireland' rising, the army vote totalled £9,722,608, nearly 10 per cent above the expenditure in 1840. The infantry stationed in the United Kingdom numbered 64,981 officers and men, the largest force retained at home since 1816.

Military expenditure would rapidly decline over the next three years, but fears of an invasion were never entirely removed. Indeed they were given a powerful boost in December 1851 when Louis Napoleon seized power in France. Within three months the Whig government had increased the regular army by 5,000 men and had introduced a Bill to form a local Militia. Palmerston opposed the Bill, favouring a national rather than a local Militia. In his 'tit for tat' with Lord John Russell, he carried his point in the Commons and defeated the government. A Tory government, under Lord Derby, took office. It introduced a new Militia Bill, with the support of Palmerston, providing for the embodiment of 80,000 Militiamen, who were to be enlisted voluntarily or, if necessary, chosen by ballot. Cobden and Bright led a desperate but despairing opposition, gathering only 150 votes against the Bill. Ironically the House of Commons, which had aroused the fears and suspicions of the Duke of Wellington for nearly twenty years, would within months of his death pass a Militia Act and earn the sobriquet from Cobden of a 'military hothouse'.[75]

In sum, the army and society co-existed in an uneasy and fluctuating relationship over the years from 1815 to 1854. The army suffered from the retrenchment policies of successive governments, but was neither the victim of rampant anti-militarism nor entirely ignored by the House of Commons and the rest of society. The army occupied the forefront of the struggles to preserve public order. It benefited from the invasion fears of the early 1850s. Governments began, albeit tardily and in a fairly limited manner, to spend more money on the army and to improve the defences of the country. The Duke of Wellington, meanwhile, had struggled successfully to maintain the prerogatives of the Commander-in-Chief. An opponent of army reform, he normally prevailed over those cabinets and subordinates, like Hardinge, who occasionally favoured innovation. The concessions of the Duke were relatively minor. Even when he permitted the army to be equipped with 28,000 Minié rifles, he wished to retain the old calibre and bayonets. Only reluctantly did he give way to technical advisers.[76] The Duke resisted new ideas and new inventions. He accepted that the army would remain an institution apart, a body estranged from the rest of society. The army, he wrote, was 'an exotic in England':

'Service in the army is an advantage to none. The officers and soldiers of the army are an object of dislike and suspicion to the inhabitants while serving with their regiments, and of jealousy afterwards, and they are always ill-treated'.[77]

Notes and references

1. J. W. Fortescue, *op. cit.*, Vol. XI, pp. 47–52; **C. Barnett,** *Britain and Her Army 1509–1970, A Military, Political and Social Survey,* Allen Lane, London, 1970, p. 278.
2. C. Woodham Smith, *op. cit.*, p. 88; **R. L. Blanco**, 'Reform and Wellington's post-Waterloo army', *Military Affairs,* **45**, Fall 1965, p. 123.
3. Quoted in **Major-General Sir L. C. Jackson,** *History of the United Service Club,* private, London, 1937, p. 6.
4. *The Black Dwarf,* **V**, No. 2, 2 July 1820, p. 62.
5. Quoted in *Political Letters and Pamphlets by William Carpenter,* 29 Oct. 1830, p. 2.
6. *The Poor Man's Guardian*, **III**, No. 161, 26 July 1834, p. 194.
7. 'Extracts from the Journals of the Major Edward Macready', *United Service Magazine,* Part III, Sept. 1852, p. 68.
8. *The Morning Chronicle,* 16 Feb. 1832, p. 2; *The Manchester Guardian,* 4 Aug. 1832, p. 3; *The Poor Man's Guardian,* **II**, No. 113, 3 Aug. 1833, p. 251; **D. Thomas,** *Charge! Hurrah! Hurrah! A Life of Cardigan of Balaclava,* Omega, London, 1976, pp. 80–1.
9. G. Bell, *op. cit.*, p. 186.
10. *The Journal of Mrs. Arbuthnot, 1820–1832,* ed. F. Bamford and the Duke of Wellington, 2 vols., Macmillan, London, 1950, Vol. 1, pp. 55–6, 69.
11. **C. T. Atkinson,** *History of the Royal Dragoons 1661–1934*, University Press, Glasgow, 1934, pp. 315–19.
12. *P.P.*, No. 88, 2 Sess. 1859, XVII, pp. 8–25.
13. *Parl. Deb.*, New Series, Vol. 21, 1 June 1829, col. 1,646, and **The Hon. Sir A. Gordon,** *The Earl of Aberdeen,* Sampson Law, London, 1893, p. 113.
14. **Duke of Wellington,** 'Memorandum on the proposed reduction of the army', 4 Aug. 1827, enclosed in a letter to Lord Goderich, 25 Aug. 1827, *Despatches, Correspondence and Memoranda of Field Marshal Arthur Duke of Wellington K.G.*, hereafter referred to as Despatches, ed. Duke of Wellington, 8 vols., Parker & Co., London, 1867–80, Vol. 4, p. 114.
15. R. L. Blanco, *op. cit.*, p. 125.
16. R. Cobden to J. Sturge, 18 July 1848, Cobden Mss., B.M. Add. Mss. 43,656, ff. 34–5.

17. **F. O. Darvall,** *Popular Disturbances and Public Order in Regency England,* O.U.P., London, 1934, p. 260.
18. **J. M. Hart,** 'The reform of the borough police, 1835–1856', *English Historical Review,* **LXX**, 1955, p. 416.
19. **F. C. Mather,** *Public Order in the Age of the Chartists,* Manchester University Press, Manchester, 1959, pp. 113–15.
20. Duke of Wellington to Sir R. Peel, 14 July 1828, Peel Mss., B.M. Add. Mss. 40,306, f. 193.
21. **W. Cobbett,** *Weekly Political Register,* **XXXI**, 6 July 1816, p. 39 and *The Black Dwarf,* **VII**, No. 11, 12 Sept. 1821, p. 378.
22. Duke of Wellington, 'Memorandum to the Earl of Liverpool respecting the state of the Guards', June 1820, *Despatches,* Vol. 1, p. 128.
23. Duke of Wellington, 'Memorandum on the proposed plan for altering the discipline of the army', 22 Apr. 1829 and 'Memorandum on Corporal Punishment', 4 Mar. 1832, *Despatches,* Vol. 5, p. 594 and Vol. 8, p. 235.
24. *The Poor Man's Guardian,* **II**, No. 92, 9 Mar. 1833, pp. 74–5.
25. A. Somerville, *op. cit.*, p. 159.
26. **M. Cunliffe,** *The Royal Irish Fusiliers 1793–1950,* O.U.P., London, 1952, p. 186.
27. Colonel D'Aguilar, report, 11 Oct. 1830, Hardinge Mss.
28. Sir H. Hardinge to Sir R. Peel, 12 and 13 Oct. 1830, Peel Mss., B.M. Add. Mss. 40,313, ff. 47–51, 63–4.
29. Sir R. Peel to Sir H. Hardinge, 15 Oct. 1830, Hardinge Mss.
30. Sir H. Hardinge to Sir J. Graham, 23 May 1843, Hardinge Mss.
31. Lieutenant-General Sir W. Napier, *The Life and Opinions of General Sir Charles Napier, GCB,* 4 Vols., John Murray, London, 1857, Vol. II, pp. 30–1, 34, 54, 62.
32. Duke of Wellington, 'Memorandum upon the Irish Yeomanry', 21 Aug. 1831, *Despatches,* Vol. 7, pp. 506–8; *Parl. Deb.,* Third Ser., Vol. 42, 7 May 1838, col. 951; Sir J. Graham to Sir R. Peel, 18 June 1843, Peel Mss., B.M. Add. Mss. 40,448, ff. 325–6.
33. Lord Palmerston to Sir R. Peel, 1 Feb. 1824, Palmerston Mss., B.M. Add. Mss. 48,420, ff. 22–8.
34. **D. Read,** *Peterloo: The 'Massacre' and its Background,* Manchester University Press, Manchester, 1958, pp. 126–40 and **R. Walmsley**, *Peterloo: The Case Reopened,* Manchester University Press, Manchester, 1969, pp. 21–40.
35. *Parl. Deb.,* Third Ser., Vol. 42, 27 Apr. 1838, col. 651.
36. Sir J. Graham to Sir R. Peel, 18 June 1843, Peel Mss., B.M. Add. Mss. 40,448, f. 325.
37. Sir R. Peel to the Duke of Wellington, 24 Aug. 1842, Peel Mss., B.M. Add. Mss. 40,459, f. 295 and F. C. Mather, *op. cit.*, pp. 148–50.
38. Sir H. Hardinge to Sir R. Peel, 12 Oct. 1830, Peel Mss., B.M. Add. Mss. 40,313, f. 56. See also Duke of Wellington to Sir

R. Peel, 5 Nov. 1828, Peel Mss., B.M. Add. Mss. 40,306, f. 52.

39. Sir R. Peel to Sir H. Hardinge, 14 Oct. 1830, Peel Mss., B.M. Add. Mss. 40,313, ff. 76–8.
40. Duke of Wellington to Sir J. Byng, 21 Oct. 1819, *Despatches,* Vol. 1, pp. 80–1.
41. Sir C. J. Napier to S. M. Phillips, 13 Apr. 1839, Napier Mss., B.M. Add. Mss. 49,129, ff. 8–9.
42. Lord Granville Somerset to Duke of Wellington, 3 Nov. 1831, *Despatches,* Vol. 8, p. 27.
43. **Sir H. Smith,** *The Autobiography of Lieutenant-General Sir Harry Smith,* John Murray, London, 1903, p. 326.
44. Sir J. Byng to Duke of Wellington, 19 Aug. 1827, *Despatches,* Vol. 4, p. 100.
45. Lt.-Gen. Sir W. Napier, *op. cit.,* Vol. II, pp. 7–8.
46. Sir J. Graham to Lord Londonderry, 14 June and 17 Aug. 1844, 19 Oct. 1845, Londonderry Mss., Durham County Record Office. F. C. Mather, *op. cit.,* pp. 62–3.
47. Lt.-Gen. Sir W. Napier, *op. cit.,* Vol. II, pp. 14–15.
48. Colonel Thorn to Sir H. Hardinge, 21 Aug. 1842, Hardinge, Mss.
49. Duke of Wellington, 'Memorandum upon the precautions to be taken to prevent any disaster to the troops in case of their being called out in the North of England', 26 Oct. 1830, *Despatches,* Vol. 7, pp. 321–2.
50. Sir H. Smith, *op. cit.,* p. 325.
51. Sir C. Napier to S. M. Phillips, 13 Apr. 1839, Napier Mss., B.M. Add. Mss. 49,129, ff. 10–11.
52. F. C. Mather, *op. cit.,* p. 89.
53. **M. I. Thomas** and **P. Holt,** *Threats of Revolution in Britain 1789–1848,* Macmillan, London, 1977, p. 128.
54. **R. H. Gronow,** *The Reminiscences and Recollections of Captain Gronow,* Bodley Head, London, 1964, p. 198.
55. **P. D. Jones,** *The British Army in the Age of Reform, 1830–1854,* unpublished Ph.D. thesis, Duke University, 1968, pp. 100–87.
56. *The National Temperance Chronicle and Recorder,* **6**, June 1846, p. 139 and **9**, Aug. 1846, pp. 171–2.
57. *Colburn's United Service Magazine,* Part III, Dec. 1843, p. 540; Part I, Jan. 1815, pp. 6–7; Part III, Sept. 1850, pp. 49–55; *North British Review,* **XII**, Feb. 1850, pp. 499–531 and **IX**, Aug. 1848, pp. 275–93; *The Quarterly Review,* **LXXVI**, Sept. 1845, pp. 404–24; *Fraser's Magazine,* **XIII**, June 1836, p. 655 and **XXXVIII**, Aug. 1848, pp. 211–19.
58. Lieutenant-Colonel J. Townsend, Evidence (Q.711) before the Military Punishments Commission, *op. cit.*
59. **J. Shipp,** *Flogging and its Substitute. A Voice from the ranks,* Whitaker, London, 1831, p. 17.
60. *Ibid.,* pp. 14–15, 20; *Political Letters and Pamphlets by William*

Carpenter, 15 Oct. 1830, p. 8; Major Fancourt and Colonel Carey, Evidence (Qs.196, 325) before the Military Punishments Commission, *op. cit.*

61. **Major-General C. J. Napier,** *Remarks on Military Law and the Punishment of Flogging,* T. & W. Boone, London, 1837, pp. 149–55.
62. Evidence (Q.597) before the Military Punishments Commission, *op. cit.*
63. *The North Devon Journal,* 30 July 1846, p. 2 and 13 Aug. 1846, p. 2.
64. *The Morning Chronicle*, 20 Aug. 1846, p. 4.
65. Sir H. Hardinge to Sir H. Taylor, 16 Mar. 1826, *Despatches,* Vol. 3, pp. 198–9.
66. Extracts from the memorandum are included in Evidence (Q.5,662) before the Military Punishments Commission, *op. cit.*
67. Duke of Wellington, Memoranda, 22 Apr. 1829 and 4 Mar. 1832, *Despatches,* Vol. 5, pp. 594–5 and Vol. 8 p. 237.
68. Appendix to the Military Punishments Commission, *op. cit.*, pp. 114, 117. See also Q.4,293.
69. *Parl. Deb.*, Third Ser., Vol. 88, 11 Aug. 1846, col. 601. For a popular, but perceptive, account of this controversy see **H. Hopkins,** *The Strange Death of Private White: A Victorian Scandal that made history,* Weidenfeld and Nicolson, London, 1977.
70. *Parl. Deb.*, Third Ser., Vol. 91, 26 Apr. 1847, col. 1,339.
71. J. W. Fortescue, *op. cit.*, Vol. XI, p. 458.
72. Duke of Wellington to Lord Cowley, 15 July 1831, *Despatches,* Vol. 7, p. 469.
73. J. Bright to R. Cobden, 15 Oct. 1852, Bright Mss., B.M. Add. Mss. 43,383, f. 254.
74. Quoted by Lieutenant-Colonel Hon. G. Wrottesley, *Life and Correspondence of Field Marshal Sir John Burgoyne, Bart.*, 2 vols., Bentley, London, 1873, Vol. 1, p. 446.
75. R. Cobden to J. Sturge, 31 Mar. 1852, Cobden Mss., B.M. Add. Mss. 43,656, f. 267.
76. **H. L. Blackmore,** *British Military Firearms 1650–1850,* H. Jenkins, London, 1961, pp. 205–34; P. D. Jones, *op. cit.*, pp. 203–6.
77. Duke of Wellington, 'Memorandum on the proposed plan for altering the discipline of the army', 22 Apr. 1829, *Despatches,* Vol. 5, p. 593.

4 The Crimean War

The Crimean War (1854-56) was a watershed in the relations between the army and society. After thirty-nine years of peace, the home army suddenly became the focal point of public concern. The fighting in the Crimea, the competence of the military administration, the capabilities of the high command and its staff, and the health and living conditions of the troops attracted the critical attention of the press and Parliament. Leading the critics was *The Times*, under the editorship of John Delane, a newspaper whose circulation of 40,000 readers exceeded the combined readership of all its rivals. The editorials of *The Times*, based upon the eloquent and provocative despatches of its war correspondent, William Howard Russell, became so scathing that the paper described itself as 'a protagonist' in the war.[1] The high command found itself embroiled in a war on two fronts, with the adversary in London even more formidable in some respects than the enemy in Sebastopol.

The war itself was immensely popular. Britain had joined forces with France on 28 March 1854 to preserve Turkey, 'the sick man of Europe'. Turkey had already declared war on Russia in October 1853; she had failed to reconcile her differences with Russia over the privileges of the Catholic and Orthodox monks in Jerusalem, and over the rights of the ten million Orthodox Christians in the Ottoman Empire. On 30 November, the Turks suffered a resounding naval defeat at Sinope. France and Britain, after some hesitation, intervened to preserve the balance of power in the eastern Mediterranean. They sent their fleets to the Black Sea in January 1854, and declared war upon Russia two months later. Lord Aberdeen, who presided over a divided cabinet, had been loath to intervene with military force. He had sought a negotiated settlement. Only the worsening turn of events, the fear of independent action by the French, and the pressure of opinion at home, both public and Parliamentary, fanned by a chauvinistic press, stiffened his resolve.

Once the news of Sinope had reached Britain on 13 December, war fever gripped the nation. Reflected in editorials and in mass meetings, this bellicosity was more than a mere reaction after a long period of peace: the prospect of war had touched the raw nerve of

Russophobia. Hatred of the Tsar, his despotic rule, and his designs upon Constantinople was not a new phenomenon. As early as 1817, Sir Robert Wilson had written an inflammatory tract warning the nation of Russian diplomatic objectives. No less alarming were the pamphlets of Lieutenant-Colonel George De Lacy Evans, written in the late 1820s, which conjured up the spectre of Russian aggrandizement unless the free nations of Europe rallied to preserve the Ottoman Empire. During the next decade, until the peaceful resolution of the Near Eastern Crisis in 1841, David Urquhart stirred the reading public with a vehement anti-Russian campaign in various pamphlets, papers and journals.[2] Between 1848 and 1854 however, the Russophobes aroused a much wider audience. After Russian troops crushed the revolution in Hungary, and the exiled Hungarian leaders arrived in England, popular indignation mounted in the large cities. Several ex-Chartists and radical leaders espoused the nationalist cause, mass meetings were held in all the large cities of the country, and many leading newspapers, including *The Times* after the battle of Sinope, kindled the Russophobe and pro-war fervour.[3]

A small but vociferous opposition to the war evolved under the leadership of Cobden, Bright and the Peace Society. In an endeavour to avert hostilities, a deputation of Quakers visited St Petersburg and gained an audience with Nicholas I. Although the visit proved abortive, the peace movement sustained its efforts, incurring considerable opprobrium as a consequence. Cobden and Bright were even burned in effigy by the crowds in Manchester. Joseph Sturge, the venerable Quaker, ruefully acknowledged 'that the Government was far less to blame than the people of England' for the bellicose passions which were sweeping the nation.[4] With the Radicals providing the noisiest support of the war, Radicals, Liberals and Conservatives united in common cause. Their motives might differ, ranging from opposition to an autocratic tyrant through upholding the claims of public law to resisting the imperial designs of Tsarist Russia, but their objectives coincided. Seeking a 'real victory', and expecting a decisive triumph before the end of 1854, British opinion would follow the course of the war with keen anticipation. The cabinet was supremely confident. Lord Aberdeen believed that Sebastopol would fall almost immediately. The Duke of Newcastle, his Secretary of State for War, expected that the army after capturing Sebastopol would winter there, or, after destroying the fortress, would return to winter on the shores of the Bosphorus.[5] Heady optimism was all-pervasive.

An expeditionary force of approximately 27,000 men was sent to the Crimea. It was composed of three battalions of Guards, twenty-five battalions of infantry and sixteen squadrons of cavalry. Of the twenty-five infantry battalions, only six had seen active service in the previous thirty years. Very few of the regimental officers and men had any previous experience of war. The Commander-in-Chief was Lord Raglan, who, at the age of sixty-six, was receiving his first independent command. Of his five generals in command of infantry divisions, only two had experience of commanding anything larger than a battalion in war; and only one of them, the Duke of Cambridge, was under sixty. His cavalry commanders, with the exception of Sir James Scarlett, commander of the Heavy Brigade, inspired even less confidence. Neither Lord Lucan, who commanded the Cavalry Division, nor his brother-in-law, Lord Cardigan, who commanded the Light Brigade, were experienced officers: both cordially disliked each other. Even less experienced in their duties were the officers who were allocated to staff appointments. Brigadier-General Estcourt, the Adjutant-General, was more interested in exploration than in the army; he had never been to war. Lord de Ros, the original choice as Quartermaster-General, was unversed in his duties and largely uninterested in them. When he fell sick at Varna in midsummer 1854, he was replaced by the much more talented and energetic General Airey. Matters of supply and transport were administered by the Commissariat Department. Staffed by civil servants, and directed by Mr James Filder, another sixty-six-year-old, the Department was utterly ill-equipped to support an army of 27,000 men. Nevertheless, *The Times* would dub this force as 'admirably efficient', able 'to act with a vigour heretofore unknown'.[6]

The Times sent its own correspondent, W. H. Russell, with the expeditionary force. Formerly British editors had either stolen war news from foreign newspapers or had hired junior officers to send letters from the battlefront. Neither arrangement had proved satisfactory; the officers, in particular, tended to be too selective and too irregular in their correspondence. Having experimented with various locally-hired correspondents, such as Lieutenant Nasmyth, during the early days of the Russo-Turkish hostilities, Delane decided to send his own correspondent from London. He secured permission from Lord Hardinge for Russell to accompany the Guards to Malta, to draw army rations, and, subsequently, to sail with the Light Division to Gallipoli. Although the Horse Guards' promises of facilities would be irregularly honoured by the officers in the field, Russell persevered. He pitched his tent alongside those of the British force, and began sending his despatches home in the form of letters to Delane. His first letter from Malta was published on 19 April 1854.

Russell soon observed appalling administrative incompetence. Only three days after his arrival at Gallipoli, he informed Delane that 'The management is infamous, and the contrast offered by our proceedings to the conduct of the French most painful. Could you believe it - the sick have not a bed to lie upon?'.[7] Encouraged by his editor, Russell continued describing events in an uninhibited, graphic, and forceful manner. Though capable of literary embellishments, he established the credibility of his reporting by detailed descriptions and by catalogues of factual information. *The Times* supported his endeavours by publishing letters from officers at the front. Often these correspondents endorsed the reports of Russell; they frequently expressed feelings of grievance and outrage.[8] Delane, too, began to mobilize his leader-writers in support of Russell's ever-expanding indictment of the military administrative system. By the end of May 1854, *The Times* was actively promoting the cause of administrative reform.

Shortcomings in the administrative system had been evident before the arrival of Russell's despatches. Prior to the departure of the expeditionary force, *The Times* had periodically criticized the divided control of military affairs. It had urged the separation of the Colonial from the War department and the unification of the various military bureaucracies under a single head.[9] Russell's complaints lent a new force and immediacy to these arguments. He described soldiers at Malta, particularly the sick soldiers, as shivering in the cold with only a 'single regulation blanket' apiece. The commissariat, he feared, was 'quite bewildered'; the four officers were not to blame; responsibility lay with 'those who sent them out without a proper staff, and without the smallest foresight or consideration'.[10] As soon as *The Times* could claim that administrative reform was more than an intrinsically worthwhile measure - that it was a precondition for success in war - its injunctions had some effect. On 9 June 1854, the government announced the creation of a new post of Secretary of State for War, a post to be filled by the Duke of Newcastle.

A partial success in administrative reform (partial inasmuch as the choice of the new Secretary of State was not to the liking of Printing House Square) did not satiate the crusading zeal of *The Times*. Over the summer and autumn of 1854, it campaigned with several other papers against various military outrages, particularly 'the outrage' perpetrated upon Lieutenant Perry of the 46th regiment. The press believed that this officer, charged with insubordination, had been victimized because he had refused to indulge in the loose living of his brother officers. The manners and morals of the mess appeared to be suspect. As *The Times* observed, 'The bottle and the brothel are the order of the day, and woe to him if he endeavours to avoid the customs of the army!'.[11] Outraged citizens raised funds for Perry's defence and for the purchase of his promotion. Civilians and officers even clashed at Windsor, where the 46th were stationed. This furore was indicative of the indignation which the officer corps could arouse; criticism of the attitudes, life-style, and competence of the officer corps would be voiced increasingly as the War proved unexpectedly protracted and as the sufferings of the troops became all too apparent.

Russell directed his attacks upon Lord Raglan and his staff. Initially he confined these criticisms to his private correspondence with Delane, a correspondence which Delane distributed to various members of the cabinet.[12] In his letter of 8 November 1854, Russell venomously disparaged the Commander-in-Chief. 'I am convinced', stated Russell, 'that Lord Raglan is utterly incompetent to lead an army through any arduous task'. The general was, in the opinion of

Russell, lacking in strategic skill and initiative, 'a mere cool and callous spectator' at the battle of Inkerman. Even worse he did not move among his troops: 'he does not cheer them and speak to them, and is in consequence almost unknown to them'.[13] As the army endured a miserable and bitter winter before Sebastopol, complaints poured forth from Russell and from the disgruntled field officers who wrote to the press. They condemned not only Lord Raglan but also his staff and some senior officers, notably Lords Lucan and Cardigan, for remaining in their quarters while the troops suffered. On 25 November Russell openly voiced these criticisms in his despatch from Sebastopol.

> It is now pouring rain - the skies are black as ink - the wind is howling over the staggering tents - the trenches are turned into dykes - in the tents the water is sometimes a foot deep - our men have not either warm or waterproof clothing - they are out for twelve hours at a time in the trenches - they are plunged into the inevitable miseries of a winter campaign - and not a soul seems to care for their comfort or even for their lives.[14]

No longer inhibited, the leader-writers of *The Times* became more personal and more specific in their accusations. The capabilities and reputation of Sir Richard England, nominally the second-in-command in the Crimea, were savaged in several articles. The possibility of his promotion, should Lord Raglan fall ill, was considered as 'absolutely disastrous' and a 'public danger'. *The Times* noted that Sir Richard, unlike his fellow general officers, had never yet seen action in the Crimea, and that his previous military record was unimpressive and uninspiring. Having reviewed his exploits as the commander of the Scinde field force in 1842, which included a reverse and a retreat in the face of an enemy he would later repulse with ease, *The Times* deplored the possibility of his ever commanding the army in Crimea. That army, it declared, should not be 'handed over to the timid or the incapable'.[15]

Had Lord Raglan been a competent and successful commander in the prime of life then the incapacity of Sir Richard England might not have alarmed *The Times* so much. But *The Times* had lost all confidence in the Commander-in-Chief and, by 23 December, could contain itself no longer. In a blistering leading article, the paper declared that the army had suffered from the 'grossest mismanagement' in the Crimea: 'Incompetency, lethargy, aristocratic hauteur, official indifference, favour, routine, perverseness, and stupidity reign, revel and riot in the camp before Sebastopol, in the harbour of Balaklava, in the hospitals of Scutari, and how much nearer home we do not venture to say. We say it with the extremest reluctance - no-one sees or hears anything of the Commander-in-Chief'.[16] The staff had failed too. These 'young gentlemen', though honourable and courageous, were 'devoid of experience, without much sympathy for the distress of such inferior beings as regimental officers and privates, and disposed to treat the gravest affairs with a dangerous nonchalance'.[17] A week later *The Times* renewed its onslaught. By comparing the French and British armies, it adduced that the French officers, unlike their British counterparts, understood their profession, and felt a 'paramount interest in the condition of the common soldier'. Lord Raglan, argued *The Times*, had provided a poor example; he had remained out of sight, unable to comprehend or to rectify the present malaise. It was 'a crime', the leader-writer claimed, 'to permit an officer to remain for a single day in the nominal discharge of duties the neglect of which has brought a great and victorious army to the verge of ruin'.[18]

So vehement an attack was partly a reaction against the disdainful treatment of Russell by Lord Raglan and his staff. Russell fumed at the refusal of the Commander-in-Chief to honour the promises of the Horse Guards - his initial reluctance to provide rations and assistance, his unwillingness to recognize the press, and his determination to prevent it from accompanying the troops in action. Denied any contact with headquarters, Russell never even spoke to Lord Raglan. He had to rely upon what he saw and upon what the men and the regimental officers told him. Of the senior officers, only Sir George De Lacy Evans showed kindness or consideration to him.[19] Undoubtedly the treatment Russell received coloured his judgement, and prevented him from correcting much of the misinformation upon which his reports were based.[20]

But even more important as an explanation of the censorious comment of *The Times* was the manner in which it had depicted the war. The early battlefield reports of Russell had lifted spirits at home with their lyrical descriptions of British heroism and valour. He had returned despatches from each of three main battles of the campaign, peppered with clichés. At the battle of the river Alma (21 September 1854), he described 'serried masses' of infantry crossing the river Alma 'through a fearful shower of round, case shot, and shell'. Under 'formidable fire', the British soldiers continued 'their magnificent and fearful progress up the hill', until they stormed the Russian batteries, leaving 'multitudes of dead behind them'. At Balaclava (25 October) Russell reached new heights of descriptive journalism. He immortalized the 93rd Highlanders in their resolute defence against a massed cavalry charge: they were a 'thin red streak topped with a line of steel' (later misquoted as the 'thin red line'). He glorified the 'sheer steel and sheer courage' of the Heavy Cavalry Brigade as it routed the Russian Horse, and watched 'in all the pride and splendour of war' as the Light Cavalry charged into 'the arms of death'. So vivid were the descriptions of Russell that the indecisive character of battle (the Russians held the positions which they had taken earlier from the Turks) lost significance for a British reader. Less satisfaction, however, would be gained from the battle of Inkerman (5 November), 'the bloodiest struggle ever witnessed since war cursed the earth'. In fierce hand-to-hand fighting British soldiers with 'noble tenacity' withstood repeated attacks by 'masses' of Russian infantry, many times their number. Victory was won, but at a fearful price of dead and wounded, leaving the allies not 'one step nearer towards the citadel of Sebastopol'.[21]

Cast in a thoroughly heroic mould, the British soldier had become the focal point of public attention. Although Russell had rightly praised the personal courage of many senior officers, *The Times* dubbed the battles of Alma and Inkerman 'soldiers' victories'.[22] Reflecting upon the first six months of war, the paper applauded the spirit and character of the other ranks. Having received shoals of letters from non-commissioned officers and private soldiers, *The Times* noted 'the tone of religious feeling' in the correspondence, and the absence of 'any sentiment of malice or vindictiveness'. Convinced that the letter-writers represented a fair cross-section of the men in the ranks (a highly dubious proposition), *The Times* insisted that the army had attracted a better stamp of recruit in recent years and had not suffered as a consequence. No longer was it the case that 'a bad man made the best soldier'; the reports from Alma, Balaclava and Inkerman had vindicated the martial valour of the contemporary soldier.[23]

Given this perspective, the sufferings of the troops, especially the sick and wounded, excited considerable anguish and wrath. It was Thomas Cherney, the Constantinople correspondent of *The Times*, and not Russell, as often supposed, who drew attention to the conditions at the hospital in Scutari. In a despatch published on 12 October, Cherney declared that '. . . no sufficient preparations have been made for the proper care of the wounded. Not only are there not sufficient surgeons - that, it might be urged, was unavoidable; not only are there no dressers and nurses - that might be a defect of the system for which no one is to blame; but what will be said when it was known that there is not even linen to make bandages for the wounded?'.[24] This article, following upon the disclosures of Russell of the hardships endured by the troops in the field, prompted *The Times* to appeal for private charity to relieve the distress. The appeal had two main consequences. First, a sum of £7,000 was rapidly raised and remitted to Constantinople in the care of John C. MacDonald, almoner of the fund. Secondly, and more importantly, Florence Nightingale offered her services as a nurse. Writing to Mrs Sidney Herbert, wife of the Secretary at War, she stated, 'I do not mean to say that I believe *The Times* accounts, but I do believe that we may be of use to the wounded wretches'.[25]

Her letter crossed one from Herbert himself asking her to go out to Scutari as the accredited head of a government nursing service. By the 21 October she had recruited a staff of thirty-eight nurses and had embarked for the Crimea. Arriving at the Barrack Hospital on 4 November, she found a state of utter confusion and was almost immediately inundated with the wounded from Inkerman. The hospital was insanitary, unventilated and appallingly overcrowded. The patients were not merely wounded, but often arrived at Scutari covered with vermin, their shirts so rotted with filth that they had to be cut from their backs.[26] The doctors were hopelessly overworked, while the store-keepers were paralysed into inactivity, preoccupied with thoughts of saving expense. With admirable determination, Miss Nightingale set about the task of reorganizing the administration. She bypassed officials where necessary, and used both her own money and *The Times* fund to supply comfort for the hospitalized troops. On account of her caring and attentive nursing, she soon became a legend among the troops and a popular heroine in Britain.[27] That she had so much to do and did it so efficiently only enhanced the influence of *The Times* and cast further doubts upon the administration of the war.

Having exposed the hospital conditions at Scutari, *The Times* was no less concerned when it learnt of the conditions endured by the ranks during the siege of Sebastopol. Russell returned harrowing accounts of fever, dysentery, and diarrhoea sweeping through the encampments, of huge sick lists, and of men ill-clothed and ill-sheltered against the winter elements. He berated the shortage of supplies, the failure to maintain the roads and communications, the want of transport horses and wagons.[28] The horrors, first described by Russell, of the siege during the weeks from November 1854 to January 1955, would be confirmed by subsequent Committees of Enquiry. Over the seven months from 1 October 1854 to 30 April 1855, 35 per cent of the average strength died in the Crimea, the vast majority from disease. The excessive mortality was not due to inclement weather, but to overwork and exposure (men often spent twelve hours on duty in the cold and wet trenches), improper food (a diet of salt beef, biscuit and execrable green coffee), insufficient clothing during the first few months of winter (no change of clothing for six weeks), and insufficient shelter (one regulation blanket apiece). Although supplies piled up on the quayside at Balaclava, the Commissariat lacked the transport, the staff, and the administrative flexibility to move them with sufficient despatch. Over 12,000 grey coats arrived in early December but by the end of the month 9,000 remained in store, as Queen's Regulations did not warrant their issue more frequently than once in every three years.[29] Many of these deficiencies would be rectified in the later months of the winter - coats, caps, waterproof leggings, and long boots would be issued much more liberally from mid-January onwards - but this was much too late for the men who had already been fatally stricken.

How then did the military react to this unprecedented degree of press coverage, the criticisms of the Commander-in-Chief and his staff, and the wholesale condemnation of the administrative system? Few doubted that the Commissariat, a civilian department, had proved defective. Lord Raglan conceded that the state of the roads, the lack of transport, and the shortage of staff had been the cause 'of irregularity in the issue of rations, and of the inadequate supply from time to time'. He blamed 'the machinery' and not the individuals, believing that Mr Filder and his staff could do no more, given their limited numbers and their want of transport.[30] Proffering a similar explanation, Brigadier-General Estcourt argued that the small port of Balaclava would always present difficulties for the unloading, storage and issue of supplies. He doubted that these difficulties could be easily overcome, and reckoned that the troops might have to bear the inconvenience: this was 'the nature of war'.[31] The Duke of Cambridge insisted that 'circumstances' and not individuals were to blame. The 'circumstances' he faulted were the forty years of peace and the failure to anticipate war on so large a scale again. As a consequence, he claimed, the country had failed to sustain the civil establishments of the Commissariat Department, and had thus precipitated the difficulties experienced in the Crimea.[32]

This line of reasoning would be used in private correspondence and in response to the criticisms of Select Committees. It offered little solace for the field officers and their men who were encamped before Sebastopol. While many bore their discomforts with stoical fortitude, a determined minority of officers either complained bitterly in their letters to the press or endorsed the writings of Russell. Colonel Charles A. Windham, Coldstream Guards, repeatedly censured the generalship of Lord Raglan: 'We have decidedly no Wellington here'. Inkerman, he thought, 'spoke volumes for the men, little for the General'. He fulminated over the plight of his sick soldiers, lying in 'the wet and muck without medicine or any single kind of comfort'. With his divisional strength dropping to 2,500 under arms out of 6,800 on the roll, he disparaged the generals in authority as merely 'a comfortable, easy-going, gentlemanlike set of do-nothings, who are only fit to scribble a despatch to the Secretary at War'. He supported the criticisms of *The Times*: 'not a word . . . is exaggerated'. Indeed he believed that *The Times* had galvanized headquarters into action,[33] an observation echoed by Captain Henry Clifford and Lieutenant Gerald Graham. Although Clifford deplored those officers who wrote letters to the press, and believed that some of the strictures of Russell were excessive, he still affirmed that *The Times* had done 'much good' by publicizing the 'misconduct and mismanagement of our Army'.[34] Graham agreed; he even claimed that 'Those attacks in the *Times* on Lord Raglan are very welcome out here. They have a marked influence on the Field-Marshal, who rides about much more frequently ever since the first article appeared in the *Times* of Dec. 23'.[35]

Many officers, particularly senior officers, disapproved heartily of the press coverage. Imbued with unquestioning loyalty and obedience, they resented the aspersions of a war correspondent and a London-based editor. Castigations of *The Times* poured forth from Sebastopol,

Horse Guards, and the military press. Having dismissed the first reports of Russell as merely 'frivolous and vexatious',[36] these officers began to prefix their comments upon the reporting with the epithets – 'horrid', 'shameful', 'infamous' – until they became convinced, that 'our newspapers are Nicholas' best friend', and that *The Times*, in particular, was simply 'rabid with Radicalism'.[37] Officers who wrote letters in this vein raised three main objections. They claimed that the criticisms of the press were unfair and unwarranted, especially undeserved in their focus upon Lord Raglan. Sir James Simpson feared that these continuous and ill-deserved criticisms bore heavily upon Lord Raglan, perhaps even contributing to his death on 28 June 1855.[38] Secondly, some believed that the press reports, whether accurate or not, should not have been published, that they simply sapped the morale of the front-line forces: 'it is an ill Bird which fouls its own nest', lamented Lord Rokeby.[39] Finally, many dreaded that the incessant reporting of *The Times* could involve breaches of security. A breach had occurred when *The Times* of 23 October 1854 published several despatches from Russell, revealing detailed information about the number of artillery pieces moved to the front, their position, and the amount of gunpowder needed to supply them. Russell would claim that his articles were out of date before the Russians received them, quoting the retrospective opinion of Prince Gortschakoff that he had learnt nothing from them. These excuses were not entirely convincing.[40]

Lord Raglan pressed for some form of censorship. Aware that information published in the English press could be rapidly transmitted via the telegraph to St Petersburg, he ordered the Deputy Judge Advocate to press upon Russell the need for discretion.[41] He prevailed upon the Duke of Newcastle to take up the cudgels in Fleet Street. The latter appealed to the patriotism of the newspaper editors to supervise carefully the content of reports from their own journalists and the letters from officers at the front. The editors of *The Morning Post, Daily News*, and *The Times* agreed to meet this requirement; Delane even assured the Duke that henceforth his correspondents would confine themselves to 'their version of past events'.[42] Such an agreement, however, did not prevent the press from probing into the conduct of the war, from criticizing the competence of the high command, and from championing the cause of army reform.

Initially, *The Times* had incurred widespread rebukes from other newspapers for its attacks of 23 and 30 December 1854. From the Liberal spectrum, *The Daily News* denounced 'the mendacious calumnies vomited forth by *The Times*' while *The Manchester Guardian* deplored 'the unaccountable recklessness and extravagance of the London journals'.[43] Even more outraged were the Conservative papers. *The Spectator* reviewed the articles of *The Times* under the headline 'Russian Allies in England'; *The Naval and Military Gazette* countered 'the diatribes and mendacious accusations of *The Times*' by claiming that 'no Army was ever more cared for than that now in the Crimea'.[44]

Only the sheer persistence of *The Times*, which published ever more letters from the front, and amassed more evidence to support its contention that the Crimean expedition was 'in a state of entire disorganization', produced a *volte face* by the more radical of its newspaper critics. By January 1855, the tide had turned dramatically. Having recognized the enormity of the military chaos, several papers pressed for sweeping reforms. *Reynolds's Newspaper* demanded the formation of a new government, the recall of 'every superannuated or incapable officer', and the abolition of the purchase system. Less vindictive, but no less forceful, *The Nonconformist* advocated the reform of the whole system of military administration, replacing the patronage of the purchase system by promotion based upon merit alone. Charles F. Greville feared that 'The Press, with *The Times* at its head, is striving to throw everything into confusion, and running amuck against the aristocratic element of society and of the Constitution'.[45]

The government wilted under the sustained attacks of the press. Sidney Herbert, though appalled by the 'violence and abuse of *The Times*', dreaded the cumulative effect of the daily assaults. Writing to Lord Raglan on 22 December, one day before the major onslaught was launched from Printing House Square, he opined that the government was in a 'very precarious' position, and that its ability to survive before an 'impatient and dissatisfied' public was by no means certain.[46] The Duke of Newcastle, aware that he would be 'the first victim of the popular vengeance', became increasingly worried. He had always been concerned about unfavourable newspaper comment; as early as 28 April, he had requested Lord Raglan to inquire into the complaints of Russell about the Commissariat and medical services at Gallipoli. By December, he was urging the Commander-in-Chief to send Sir Richard England home and so appease 'public anxiety'. He professed concern about 'the want of method' in the Crimea, particularly 'a want of foresight or of ability on the part of some of your Lordship's staff . . .'. Such shortcomings, he claimed, had precipitated 'the suffering and sickness' endured by officers and men, the nub of the complaints passed on to him by Members of Parliament and by private citizens. In search of a scapegoat, he appealed to Lord Raglan to replace the principal members of his staff.[47]

Lord Raglan was unmoved. He refused to entertain any criticisms of Generals Airey and Estcourt. He attributed the irregularity of supplies to the want of transport over which he had no control. He testified to the 'zeal, ability, and unceasing devotion' of these officers. Insisting that Airey and Estcourt were 'perfectly efficient', he could not justify their removal from staff appointments. Over a period of five months, he repulsed the demands of Herbert, Newcastle, and his successor, Lord Panmure, for the removal of these officers. Unable to fault their record as staff officers, he viewed their dismissal as an act of injustice 'in direct opposition to the bright example of the Duke of

Wellington . . .'.[48] Unwilling to bow before the indiscriminate attacks of the press, Lord Raglan denied the government its sacrificial scapegoat.

Baulked by the Commander-in-Chief, Lord Aberdeen's ministry had to face the wrath of the House of Commons. On 23 January 1855, John Arthur Roebuck, the independent-minded Member of Parliament for Sheffield, cast the first stone. He requested the creation of a Select Committee of enquiry into the conditions of the army before Sebastopol, and into the conduct of those government departments responsible for army administration. Faced with this embarrassing debate, the government was undermined by the resignation of Lord John Russell. In the debate upon Roebuck's motion, the Whig-Peelite ministry was defeated by 305 votes to 148: it promptly resigned. The new government was formed by Lord Palmerston, and it was supported by a Parliamentary majority only inasmuch as it favoured the cause of administrative reform. As Professor Briggs has aptly remarked, 'Palmerston, in February 1855, was the creature of the people rather than their master'.[49]

Lord Panmure succeeded the Duke of Newcastle as Secretary of State for War. Combining the offices of Secretary for War and Secretary at War, Panmure accepted the overriding importance of administrative reform. He ascribed 'the lamentable results' of the Crimean expedition to 'the want of proper control by a single Minister of every department of the Army'.[50] A brusque, impatient man, Panmure had been advocating the case for a unified control of the army since 1850; now his objective was embraced by the incoming Government. Within three months sweeping changes were completed. The Board of Ordnance was abolished; its command and discipline of the Royal Artillery and Royal Engineers was transferred to the Commander-in-Chief, while its civil duties were vested in the Secretary of State for War. The War Department became responsible for clothing the whole army, for examining the cash and store accounts, for administering the Commissariat and Medical departments, the Ordnance office, and the Militia business of the Home Office. Only the Commander-in-Chief's office remained apart from the War Office, retaining its control over command, discipline, appointments to and promotions in the army.

Supported by Palmerston, Panmure pressed ahead with the reform of the military administration at home and in the Crimea. At a cabinet meeting on 12 February 1855, Panmure secured approval for the appointment of Lieutenant-General James Simpson as Chief of the Staff in the Crimea. Simpson was required to convey Lord Raglan's orders to the staff and to ensure their prompt compliance. He was also expected to inquire into and report upon the efficiency of the staff officers including Generals Airey and Estcourt. At the same meeting Palmerston listed the other measures which had been authorized 'to establish a better order of things in the Crimea'. Several new organizations would be formed, including a Land-Transport Corps, a Corps of Scavengers to clean up the camp, and a Sea-Transport Board at the Admiralty. Civilian doctors would be dispatched to the East. Sanitary Commissions would be sent to advise Lord Raglan on the measures necessary for keeping the camp in good order. Another Commission, headed by Sir John McNeill, would be sent out to enquire into the working of the Commissariat.[51] The government, as Panmure informed Lord Raglan, had no wish to see Roebuck's committee convened. Only reforms and new appointments could forestall it; the removal of Airey and Estcourt was the minimum which would 'satisfy the public . . .'. Claiming that the staff had 'misled' Lord Raglan, he added in a severe and brutal despatch that 'your staff seem to have known as little as yourself of the condition of your gallant men'.[52]

Appalled by the abrasiveness of Panmure, Raglan became ever more resolute in defence of his staff. Relations between Lord Raglan and the home authorities reached their nadir. The Parliamentary position of the government weakened as Palmerston tried and then failed to suppress the Roebuck committee. When he capitulated the three remaining Peelite ministers, Graham, Gladstone, and Herbert resigned. In these delicate circumstances another potentially critical challenge arose over army reform. On 1 March, Viscount Goderich introduced a motion in the Commons condemning the effects of the promotion system, particularly the rarity of non-commissioned officers attaining commissioned rank. Lieutenant-General De Lacy Evans, who had recently distinguished himself at the battle of Alma, supported the motion. Describing the purchase system as a 'corruption', he insisted that it was riddled with favouritism, benefiting 'the sons of gentry and nobles' while excluding others, including the more able non-commissioned officers. By adopting a more liberal system, based on merit, he claimed that the army would attract a higher quality of recruit into the ranks, and that the Service as a whole would benefit. These views were too radical to find widespread acceptance. Although Goderich and Evans denied that their remarks were conceived in a levelling or an anti-aristocratic spirit, such fears gripped the Commons. Ministers did not deny that purchase was an anachronism, even 'an evil' in theory. They argued, however, that some NCOs were promoted (219 in the past five years, 90 of whom were promoted in the Crimea), that a promotion system based on merit would prove unworkable and prone to jobbery, and that abolishing purchase would be extremely expensive (to buy out the officers who were serving in the Crimea alone would cost £2,000,000). By 158 votes to 114, the Commons backed the government and dealt the cause of army reform a fatal blow.[53]

The consequences did not appear to be fatal at the time. The press either viewed the reverse as temporary or the debate as irrelevant. The Commons, declared *The Daily News*, had tried to 'burke' the subject of army reform; but it would not do so indefinitely. Within six months, it prophesied, the Commons would have to bow before public indignation: the nation 'will have no more buying and selling of commissions, no more trafficking in commands as if they were so many bales of cotton'.[54] *The Times* was less convinced. Suspicious of Goderich's radical views as well as the levelling tone of the debate, it affirmed that army reform 'should proceed from less suspected hands, and should be considered as a whole'.[55] Considering the topic as a whole would lead the unwary into a more general and ill-fated demand for administrative reform. Already there was ammunition available for a broader attack upon the 'aristocratic monopoly of power and place' in the *Report on the Organization of the Civil Service,* compiled by Sir Charles Trevelyan and Sir Stafford Northcote. Reformers who wished to introduce the drive and efficiency of business and the competence of the professions into the military and civil services formed various Administrative Reform Associations in different parts of the country. In June, the metropolitan organization staged two mass meetings at the Theatre Royal, Drury Lane. It had Samuel Morley, the wealthy hosiery manufacturer, as its president, and Charles Dickens as one of its speakers.

Several Members of Parliament sympathized with the demand for administrative reform. Thirty-three Members attended the first meeting of the London Association, and two days later, on 15 June 1855, Henry Layard, a Radical MP, raised the issue on the floor of the House. He launched a wide-ranging attack upon 'party and family influences' and upon 'a blind adherence to routine' in the government departments. He attacked all branches of the State service. The government, he asserted, was a monopoly of 'a few families'; the army was officered by those 'who have influence and family connections', the consular and diplomatic service were the preserves of a small coterie of people, and the civil service remained confined to those who have 'family and political influence'. Entry into the civil service, he declared, should be based upon the results of competitive examination. So broad an attack was bound to offend the vast majority in the Commons. Although Members might support different aspects of the critique - Gladstone agreed that admission to the public service should be 'thrown open', and Sir Edward Bulwer Lytton, a Tory, condemned 'the family exclusiveness of successive Whig ministries' - few would proffer whole-hearted support. Henry Drummond, an Independent, denounced the Utopian ideas of the reformers, their attack upon 'every kind of rule and order'. He doubted that the middle classes would prove better administrators than the aristocracy; their record in local government was none too good, in Newcastle they had lacked sufficient administrative talent 'to clean and drain their own town'. Such sarcasm, coupled with an angry speech by Palmerston, denouncing the Drury Lane 'theatricals', ensured a resounding defeat for Layard's motion by 359 votes to 46.[56]

In spite of this defeat and another Parliamentary reverse in July, the reform movement would continue campaigning until the end of the war. The movement was never more than a loose coalition of people. They had joined together in revulsion at the mismanagement of the army. Morley and his associates lacked any political sagacity, never established any unity on issues of policy, and failed to channel their mass popular support into a movement of political consequence. Without policy objectives, the movement relied too much upon the original emotion, kindled by the reports of army mismanagement before Sebastopol.[57] Since the middle of February, however, the news from the Crimea had been steadily improving. With the passing of winter, the track from Balaclava had been opened. Supplies, huts and food had been reaching the troops in vast quantities. Some men had so much clothing that they were trying to sell it for drink.[58] Starved of harrowing accounts from the Crimea, popular indignation began to wane. When Henry Rich launched another attack on the purchase system in the Commons on 3 July 1855, the House was counted out as less than forty Members were present.[59]

The Roebuck Committee, meanwhile, had taken evidence in open sessions over a period of four months. The meetings were always well attended and the evidence extensively reported in the daily press. The Committee asked over 20,000 questions, taking evidence from a varied array of witnesses, among whom were the Duke of Cambridge, Lieutenant-General De Lacy Evans, and several members of the Aberdeen cabinet. Witnesses testified repeatedly that the administrative system and not individuals were responsible for the mismanagement. Even De Lacy Evans, who was fairly forthright in his complaints about the Commissariat department, attributed the blame to Treasury regulations and to 'the spirit of the Treasury authorities of the Cabinet'.[60] It became apparent that the individual ministers of the Aberdeen government had been unjustly blamed. It appeared that the causes of the mismanagement were more fundamental, rooted in the administration of the pre-war army and, to some extent, in the whole structure of government. In the final report, published on 18 June 1855, the Committee found that the troops had lacked sufficient care from mid-November onwards, and that the transport and hospital arrangements had been grossly mismanaged. Only upon the insistence of Roebuck, however, did the Committee include its most damning indictment. The administration, it stated, had authorized an expedition without adequate information about either the armament of the forces in the Crimea or the strength of the fortress in Sebastopol. The administration, it concluded,

> hoped and expected that the expedition would be immediately successful, and, as they did not foresee the probability of a protracted struggle, they made no preparation for a winter campaign; what was planned and undertaken without sufficient

> information, was conducted without sufficient care or forethought. This conduct on the part of our Administration was the first and chief cause of the calamities which befel our army.[61]

Determined to act upon his report, Roebuck insisted upon moving a vote of censure in July. Despite 'the sting in the tail of the report', Lord Panmure was not perturbed by the prospect of a vote of censure. 'I do not imagine it will come to anything', he assured Lord Raglan.[62] His confidence would prove well-founded. When Roebuck brought forward his motion, demanding the punishment of everyone 'who deserves it', he found much less support than he might have done five or six months previously. A retrospective indictment of Lord Aberdeen's administration attracted little enthusiasm; indeed, a large proportion of Palmerston's cabinet would have been compelled to resign had the motion been carried. Various Members of Parliament recoiled before the 'acrimonious and vindictive' sentiments of Roebuck; even more were swayed by the deft arguments of Palmerston. The Premier attacked Roebuck for moving a vote of censure against the present government on account of the actions of a previous administration. He doubted, too, that the time was appropriate for such motions - the war had to be fought and the state of the army was much improved. 'The army now', claimed Palmerston, 'is in as fine a condition as any army which ever existed on the face of the earth'. This was not the time for party squabbles, but for a vigorous prosecution of the war until victory was won.[63] Roebuck's motion, though not formally defeated, was shelved. General Peel moved that 'the previous question' be put and carried the House by 284 votes to 182.

Privately, Palmerston was less confident than he appeared in public. On 18 June, the anniversary of Waterloo, the allies had launched a major assault upon the defences at Redan, only to be repulsed with severe loss of life. Notwithstanding Russell's evocative descriptions of British heroism, the reverse was a sad reflection upon Raglan's capacities as a general. Within ten days the brooding and disconsolate Commander-in-Chief died. Reports in *The Times* about the failure to complete proper medical preparations before the assault on Redan alarmed the Prime Minister. He requested Panmure to require that Simpson, Raglan's successor, appoint a Court of Inquiry to investigate and report upon these newspaper allegations.[64] New reports of cholera sweeping sections of the camp prompted another letter from Palmerston on 16 August. He urged Panmure to press upon General Simpson the importance of regular visitations to the men in their huts, tents and trenches. Keeping 'soldiers alive and in good health', was rated by Palmerston as 'the most important military consideration'.[65] Pending a decisive military triumph, it was also the most important political consideration.

That military triumph would be forever denied. On 8 September

1855, the French captured Sebastopol and the main fighting of the war was over. Although there was widespread relief at the fall of the fortress, the news divided opinion at home. Many Members of Parliament and, more importantly, the French wanted peace; others, including Palmerston, the more militant Radicals, and many newspapers wished a renewed military effort to redress the disaster of Redan. Panmure informed General Simpson that 'the papers have been discussing your affair of the Redan, and pulling you all to pieces'. Quite properly, the General replied: 'I care not for the newspapers. I am not trying to please the Mob, but am endeavouring to do my duty'.[66] When Russell berated Colonel Windham for looking forward to peace 'before he has wiped the dust of the Redan off his jacket', Windham queried what Russell expected the army to do when faced with 100,000 Russians, under the command of Muravieff, with another 70,000 in reserve.[67] Ultimately the French reluctance to continue the war forced the hand of Palmerston. After many secret negotiations, peace talks were begun in Paris in February 1856, and a treaty was signed in the following month.

From the late summer of 1855, the army reform movement had begun to disintegrate. The administrative shortcomings of the previous winter, confirmed by the reports of the Hospital and Sanitary Commissioners, excited little interest in the press and Parliament. Much more attention would be focused upon the report of the McNeill and Tulloch Commission, published in January 1856, which criticized specific officers and individuals who had served in the Crimea. Attacking individuals suited the purposes of the residual members of the reform movement. Such an attack avoided the need to formulate an agreed programme of reform. It enabled the reformers to maintain their high degree of indignation, 'their sole source of unity'. It suited, too, the temperaments of the Parliamentarians who still headed the movement. Layard and Roebuck were, naturally, vindictive men; their sense of bitterness mounted as their Parliamentary and national importance diminished.[68]

For these reformers, the McNeill and Tulloch report confirmed their suspicions about the personal competence of several senior officers. In a comprehensive review of the failure of army supplies in the Crimea, the report found fault with four senior officers and with Mr Filder, the Commissary-General. It implied that Lord Lucan could have reduced the death rate of cavalry horses, during the months from October to March, by ensuring the provision of temporary shelter and by proceeding more quickly with the construction of huts for his horses. It charged Lord Cardigan with stationing the Light Cavalry Brigade some seven or eight miles from Balaclava, at a time when the roads were extremely bad, so compounding the difficulties of supplying forage. After a month, the report noted, the horses were so weak that they could no longer bear the weight of their riders. Seventeen horses died on the road before they could return to their former station, a distance of only six miles. The report was even more critical, though obliquely, of Sir Richard Airey, the Quartermaster-General. It criticized the failure to recover knapsacks, to issue and distribute warm clothing, and to supply rugs, blankets and greatcoats. It also condemned the non-issue of palliasses, and the shortage of tents and hutting. The report compared the evidence of Colonel the Hon. A. Gordon, Deputy Quartermaster-General, with that of other officers, and found it wanting in several respects. Finally the report censured the Commissary-General over the quality and quantity of the rations, the inefficiency of the land transport and fodder, and the lack of adaptation in his organization procedures.[69]

A storm of indignation erupted over the report. The four officers blamed were furious. Lords Lucan and Cardigan delivered speeches of protest in the House of Lords. Four days later, on 15 February, their replies to the charges against them were laid on the table of the House of Commons. Many Members of Parliament were appalled by the report; Roebuck viewed it as the equivalent of 'an indictment from a grand jury' and sought a trial of 'the persons accused'.[70] Lord Panmure found himself in the middle of the ferment, being criticized on all sides, not least by the Crown. The prospect of officers replying to accusations from a Parliamentary Commission did not amuse the Queen. She rebuked Lord Palmerston: 'It is quite evident if matters are left so, and military officers of the Queen's Army are to be judged as to the manner in which they have discharged their military duties before an enemy by a Committee of the House of Commons, the command of the Army is at once transferred from the Crown to that Assembly'.[71] To mollify the Queen and escape from the controversy, the government recommended the appointment of a Commission of Enquiry, consisting of General Sir Alexander Woodford and six other generals including the Judge Advocate-General.

By announcing a Commission of Enquiry the government doused the last remaining hopes of the army reformers. Even before the Commission assembled *The United Service Gazette* predicted its outcome. The disposition of the Commissioners, it claimed, 'will be to make all smooth'. They will establish that 'Lord Lucan was right, and Lord Cardigan was right, and that the Crimean Commissioners were right too . . .'.[72] By the end of July, the Board reported exonerating all concerned. Lord Palmerston upheld, simultaneously, the findings of the Crimean Commission and those of the Board of Enquiry. Lord Panmure duly informed the Queen that further action need not be taken in respect of statements contained in the report of Sir John McNeill and Colonel Tulloch. Meetings of protest would be held in many large towns, many papers were severely critical, and Members of Parliament would not let the matter rest. Eventually, in March 1857, Palmerston accepted the suggestion of Sidney Herbert that Her Majesty should honour the Crimean Commissioners. Colonel Tulloch was created a KCB and Sir John McNeill was created a Privy Councillor.

Tardy recognition was but poor compensation for a report which was never acted upon.

However tame the Parliamentary dénouement, the army reform campaign had been instructive and, in some respects, productive. It had indicated the enormous scope and influence of an uncensored press in wartime. Having galvanized public interest, *The Times* had riveted attention upon the plight and privations of the ordinary soldier. It had raised and administered a charitable fund. It had pressurized a government into sending Miss Nightingale and her nurses to the Crimea. By its revelations and exposures, it had effectively toppled one government and had influenced another considerably. Army commanders in the Crimea were aware, perhaps too aware, of the power of the press. Lord Raglan and his successors as Commander-in-Chief, Sir James Simpson and Sir William Codrington, bemoaned the indiscretions of *The Times*, and sought a degree of control and censorship. Simpson felt that 'the Press is our "Commander" at home', an intolerable circumstance for an 'English gentleman' in command of the army.[73] Ultimately these protests bore fruit; in the last month of the war the first ever press order was issued which placed restraints upon wartime reporting.

Military fears were misplaced in some respects. The wartime press, though influential and provocative, revealed inherent shortcomings as an instigator of an army reform movement. The war correspondents, essentially, were recording their impressions of day-to-day events; they were not formulating detailed programmes of army reform. When Russell returned from the Crimea, Palmerston invited him to breakfast and asked him what he would do were he charged with command of the army. After thirty minutes Russell slunk away from the meeting, 'feeling that I had cut a rather poor figure in the interview'. It became apparent that Palmerston, a former Secretary at War, knew more about the army than the war correspondent did. Russell had 'not even thought out' the priorities of army reorganization.[74]

Admittedly, editors and leader-writers could adopt a longer-term perspective, suggest ameliorative measures, and either mount or support campaigns for administrative reform. But their interest in reform derived mainly, though not exclusively, from the 'scandalous' exposures of the war, and from the purported failings of individual officers, politicians and civil servants. Their campaigns, as a consequence, were shortlived and emotional. They thrived upon news of maladministration, incompetent staff work, and inept generalship. Without such news, their campaigns attracted less interest and attention, and consequently faded. Even more deleterious were the emotional overtones of the reform movement. By concentrating upon individual failings, the campaign quickly degenerated into a vindictive and vituperative crusade. Inevitably a 'backlash' of sympathy erupted, when maligned individuals either died in active service (as did Lord Raglan and

General Estcourt), or were exonerated by subsequent committees of enquiry (e.g., the Duke of Newcastle). Once the credibility of the reform movement was punctured, the government could regain its ascendancy over the Commons and so control the pace and content of army reform.

Yet the revival of ministerial fortunes was by no means absolute. By seizing the initiative in administrative reform, the Government had contributed to the freer flow of supplies from Balaclava. The government, too, had less to fear from the House of Commons. In March 1856, Lord Panmure defused the demands of De Lacy Evans for another Commons debate over the abolition of purchase. He secured the appointment of a Royal Commission to enquire into the subject, and included Evans among the Commissioners, where he 'can do no harm'.[75] On the other hand, the government found it much more difficult to resist Florence Nightingale, who returned to England, fired with a resolve to improve the health and living conditions of the ordinary soldier. Having conferred with experts she had known in the Crimea, Sir John McNeill, Colonel Tulloch and Colonel Lefroy, Miss Nightingale instigated a new campaign in favour of army reform. Immensely prestigious and determined, she used her influence at Court, a public campaign in the press, journals and Parliament, and the threat of publishing her Crimean experiences to move Lord Panmure. Unmoved by partial concessions (a Royal Commission whose Commissioners would have nullified the enquiry), Miss Nightingale persevered until she secured not only her Sanitary Commission, but also Sidney Herbert as chairman, supported by an array of Commissioners who held out the promise of seeking some far-reaching reforms.[76]

Reform could not have prospered in the post-war years without the other major dividend of the Crimean War, namely the enhancement of the image and reputation of the British soldier. The army returned from the East to be fêted and feasted. In an order, issued from the Horse Guards on 5 August 1856, the Queen formally praised the British soldier for his 'patient endurance of evils inseparable from war'. The nation followed up this Royal expression of gratitude with public thanksgivings and dinners and presentations to individual regiments. The last ceremony of the war took the form of a grand military review in Hyde Park on 26 June 1857. On this occasion, the Queen distributed the newly-instituted Victoria Cross, an award earned by officers and men alike. *The Times* would claim that 'any hostility which may have existed in bygone days towards the army has long since passed away. The red coat of the soldier is honoured throughout the country'.[77]

A transformation had occurred in attitudes towards the army. The war had attracted widespread popular support. The valour and heroism of the troops had been widely admired. The patient fatalism of the ranks as they endured the hardships of the camp before Sebastopol had aroused immense emotional feeling, an unprecedented interest in their plight and welfare. It became a commonplace to assert that the nation should, in the post-war years, recognize its responsibilities towards the rank and file. The Reverend Henry P. Wright noted that, hitherto, the upper classes had merely regarded soldiers as instruments 'for keeping down riots' and 'for figuring at reviews'; 'the public', he claimed, had looked upon soldiers as fitted only for 'swearing, drinking, and fighting'. The war had altered these impressions. From the wartime correspondence, published in the press, it was apparent that these 'gallant soldiers' had 'souls to be saved'. Their appeal 'to the gratitude of a generous nation cannot go forth in vain'.[78] Such were the hopes of army reformers. The return of peace would test these assumptions; it would reveal the depth and significance of the transformation of public attitudes, and would confirm whether these attitudes had changed sufficiently to sustain a programme of army reform.

Notes and references

1. *The History of the Times: The Tradition Established 1841-1884*, London, 1939, p. 166.
2. **J. H. Gleason,** *The Genesis of Russophobia in Great Britain*, Harvard U.P., Cambridge, Mass., 1950, pp. 50-4, 101-4, 164-204.
3. **A. Briggs,** *The Age of Improvement,* Longmans, London, 1959, p. 380.
4. *The British Banner,* 24 May 1854, p. 375.
5. Evidence (Qs.21,306, 15,183) before *The Select Committee appointed to Inquire into the Condition of our Army before Sebastopol,* hereafter referred to as the Sebastopol Committee, Fifth Report, C.318, 1854-55, IX.
6. *The Times,* 14 Feb. 1854, pp. 6-7.
7. W. H. Russell to Delane, 8 Aug. 1854, quoted in *The History of the Times,* p. 171.
8. For example the letter published in *The Times*, 2 June 1854, p. 10.
9. *The Times*, 27 Feb. 1854, p. 8.
10. **W. H. Russell,** *The War: from the landing at Gallipoli to the death of Lord Raglan*, Routledge, London, 1855, p. 33.
11. *The Times,* 7 Sept. 1854, p. 6.
12. **J. B. Atkins,** *The Life of Sir W. H. Russell,* 2 vols., John Murray, London, 1911, Vol. 1, p. 146.
13. *Ibid.,* Vol. 1, p. 174.
14. W. H. Russell, *op. cit.,* pp. 279-80.
15. *The Times*, 11 Dec. 1854, p. 8 and 14 Dec. 1854, pp. 6, 8.

16. *Ibid.*, 23 Dec. 1854, p. 9.
17. *Ibid.*, 23 Dec. 1854, p. 9.
18. *Ibid.*, 30 Dec. 1854, p. 6.
19. J. B. Atkins, *op. cit.*, Vol. 1; compare pp. 133-5, 139 with 152, 156, 157.
20. **C. Hibbert,** *The Destruction of Lord Raglan: A Tragedy of the Crimean War,* Pelican, London, 1963, p. 262.
21. W. H. Russell, *op. cit.*, pp. 180-2, 227-31, 247-54.
22. *The Times,* 6 Dec. 1854, p. 8.
23. *Ibid.*, 4 Dec. 1854, p. 6.
24. *Ibid.*, 12 Oct. 1854, p. 7.
25. **Lord Stanmore,** *Sidney Herbert; Lord Herbert of Lea: A Memoir,* 2 vols., John Murray, London, 1906, Vol. 1, p. 336.
26. *Report of the Commission of Enquiry into the Supplies of the British Army in the Crimea,* hereafter referred to as the McNeill and Tulloch Report, C.2,007, 1856, XX, p. 23.
27. **C. Woodham-Smith,** *Florence Nightingale, 1820-1910,* Constable, London, 1950, pp. 135-257.
28. W. H. Russell, *op. cit.*, pp. 281-2, 287, 291.
29. McNeill and Tulloch Report, pp. 3-28.
30. Lord Raglan to the Duke of Newcastle, 13 Jan. 1855, Raglan Mss., N.A.M., 6807/28.
31. Brig.-Gen. Estcourt to Herbert, 23 Jan. 1855, quoted in Lord Stanmore, *op. cit.*, Vol. 1, pp. 298-9.
32. Duke of Cambridge to Sir G. Brown, 17 Oct. 1855, Brown Mss., N.L.S., Ms. 1,851, ff. 159-60.
33. Col. C. A. Windham to W. Windham, 22 Oct. 1854, to H. Beresford Pierce, 1 Dec. 1854, to R. Hook, 5 Jan. 1855, to Mr Hudson, 16 Jan. 1855 quoted in *The Crimean Diary and Letters of Lieut.-General Sir Charles Ash Windham, K.C.B.*, ed. Mjr H. Pearse, Kegan Paul, London, 1897, pp. 41, 77-9, 96, 104.
34. **C. Fitzherbert,** *Henry Clifford V.C. his letters and sketches from the Crimea,* Michael Joseph, London, 1956, pp. 155, 170.
35. G. Graham to his sister, 21 Jan. 1855 quoted in **Col. R. H. Vetch,** *Life, Letters and Diaries of Lieut.-General Sir Gerald Graham V.C., G.C.B., R.E.*, Blackwood, London, 1901, p. 72.
36. Lord Raglan to the Duke of Newcastle, 14 May 1854, Raglan Mss., N.A.M., 6807/284.
37. Capt. Higginson to his father, 12 Jan. 1855 quoted in General Sir G. Higginson, *op. cit.*, p. 222 and Lord Hardinge to Lord Cowley, 15 Feb. 1855, Hardinge Mss.
38. Sir J. Simpson to Sir G. Brown, 29 June 1855, Brown Mss., N.L.S., Ms. 1,850, f. 153.
39. Lord Rokeby to the Duke of Cambridge, 27 Nov. 1855, Cambridge Mss., R.A. Add. Mss. E/1/394.
40. *The Times*, 23 Oct. 1854, p. 7; J. B. Atkins, *op. cit.*, Vol. 1, pp. 255-6.

41. Mr Romaine to Lord Raglan, 12 Nov. 1854, Raglan Mss., N.A.M., 6807/293.
42. The Duke of Newcastle to Lord Raglan, 7 Dec. 1854, enclosing letters from the editors of *The Times, The Morning Post* and *The Daily News*, Raglan Mss., N.A.M., 6807/283.
43. *The Daily News*, 25 Dec. 1854, p. 4; *The Manchester Guardian*, 27 Dec. 1854, p. 4.
44. *The Spectator,* 30 Dec. 1854, pp. 1,379–1,380; *The Naval and Military Gazette,* 6 Jan. 1855, p. 9.
45. Diary, 17 Feb. 1855, *The Greville Memoirs 1814–1860,* ed. L. Strachey and R. Fulford, 8 vols., Macmillan, London, 1938, Vol. 7, p. 115; *Reynolds's Newspaper*, 7 Jan. 1855, p. 1; *The Nonconformist,* 24 Jan. 1855, p. 67.
46. S. Herbert to Lord Raglan, 22 Dec. 1854, quoted in Lord Stanmore, *op. cit.*, Vol. 1, pp. 308–9.
47. Duke of Newcastle to Lord Raglan, 28 Apr., 15 and 29 Dec. 1854 and 6, 8 and 22 Jan. 1855, Raglan Mss., N.A.M., 6807/283 and P.R.O., W.O.33/1/63.
48. Lord Raglan to the Duke of Newcastle, 13, 15, 20 and 22 Jan. 1855, Lord Raglan to Lord Panmure, 5 May 1855 and Lord Raglan to Herbert, 23 Jan. 1855, Raglan Mss., N.A.M., 6807/284, 287, 290.
49. **A. Briggs,** *Victorian People*, Pelican, London, 1965, p. 77.
50. 'Observations by Lord Panmure on Military Organisation', Feb. 1855 quoted in *The Panmure Papers*, ed. Sir G. D. Bart and Sir G. D. Ramsay, 2 vols., Hodder and Stoughton, London, 1908, Vol. 1, pp. 47–8.
51. 'Memorandum of measures taken to establish a better order of things in the Crimea', 12 Feb. 1855, *ibid.*, Vol. 1, pp. 53–4.
52. Lord Panmure to Lord Raglan, private letter and official despatch, 12 Feb. 1855, *ibid.,* Vol. 1, p. 59 and Appendix, Vol. 2, p. 522.
53. *Parl. Deb.*, Third Ser., Vol. 136, 1 Mar. 1855, cols. 2,091–171.
54. *The Daily News,* 15 Mar. 1855, p. 4.
55. *The Times,* 2 Mar. 1855, p. 7.
56. *Parl. Deb.*, Third Ser., Vol. 138, 15–18 June 1855, cols. 2,040–225.
57. **H. S. Wilson,** 'The British army and public opinion from 1854 to the end of 1873', unpublished B.Litt. thesis, Oxford University, 1954, pp. 22–6.
58. C. Fitzherbert, *op. cit.*, p. 158.
59. *Parl. Deb.*, Third Ser., Vol. 139, 3 July 1855, cols. 429–30.
60. Evidence (Q.669) before the Sebastopol Committee, Second Report, C.156, 1854–55, IX.
61. Fifth Report of the Sebastopol Committee, C.318, 1854–55, IX, p. 23.

62. Lord Panmure to Lord Raglan, 23 June 1855, *The Panmure Papers*, Vol. 1, p. 250.
63. *Parl. Deb.*, Third Ser., Vol. 139, 19 July 1855, cols. 1,172-4.
64. Lord Palmerston to Lord Panmure, 19 and 20 July 1855, *The Panmure Papers*, Vol. 1, pp. 303, 308.
65. Lord Palmerston to Lord Panmure, 16 Aug. 1855, *ibid.*, Vol. 1, pp. 350-1.
66. Lord Panmure to General Simpson, 6 Oct. 1855, and General Simpson to Lord Panmure, 20 Oct. 1855, *ibid.*, Vol. 1, pp. 431, 453.
67. J. B. Atkins, *op. cit.*, Vol. 1, p. 247.
68. H. S. Wilson, *op. cit.*, p. 28.
69. McNeill and Tulloch Report, pp. 3-37.
70. *Parl. Deb.*, Third Ser., Vol. 140, 29 Feb. 1856, col. 1,585.
71. *Letters of Queen Victoria*, 2nd Ser., Vol. III, p. 222.
72. *The United Service Gazette*, 1 Mar. 1856, p. 4.
73. Sir J. Simpson to Lord Panmure, 20 Oct. 1855, *The Panmure Papers*, Vol. 1, p. 453.
74. J. B. Atkins, *op. cit.*, Vol. 1, pp. 261-2.
75. Lord Panmure to Queen Victoria, 20 Apr. 1856, *The Panmure Papers*, Vol. 2, p. 200.
76. C. Woodham-Smith, *Florence Nightingale*, pp. 258-81.
77. *The Times*, 22 Oct. 1856, p. 6.
78. **Rev. H. P. Wright,** *England's Duty to England's Army*, Rivingtons, London, 1858, pp. 6, 36.

5 The Indian mutiny

Less than fourteen months after the Treaty of Paris was signed, the Indian Mutiny erupted.[1] The revolt of the sepoy troops at Meerut (10 May 1857) and their capture of Delhi, the old imperial capital, on the following day, posed a fundamental challenge to the rule of the British in India. Only 40,000 British troops were stationed in India in May 1857. They were composed of regular British forces and of troops employed by the East India Company. They were outnumbered by approximately 300,000 Indians, including 'irregular' and 'contingent' soldiers, a ratio of about 8:1. Confronted by a challenge so significant and so daunting, Britain became absorbed in the new conflagration. The outcome would depend upon the resources and capacities of Britain as a military power. For the army, this was another major test less than two years after the Crimean War. How it responded would be eagerly followed in Britain.

The Indian Mutiny derived from the reaction of the more traditional elements in Indian society to the modernizing zeal of successive British administrations. Ever since the end of the third war against the Marathas (1818), the British had endeavoured to consolidate their power and to reform Indian society, morally and politically. Religious customs, practices and sensibilities were ignored as the British proscribed widow burning and female infanticide, and crushed the criminal gangs known as the Thugs. Traditional beliefs and values seemed to be threatened by the introduction of Western education and by the activities of Christian missionaries. The pace of reform and innovation quickened under the Governor-Generalship of Lord Dalhousie (1848–56). Customary laws and traditions were set aside, as he refused to recognize the right of a childless ruler to adopt an heir. He seized, as a consequence, a number of states, including Satara, Nagpur and Jhansi. He annexed, too, on grounds of misgovernment, the Muslim kingdom of Oudh. He pressed ahead with the rapid modernization of the Indian economy, building roads, laying the first railway lines, and installing thousands of miles of wire for the electric telegraph. A small number of Indians welcomed these Westernizing tendencies; many others feared their repercussions upon the traditional order, especially upon their religion.

These fears were not entirely misplaced. Although the government of India repeatedly denied any proselytizing policy, many missionaries and Company employees were horrified by the practices of widow burning (Suttee) and female infanticide. They came to disparage the Hindu religion, viewing it as pagan and barbaric. Many officers of the Company's army shared this opinion; they continually endeavoured to convert their men to Christianity. Lieutenant-Colonel Wheler admitted: 'As to the question whether I have endeavoured to convert Sepoys and others to Christianity, I would humbly reply that this has been my object, and I conceive is the aim and end of every Christian . . . that the Lord would make him the happy instrument of converting his neighbour to God, or, in other words, of rescuing him from eternal damnation'.[2] Some officers joined missionaries in public meetings and sought to wean both Hindus and Muslims from their religious creeds.[3] Such 'impudence', argued the Duke of Cambridge, was 'a fatal error however well intended'. In his opinion, it simply compounded the other major failing of 'the officer of the present day' - his 'treating the men and especially the Native Officers with great contempt, in fact looking down upon them, calling them niggers etc.'.[4]

Overt proselytizing and personal snobbery, though baleful influences where they occurred, were not all-pervasive within the Company's army. Some British officers, particularly those who were stationed in the remote frontier posts, were largely preoccupied with their professional duties. Unlike their colleagues in the rest of India, these officers lived alongside their men and endured a relatively spartan life. For these officers rugged field sports, tent pegging, and polo took the place of the balls and entertainments of the more civilized parts of India. Several officers learnt and became proficient in native languages, notably Colonel J. Luther Vaughan who wrote the first Pushtoo grammar in English.[5] Several followed the example and precepts of Generals Sir Henry Lumsden and John Jacob; they devoted themselves to drilling their men, and to studying their character, each tried to remain 'a thoroughly English gentleman', in hope of earning 'the respect and regard of every Native around him'.[6] Within the Bengal army, however, the rot had firmly set in by the late 1840s and early 1850s. Promotion was by seniority and not by merit as in the Bombay army. Relatively few European officers remained with their regiments: in 1849, more than a third held lucrative detached appointments on the staffs of either the Governor-General or the Commander-in-Chief. Senior officers, like Sir Charles Napier and Sir Thomas Munro, berated their European subalterns for their aloofness, and for their lack of contact with native officers.[7] Maintaining order and discipline, finally, was a constant problem within the Bengal army. That army contained a large proportion of Brahmin recruits, whose notions of caste cut across British ideas of military discipline.

Caste, the mechanism by which Hindus ordered their social relations, profoundly troubled the British. The sight, off parade, of a low-caste subahdar (a native captain) crouching in abject submission before a Brahmin recruit horrified British observers. It could not be reconciled, in their eyes, with the requirements of military subordination. Even worse, caste and religious prejudices sometimes conflicted with military requirements. A regiment refused to cross the sea to Burma in 1852, because crossing over water would break their caste. Over the years, various concessions had been made to the religious prejudices of the Indian soldiers. Turbans, caste marks, and beards were still worn by sepoys after an order banning them had provoked a revolt in the Madras army in Vellore in 1806: the regulation was withdrawn after the mutiny had been brutally suppressed. In the 1830s, corporal punishment was abolished in the sepoy army. Rarely inflicted, flogging had been a terrible degradation for the native soldier; it had carried dismissal with it, the victim leaving the army as an outcast, deprived of social and civil rights. The Bengal army had a further privilege inasmuch as a mere six of its seventy-two battalions enlisted for general service; the remainder enlisted only for service in places to which they could march. Many British observers believed that the Indian government had truckled to caste prejudices, and had 'pampered' the Bengal army.[8] It became, too, increasingly inconvenient to recognize the Brahminical principles of the Bengal army. During the Second Burmese War of 1852, the government was virtually in a position of having to beg for volunteers to undertake garrison duty in Burma. This was peculiarly embarrassing, as Brahmins from the Bengal army had been known to volunteer for overseas service. Seeking a more uniform and serviceable sepoy army, Lord Canning, who succeeded Lord Dalhousie as Governor-General, and his Council issued the General Service Enlistment Act on 25 July 1856. Under this Act, the grouping in the armed services according to caste was to be abolished, and future recruits would be required to march wherever ordered.

This Act merely compounded the fears of the Indian soldiers. Already the high-caste sepoys from the Oudh, who were serving in the Bengal army, had lost privileges and status after the annexation of the province. Rumours began to circulate that the British were about to default on their contract with the sepoys, to break their caste, and convert them to Christianity. The introduction of the new Lee-Enfield rifle in 1857 seemed to confirm these fears. To load the new rifle, soldiers had to bite the end of each greased cartridge. Fearing that the grease was made from cow or pig fat, both Muslim and high-caste Hindu sepoys were appalled (pig is considered unclean by Muslims and the cow is held sacred by Hindus). Viewing the cartridge issue as an attack on their religions, sepoy regiments began to protest. On 26 February 1857, the 19th Native Infantry refused to accept the cartridges at Berhampur, but their commander, Colonel Mitchell, regained control of the situation. He had the regiment marched to Barrackpur, where it was immediately disbanded without incident. Sepoy fears were to spread, however. On 29 March, a sepoy of the 34th Native

Infantry seized a musket and ran amok, shooting the adjutant and threatening other officers (he had the active sympathy of the guard). The sepoy, finally, tried to shoot himself, but was revived and executed. The regiment was not disbanded until 6 May; its British officers insisted that this was an isolated incident and that the majority of the men were not mutineers.[9] Neither civil nor military authorities believed that a serious revolt was likely and imminent. Mutinies and near mutinies had happened before, but not a revolt. On 10 May their complacency was confounded. At Meerut, the native cavalry released comrades who had been jailed on the previous day for refusing to use the greased cartridges. They burnt bungalows and offices, murdered isolated British officers and their families, and set alight the Indian Mutiny.

News of the Mutiny shocked British opinion. The supreme confidence and self-satisfaction of the British in Imperial matters was only matched by their vast ignorance of Indian affairs. As *The Times* acknowledged, 'there are few countries and few histories about which the English know less than they do about India'.[10] Hitherto the Empire had never really attracted national or popular interest. It had been acquired, preserved, and expanded by a relatively small number of individuals. Knowledge of India was extremely limited. The British at home had derived their impressions of Indian society from the writings and reports of Christian missionaries. These missionaries, in seeking support for their evangelical efforts, had generally depicted Indians as abominably depraved and superstitious. Nevertheless, until 1857, the Indian subcontinent had remained remote, its depravity of little immediate significance. Once tales of atrocities against British men, women and children began to filter home, they riveted attention upon the Indian scene.[11]

The immediate reaction of *The Times* was 'to put down force by force'. It derided the causes of the revolt. 'Never', it declared, 'were acts of insurrectionary violence based on more insubstantial grounds, or committed with more indefinite views'.[12] The religious fears and apprehensions of the sepoys found few sympathizers in the British papers. Many shared the view of *The Nonconformist* that the government in India had 'demeaned' itself to no purpose by sanctioning and preserving caste, 'an abominable superstition', in the Bengal army. The paper complained that 'the discarding of every Christian idea, lest it should prove an occasion of offence, and that open indulgence of a pestilent social wrong in compliance with the prevalent superstition of the Hindoos, has been a prolific source of trouble and danger'.[13] Utterly contemptuous of native religions, several papers refused to accept that superstition alone, in their terminology, had precipitated so widespread a revolt (forty-five of the seventy-four infantry regiments in the Bengal army mutinied, and all except five of the remainder had to be disbanded or disarmed in case they mutinied too). The more simplistic and prejudiced papers regarded plunder as a 'chief cause' of the sepoy rebellion. 'The lust for plunder', argued *The Naval and Military Gazette,* 'is inherent in the Asiatic soldier'; the capture of Delhi, with its treasury and arsenal, had tempted the sepoys to revolt.[14] Credence was also given to theories of a conspiracy among the sepoys, fomented possibly by agents of a foreign power, or by agents of the disaffected princes of northern India.[15]

The Times found solace in a further theory - that the uprising was merely a 'mutiny and nothing else', a rebellion of 'a pampered soldiery', aided by 'rabid desperadoes'. The peasantry, it reckoned, had no sympathy with the rebels; the mass of Indians, it affirmed, would not renounce the order, toleration, justice, and peace of British rule for the 'wanton cruelty', 'malicious vengeance', and, above all, the 'treachery' of their Asiatic princes. 'The Asiatics', it stated, 'were always especially barbaric, and they are now much what they were thousands of years ago'.[16] *The Times* insisted that Britain was in India as part of a providential design, and that she ruled over the various races and regions in 'the interest of civilization and humanity'. Britain's objective in India, it claimed, was 'the future Christianity and civilization of the people'.[17] Not everyone shared these views. Richard Cobden, for example, argued 'that sending redcoats as well as black to Christianize a people is not the most likely way to insure the blessing of God on our missionary efforts'. He prudently refrained from saying so in public. As he informed Mr Ashworth, 'it is quite useless to preach these doctrines in the present temper of the people of this country'.[18]

Confidence in the innate superiority of Western values, and in the rectitude of Britain's civilizing mission, was not reassuring in and of itself. *The Inquirer* dreaded a repetition of the Crimean blunders. Another twelve-month delay before British power was brought to bear would damage the military prowess and reputation of the United Kingdom.[19] *The Times,* by contrast, would brook no misgivings. It rejoiced that the revolt had coincided with neither the Crimean War nor the military operations in Persia. It professed every confidence in the leadership and capacities of the British army. It never doubted that the army could defeat the sepoys in open battle, or hunt them down should they flee to the hills. Delhi could not be held: 'a British force must take a city garrisoned only by Asiatics . . .'[20]

A reaction, so blustering and belligerent, was widely but not uniformly endorsed. Several papers paused to criticize the shortcomings of the East India Company and the administration of India;[21] some ultra-radical papers attributed the revolt to British perfidy, greed and exploitation. *Reynolds's Newspaper* took up the cudgels on behalf of the rebels. The revolt, it contended, was a national one, in which the people were supporting the soldiers in fighting for their religion and national independence. It rejoiced that slavery had not utterly crushed the 'manhood' of 'the long-oppressed people of India'. It rejoiced that Britain had suffered a 'terrible and salutary lesson', and that the 'rapacious' policies of the Company had rebounded upon the government. 'British oppression', it declared, 'has been so fierce, powerful, and terrible, that it has fused and welded into one harmonious phalanx the hitherto discordant, antagonistic elements of Indian society'.[22]

Ernest Jones, the Chartist leader, also defended the Indian cause. In various speeches, and in the columns of *The People's Paper*, he defended the cause and the actions of the Hindu rebels. Nevertheless, the pronouncements of Jones and of *Reynolds's Newspaper* do not mean, as has been implied, that there was a significant rift in British reactions to the Indian Mutiny, largely reflecting the class divisions of British society.[23] On the contrary, these editors and spokesmen were examples of relatively isolated and courageous individuals, who defied the flood-tide of popular indignation. Many other radicals who might have spoken out either refused to do so or endorsed the policy of repression. Cobden and Bright, who lost their Parliamentary seats in the general election of 1857, refused to champion another unpopular cause. Cobden urged Sturge to refrain from criticizing ministerial policy: indeed he affirmed that 'The only possible course for our authorities to pursue is to put down by any means in their power the murderous rebels who have cut the throats of every white women and child that has fallen into their hands'.[24] Bright was equally obdurate. Like Cobden, he doubted that Britain had any right to be involved in India, but he accepted, too, that once the Mutiny had erupted order must be restored. Seeking to reassure the chairman of the Birmingham Liberal Committee, prior to his adoption as the Liberal candidate in the city, Bright insisted that 'the success of the Indian revolt would lead to anarchy in India, and I conceive that it is a mercy to India to suppress it'.[25]

Reports of sepoy atrocities dominated the early newspaper accounts of the Indian Mutiny. Publishing despatches from its correspondent in Bombay, and reprinting accounts from the English press in India, *The Times* carried lurid accounts of the massacre of Europeans in Delhi and of the murder of isolated European families. These reports were embellished by letters from India, especially from clergymen. Many of these letters repeated wildly exaggerated rumours, reflecting more about the phobias of the horror-stricken correspondents than about events in the northern provinces. Several correspondents focused upon the killing of women and children; they took their cue from the butchered remains of Mrs Chambers, an officer's pregnant wife, found near Meerut at the outset of the Mutiny. Having placed women upon a pedestal, viewing them as chaste, delicate, and refined creatures, Victorians were appalled at the thought of black sepoys laying their hands upon them. Ever-recurring was the fear that rape had preceded murder. Writing from the safety of Bangalore, a clergyman reported that forty-eight 'delicately nurtured ladies' and girls had been raped in Delhi, stripped naked, abused in broad daylight, and then tortured to death.[26] Although rape may have occurred during the Mutiny, there is no evidence of it in the massacres of which there is record.[27] Nevertheless, these fears and fantasies were widely and vividly reported, ensuring the horrified fascination and fury of the English reading public.

Distortion and exaggeration were hardly necessary, as real atrocities were all too common. Reports of murders, massacres and mutilations were avidly read. Rage and fury erupted over the details and embellishments of what had happened at Meerut and Delhi. Of the various outrages, the massacre of the Cawnpore garrison exceeded all others in the depth and intensity of its impact. General Wheeler's beleaguered and vastly outnumbered force had surrendered to the army of Nana Sahib on the promise of safe passage to Allahabad. That promise was never honoured. As the survivors embarked in their boats at Sati Choura Ghat, the men were massacred and about 200 women and children were rounded up and retained in Cawnpore. Over two weeks later, on 15 July 1857, as the British under General Havelock approached the town, the women and children were hacked to death and their bodies thrown down a well. The massacre was dubbed 'the crowning atrocity', ranking among 'the foulest crimes' of the human race; Nana Sahib became a fiend incarnate, a legendary monster in British eyes. *The Times*, which had always favoured meting out 'a terrible example' to suppress the Mutiny, now demanded the destruction of 'this foul, craven mob'. 'Retribution' became the rallying cry of Printing House Square. Chastizing these 'infamous assassins', it declared, was now a duty, a burden which Britain must discharge in the cause of self-preservation.[28]

The desire for vengeance swept most of the nation. A few politicians and newspapers deplored the over-reaction. Taking its cue from Gladstone, *The Inquirer* urged the army to 'wield the sword of retributive justice', but not 'to meet atrocity by atrocity' and exact a savage vengeance. Such action, it claimed, would lose 'our influence in India as a Christianizing nation'.[29] *Reynolds's Newspaper* advanced the argument one step further, noting that the barbarous atrocities merely testified to the failure of the civilizing mission over the past hundred years: Britain, in short, should abandon India.[30] These views were not widely shared. As Thomas Macaulay wrote, 'The cruelties of the sepoys have inflamed the nation to a degree unprecedented within my memory. Peace Societies, and Aborigines Protection Societies, and Societies for the Reformation of Criminals are silenced. There is one terrible cry for revenge'.[31] Nor was the cry for revenge short-lived. As late as 18 May 1858, Joseph Sturge reported to the annual meeting of the Peace Society that the desire for blood was still pervasive, extending beyond the military and the capitalists to engulf the President of the Bible Society and the ministers of various denominations.[32] The nation expected vengeance, and wished the military to administer that vengeance as swiftly and as firmly as possible.

Crushing the mutineers would prove an exacting proposition. Not only were the British troops vastly outnumbered, but they were also scattered across the subcontinent. Reinforcements would take months to arrive from England, travelling via the Cape of Good Hope. Only a few thousand men could be sent from Burma, Ceylon and Mauritius, and from the troops *en route* to China. The British had to rely initially upon the Queen's and Company's troops already in India, especially those in the Bengal region. Of these forces, the vast majority were concentrated in the Punjab, close to the troubled frontier with Afghanistan. On account of this concentration the British could disarm the sepoy regiments in the Punjab, and thereafter use the region as a base for their operations against Delhi. On the other hand they had to give ground in the Oudh and Rohilkhand, conceding Delhi and Cawnpore to the rebels while leaving Lucknow and Agra beleaguered. Having failed to forestall the Mutiny, the British were faced with a formidable army, thoroughly trained, endowed with considerable artillery and ammunition, and supported by a disciplined and well-horsed cavalry.

Once they had perceived the scale of the Mutiny, many officers in India were more perturbed than their compatriots at home. Their confidence and complacency had been rudely shattered. They could never trust the sepoys again. As Colonel, later Major-General Sir, Herbert Edwardes reflected, the British had witnessed a cataclysm in India: 'The system and confidence of a hundred years has passed away for ever like a breath. The Government can never again trust the Sepoys, nor the Sepoys believe themselves trusted. The wonderful spectacle of thirty or forty thousand Europeans ruling India will be seen no more. The natives have counted us at last'.[33] He was not downcast, however. Like the majority of his colleagues, he believed that Englishmen were innately superior 'in character and in physique', and that the Lord was on their side.[34] Many of the younger subalterns looked forward to the campaign as an opportunity to see 'some action' and win a few medals, including the much coveted Victoria Cross. Lieutenant, later Field Marshal Earl, Roberts wanted this reward more than any other: 'Oh! if I can only manage it', he confided to his mother, 'how jolly I should be!'.[35]

Yet the military did not approach the campaign in a mood of supreme and light-hearted confidence. They were not embarking upon another small colonial war; they were not confronting an undisciplined and ill-equipped enemy. As 'our own army was the enemy', Edwardes mused, 'the issue was very doubtful indeed'.[36] Nor was it the case, as earlier rumours had indicated, that the rebels lacked popular support in the northern provinces and were fighting amongst themselves. Reading such accounts in the London-based newspapers, which were always behindhand in their reporting of the Mutiny and took several weeks to reach India, irritated the officers in India. While encamped before Delhi, in July 1857, Lieutenant Arthur M. Lang,

R.E., fumed at the 'sickening twaddle in the leaders from *Times, Examiner*, etc.'. He derided their confident assertions that British supremacy over her conquered subjects would never be endangered, and that the Muslim sepoys would join the British against the Hindus.[37] Roberts was equally contemptuous of the 'nonsense' in *The Times* 'about the Mutiny being confined to the army'. While advancing on Agra, in September 1857, he had passed through a district in which the sepoy presence was minimal, but which had rebelled under the command of the local rajahs, aided by the police and native civil authorities, and supported by almost every villager.[38] Unlike the London press, the military soon perceived that their operations would be difficult and daunting, though not insuperable.

In one respect, the opinions of officers in the field coincided with the views expressed in Printing House Square. Officers, generally, were appalled by the accounts and by the evidence of native atrocities upon women and children. Their inflamed passions were not short-lived; they would influence the character of the subsequent fighting and would contribute to the legacy of hatred and distrust between the British and the native communities. Writing to the Deputy Commissioner at Simla, in May 1857, Lieutenant Macdowell relayed stories from the men who had escaped from Delhi of the mangled, but not outraged, bodies of women and children being displayed in the city. 'The very idea', he added, 'of a sister or wife being exposed to the fury of these black devils makes one shudder'.[39] Lieutenant, later General Sir, George Barker was horrified, too, by the atrocities of these 'murderous hounds'. Where the murders consummated treachery, after the victims had surrendered on the promise of escort to a place of safety and were then slaughtered, he found them even more vile. 'It is all Mussulman fanaticism', he assured his mother. 'They are taught that a man who kills a Christian is sure to go to heaven'.[40] Senior officers were no less moved by the tales of murder and carnage. Colonel, later General Sir, Hope Grant recorded in his journal the constant receipt and confirmation of 'terrible accounts' of atrocities, while Brigadier Sir Neville Chamberlain accepted that a 'death-struggle between civilisation and barbarism' had ensued.[41]

Although Cawnpore became the focus of military wrath, it was neither the source of that wrath nor the inspiration of the first reprisals. Within a month of the Mutiny at Meerut, the British were exacting a fearful retribution. In the Punjab, they were not merely disarming native regiments and hanging deserters, they were also blowing mutineers away from their guns. On 10 June, forty mutineers from the 55th regiment were paraded before the whole garrison of Peshawar, with thousands of spectators watching, and then blown away from the British guns. On the following day, over 800 miles away, Colonel Neill led his forces into Allahabad. Thereupon he enforced martial law and unleashed 'the holy work' of retribution. Over a period of three months, the retribution continued; soldiers and civilians alike began 'holding Bloody Assize, or slaying Natives without any assize at all, regardless of sex or age'. The British, as J. W. Kaye noted, were reacting to the first bitterness of their degradation - the degradation of fearing natives whom they had taught to fear them.[42] This bitterness would reach new heights of intensity when General Havelock's relief force reached Cawnpore, on 17 July, one day too late to save the women and children from massacre.

Soldiers shuddered and some even wept as they entered the blood-stained slaughter-house. 'Eager and maddened', wrote Lieutenant North, 'we sped round the dreary house of martyrdom where their blood was outpoured like water; the clotted gore lay ankle deep on the polluted floor'.[43] 'Every British soldier in this place', wrote Lieutenant Barker, 'is fired with indignation and longing to avenge the slain'.[44] General Havelock tried manfully to stem the thirst for vengeance; he prevented Neill, who had been promoted Brigadier-General, from issuing any punitive orders when he arrived in Cawnpore. As soon as Havelock left the town, however, Neill acted. In an order dated 25 July he required all 'apprehended miscreants' to clean a portion of the house (usually by licking the blood-stained floor), before being hanged. Few countrymen criticized Neill at the time. Many visited Cawnpore in the subsequent months, inspecting the house and compound where remnants of clothes, shoes and garments were left strewn around. The well, covered over with earth, became a shrine before which soldiers knelt, and vowed vengeance on the native community. William Howard Russell, on his tour of India, visited Cawnpore in February 1858. He noted in his dairy that the massacre, though neither unprecedented nor unparalleled in human history, had a peculiar significance for his contemporaries. The deed had been perpetrated by 'a subject race - by black men who dared to shed the blood of their masters, and that of poor helpless women and children'. The war, thereafter, had become not merely a re-conquest of India, but a war of race, a war of religion, a war of revenge.[45]

The desire for reprisals had several significant aspects. In the first place, it embraced soldiers of all ranks. Private soldiers were not ordered to swear vows of vengeance at Cawnpore; they did it of their own accord. As Private Mackintosh wrote in his dairy, 'I wanted to have some share in revenging the *horrid atrocities* committed there on our *women* and *children* by those fiends'.[46] Civilians, attached to the military columns, frequently shared the anguish and desire for retribution; some were shocked by their own inability to feel any pity or compassion for the victims of military lynchings.[47] Some officers, admittedly, recoiled from the spectacle of wanton and indiscriminate killing by British and by loyal Indian soldiers. Macdowell deplored the random lynchings, while Roberts, distressed by the sight of innocent deaths, sadly accepted that soldiers 'in the heat of the moment' could not be expected to distinguish between the guilty and the innocent.[48] But few doubted the need for crushing the rebels with maximum force.

Generals, indeed, were required 'to act with vigour' by the Horse Guards. The Duke of Cambridge, in the second of his thirty-nine years as Commander-in-Chief, urged Sir Patrick Grant to ensure that 'feelings of humanity' did not check 'punishment so richly deserved'.[49]

The reprisals, also, fuelled the spiral of outrage, murder and arson. The savagery of the British left the mutineers without any inducement to show mercy or to consider trading their hostages. The hangings and burnings of Neill at Allahabad may have occasioned the massacre of women and children at Cawnpore. Undoubtedly Lord Canning feared the consequences of excessive and indiscriminate punishments. By proclaiming, publicly, the virtues of just punishments and the importance of reconciliation once the Mutiny was over, he earned the nickname 'Clemency Canning' and opprobrium in many quarters, including the Horse Guards. The Duke of Cambridge feared that the Proclamations of Canning, if acted upon, would enable the mutineers to escape their fate. While insisting upon the punishment of troops, caught burning villages and slaughtering 'defenceless natives', he exhorted Sir Colin Campbell to press ahead with the suppression of the mutinous sepoys.[50] Encouraging the troops to crush the rebels, however, did not ensure that discretion would be used in the retribution inflicted. Russell saw the long-term folly of the British reprisals: 'All these kinds of vindictive, unchristian, Indian torture, such as sewing Mahomedans in pig-skins, smearing them with pork-fat before execution, and burning their bodies, and forcing Hindoos to defile themselves, are disgraceful, and ultimately recoil on ourselves. They are spiritual and mental tortures to which we have no right to resort, and which we dare not perpetrate in the face of Europe'.[51]

Nevertheless, British reprisals evoked relatively little outrage in the United Kingdom. *Reynolds's Newspaper,* inevitably, denounced the 'English cut-throats' in India, especially those who embarked on an orgy of murder, plunder and destruction in the recapture of Delhi. The paper deplored not merely the atrocities, but also the 'fiendish glee' with which some officers recounted their experiences to friends at home.[52] Such criticism was exceptional. Jubilation greeted news of the recapture of Delhi and of the methods used to subdue the city. The order of Major-General Wilson that 'no quarter should be given to the mutineers' was widely applauded. Lord Brougham assured a Cumberland audience that severe punishment and retribution were now essential: 'justice', he said, 'must be placed above mercy'. Lord Shaftesbury, addressing an Indian Relief Fund meeting, was equally definite; he rejoiced in the sentiments of Wilson, fondly, but erroneously, believing that women and children would be spared as the General had ordered.[53]

British politicians could hardly be expected to grasp the full extent of the atrocities committed by the liberators of Delhi. Officers who sent letters from the front did not dwell upon the sight of British soldiers, deranged by fatigue and liquor, disobeying orders, and embarking on a spree of murder, plunder and arson. Yet they were far from reticent. One officer forecast that retribution would be heavy once the city had fallen, 'a work of extermination'. After the capture of Delhi, another officer recorded the shooting of three or four hundred suspects; a third re-told the bayoneting of residents and not mutineers, sometimes forty or fifty in a house all pleading for pardon or mercy.[54] Even this evidence did not rouse many qualms. As the reprisals frequently, though by no means invariably, followed a British triumph – the relief of Allahabad and Cawnpore, the recapture of Delhi – the euphoric adulation dwarfed any concern over the excesses of retributive zeal. These were occasions of rejoicing, not of recrimination.

Many comparisons would be struck between the performance of the army in India and the army in the Crimea. *The Times*, lacking the on-the-spot reporting of Russell, gloried in the successes of British arms. In contrast to the Crimean experience, it noted, 'we hear of no commissariat difficulties, no "requisitions", no embarrassments of system, no complications of routine . . .'. The army, it added, had encountered enormous logistical problems – huge distances, a hot and unhealthy climate, the difficulty of keeping communications open, and a country that was hostile and 'on the point of rising'. Yet the army had surmounted these problems; it had withstood an 'unprecedented' siege at Lucknow, it had retaken Delhi, overcoming an army four times its number, and it had dispersed the sepoy army. By the winter of 1857, *The Times* was confident of ultimate success.[55]

No aspect of the campaign was praised more lavishly than the generalship of Havelock, Neill, Lawrence, Nicholson, and latterly Campbell. Comparisons with Cardigan, Lucan, Cambridge and Codrington were odious, superficial, but all too common. During the Crimean War, the victories had been described as 'soldiers' victories', with the bravery and fortitude of the troops acclaimed. The generals, with a few notable exceptions, were largely condemned. In India, on the other hand, the vast terrain, isolated garrisons, and scattered enemy offered scope for a multitude of independent initiatives by the various generals, commanding relatively small bodies of men. Wilson stormed Delhi with about 5,000 soldiers, Havelock marched from Allahabad to Cawnpore with less than 2,000 troops. Campbell relieved Lucknow with nearly 5,000 men and forty-nine guns. By recording a host of small, localized successes, the generals earned paeans of praise from the British press. Their tactical finesse, coupled with the courage and character of the British troops, were applauded; their technical advantages in the possession of the telegraph and Enfield rifle were barely mentioned. Some marches, battles, and defensive engagements were remarkable, overcoming serious logistic difficulties, numerical odds, and a tenacious and resourceful enemy; but, invariably, these achievements were extolled and magnified. Shocked at the outbreak of the Mutiny, and appalled by outrages of the mutineers, the press over-reacted to news of a military triumph, lapsing into panegyrics and lyrical descriptions.

Of the generals praised, Sir Henry Havelock received the greatest adulation. Virtually unknown before the Mutiny, he gained a reputation of legendary proportions after the march from Allahabad, the victories at Cawnpore and Alambagh, and the heroic, though personally fatal, attempt to relieve Lucknow. Revered for his energy, character and bravery, Havelock was lauded as a man of action, and above all as a Christian man of action. A practising Baptist, whose religious activities had probably hindered his military career, his wartime exploits were lionized by the nonconformist papers. While *The Inquirer* rated his march as 'one of the most glorious achievements in our history', *The Nonconformist* characterized him as 'a resuscitation . . . of the Puritan warrior' of the seventeenth century.[56] No less important were the middle-class origins of Havelock. He was described as a middle-class officer who had proved his worth, and had proved that military prowess and leadership were not confined to the scions of the aristocracy. Like Campbell, Neill and Nicholson, Havelock had not advanced his career by wealth and patronage. After thirty-four years of Indian service, in which he had fought in Burma, central India, Afghanistan, the Punjab, and Persia, Havelock, aged sixty-two, still languished as a colonel when the Mutiny broke out. Having emerged from obscurity in so dramatic a fashion, Havelock was hailed as proof that a man from his background could serve with distinction.

Rewarding Havelock for this distinction became, briefly, a bitter and acrimonious controversy. In November 1857, the first honours of the Mutiny were awarded - a GCB for Sir John Lawrence and KCBs for Havelock and Wilson. The same rewards, in other words, were being bestowed upon the Indian generals as were conferred on their Crimean predecessors. Havelock and Wilson were to receive the same honour as Lord Lucan, Lord Cardigan and Sir Richard Airey received for their much criticized services in the Crimea. Many papers were appalled; *The Times* and *Reynolds's Newspaper* even joined forces in the crescendo of criticism. *Reynolds's* deplored the 'insult' of gazetting Havelock to a baronetcy, the same award that Sir Fenwick Williams had received after losing the city of Kars. It feared that the jealousy and prejudice of the aristocracy would deny the 'able and efficient generals' in India of their just deserts. 'The highest honours, dignities, and rewards', it thundered, 'are reserved for princely boobies and noble blunderers, Cambridges, Cardigans, and Codringtons'.[57] *The Times* was equally vitriolic. Only as interim awards could these honours be accepted. The middle-class generals, serving in India, had confirmed their merit, had proved their military competence. 'High honours', declared *The Times*, 'do not suit our aristocracy alone . . . they suit these men of middle classes also; they suit them admirably, suit them perfectly'.[58] The controversy soon blew over; Havelock, like Sir Henry Lawrence, Neill and Nicholson, died in action, while the government, in the course of the Mutiny, doled out further honours, even elevating Sir Colin Campbell to the peerage. Yet the controversy had been indicative of the esteem and respect which able officers from relatively humble origins had earned in Britain.

Under these officers British soldiers were depicted, by the press and by some early historians of the Mutiny, as performing heroic deeds, against formidable odds, defying and later defeating the mutineers. This impression, which enhanced the image of the army and accounted partially for the rapturous receptions accorded some regiments on their return from India, was not entirely true. It overlooked the vital role played by Indian troops fighting on the British side. Only two battalions mutinied in the Bombay army. Indian soldiers from the Bombay regiments comprised the bulk of the forces used by Sir Hugh Rose in his drive against the rebel strongholds of Jhansi and Kalpi in central India. In the Madras army not a single regiment mutinied. Madras artillery was used at Cawnpore and in the Oudh campaign; six battalions of native infantry were employed in central India. Of the Bengal army, a few loyal remnants remained, mainly irregular cavalry, the Gurkhas, and the Punjabis both Sikhs and Muslims. Indians supplied two-thirds of the army which stormed Delhi. Sikhs and sepoys lent staunch assistance in the defence of Lucknow. Indian auxiliaries, finally, rendered invaluable service throughout the Mutiny. Indians groomed horses, fed elephants, managed the transport, supplied the commissariat, cooked, carried water, waited on officers, even manned the outposts. These services received scant recognition.

In promoting the image of an all-conquering army, the British press glossed over the incompetence, indecision and chaotic organization, characteristic of so many campaigns. The press was not unaware of the misgivings voiced in India. *The Times*, for example, received letters from 'A Disabled Officer', deriding the over-cautious tactics of Sir Colin Campbell. He claimed that Campbell could have completed the conquest of Lucknow in November 1857, instead of retiring and escorting the garrison to safety; that he spent too much time in preparation before the final assault on Lucknow in March; and that subsequent operations had to be undertaken in the heat of an Indian May, so increasing the casualties from sickness or sunstroke. *The Times* dismissed these complaints. Rallying to the defence of 'the old Highland general', it claimed that the relief of the garrison was 'the one great object of anxiety in this country', an all-important objective. It could not accept that Campbell had incurred greater casualties in the long term on account of his caution. It dismissed this theory as mere conjecture, evidence of jealousy in India of any officer other than a Company officer. Slow and sure methods, involving 'the least possible loss', were hailed by *The Times*, as admirable tactics.[59] Had these tactics involved the least possible loss, they would have been admirable. Campbell, in taking Lucknow, had lost only 127 officers and men killed, and 595 wounded. During the month of May, in the following year, he lost 100 men in action and not less than 1,000 who died from sunstroke, fatigue, and disease. These men, as an historian of the Mutiny has claimed, 'died fighting the rebels Campbell could have prevented from leaving Lucknow'.[60]

The press, apart from the more radical papers, also barely mentioned the shortcomings of the medical and supply services, and the effects upon the soldiers of drink, disease, and the desire for plunder. The army was not smoothly and efficiently supplied, as *The Times* implied. Sir Colin Campbell had found it lacking in shoes, ammunition, sets of harness - 'deficient in *everything*', as the Duke of Cambridge concluded.[61] For the winter campaign of 1857-58, the army in India had to be re-equipped from home. The troops were not any more free from the ravages of disease and sickness than their predecessors in the Crimea. Of 11,021 officers and men who perished during the Mutiny, 8,987 died from sunstroke and sickness. Drunkenness was a recurrent problem. On the line of march, in camp, and in towns and villages, soldiers were forever finding liquor and drinking to excess. Havelock had to order his commissariat to purchase 'every drinkable thing at Cawnpore', while Campbell had to order a roll-call every two hours, and two parades a day, to check the irregularities committed on the march from Lucknow to Cawnpore.[62] Occasionally discipline collapsed altogether when some towns were seized. Russell described the soldiery as 'literally drunk with plunder' during the capture of Kaiserbagh. Oblivious of their officers, the men ran amok, looting, burning, pillaging, quarrelling and fighting over their spoils.[63] Such excesses received relatively little coverage. Lord Palmerston could say, without much fear of contradiction, that the nation felt 'proud' of its accomplishments in India. Never 'in the history of the world', he asserted, had 'such splendid examples of bravery, of intrepidity, of resource, and self-reliance been witnessed'.[64]

The army acquired more from the Mutiny than an enhanced image in Britain; it also assumed greater responsibilities in India. By late summer 1858, when the Mutiny was virtually over, the European forces in India had more than doubled, rising to nearly 100,000 officers and men. The Queen's army had provided three-quarters of the personnel. That more European troops should be permanently stationed in India, and that the proportion of Indian to British troops should be sharply reduced, was a widely supported reform. It had been mooted before the uprising, generally endorsed during the Mutiny, and then examined by the Royal Commission which convened in London in 1858 to consider the reorganization of the Indian Army. Lacking any detailed assessment of the likelihood of internal disturbance or of external aggression, estimates of the necessary European force varied considerably. The estimates of those witnesses who had given the matter any consideration ranged from 50,000 to 100,000 Europeans. The Commissioners, without disclosing their reasons, reckoned that about 80,000 British troops should be retained in India, of whom 50,000 should be in northern India, 15,000 in Madras, and 15,000 in

Bombay. The Commission also recommended that new ratios of British to Indian soldiers should be enforced; it proposed 1:2 in Bengal and 1:3 in each of the two southern Presidencies.[65]

Another reform aroused bitter passions and a fierce controversy, namely the future constitution of British forces. Even before the passage of the Government of India Act of 1858, by which responsibility for governing India was transferred from the Company to the Crown, the future role, if any, of the Company's locally-raised regiments was keenly disputed. Lord Panmure favoured radical reform. 'All European troops in India', he claimed, 'ought to be Queen's troops',[66] a view shared by several senior officers. Sir Colin Campbell had always favoured the amalgamation of the Company's troops. He believed that 'discipline is not asserted as it ought to be' in the Company's regiments, and that a sense of 'duty' was not the paramount consideration of the Company's officers.[67] Major-General Mansfield endorsed these criticisms in a memorandum forwarded to the Duke of Cambridge. He emphasized that prolonged service in India was morally and physically debilitating. Only exceptionally zealous commanding officers, he claimed, could prevent a regiment, in peacetime, from succumbing to the influences around it. These officers were few in number, argued Mansfield; hence the regiments of the Company were prone to lapse into undisciplined ways, even into 'sloth and debauchery'.[68]

Advocates of a local army, headed by Lord Canning, pressed their views upon the Royal Commission. They maintained that a local army would remain as a check upon the precipitate withdrawal of European troops from India. A locally raised army would comprise men, who possessed an intimate knowledge of the customs and languages of India. Officers from a local army could also be seconded to various staff appointments of the Governor-General, and the Governors of the several Presidencies. Officers from a force stationed temporarily in India and relieved periodically might lack the inclination to undertake such tasks. Opposing these views were advocates of a line army, led by Lord Elphinstone, Governor of Bombay. These witnesses derided the possibility of a precipitate withdrawal from India. They feared that two distinct armies, serving the same Sovereign, would excite professional jealousies and impair recruiting. Maintaining a double army would deprive the line army of valuable service in India, while debarring the Crown from using local troops in the battlefields of Europe. A local force, finally, would suffer from the same debilitating influences which had undermined the Company's army. The Commission, which included four officers of each of the line and local armies, were unable to agree. Reporting in March 1859, the Commission recorded majority and minority viewpoints, with a bare majority favouring an exclusively line formation.[69]

Queen Victoria made her views abundantly clear. Concerned about the Sovereign's prerogative at titular head of the army, she informed Lord Derby, the Prime Minister, 'of her firm determination not to sanction, under any form, the creation of a British Army, distinct from that known at present as the Army of the Crown'.[70] As she explained, in a subsequent letter, the Queen did not object to 'the *continuance*' of local forces but to 'the *creation* of a British Army distinct [in its existence and constitutional position] from that of the Crown'.[71] The Indian Council contested these views. Composed of former directors and civil and military servants of the Company, it favoured the retention of a large local army. The cabinet, lacking any clear recommendation from the Royal Commission, was divided internally. Lord Stanley, the Secretary of State for India, advocated a local army, while General Peel, the Secretary of State for War, favoured an exclusively line organization.[72] In June 1859, just before it left office, the cabinet agreed a compromise by which two-fifths of the minimum European army might consist of local forces. Although the Queen and her cousin, the Commander-in-Chief, accepted the proposal, the Indian Council remained intransigent; it insisted upon local forces comprising two-thirds of the infantry and three-quarters of the cavalry in India.[73]

Events in India would resolve the controversy. Ever since the Queen's proclamation of November 1858, converting former Company troops into servants of the Crown, protests had been aired, and had been printed in the English-language press. Critics claimed that the rights of freeborn Englishmen had been infringed. Objecting to the switch of allegiances without prior consent, some men believed that they should have been discharged from the Company's service, and offered a bounty to re-enlist with the Queen. During May and June 1859, the rumours of discontent, even of mutinous behaviour, spread; they became so persistent that the new government permitted NCOs and men to take their discharge and return to Britain at the State's expense. But re-enlistment was not permitted. As the soldiers eagerly claimed their discharges, the protests, known as the 'white mutiny', petered out and died. The only serious incident, the refusal of the men of the 5th European Regiment at Barrackpur 'to do any duty', was promptly crushed, without bloodshed, by the dispatch of 500 men from the Royal army. Of the 15,000 men of the old Company's regiments, 10,116 claimed their discharges and returned to Britain, costing the State £250,000.[74]

The white mutiny dashed the prospects of raising a local army. Following so closely upon the sepoy mutiny, it damaged still further the reputation of the Indian forces. It confirmed doubts about the discipline within former Company regiments. It enabled Lord Clyde, formerly Sir Colin Campbell, and his colleagues to resume their attacks upon the reliability of a local army. The white mutiny, claimed Lord Clyde, had almost completed 'the circle of revolution which has overtaken the Indian Services . . .'. The local European army, he affirmed, had to be punished and their crime 'marked with a sufficient stigma':

he suggested amalgamating their units within the regular line.[75] Preserving the existing local forces, was, in any case, no longer feasible. As approximately two-thirds of the men had taken their discharges, a local army would need to be recreated. It would also have to be established on a much larger scale than even before (at least 40,000 recruits would have to be enlisted to meet the two-thirds criterion of the Indian Council). After considerable deliberation the cabinet, in May 1860, resolved upon discontinuing a separate European army.[76]

Henceforth at least 60,000 regular British soldiers or roughly three times the pre-Mutiny number, were stationed in India. Approximately one British to every two Indian soldiers was maintained as a ratio over the next fifty years, until 1914. In 1869 the garrison included 64,858 British and 120,000 Indian troops; in 1908, 75,702 British and 148,996 Indians.[77] To preserve internal order, the number of Indian regiments in the Bengal army was halved, and all artillery was concentrated in European hands. All arsenals and principal forts were to be held by white soldiers. Britain was determined to overawe the Indian soldiery and to minimize the possibility, or at worst the seriousness, of another mutiny. To fulfil this objective over the next half-century imposed an immense manpower strain upon the army. Soldiers could not be left indefinitely in the tropics; they had to be relieved by drafts from Britain, and the regular rotation of troops required a larger home army and the attraction of additional recruits. By the early 1860s, the strain was already visible. Recruiting standards had had to be lowered. Recruits were being accepted, as Sir William Butler recalls, 'who would have been rejected with scorn a few years ago'. Seeking a larger number of recruits each year, the army came to rely increasingly upon the slums of the big cities. 'Even from these sources', Butler observed, 'we find it difficult to obtain them in sufficient numbers'.[78]

Notwithstanding the persistent recruiting difficulties, the military commitment to India would never be significantly modified. Popular interest in Indian affairs, once aroused by the Mutiny, was not subsequently lost. After the imposition of direct Crown rule, Indian government became a national concern: India 'belongs to us', as Miss Martineau insisted.[79] Having survived the year of turmoil, the British were resolved upon the imposition of firm and effective control of the Indian subcontinent. Such control could only rest upon the complete subordination of the Indian communities. Racial fears and hostility were clearly evident; they did not begin in 1857, a change of attitudes had already set in before the Mutiny erupted, but the rebellion undoubtedly hardened and intensified the inter-racial bitterness. Arriving in Calcutta in January 1858, Russell observed the lack of *rapprochement* between Indians and Englishmen. During his travels through India, he noted 'the utter absence of any friendly relations between the white and black faces when they are together'. He feared that 'Many years must elapse ere the evil passions excited by these disturbances expire;

perhaps confidence will never be restored; and if so, our reign in India will be maintained at the cost of suffering which it is fearful to contemplate'.[80]

Racial tensions persisted, and fears of another rising recurred periodically. In 1870, General Vaughan, commander of the Allahabad division, heard rumours for the third or fourth time since 1857 of another mutinous outbreak afoot. Though reluctant to make an official report over bazaar rumours, he ordered officers commanding batteries of artillery to march their batteries through the street 'to remind the ill-disposed that things were not as they had been in 1857'.[81] 'Dislike and distrust' between Europeans and Indians was unlikely to decrease, reported Lieutenant-General Sir Frederick Roberts in 1883. Opposing the admission of educated Indians to the civil service, or to positions of equality with European army officers, he feared that the spread of education had merely aggravated the racial tensions. He doubted

> that the race antagonism, which was brought to such a pitch during the Mutiny, has been gradually disappearing, as I see it often asserted.
>
> In the Army, especially amongst the northern regiments, it is kept under, and no doubt considerably lessened by that mixture of camaraderie and respect which sharing dangers and hardships in common has engendered, and which will last so long as nothing occurs to excite the religious, or in some future time the *political* feelings of the soldiery.[82]

Shaken by the events of 1857, army commanders neither relaxed their guard nor shelved their suspicions for many years after the Mutiny.

However daunting the additional responsibilities and the persistent concerns of the army in India, the Mutiny heightened the reputation of the army at home. After experiencing years of public disinterest, officers did not expect a hero's welcome. Lieutenant Barker suspected that the 'good folks in England will be too busy with Reform Bills, elections and so forth, to pay much attention to the war-worn soldiers of Havelock, when they land in England . . .'.[83] But returning regiments received ecstatic receptions. Barker's 78th Highlanders were feted and feasted on their arrival in Edinburgh. Received by a prestigious deputation, 'the heroes of India and the survivors of beleaguered Lucknow' attracted a crowd of 50,000 to 60,000 people in Princes Street. So crushed were the spectators that the regiment took two hours to march the mile from Waverley station to Edinburgh Castle.[84] Similar demonstrations awaited the 32nd Foot on its return after fourteen years of overseas service. Reviewed by the Queen at Portsmouth, the regiment travelled to Dover where flags, bunting, and enormous crowds greeted the 'heroes of Lucknow'. The reception culminated with a banquet and ball, as the people of Dover paid tribute to the 'suffering, bravery and endurance' of the 32nd.[85]

Estimating the depth and significance of mid-nineteenth century opinion is inherently difficult. Regiments had received triumphant receptions in previous years. Politicians and the press had saluted martial triumphs in earlier campaigns. Yet the feelings engendered by the Indian Mutiny had a peculiar intensity. The Mutiny had aroused a profound sense of shock, anguish and indignation; these feelings had ensured that the progress of the campaign was feverishly followed, and that the military successes were loudly acclaimed. Officers and men earned plaudits from the press. New middle-class heroes were found in Havelock, Lawrence and Nicholson. Unlike the Crimean War, this distant and more decisive campaign never received close and critical scrutiny from the London press. The exploits of various generals assumed legendary proportions, as the nation revelled in the spectacle of a relatively few white troops routing a multitude of black mutineers. The manner in which the campaign was depicted added a new lustre to the reputation of the army in general, and of a few regiments in particular.

Enhancing the reputation of the army, however, did not, as some officers hoped, attract a large and sustained flood of new recruits. Recruiting boomed, but only briefly. By January 1858, the Duke of Cambridge accepted that the boom had begun to taper off, and that establishments could not be filled by the declining intake.[86] The appeal of the army as a career had not been suddenly transformed. People clearly distinguished between the army as a popular national institution, and the army as a worthwhile career into which they would enter themselves, or would encourage friends and family to enter. By its successes, too, the army checked the progress of its own reform, and, to that extent, dampened the prospects of improving its appeal as a career. Reforms promoted during and after the Crimean War were delayed; from 1 September 1857, officers were accepted for commissions without examination. Apart from the opening of the Staff College in 1858, few reforms were accomplished, and the interest in reform tended to wane. The unreformed army had triumphed; it had proved its mettle, preserving India from the rebels and assuming more onerous responsibilities in Imperial defence.

Notes and references

1. The uprising of 1857 will be described as a mutiny because this was the term used by the British at the time, and because contemporary opinion is of prime importance in assessing the evolution of the relationship between the army and society. Recent scholarship indicates that the original mutiny soon assumed the character of a popular rebellion. See **T. R. Metcalf**, *Aftermath of Revolt: India, 1857–1870*, Princeton University Press, Prince-

ton, 1964, and **S. N. Sen**, *Eighteen Fifty-seven*, Government of India, Ministry of Information and Broadcasting, Calcutta, 1957.

2. Lieutenant-Colonel Wheler to Government, 15 Apr. 1857, quoted in **J. W. Kaye**, *A History of the Sepoy War in India 1857-58*, 3 vols., Allen, London, 1864-76, Vol. 1, pp. 480-1.
3. **Quarter-Master-Sergeant A. Laverack**, *A Methodist Soldier in the Indian Army*, Woolmer, London, 1885, pp. 74-5.
4. Duke of Cambridge to Major-General Anson, 26 June 1857, Cambridge Mss., R.A., E/1/656.
5. **General Sir J. Luther Vaughan**, *My Service in the Indian Army and After*, Constable, London, 1904, p. 41.
6. **General J. Jacob**, *A Few Remarks on the Bengal Army and Furlough Regulations with a view to their improvement*, Smith Elder, London, 1857, p. 10.
7. *Defects, Civil and Military of the Indian Government by Lt.-Gen. Sir Charles Napier*, ed. Lieutenant-General Sir W. F. P. Napier, Westerton, London, 1853, pp. 250, 255, 257, 259.
8. Maj.-Gen. Anson to the Duke of Cambridge, 3 May 1857, Cambridge Mss., R.A., E/1/634; *The Naval and Military Gazette*, 11 July 1857, p. 440; *The Nonconformist*, 22 July 1857, p. 571; **T. R. E. Holmes**, *A History of the Indian Army*, Allen, London, 1883, p. 60.
9. **M. Edwardes**, *Battles of the Indian Mutiny*, Batsford, London, 1963, pp. 23-4.
10. *The Times*, 16 Sept. 1857, p. 6.
11. **F. G. Hutchins**, *The Illusion of Permanence*, Princeton U.P., Princeton, 1967, pp. 83-5.
12. *The Times*, 29 June 1857, p. 8 and 1 July 1857, p. 9.
13. *The Nonconformist*, 22 July 1857, p. 571.
14. *The Naval and Military Gazette*, 29 Aug. 1857, p. 552.
15. *The Nonconformist*, 19 Aug. 1857, p. 651 and *The Spectator*, 4 July 1857, p. 699.
16. *The Times*, 1 Sept. 1857, p. 6 and 30 Nov. 1857, p. 6; 29 Jan. 1858, p. 8.
17. *The Times*, 15 Aug. 1857, p. 9 and 7 Oct. 1857, p. 8.
18. R. Cobden and H. Ashworth, 16 Oct. 1857, quoted in **J. Morley**, *The Life of Richard Cobden*, 2 vols., Chapman and Hall, London, 1881, Vol. II, p. 206.
19. *The Inquirer*, 15 Aug. 1857, p. 513.
20. *The Times*, 27 June 1857, p. 9, 9 July 1857, p. 8 and 23 July 1857, p. 8.
21. **J. Bryne**, 'British opinion and the Indian revolt', *Rebellion 1857: a symposium*, ed. P. C. Joshi, People's Publishing House, New Delhi, 1957, pp. 294-5.
22. *Reynolds's Newspaper*, 2 Aug. 1857, p. 1 and 16 Aug. 1857, p. 7.
23. J. Bryne, *op. cit.*, p. 311.

24. R. Cobden to J. Sturge, 1 July 1857, Sturge Mss., B.M. Add. Mss. 43,722, f. 249.
25. **G. M. Trevelyan**, *The Life of John Bright*, Constable, London, 1913, p. 261.
26. *The Times*, 25 Aug. 1857, p. 6.
27. **P. Mason**, *A Matter of Honour: an account of the Indian Army, its officers and men*, Jonathan Cape, London, 1974, p. 296; J. W. Kaye, *op. cit.*, Vol. 2, p. 373.
28. *The Times*, 6 Aug. 1857, p. 6, 17 Sept. 1857, p. 8, 26 Oct. 1857, p. 8 and 30 Nov. 1857, p. 6.
29. *The Inquirer*, 17 Oct. 1857, p. 657.
30. *Reynolds's Newspaper*, 8 Nov. 1857, p. 7.
31. **G. O. Trevelyan**, *The Life and Letters of Lord Macaulay*, 2 vols., Harper, New York, 1876, Vol. II, p. 366.
32. *The British Banner*, 20 May 1858, p. 312.
33. Lieutenant-Colonel H. B. Edwardes to Sir J. Lawrence, 11 June 1857 cited in **E. Edwardes,** *Memorials of the Life and Letters of Major-General Sir Herbert B. Edwardes, K.C.B., K.C.S.I.*, 2 vols., Kegan Paul, London, 1886, Vol. 1, p. 390.
34. *Ibid.*
35. Field Marshal Earl Roberts, *op. cit.*, p. 29.
36. Lt.-Col. H. B. Edwardes to his wife, 17 June 1857, cited in E. Edwardes, *op. cit.*, Vol. 1, p. 397.
37. Lieutenant A. M. Lang to his mother, 22 July 1857, 'The diary and letters of Arthur Moffat Lang, 1st Lieutenant Bengal Engineers', *JSAHR*, **IX**, Apr. 1930, p. 92.
38. Field Marshal Earl Roberts, *op. cit.*, p. 75.
39. Lieutenant Macdowell to H. Tweddle, 24 May 1857, cited in *Letters from the Field during the Indian Mutiny*, Waterlow, London, 1907, p. 5.
40. Lieutenant G. D. Barker to his mother, 1 July 1857 cited in *Letters from Persia and India 1857–1859*, ed. Lady Barker, Bell, London, 1915, p. 46.
41. H. Knollys (ed.), *op. cit.*, Vol. 1, p. 229; N. Chamberlain to C. Chamberlain, 22 May 1857 quoted in **Sir G. W. Forrest**, *Life of Field Marshal Sir Neville Chamberlain*, Blackwood, London, 1909, p. 331.
42. J. W. Kaye, *op. cit.*, Vol. 2, p. 269.
43. **Lieutenant C. N. North**, *Journal of an English Officer in India*, private, London, 1858, p. 76.
44. Lt. G. D. Barker to his mother, 19 July 1857, cited in Lady Barker (ed.), *op. cit.*, p. 58.
45. **W. H. Russell**, *My Diary in India, in the year 1858–9*, 2 vols., Routledge, London, 1860, Vol. 1, p. 164.
46. E. and A. Linklater, *op. cit.*, p. 105. See also *The Chronicle of Private Henry Metcalfe,* ed. Lieutenant-General Sir F. Tuker, Cassell, London, 1953, p. 68 and **Lieutenant-Colonel W. Gordon**

Alexander, *Recollections of a Highland Subaltern*, Arnold, London, 1898, p. 37.

47. **Surgeon-General W. Munro**, *Reminiscences of Military Service with the 93rd Sutherland Highlanders*, Hurst & Blackett, London, 1883, pp. 120–1. See Also **H. H. Greathead**, *Letters written during the siege of Delhi*, Longmans, London, 1858, p. 229.
48. Lt. Macdowell to H. Tweddle, 7 June 1857, *op. cit.*, p. 12 and Field Marshal Earl Roberts, *op. cit.*, p. 140.
49. Duke of Cambridge to Sir P. Grant, 25 Aug. 1857, Cambridge Mss., R.A., E/1/710.
50. Duke of Cambridge to Sir C. Campbell, 26 Oct. and 9 Nov. 1857, Cambridge Mss., R.A., E/1/785, 798.
51. W. H. Russell, *My Diary in India*, Vol. 2, p. 43.
52. *Reynolds's Newspaper*, 29 Nov. 1857, p. 7.
53. *The Times*, 31 Oct. 1857, p. 5 and 2 Nov. 1857, p. 6.
54. *The Times*, 24 Oct. 1857, p. 7 and *Reynolds's Newspaper*, 29 Nov. 1857, p. 7.
55. *The Times*, 27 Nov. 1857, p. 6 and 16 Dec. 1857, p. 6.
56. *The Inquirer*, 19 Sept. 1857, p. 594 and *The Nonconformist*, 18 Nov. 1857, p. 911.
57. *Reynolds's Newspaper*, 29 Nov. 1857, p. 8. See also 20 Sept. 1857, p. 8.
58. *The Times*, 19 Nov. 1857, p. 6.
59. *The Times*, 5 Aug. 1858, p. 6 and 6 Aug. 1858, p. 8.
60. M. Edwardes, *op. cit.*, p. 136.
61. Duke of Cambridge to Lord Panmure, 2 Oct. 1857, *The Panmure Papers,* Vol. 2, p. 441.
62. J. W. Kaye, *op. cit.,* Vol. 2, pp. 384–5 and *With H.M. 9th Lancers during the Indian Mutiny: the Letters of Brevet Major O. H. S. G. Anson*, ed. H. S. Anson, Allen, London, 1896, p. 209.
63. W. H. Russell, *Mr Diary in India*, Vol. 1, pp. 329–34.
64. *The Examiner*, 14 Nov. 1857, p. 721.
65. *Report of the Commissioners appointed to inquire into the Organization of the Indian Army,* hereafter referred to as the Indian Army Commission, C.2,518, 1859, V. p. ix.
66. Lord Panmure to the Duke of Cambridge, 23 July 1857, *The Panmure Papers*, Vol. 2, p. 408.
67. Sir C. Campbell to the Duke of Cambridge, 21 Oct. 1857, Cambridge Mss., R.A., E/1/774.
68. Major-General Mansfield to the Duke of Cambridge, 20 Oct. 1857, Cambridge Mss., R.A., E/1/775.
69. Report of the Indian Army Commission, *op. cit.*, pp. x–xii.
70. Queen Victoria to Lord Derby, 5 Feb. 1859, *Letters of Queen Victoria*, Vol. III, p. 404.
71. Queen Victoria to Lord Derby, 7 Feb. 1859, *ibid.*, Vol. III, p. 408.

72. Queen Victoria to General Peel, 13 Feb. 1859, *ibid.*, Vol. III, p. 410. See also **R. J. Moore**, *Sir Charles Wood's Indian Policy 1853-66*, Manchester University Press, Manchester, 1966, pp. 208-10.
73. *Report of the Political and Military Committee of the Council of India, the 30th June 1859*, C.330, 1860, L, p. 7.
74. *A Return of the number of soldiers discharged from the Indian Army*, No. 468, 1860, LI, p. 833.
75. Lord Clyde to the Duke of Cambridge, 24 July 1859, Cambridge Mss., R.A., E/1/2,325.
76. R. J. Moore, *op. cit.*, pp. 214-16.
77. *P.P.*, No. 208, 1908, LXXIV, p. 2.
78. Lt.-Gen. the Rt. Hon. Sir W. F. Butler, *op. cit.*, p. 41.
79. H. Martineau, *British Rule in India*, Smith Elder, London, 1857, p. 3.
80. W. H. Russell, *My Diary in India*, Vol. 1, pp. 105, 189; quotation, Vol. 2, p. 259.
81. Gen. Sir J. Luther Vaughan, *op. cit.*, p. 156.
82. Lieutenant-General Sir F. Roberts to the Duke of Cambridge, 21 Mar. 1883, Cambridge Mss., R.A., E/1/10,360.
83. Lt. G. D. Barker to his sister, 6 Apr. 1859, cited in Lady Barker, ed., *op. cit.*, p. 156.
84. Lt.-Gen. J. A. Ewart, *op. cit.*, Vol. 2, pp. 224-9.
85. Lt.-Gen. Sir F. Tuker, ed., *op. cit.*, pp. 99-107.
86. Duke of Cambridge to Sir C. Campbell, 17 Jan. 1858, Cambridge Mss., R.A., E/1/884.

6 The post-Crimean period

The six years which encompassed the Crimean War, the Indian Mutiny and the invasion panic of 1859 represent a pivotal period in relations between the army and society. During those years, the state of the army attracted considerable attention in the press and Parliament, albeit in a periodic and somewhat desultory fashion. Reformers, both military and civilian, campaigned for sweeping changes in the purchase system, the standards of military education, the social conditions of the rank and file, and the organization of the reserve forces. Their campaigns, launched in the 1850s, would be sustained in some instances throughout the next decade. They would take place against a background of bewildering military events - wars and the threat of wars in various parts of the Empire, a civil war in the United States, and the rise of Prussia as a military power. How these campaigns fared, in years 'unusually full of anxious changes',[1] will now be examined.

Sir De Lacy Evans had raised the most controversial reform - the abolition of the purchase system - during the Crimean War. Having returned from the war wounded, but popularly acclaimed for his generalship at the battle of the Alma, this irrepressible reformer had tabled a motion in the Commons, proposing the abolition of purchase. The cabinet, unwilling to debate the issue openly, had set up a Royal Commission. Determined to muzzle Evans, the cabinet had chosen a ten-man Commission, headed by the Duke of Somerset, which would include only one committed army reformer - Evans himself.[2] So transparent a manoeuvre had enraged the radical supporters of Evans. *Reynolds's Newspaper* condemned 'the crafty old Premier [Lord Palmerston] . . . for burking unpleasant matters by referring them to a committee of his own appointment'.[3] M. J. Higgins, another radical journalist, writing in *The Times* under the pseudonym 'Jacob Omnium', deplored the secretive character of the Commission's proceedings. Unlike a Parliamentary Select Committee, he argued, the deliberations of a Royal Commission would enhance the power of the executive, enabling it to influence 'the result of such a tribunal, against which the intelligence and energy of one or two members of the Board must struggle in vain'.[4]

The Royal Commission, however, did not endorse the purchase system in its entirety. It took evidence from several senior officers, including Lord West and Sir Colin Campbell, who were critical of the purchase system. It heard of the trafficking in illegal over-regulation payments, the advantages enjoyed by the wealthy, and the deadening effects of a system in which promotion and advancement bore little relation to personal merit. It learnt, above all, that the system rendered men eligible for regimental command without any guarantee of their professional competence. Of the witnesses questioned, none was more critical of the purchase system than Sir Charles Trevelyan, the official responsible for military questions in the Treasury. He favoured a radical restructuring of the military profession. He wished to replace the present entry system by the competitive examination of the candidates nominated by the Horse Guards, followed by two years' professional instruction at a military college. He advocated, too, that the pay of subalterns should be increased, and that their promotion should be on the basis of merit. He hoped, thereby, to broaden the social composition of the officer corps and to enable more non-commissioned officers to seek promotion. In spite of this testimony, the Commission recognized that the majority of officers favoured the maintenance of the purchase system, or at least some scheme which preserved the benefits commonly ascribed to the existing system. It accepted that purchase accelerated promotion within the peacetime army, and protected officers against jobbery and favouritism. Indeed it rejected any general scheme of promotion by selection, as advanced by Trevelyan, because it 'would not be favourably received by the officers of the British army'.[5]

The report of the Commissioners, issued in August 1857, revealed disagreements within the Commission. Six members, a bare majority, recommended a modification of the purchase system. They proposed that the purchase of the rank of lieutenant-colonel should be abolished and replaced by selection from the list of majors. This recommendation, they hoped, would reduce the likelihood of incompetent officers reaching the position of regimental command.[6] It would also curb the scale of the over-regulation payments, as the largest amounts were paid for lieutenant-colonelcies. De Lacy Evans signed the report, although its recommendation fell short of his ultimate objectives. From his point of view the inquiry had been successful. The Commission had proved itself an independent and an impartial body. It had enabled some officers to air their grievances against the existing system. The report, having exposed the abuses and shortcomings of purchase, had compared, fully and fairly, the arguments for and against the system and had recommended a modest reform. For De Lacy Evans, the report was a useful beginning and an invaluable work of reference. He would urge successive governments to implement its findings. He signed the report, convinced that evidence demonstrated that purchase should be terminated sooner than his colleagues envisaged.[7]

Four Commissioners, including a majority of the military representatives, refused to sign the report. Three of their dissenters, headed by Edward Ellice, a former Secretary at War, produced a separate minority report. They did not defend the principle of purchase, but accepted the expediency of leaving the established system untouched. The majority recommendation, they argued, would neither remove the objections to the principle of purchase nor arrest the evils associated with it. If implemented, the recommendation would undermine the regimental commitment of the junior officer - 'the greatest incitement to professional exertions . . .'. Promotion by selection in peacetime, they feared, 'would naturally be ascribed to favouritism or influence'. Incompetent appointments, they claimed, could be prevented by greater stringency in professional examinations and by more rigorous use of the Commander-in-Chief's veto over purchase promotions. The recommendation, in short, was neither necessary nor liable to allay the abolitionist clamour. Even worse, from the dissenters' viewpoint, it could prove positively harmful, a fatal blow to regimental *esprit de corps*.[8] By revealing so sharp a division of opinion, and by couching their objections in largely pragmatic terms, the dissenters had damaged the credibility of their colleagues' report.

Evidence of internal disagreements cannot entirely explain the limited impact of the Purchase Commission. Equally important was the timing of its publication. Ministerial initiatives in the wake of the report could not be expected in August 1857, at the height of the Indian Mutiny. Government ministers shelved the issue temporarily, pending the defeat of the mutineers. Moreover they were not embarrassed by the same scale of dislocation in the officer corps as had occurred during the Crimean War. Although an officer shortage recurred, requiring the commissioning of 780 officers without purchase, this compared with 1,398 officers commissioned without purchase in 1855.[9] The military press was not as enraged as it had been two years previously. In 1855 *The United Service Gazette*, appalled by the dislocation, had advocated the abolition of purchase; even the more conservative journal *The Naval and Military Gazette* had criticized the hardship which the dislocation could cause the veteran officer. The influx of non-purchase officers would not assist the older officer who might wish to sell his commission after the war.[10] Such criticism mellowed once the Crimean War was over. *The Naval and Military Gazette*, though prepared to support the recommendation of the Purchase Commission, if the Horse Guards felt able to select from the list of majors, preferred to leave the purchase system untouched.[11] More committed to abolition, *The United Service Gazette* disliked the modest, and in its view inadequate, proposals of the Commission. By the end of the decade, it had become thoroughly disillusioned with the gradualist approach and the ineffectual campaign of De Lacy Evans. Modifying its earlier views, it accepted that purchase and military education could be combined successfully. By 17 May 1862, it announced a complete *volte-face*, decrying 'those journals which sought to cultivate a cheap popularity by raising a cry against the system upon which so much of the promotion, in the commissioned ranks of the British Army, is based'.[12]

So swift an erosion of support underlined the flimsy commitment to abolition of the military papers. Founded upon administrative experience rather than opposition to purchase in principle, this commitment weakened with changes in circumstance and with movements of opinion. Military events did not assist the reformers. The catastrophes and administrative failures of the Crimea were not repeated on the same scale in India. Indeed the victories of 1857-58, coupled with the exultation they engendered at home, diluted criticism of the purchase system. The victorious generals, whether beneficiaries or sufferers from the purchase system, had demonstrated their competence; they had restored confidence in the officer corps. The reformers never sustained the momentum of their own campaign. The Parliamentary protests began to founder under the determined, but largely ineffectual, leadership of De Lacy Evans. By 1857, this Peninsular veteran was seventy years of age, somewhat infirm, an isolated military radical, and a poor, frequently inaudible, speaker. Apart from occasional letters to the press and to his constituents in Westminster,[13] he neither mobilized extra-Parliamentary support nor even prepared written hand-outs of his largely unheard speeches. Critics would repeatedly complain that his indifferent Parliamentary performances impaired the prospects of the abolitionist cause.[14]

Had not Sidney Herbert intervened, as Secretary of State for War (1859-61), the abolitionist campaign might have collapsed even more swiftly than it did. Herbert, like Evans, had served on the Purchase Commission, and had endorsed the majority report. He was not an abolitionist, however. As he informed the Duke of Cambridge on 7 December 1859, 'I have always believed that if the scandals and abuses which beset the Purchase System could be removed, much of the Feeling against the System itself would die out'.[15] In the same letter, Herbert proposed two plans with the aim of curbing the size of over-regulation payments. First, he suggested that regimental commands should not be held for longer than seven or ten years, so encouraging officers to sell out early in search of a high price (those who failed to do so would be placed on half-pay until appointed to a staff post). Secondly, he advocated that the purchaser of a lieutenant-colonelcy should not come from the same regiment as the retiring officer. He argued that this would check 'the vice' of over-regulation payments, because the outsider 'would have no pressure put upon him to give more than the regulated Price'.[16]

The Duke of Cambridge firmly rejected these proposals. Opposing the first plan, he described all limitations on length of service as objectionable; he also dreaded a vast increase in the number of half-pay officers. He found the second plan even more odious, fearing that it would shake the foundations of regimental *esprit de corps*. Preventing officers from commanding their own regiments could only undermine their regimental interest. The Duke preferred 'to leave matters as they are', believing that the purchase system had been maligned as a cause of the over-regulation payments. 'The wealth of the country', he insisted, 'is the cause of the evil and money will somehow obtain its worth, do what you wish to prevent it'. He deprecated any tampering with the existing system, which had furnished the infantry and cavalry with a young and active officer corps. He feared, above all, 'that the class of man entering the army would be lowered were the purchase system abolished and this would be an evil that ought to be avoided . . .'.[17]

Although Herbert heeded these objections and withdrew his plans, he still favoured reform. In the House of Commons he faced another challenge from his former co-Commissioner, De Lacy Evans. The General had given notice that he would re-introduce, in March 1860, a motion postponed from the previous year, calling for the gradual abolition of purchase. Herbert may also have been pressed to act by his Under-Secretary of State, Earl de Grey, the former Viscount Goderich, who had led the campaign against purchase during the Crimean War.[18] Whatever his immediate motive, Herbert resolved to implement the recommendation of the Commissioners and abolish the sale of the rank of lieutenant-colonel. The Queen and the Prince Consort were appalled. Briefed by her cousin, the Duke of Cambridge, the Queen deprecated any move from promotion by purchase to promotion by seniority and selection. Such a reform, she feared, would undermine the principle of purchase itself.[19] Prince Albert was even more blunt; he dreaded the constitutional implications of the Commander-in-Chief, in consultation with the Secretary of State, selecting majors to become lieutenant-colonels. This reform, he argued, would transfer the patronage of the army from the Queen to the House of Commons '- a change striking at the root of the prerogative of the Crown'.[20]

Herbert persevered. He submitted his proposals to the cabinet in early March, where they were scrutinized for several days. In spite of the presence of the Duke of Cambridge, whose attendance at the later deliberations of the cabinet was insisted upon by the Queen,[21] the cabinet supported the Secretary of State. Herbert insisted that he could not speak against his recorded opinions in Parliament, a view accepted by Palmerston.[22] When De Lacy Evans moved his motion on 6 March 1860, Herbert could reply on behalf of the government with complete consistency. Reiterating his opposition to the entire abolition of purchase, he intimated his support, in principle, for the removal of 'the abuses and scandals that overlay the practice of purchase'.[23] He had effectively thwarted Evans, for without ministerial backing the motion was doomed. Only 59 Members voted in favour of abolition while 213 voted against; a majority of 154. *The Times*, which had supported Evans before the debate, accepted that 'the advocates of established usage had it all their own way', and that the 'debate was entirely one-sided'.[24] Edward Ellice, the former Secretary at War, Colonel North, and other military Members had opposed recourse either to seniority or selection as a means of promotion. Captain Jervis had added an even more telling point: he claimed that, unless the House was 'prepared for a large pension list and increased pay, the resolution of the gallant General would mean nothing at all'.[25]

With the supporters of purchase so firmly entrenched in the Commons, the prospects of reform were gloomy. The Duke of Cambridge made it abundantly clear that he did not wish to implement the recommendation of the Purchase Commission, which Herbert had endorsed in the Commons. Addressing the House of Lords on 23 March 1860, he stated that 'it shall be my earnest and anxious endeavour - difficult as it may be, and, as I may perhaps consider it, impossible - to carry out that decision in such a manner as to promote the best interest of the Army . . .'.[26] Lacking cooperation from the Horse Guards, and burdened by the increasing demands of Florence Nightingale to promote other reforms, Herbert never formulated a detailed reform of the purchase system. Suffering in the last year of his life from an incurable disease, he died on 2 August 1861 with his purchase proposals still-born.

The tide had turned decisively against reform. When Evans tabled another moderate abolitionist motion in May 1862, proposing the abolition of purchase of the rank of lieutenant-colonel, he encountered an even greater defeat. Although he had the eloquent support of Lord Stanley, a fellow Commissioner, the motion was defeated by 185 votes. As *The Times* ruefully observed, 'The large majority which rejected the General's motion shows that the tide, which ran strongly towards reform in the days of the Crimea has now turned. Until further experience be gained or some unforeseen calamity causes a new agitation the long-threatened anomaly will plainly continue an institution of the country'.[27]

Notwithstanding the failure of purchase reform, the 1850s had witnessed changes in the Victorian army, particularly in military education. Again the main instigator was Sidney Herbert, the moving force of mid-nineteenth-century army reform. Immensely rich and attractive, he was a modest, gentle, and unassuming politician. Socially charming, a Peelite, a philanthropist, a devoted Christian, he was imbued, above all, with a high sense of public duty. He could always command the ear of the House of Commons and the respect of his cabinet colleagues. As Secretary at War (1844-46) he had authorized the reform of army schools, reorganizing the instruction and management of the Duke of York's School. He had instituted a system of training for army schoolmasters, and had created the office of Inspector-General of Military Schools. On his return to the War Office in 1853, Herbert had embarked upon the reform of officer education. Writing to Viscount Hardinge in January 1854, he had proposed the creation of a Board of Examiners to supervise the examination of candidates for commissions and of officers awaiting promotion. He recommended that a military instructor should be appointed in each divisional headquarters to prepare subalterns for promotion, and that the senior department at Sandhurst should be converted into a staff school.[28] The scheme was approved by Hardinge and sanctioned by the cabinet. A sum of £2,000 was voted on the Estimates for 1854-55 to meet the initial expenses of district instruction, but this money was never spent. The outbreak of war, followed by the resignation of Herbert in February 1855, ensured that the scheme was suspended. The money was omitted from the Estimates for 1855-56.

Military education nonetheless attracted considerable interest during the Crimean War. The press and Parliamentary criticisms of Lord Raglan's staff injected a fresh sense of urgency into the educational debate. Lord Panmure accepted that incompetent staff work had bedevilled the organization of supplies, transport, and the auxiliary services in the Crimea. An indication of this new urgency was the presentation of the report of the Select Committee on the Royal Military College, Sandhurst, on 18 June 1855 - in the middle of the war. Although overshadowed in press coverage by the Sebastopol Report, which appeared on the same day, the findings of the Sandhurst Committe, especially the opinions recorded in the minutes of evidence, bolstered the case for reform. Several witnesses deplored the current state of military education. Lieutenant-Colonel W. H. Adams, Professor of Military Science at the Royal Military College, insisted that 'military education is but little valued by the greater part of the high military authorities'.[29] He urged the formation of a proper military staff, with all staff officers required to receive a 'high professional education' at a staff school. Hitherto a certificate from the senior department at Sandhurst had rarely assisted officers in obtaining staff employment. As General Sir Howard Douglas revealed, 216 officers had received certificates since 1836, of whom only seven held staff appointments in 1852 and fifteen in May 1854.[30] The army of the Duke of Wellington, in short, had placed little value upon studying the science of war and the acquisition of professional qualifications. A quick eye, personal courage, and the qualities of an English gentleman had been all-sufficient. It was significant that Adams felt obliged to argue that 'a very clever and educated man is as likely to be a brave dashing officer as an ignorant man. . .'.[31]

Lord Panmure followed up the Committee by appointing a three-man Committee to report on the best means of reorganizing the training of officers for the scientific corps (the Royal Artillery and

Royal Engineers). The Committee, comprising Lieutenant-Colonel W. Yolland, R.E., Lieutenant-Colonel W. J. Smythe, R.A., and Rev. W. C. Lake, M.A. (Fellow of Balliol College, Oxford), visited the military institutions of Austria, France, Prussia and Sardinia. Reporting in January 1857, the Committee recorded that foreign armies attached much greater importance to scientific training than did the British army. Foreign schools were accorded 'more importance', the teaching standards were 'higher', the discipline 'more strict', the number of teachers 'greater', the sums expended were 'larger', and the whole education 'conducted on a more complete system'. While Britain spent about £1,300 annually on military education, Prussia spent £26,000, France £48,000, and Austria at least £127,000. The Committee recommended that cadets should enter Woolwich at a later age, that admission should be partially competitive, and that Queen's Cadetships should be awarded to the most successful candidates. It proposed that all officers should have to pass a general examination and undertake a course of professional study. It reiterated the view of the previous Committee that the senior department at Sandhurst should be much improved, adding that graduation should be a prerequisite for staff appointments. It advocated, above all, that a Board of Education, headed by the Secretary of State, should be formed to draft regulations on discipline and instruction, supervise textbook changes and the examination of candidates, and make annual reports. Were such a Board established, with sufficient independence and pecuniary support, the Committee believed that 'all important improvements in Military Education would follow in time almost as a matter of necessity. . .'.[32]

Both reports buttressed the case for educational reform. Their findings were welcomed by the military press. *The Naval and Military Gazette* yearned for a more professional army to replace the present 'congregation of sporting men and loungers'. Condemning the 'gross ignorance' of the officer corps, it favoured examining staff officers to assess their competence. 'The Army', it thundered, 'can no longer be left as a refuge for ignorant, stupid, and vicious young men. . .'.[33] The Prince Consort rendered less vituperative, but probably more influential, support. Keenly interested in the practicalities of staff work, he worked behind the scenes, pressing the case for a staff corps to train subordinate officers and for a staff of competent general officers.[34] From Parliament, too, there was sustained pressure in favour of educational reform. On 5 June 1856, Sidney Herbert, speaking from the back benches, reminded the House of his pre-war proposals. He argued that the army should reap the benefit of its unprecedented popularity and of the general desire to see it efficient. He urged that the time was ripe to implement his pre-war proposals, to reorganize the army in large brigades or divisions, and 'to inoculate the whole army with a more professional spirit'. Supported by Edward Ellice, De Lacy Evans, Viscount Goderich, and other back benchers,

Herbert pressed the government to rejuvenate the senior department. Specifically, he recommended that the senior department should be moved back to Farnham, and that the course of instruction should be more practical and military. Officers, he argued, should not be eligible for staff appointment unless they had a staff school certificate, or an equivalent educational certificate, and had served for three years in each branch of the service.[35]

Though reticent during the debate, ministers had accepted the need for a thorough reorganization of military education. Both the War Office and the Horse Guards began drafting schemes of reform. The Duke of Cambridge, an ardent educational reformer, brought together Rev. G. R. Gleig, Major-General Duncan Cameron, and several other officers to formulate the Horse Guards' proposals. Working independently on similar schemes, Lord Panmure drew on the expertise of John Henry Lefroy, the brilliant young artillery officer who had aided Florence Nightingale in the Crimea. Lefroy reckoned that the new staff school should be established in London, catering for fifty students on two-year courses, and emphasizing competition in its grading with special distinctions for success.[36] Lord Panmure wished to appoint Lefroy as the first Director-General of Military Education.[37] The Queen protested; she insisted that military education should be under the direct control of the Horse Guards. She objected to the junior rank of Lefroy and to his position as Lord Panmure's adviser.[38] Eventually a compromise was found by which the Department of Military Education was placed under the Commander-in-Chief, but subject to the overall control of the Secretary of State. When the New Council of Military Education was established in April 1857, the Duke of Cambridge became its president, with most of the work devolving upon Major-General Duncan Cameron, the Vice-President. Lefroy was left with the post of Inspector-General of Army Schools.

Creating a Council of Military Education did not, as some reformers had hoped, ensure the immediate foundation of a separate staff school. Instructions were issued by the Duke of Cambridge on 9 April 1857 outlining the qualifications required of all staff officers from 1 January 1858. These were essentially practical, based upon an ability to ride well and write legibly, requiring proficiency in sketching, trigonometry, military history and geography, the knowledge of at least one foreign language, an understanding of the principles of fortification, an ability to judge ground and its occupation by all arms.[39] However, a separate Staff College remained in abeyance, or so it seemed to De Lacy Evans and Sidney Herbert. On 28 July 1857, they initiated another important Parliamentary debate, persuading the Commons to support a higher standard of professional instruction 'for the commissioned ranks of the Army, but especially for the Staff. . .'.[40] The Purchase Commission, which reported in the following month, echoed these sentiments. 'Promotion to the staff', it urged, should be a 'means of stimulating military education, rewarding meritorious officers and obviating some of the hardships which must arise under the purchase system'.[41]

Within three months, the Council of Military Education had drafted a syllabus for the entrance examination and course of study at the Staff College. The recommendations disappointed the hopes of the more optimistic reformers. An excessive emphasis in the curriculum upon pure mathematics incurred the displeasure of the Prince Consort and the Duke of Cambridge. The Council, which included two officers from the Ordnance Corps, proved reluctant to modify its mathematical requirements. Consequently, the trained staff officer, in the early years of the Staff College, became identified 'too closely with the scientific specialists of the Ordnance Corps, whose education and duties related only very indirectly to the movement of large bodies of the troops in the field'.[42] The Council also rejected the suggestions of Lefroy, Herbert, and others that the new Staff College should be removed from Sandhurst. Unable to afford the price of building land in London, and reluctant to expose officers to the social distractions of living in the capital, the Council decided to build the new College at Camberley, and leave it subordinated to the Royal Military College. The number of students was increased from fifteen to thirty and the number of instructing staff from two to nine, four of whom were serving officers. Admission was to be by competitive examination, the course was to last for two years, followed by six-month attachments in each of the two arms other than the officer's original arm. Full attendance at the Staff College, however, was not made a prerequisite for staff appointments. Officers who satisfied the conditions of entry could either sit the final examination, or sit the examination for the Junior Division at the end of the first year and attend for the second year. The Staff College regulations, though less radical than either Herbert or Lefroy had envisaged, emerged as one of the few tangible reforms of the post-Crimean period.

Reforms were also implemented in connection with the R.M.A. Woolwich and the R.M.C. Sandhurst. Hitherto both institutions had been a mixture of a public school and a military college - neither a good public school nor an adequate military college. Henceforth the age of admission to Sandhurst was raised to sixteen years, or eighteen by competitive examination (and from seventeen to twenty years at Woolwich). The rates of payment were altered to incorporate a subsidy for the sons of officers. This subsidy, along with the cost of the twenty Queen's Cadetships, was to be paid by Parliamentary grant. The Queen's Cadetships were at the disposal of the Commander-in-Chief and the First Lord of the Admiralty. They could be awarded to the sons of officers, who were killed or wounded, or died of disease on service, and whose families were financially embarrassed. All Sandhurst cadets were given priority of appointment to commission over those who bypassed the College and sought a direct commission.

More fundamental reforms encountered increasing opposition

during the late 1850s and early 1860s. The Council recommended an amalgamation of Sandhurst and Woolwich to ensure that all candidates for Woolwich received two years of theoretical study at Sandhurst before passing on to Woolwich for practical instruction. The proposal was adopted by the cabinet and approved by the Queen before the fall of Lord Palmerston's government in March 1858. General Peel, who succeeded Lord Panmure at the War Office, took up this scheme and tried to effect the amalgamation. The House of Commons interceded. On 26 April 1858, W. Monsell, a Member with a keen interest in education, tabled a motion condemning the proposed amalgamation. Giving a monopoly of education to Sandhurst filled him with horror. The College, in his opinion, 'had not entitled itself to any very large amount of public favour'. Amalgamation, he claimed, would reduce the standard of education of the scientific corps to the level required for the line.[43] Other Members rebutted the arguments of ministerial spokesmen that amalgamation would provide a new competitive stimulus for the Woolwich cadets. They perceived that the new competition would be much less demanding as it would exclude boys who had just left the public schools or universities. To the dismay of the Duke of Cambridge,[44] Monsell's motion was carried by a large majority.

Having failed over amalgamation, the Council pressed for the abolition of direct commissions. While retaining Woolwich as the means of entering the artillery and engineers, the Council proposed that all candidates for commissions in the other arms should pass through Sandhurst. This would ensure that all officers underwent a preliminary course of military instruction; it would also, if implemented, justify the vast enlargement of Sandhurst which the Council desired. Herbert, who had deplored this idea five years earlier,[45] reluctantly accepted it while Secretary of State. Aware, by January 1861, of his failing strength and imminent demise, he possibly viewed this measure as the only way in which he could effect a lasting improvement in the education of junior officers. The military press rejoiced. Discounting any alternative to professional instruction in the military colleges, *The United Service Gazette* declared that 'Our military system must be exclusive or it is nothing and every attempt to blend the character of the soldiers with that of the civilians must land between the two classes'.[46] Some civilian papers demurred. Military officers, claimed *The Press*, were unfit to educate the young: 'their outlook being jesuitically professional and that is quite enough to condemn it'. It argued that 'Sandhurst is a bad school for it is a military school and military schools are bad. They are a foreign innovation in England . . . their vices are rooted in the depths of their nature: they are only to be eradicated by the destruction of the Establishments themselves'.[47]

The issue of exclusivity obscured the more fundamental and contentious questions concerning the character of the education required for the officer corps, and, ultimately, the kind of officer corps desired. All save some ultra-radical observers agreed that officers had to be gentlemen, as a means of ensuring a small, cheap, and safe army. Restricting entry to gentlemen preserved a convivial mess, an agreeable social life, and a 'natural' bond between officers and men. On this premise competitive entry had to be limited; candidates for the Sandhurst entrance examination had to be nominated by the Commander-in-Chief. As inhibiting in the development of a purely professional ideal was the emphasis upon the physical attributes and qualities of an army officer. It was commonly felt that books and study were not the prerequisites of military competence. Lord Palmerston, in replying to Herbert's speech on military education, in June 1856, did not deny that some literary and mathematical knowledge would be proof of an officer's 'general capacity'. He believed, nonetheless, that personal courage, initiative, and resourcefulness were all important. Exhorting officers to follow the example of the Duke of Wellington, and sustain an enthusiasm for hunting and field sports, he claimed that the main qualities of an officer were

> contempt of danger, fearlessness of responsibility, a quick eye to estimate the nature of surrounding circumstances, a rapid decision how to act in every emergency, and resolution to take course which upon reflection he may think best. . . . What I want to impress upon the House is that no examination which you can institute will afford a decisive test of the qualities which I have mentioned.[48]

Palmerston was not alone in voicing these reservations. He was supported by several civilian and military papers,[49] and probably by the vast majority of officers outwith the military colleges. These doubts, coupled with the loyalty of many Members of Parliament to the existing public schools, and their dislike of any large scale extension of Sandhurst, limited the extent of educational development. Even some who favoured professional education opposed the order that all prospective officers should pass through Sandhurst. As this would compel artillerists and engineers to bear the expense of two years at Sandhurst, as well as the existing course at Woolwich, reformers feared that it would alter the character of the non-purchase corps, reducing the proportion of less wealthy officers.[50] As the removal of direct commissions would require the extension of Sandhurst, this was bound to be costly and would not be supported by either the Treasury or the House of Commons. By the early 1860s fiscal retrenchment had doused the last remaining embers of army reform.

Educational reform in the late 1850s had at least had the active support of the Horse Guards and the War Office; the movement in favour of sanitary reform had no such advantage. Headed by Florence Nightingale and Sidney Herbert, the movement included several other influential but less well-known reformers: J. H. Lefroy, the artillerist,

Douglas Galton, a captain in the Royal Engineers who specialized in barrack and hospital construction, Thomas Longmore, professor of military surgery at the Army Medical School, T. G. Balfour, the first head of the statistical branch of the army medical services, Sir John Sutherland, an army doctor, and Sir John Richardson, a navy doctor. Florence Nightingale, though immensely knowledgeable, relied considerably upon the expertise of her colleagues, especially upon the knowledge of Sutherland in sanitary matters.[51] Nevertheless she dominated the reform movement, supplying the driving force in the cause of barrack and hospital reform. She constantly harassed and exhorted her colleagues into further endeavours, immersed herself in painstaking research and prolific writings, and inspired the others by her tireless vitality and passionate commitment.

She saw herself embattled against the forces of inertia and parsimony in the War Office. Only publicity, as J. H. Lefroy advised, could move the government; only remorseless pressure, through private channels and through several campaigns in the press, journals, and Parliament, could ensure that Ministers did not give way to their bureaucratic advisers. Chronicling the remarkable efforts of Miss Nightingale, her most recent biographer has portrayed the struggle as between the reformers, aided by public opinion, and 'the reactionary party within the War Office'.[52] Undoubtedly Miss Nightingale saw herself as locked in a struggle against the forces of reaction, headed by Sir Benjamin Hawes, the Permanent Under-Secretary of State at the War Office, and Dr Andrew Smith, head of the Army Medical Department. This view, however, simplifies and distorts the attitudes of her opponents. Sir Benjamin Hawes was not a blinkered reactionary. A Liberal Member of Parliament for nearly twenty years, he had held office as Under-Secretary of State for the Colonies (1846–51) and as deputy-secretary at the War department (1851–52). A son-in-law of the elder Brunel, he was deeply interested in technology, particularly in the electric telegraph and the possibility of a Thames tunnel. He was largely responsible for the adoption of the Armstrong gun by the Royal Artillery. Like Hawes, Dr Smith was an immensely able man. Having risen rapidly through the army medical profession, he became a specialist and a voluminous writer upon the zoology of Southern Africa. Neither of these men were merely bureaucratic functionaries; they had reasons other than purblind conservatism for resisting the views of Miss Nightingale and her cohorts.

They did not accept that the reformers possessed a monopoly of wisdom. Sanitation was not an exact science. There were several schools of thought about the best method of ventilation; even Hawes had his own theories and had persuaded Dr Reid to ventilate the Legislature. Dr Smith maintained that his department was 'perfectly aware' of the sanitary requirements of the army, but had lacked, in the pre-war years, the power to enforce them.[53] As departmental heads, these officials were also easy targets of criticism. Smith, in particular, had endured withering attacks upon his staff and himself during the Crimean War. Although the calumnies had been largely refuted by the wartime Committees of Inquiry, the resurgence of demands for reform revived the bitter memories of previous criticism. Even worse, the reforming initiative in the post-war years had been seized by activists outside the War Office itself. Should the reformers prove successful, then the departments were liable to see fairly sensitive issues, like the pay and promotion prospects in the army medical services, examined by external commissions over which they had no control. Ultimately, reforms could be foisted upon their departments with relatively little concern for the 'departmental' view. Sensitive and suspicious, the War Office and the Army Medical Department wished to restrict the remit and to delay the formation of any Royal Commissions, which were committed to proposing and, possibly, to imposing reforms upon the army.

Procrastination, however, was not an effective tactic immediately after the Crimean War. Confronted by censorious editorials and Parliamentary criticism,[54] the government conceded the appointment of a Commission of Inquiry into the sanitary state of the army. Asked to preside over the Commission, Sidney Herbert insisted upon the presence of several reformers on the Commission, notably Drs Sutherland and Alexander as well as Colonel Lefroy. He also ensured that the Commission had the right to examine any factor bearing upon the sanitary condition of the troops in barracks and in military hospitals. He secured, too, the right to examine the organization, education and administration of the Army Medical Department. After about six months' delay, the Commission began its deliberations in May 1857. Miss Nightingale worked enthusiastically behind the scenes. She supplied statistics for the Commissioners, commented on the evidence of witnesses, and advised Herbert before each sitting of the Commission. Within four months, the Commission completed its labours and presented a stunning revelation of the living conditions within the peacetime army.

The Commission used dramatic civil-military comparisons to highlight the deplorable living conditions of the home-based army. It focused on the rate of mortality in the army, which was more than double the rate endured by the civilian population. Believing that the main cause of the excessive mortality was overcrowding in barracks, insufficient ventilation, and defective sewerage and water supplies, it proposed a host of new regulations to remedy these defects.[55] The reformers forced the government to act on these findings. Herbert pressed Lord Panmure to appoint four sub-commissions to supervise the implementation of the proposals. Each sub-commission, he suggested, should have a separate task: (1) to supervise the ventilating, drainage and re-arrangement of barrack and hospital buildings; (2) to found a statistical branch in the Army Medical Department; (3) to institute an Army Medical School; (4) to revise hospital regulations, reconstruct the Army Medical Department, and draw up a new warrant for the promotion of medical officers.[56] As the government could not afford to be seen to be indifferent to these recommendations, it accepted Herbert's suggestions and appointed him chairman of each sub-commission. The War Office retained misgivings about delegating powers to independent sub-commissions concerning the pay and promotion within the medical service. Within three months, Panmure was trying to revoke the fourth sub-commission; only the insistence of Herbert ensured its appointment.[57]

Such vacillation by the Secretary of State convinced Miss Nightingale of the need to sustain public pressure upon the government. She mounted a publicity campaign to publicize the Commission's report. She persuaded Lord Stanley, Sidney Herbert and Edwin Chadwick to write articles about the report. She urged journalists to review the Commission's findings. She compiled a pamphlet, *Mortality in the British Army*, from the charts and statistical data appended to the Commission's report. She sent 2,000 copies of the pamphlet, unsigned, to the Queen, the Commander-in-Chief, Members of both Houses, the War Office, commanding officers and various doctors.[58] By these tactics she guaranteed an extensive coverage and readership of the report, although its findings occasioned considerable interest in their own right. 'There can be little doubt', wrote *The Times*, 'that the chief cause of the evil is the deficient accommodation and the consequent overcrowding in barracks . . . the closeness, the dirt, the indecency spoken of remind one of a slave-ship more than of a place for English soldiers to inhabit . . .'.[59] In *The Edinburgh Review*, J. T. Howell, one of Florence Nightingale's nominees, grasped the essence of the reformers' case. 'The truth is', he stated, 'that the barrack accommodation of the United Kingdom is utterly insufficient to provide healthy quarters for any considerable body of troops'.[60] Large additional barracks were essential.

The flood of criticism and publicity provoked an immediate reaction from the Horse Guards. On 26 March 1858, the Duke of Cambridge assured the House of Lords that the soldier had not been neglected in the past; he was simply more appreciated at the present. Echoing these sentiments, the Earl of Cardigan insisted that the discomforts of the soldiers' living conditions had been grossly exaggerated.[61] The reformers were not surprised. Having already encountered such attitudes from several military witnesses who had appeared before the Sanitary Commission, they simply re-doubled their efforts. Herbert and Miss Nightingale persuaded Lord Ebrington to raise the sanitary issue in the House of Commons. On 12 May 1858, he moved resolutions which attributed the excessive mortality of the army to bad sanitary conditions and demanded an improvement of barracks and hospitals forthwith. As Ebrington gained overwhelming support from fellow back benchers, the government accepted these resolutions.[62]

Administratively, the reformers pressed ahead with the arduous work of the four sub-commissions. Herbert had to travel throughout the country, physically inspecting barracks and dealing with unco-operative and sometimes insolent commanding officers. Compounding this exhausting and wearing ordeal was the voluminous correspondence required of him as chairman of all four sub-commissions. He became immersed in lengthy arguments with the War Office over the minutiae and details of the new reforms and regulations. Only from the Army Medical Department did he gain some respite. Once Dr Smith retired as Director-General, the reformers lobbied the government to appoint Dr Alexander as his replacement. After several months' deliberation, the government accepted the recommendation; henceforth the Medical Department would work with, and not obstruct, the sub-commissions. By June 1859, when Herbert accepted the invitation of Lord Palmerston to become Secretary of State for War, the reformers appeared to be on the brink of triumph.

Herbert's tenure of office disappointed the more sanguine reformers. Some reforms were accomplished. The statistical branch of the Army Medical Department was established; it issued its first report on the health of the army in 1860. The Army Medical School was founded at Chatham for the study of gun shot wounds and the special diseases which were liable to inflict armies in the field. The Army Medical Department was reorganized and a new warrant for army medical officers was issued. But army doctors still remained dissatisfied with their pay and professional status. The new warrant did not attract a vast influx of army doctors; on the contrary, recruitment deteriorated during the 1860s and 1870s, militating against the standards of medical care. In spite of salary increases in 1858 and 1879, it was not until 1889 that the salary scales of army doctors became even remotely competitive with civilian rates. Army doctors were not accorded the rights and privileges of combatant rank until 1886; they were not organized into a professional corps, the Royal Army Medical Corps, until 1898.[64]

Herbert failed, moreover, to sustain the interest of the government in barrack and hospital renovation. During his term of office, the barrack repair and improvement programme expanded considerably in its operations. Expenditure upon the construction, enlargement, and repair of barracks rose to an unprecedented £726,841 in 1859-60. Following the principles laid down by the Sanitary Commission, new methods of ventilating and heating barracks were introduced, drainage, gas lighting, and the provision of water supplies were either introduced or extended, kitchen facilities were remodelled, and separate married quarters were added to the living accommodation. The annual reports of the medical officers from the major stations drew attention to sanitary defects in barracks and hospitals. The Barrack and Hospital Improvement Commission, later known as the Army Sanitary Committee, supervised the sanitary improvements; it visited every barrack and hospital in the United Kingdom between 1857 and 1861.

Notwithstanding this vast expenditure, careful supervision, and the sustained interest and stimulus of Herbert himself, much remained to be done. The task was always daunting in view of the scale and cost of rebuilding, the recurring problems of maintenance, the opposition of civilians to the construction of army barracks in their neighbourhood, and the difficulty of meeting ever-rising standards of health and sanitation. By 1861, the Army Sanitary Committee reported upon its inspection of 108 barracks and 59 hospitals. Although it catalogued the vast improvements which had recently been accomplished, it underlined that these achievements were merely a small beginning and had to be sustained. It found that overcrowding was endemic throughout the major stations: the worst example was at St Mary's casemates, Chatham, where in a space sufficient for 600 men, the regulation number was 1,128 men and the actual number was 1,410. Ventilation had been introduced in 2,996 barrack rooms, 346 NCOs' rooms, 86 guard-rooms, 67 school-rooms, libraries and workshops, and 500 hospital wards; but this still left approximately 30 per cent of the barracks and 10 per cent of hospitals without adequate ventilation. Water had only been piped into one-third of the barracks and one-fifth of the hospitals. Latrines had replaced privies and cesspits in 45 barracks, less than one-half of the total number. Only 9 barracks and 8 hospitals had been lighted throughout with gas.[65] Admittedly these statistics reflected the massive improvement of some barracks and hospitals since 1858, but further progress would depend upon the continuing readiness of the government to finance the necessary renovations. Herbert never secured this on-going commitment: expenditure upon barrack construction and repair slumped to £453,074 in his last Estimates, and fell further in subsequent years, totalling £313,112 in 1864-65.[66]

To explain this failure of Herbert, his protracted illness, though an important contributory factor, cannot alone suffice. Renovating barrack accommodation required, in essence, substantial and sustained financial expenditure. Herbert proposed to raise the money by selling off unhealthy barracks and using the sums obtained for the modernization of other buildings. Gladstone, the Chancellor of the Exchequer, deplored the idea; he insisted that any money raised by the sale of barracks should be paid into the Consolidated Fund as part of the general revenue for the year. Consequently, all proposed expenditure upon barracks had to be vetted by the Treasury and voted upon by Parliament. Had interest in army reform remained at the level witnessed in 1856 and 1857, Herbert might have overcome the resistance of Treasury officials and his Parliamentary critics. The health of the army, however, no longer provoked fierce passions and lengthy editorials. Even the fears of a French invasion proved remarkably short-lived. As Gladstone remarked, in January 1861, 'Last year there was a sentiment of danger at home which disposed people to wish for a strong army as well as a strong navy. This year the sentiment of danger has materially abated; and a cry for economy has become audible'.[67]

With the death of Herbert and the onset of retrenchment, the influence of the reformers, including Florence Nightingale, began to wane. They failed, despite repeated efforts, to improve the pay and status of the army doctor; they also split among themselves, unable to act in unison over the Contagious Diseases Acts. This legislation had been introduced by the government to curb the alarming incidence of venereal disease in the home army. By 1862, 25,787 men, or 33 per cent of the home-based troops, were hospitalized on account of venereal disease. Captain Pilkington Jackson's report on the Soldiers' Institutes at Aldershot and Portsmouth had highlighted the degree of military immorality; it had convinced the government and *The Times* that the soldier must be protected against his passions.[68] Acting upon the advice of the Army Medical Department, the government introduced legislation akin to similar continental statutes, by which prostitutes were restricted in their movements, inspected, and forced, if necessary, to submit to hospital treatment. The Acts, passed in 1864, 1866 and 1869, established 'protected areas' round fourteen large naval and military bases. Women, if accused by a policeman, before a single magistrate in a closed court, of acting as a prostitute within these areas, were liable to compulsory hospitalization, and, under the 1869 Act, to five days compulsory incarceration before being examined. The victims, in short, lost their rights of *habeas corpus*.[69]

While the Army Medical Department, *The Times*, and the House of Commons favoured the Acts, Florence Nightingale, Harriet Martineau, *The Daily News*, and a large body of liberal and religious opinion opposed them. Opponents deplored the Acts on moral and libertarian grounds. Florence Nightingale, incensed by the legislation, believed that it would prove unworkable and largely ineffectual. She advocated the introduction of more and better recreational facilities in the army: 'You cannot reclaim prostitutes', she argued, 'you must prevent prostitution . . .'.[70] But she never shared the acute sense of feminist outrage expressed by some opponents of the legislation. Nor did she approve of the tactics employed by the abolitionist associations.[71] Even without her active assistance, the abolitionist movement proved ultimately successful, securing the repeal of the Acts in 1886.

Although officers and other ranks attracted periodic attention throughout the late 1850s and early 1860s, the non-regular forces attracted even more interest in the press and Parliament. Initially the Militia, re-constituted in 1852, had enjoyed wide support apart from the peace party of Cobden and Bright. In framing the 1852 Act, the government of Lord Derby had acted upon the insistence of Palmerston; it had ensured that the Militia became a general and not a local force, an instrument of national and not purely county defence. During the Crimean War, the force had served the country admirably. Its strength, which numbered 38,000 men in 1855, rose to 66,000 by the following year. Eleven regiments had volunteered to undertake garrison duty in the Mediterranean; another thirty-eight had offered themselves for the same service. The Militia had also supplied the army with 33,000 recruits. Again the force responded during the Indian Mutiny; 25,000 Militiamen were embodied to reinforce garrisons which might be depleted by the withdrawal of troops to India. Eight thousand Militiamen volunteered for the regular line.

During the Crimean War, the Militia had escaped the censure which the army periodically incurred. The billeting procedures of the Militia were criticized, especially in Scotland where Militiamen were billeted on private citizens and not on licensed victuallers as in the rest of Britain.[72] Officer appointments were condemned occasionally, inasmuch as aristocratic connections and county influence seemed to rate more highly than either professional merit or seniority.[73] These criticisms were rare, however; they were too readily associated with the opinions of Cobden and Bright, whose views on military matters were no longer in vogue. In the late 1850s, liberal and radical papers hailed the Militia as the 'old Constitutional Force', a traditional, distinctively English force, a bastion against the standing army of the Crown.[74]

Unfortunately, the Militia as a bastion was less than impressive. Furnishing the regular army with recruits had severely depleted its own ranks. By calling upon the Militia for overseas service, the Government had checked the enlistment of officers and men. Prolonged embodiment, involving the loss of valuable labour at crucial times, had not enhanced the appeal of the force in rural communities: many regiments were unable to maintain their establishments. A Royal Commission, which reported in January 1859, found that the Militia was in a fairly parlous condition.[75] Volunteering, as an alternative to the Militia, had a staunch body of advocates. The concept was not new. A Volunteer Corps had survived from the Napoleonic Wars – the Duke of Cumberland's Sharpshooters, formed in 1794, continued to meet as a rifle club; in 1835 they became the Royal Victoria Rifle Club by permission of the Duchess of Kent.[76] Offers to form Volunteer Corps had flooded into the Home Office during the Chartist disturbances, but they had always been dismissed as too provocative. General Sir Charles Napier had proposed the enrolment of volunteers during the invasion scare of 1852; similar demands had been voiced during the Crimean War and the Indian Mutiny. All offers to form corps were either rejected or rebuffed by the governments of the day, save two: an Exeter and South Devon Corps was sanctioned in 1852 to ward off any local danger to the Devon coast, and the Royal Victoria Rifle Club was allowed to become a corps in 1853.[77]

Prior to 1859, the Volunteer concept had three main advocates in Hans Busk, Alfred B. Richards and Nathaniel Bousfield. Busk, a barrister and High Sheriff of Radnorshire, had championed the Volunteer idea ever since his undergraduate days (he had sent a plan for a national volunteer force to Lord Melbourne as early as 1837).

In promoting the Volunteer movement between 1856 and 1859, he travelled more than 30,000 miles and spent about £1,000 of his own money. Between March 1858 and August 1861, he delivered 147 lectures to promote the cause.[78] A. B. Richards, the first editor of *The Daily Telegraph and Courier*, wrote numerous articles on the need for a Volunteer Corps. Nathaniel Bousfield, a cotton broker, attempted repeatedly to form a Corps in Liverpool but, lacking official approval, formed a drill club for cotton workers. Along with other propagandists, the trio attracted support from merchants, professional men, tradesmen, and other respectable citizens. The earliest offers to form Corps came from upper middle-class citizens who were unable to join the socially exclusive, largely rural-based Militia, and who were too respectable to join the army.[79] These enthusiasts had the whole-hearted backing of *The Times*. During the Indian Mutiny it urged that a Volunteer Corps should be formed for Indian service, composed of men 'of a rank which would not permit them to enlist as common soldiers'.[80]

The Duke of Cambridge deplored this suggestion. Writing to Lord Panmure, on 25 September 1857, he declared that Volunteer Corps would become 'unmanageable bodies, and would ruin our Army'. Seven days later, he wrote again, dismissing Volunteers as merely 'an armed and a very dangerous rabble'.[81] Lord Panmure agreed; he believed that 'Gentlemen Volunteers' would prove utterly useless, more of a danger to their friends than to their foes.[82] Lieutenant-General Sir George H. Wetherall, the Adjutant-General, underscored the objections of the Horse Guards to the Volunteer concept in his evidence before the Royal Commission on the Militia. Asked if Volunteers should be formed as an alternative to the Militia, he replied 'that it would be a very bad principle, because they are not under martial law; they might serve or not, as it pleased their fancy'. Even if they did serve, he doubted that they could ever match regular troops.[83]

The invasion scare of 1859 swept aside any ministerial and military reticence. The immediate cause of the 'Third Panic', as Cobden dubbed it, was the explosive French reaction to the discovery that the bomb thrown by Orsini at Napoleon III had been made in England. Reports of the hysterical French reaction, especially by the French army, alarmed the British press. The French development of the port of Cherbourg perturbed the Queen and the Prince Consort on their visit to France in August 1858.[84] The French creation of an ironclad fleet, armed with breech-loading rifled cannon, worried the Admiralty. The aims and objectives of Napoleonic diplomacy caused constant concern, with British suspicions reaching a climax as France intervened in the Austro-Sardinian War in April 1859. Panic erupted in official circles and in the editorial columns. As the government sought to strengthen the navy and stiffen the south coast fortifications,[85] Volunteer enthusiasts gathered at St Martin's Hall, Long Acre, on 16 April.

Although the hall was only a third full, the speeches of Sir Charles Napier, Sir Duncan MacDougall, General Taylor, Sir Allan McNab, A. B. Richards and others received extensive press coverage. Three days later, *The Times* proclaimed that 'There can be only one true defence of a nation like ours - a large and permanent volunteer force . . .'.[86] The bulk of the press echoed these views; *The Times* sustained a stream of clamorous leading articles, published numerous letters from gentlemen wishing to form Volunteer Corps, and, on 9 May, published Tennyson's famous poem, 'Riflemen Form'.

Responding to this pressure, the government issued a circular from the War Office on 12 May 1859, which required the Lords Lieutenant to raise a Volunteer Force under the provisions of the Yeomanry and Volunteers Consolidation Act of 1804. General Peel would claim, subsequently, that the government had simply deferred to popular opinion in recognizing the Volunteers,[87] but his claim warrants an explanation. The minority Conservative government of Lord Derby was not in any electoral danger, as it had just won another thirty seats in the recent general election. It had, however, been propelled into office, in the previous year, on a wave of anti-French hostility. It had to make some concession to these sentiments and to allay the fears of invasion. To propose an increase of the regular army or the imposition of the Militia ballot would have involved political suicide. Accepting the Volunteers, conversely, satisfied the journalistic clamour, cost the State nothing, and could possibly prove beneficial.

According to the circular of 12 May, Volunteers were liable to be called out in case of actual or apprehended invasion. Exempted from the Militia ballot, they would be considered as 'effective' if they participated in twenty-four drills per year, but were able to resign on fourteen days' notice except on active service. The property of a Corps was invested in the commanding officer, who could recover subscriptions and disciplinary fines before a magistrate. The circular did not comment upon the military function or purpose of the Volunteers; this was left to a second circular, drafted by the Prince Consort, and issued from the War Office on 25 May. Prince Albert believed that the Volunteers should be composed of men from 'those classes . . . who do not, under our present system, enter either into the Regular army or the Militia'. Although these men should be amenable to military discipline, their system of drill and instruction should not be 'unnecessarily irksome'. Proficiency in rifle shooting and not drill should be their aim; they should be enrolled in small bodies or companies and should rarely, if ever, form larger corps. In war, their skill in the use of the rifle, close support of each other, and knowledge of the local countryside should enable them to 'hang with the most telling effect upon the flanks and communications of a hostile army'. The Artillery Volunteers would be organized in even smaller bodies and would be expected to man the batteries in coastal towns.[88]

Lord Derby's Government had dealt with the Volunteers in a less than benevolent fashion. Offering exemption from the Militia ballot was an empty gesture as there was not the slightest likelihood of the ballot being revived. The issue of arms and ammunition, conceded in the second circular, was also disappointing – Volunteers had to purchase these items at cost price. On 10 June 1859, the government was defeated and a new ministry, headed by Lord Palmerston, replaced it. Herbert, the new Secretary of State, had little enthusiasm for the Volunteer cause; he believed that the Militia under military discipline would prove a more reliable force for home defence. The Volunteers he rated as merely an auxiliary force, preferably 'composed of men who will do the work *for the liking of it, and maintain themselves*'.[89] He delegated the work of organizing and directing the nascent Volunteer movement to his Under-Secretary of State, Earl de Grey. The latter had more sympathy with the Volunteers than Herbert; as Under-Secretary, and later as Secretary of State (April 1863 to February 1866), he would ensure that the Volunteers became a financially supported and an integrated part of the military system. At the same time, the government curbed the virtual independence of the Volunteer movement. By issuing twenty-five Enfield rifles per one hundred Volunteers, and by providing free ammunition and access to guns for the artillery units in July 1859, the government secured a lever over the Volunteer Corps. Awarding a capitation grant for effective Volunteers, in 1863, enhanced the degree of ministerial control.

Enrolment in the Volunteers mushroomed during the winter of 1859–60. By 1861, 161,239 men were enrolled, and the number rose to 199,194 by 1868. In the early years of its growth the movement enjoyed a good press and a reasonable degree of public support. Liberal enthusiasm switched from the Militia to the less aristocratic and less expensive Volunteers, who were more clearly removed from the forms and traditions of the standing army. Military spokesmen became increasingly circumspect in their criticisms of the Volunteers. Lord Melville, Commander-in-Chief of the army in Scotland, had to apologize through the Secretary of State for disparaging comments which he had made in the quarter sessions of the county of Midlothian.[90] Even the Duke of Cambridge concealed his distaste for the Volunteer movement. Speaking at the Easter dinner in the Mansion House on 9 April 1860, he praised the 'admirable spirit', displayed by the country in volunteering. If properly organized, he stated, the Volunteers could prove 'a great auxiliary to the army and navy'.[91] Only the Peace Society and the more pacifically inclined radicals remained ardent critics of the movement. Henry Richard, who devoted his life to running the Peace Society, viewed the State encouragement of the Volunteers as an attempt to diffuse 'a martial spirit and a love of arms among the people . . .'. He feared that the Volunteers were more likely 'to turn their rifles against the working classes than [to use them] in their defence'.[92]

Though quickly established and widely accepted, the Volunteer movement experienced a rapid metamorphosis. The enthusiasm of the press and of some Volunteers, engendered by the invasion scare of 1859, rapidly waned. Drilling, outside the large towns where spectacular field days and reviews could be staged, became more and more a matter of routine. The time and expense lavished upon the movement in its early days was not sustained. By 1863 a distinct change had occurred in the social composition of the Volunteer force: the upper middle-class elements had begun to drift away, and the shortage of officers had become even more pronounced. One cause of this shortage, which would persist throughout the rest of the century, was the expense of becoming a Volunteer officer. Although the scale of expenditure varied from unit to unit, all officers had to buy their own uniform and meet the annual costs of band expenses, prize money, and camp, if applicable.[93] Commanding officers had to be wealthy, as they were liable in law for the debts of the whole Corps. On the other hand, volunteering carried little social status. Just as the movement itself attracted increasing ridicule on account of its military pretensions and gaudy uniforms, so the social aspirations of the officer corps attracted scant respect. Volunteer officers, argued N. Taillefer, 'are men of intensely vulgar, conceited and ignorant manners, men who still drop their h's, and are among the uneducated *nouveau rich* [*sic*] in local society . . .'.[94] As Volunteering attracted proportionately fewer participants from the middle class, the rank and file, of whom a majority were working-class as early as 1862, attracted an increasing proportion of artisans and unskilled workers. Eventually working-class members would comprise about three-quarters of the whole force.[95]

In spite of the change in social composition, the Volunteers proved a strong and resilient movement. A steady stream of recruits came forward, motivated partly by patriotism but also by the appeal of rifle shooting, camp, sporting facilities, and the social attractions of Volunteer involvement. Yet the role and responsibilities of the Volunteers were by no means clear. When Parliamentarians and newspapers suggested that the numerical strength of the Volunteers could ultimately enable the State to reduce the regular army, this merely alarmed the military and underlined the confusion.[96] An often mooted role for the Volunteers was assisting the civil power in the case of local disturbances. As Volunteers had rifles, and a smattering of military discipline, they could not be ignored during a local riot: their rifles, in any case, might become a target for the rioters. During the Fenian crisis of 1866–67, there was a double problem in this respect. While the authorities feared Fenian infiltration into certain Volunteer Corps (and into several regiments of the line),[97] they were not sure what role the Volunteers should play in warding off the anticipated Fenian rebellion. A War Office circular, issued in October 1867, permitted Volunteers to defend their own armouries with arms, but insisted that any aid to the civil power should be provided by unarmed individuals enrolled as special constables. Only magistrates could use Volunteers as an armed body if necessary. Throughout the country Volunteers enrolled as special constables. Some 4,000 special constables enrolled in Edinburgh, under the command of J. H. A. Macdonald, a prominent Edinburgh Volunteer. 'The whole drilling', he recalled, 'was done by Volunteers, and all the commanders of divisions and sections were Volunteers . . .'.[98]

However useful in keeping the peace, the Volunteers had not been intended to perform that task. Expected to defend the homeland, their capacity to do so was increasingly questioned from 1864 onwards. In his circular of 25 May 1859, Prince Albert had emphasized the two main skills which the Volunteers should develop, namely sharpshooting and skirmishing. As a means of defending the homeland, these skills seemed less than entirely adequate after the Prussian victories in Denmark (1864) and in Austria (1866). The performance of irregular troops, too, had not left a profoundly favourable impression upon British observers of the American Civil War.[99] The Prussian military efficiency, and above all the organization of her reserves, attracted considerable comment in *The Pall Mall Gazette, The Times* and *Broad Arrow*. Comparing British forces with Prussia's, *The Times* declared that 'We have no plan, no system, no ready machinery of combination, no connexion subsisting between our Army and its Reserves, no schemes for keeping these Reserves effective'.[100]

Prussia, argued the critics, had not merely exposed the shortcomings of the British military system, but she had also furnished a model from which Britain could profit. As Prussia had formed her reserve army from a localized militia, well-armed and well-led, the British government was urged to do likewise. Reviving the Militia became a popular idea. Various schemes were mooted by journals and newspapers; they favoured, either jointly or separately, three main objectives - a closer connection between the Militia and the line, a greater degree of compulsion, and a more professionally competent reserve. Although the first objective reflected a clear attempt to emulate the Prussian system, allowance had to be made for the responsibilities of Britain in Imperial defence. Consequently, two separate armies were proposed - a long-service army for Imperial defence and a short-service, home-based army, linked to the reserve. A restoration of the Militia ballot was recommended to solve the recruiting problem, and the drafting of enrolled pensioners into the Militia was thought likely to enhance its professional competence.[101] As journalists lauded the potential of a revived Militia, the Volunteers suffered by comparison. Their lax discipline, lack of formal military organization, and independence from the military authorities seemed almost anachronistic. The defeat of Garibaldi's forces at Mentana, in 1867, dealt a further blow to the Volunteer idea. In December 1867 Lord Ranelagh, a prominent Volunteer commander, derided the Volunteers as a 'sham army'. He had campaigned for several years in favour of an independent Volunteer army, and was primarily concerned about the inability of the Volunteers to take the field as an organized military force. By 1868, the epithet 'sham' seemed all too appropriate.

The press campaign in favour of an enhanced reserve coincided with the recognition of a recruiting crisis in the regular army. In March 1866 the government belatedly acknowledged a serious shortage of recruits and appointed a Royal Commission to examine the problem. The Commission, chaired by Lord Panmure, heard considerable criticism of the Reserve Warrant of 1859, by which the War Office had tried to form a reserve of regular soldiers from those who took their discharge after ten years instead of serving for a full twenty-one years. Although the Warrant had produced a paltry reserve of less than 3,000 men, the Duke of Cambridge and other officers condemned it for seducing men from the ranks and thus exacerbating the man-power shortage.[102] Earl Grey defended the policy of the War Office; he argued that it was more important to have a reserve of trained men in the country than to retain every ten-year man in the Colours.[103] The Commission, though primarily interested in alleviating the recruiting problem, accepted the need for an army of reserve. It recommended an increase of the enrolled pensioner force and a reorganization of the Militia to provide 'a solid and constitutional Reserve'.[104]

Acting upon these recommendations, General Peel, the Secretary of State for War, introduced a new reserve scheme in the House of Commons in March 1867. He proposed the formation of two distinct reserves - a first reserve of 50,000 men, earmarked for overseas service, and intended to bring the regular regiments up to their war establishments, and a second reserve of 30,000 men intended for home defence. Prospective reservists would be allowed, as a favour and not as a right, to commute their last four or five years' service in the Colours for service in the reserve. Those who commuted their service on the original twelve years' engagement would enter the first reserve; those who commuted on their second engagement would enter the second reserve, joining the 14,000 pensioners. Peel also envisaged that one-quarter of the Militia establishment of 120,000 men would be tempted to enter the first reserve by the offer of a double bounty. From these relatively modest and inexpensive proposals, he sought a reserve of 80,000 men.[105] *The Daily News* applauded the General for eschewing any crude imitation of the Prussian model, but perceived the complete inadequacy of his recommendations. Given the recruiting shortfall, it argued, the loss of these soldiers could 'seriously embarrass our active army'. At the same time, it feared that the government, by failing to offer any reserve pay other than normal Militia rates, would attract a derisory number of reservists. The forecast proved abundantly correct. By 1870, the first reserve numbered 1,939, the second reserve 18,528, and the Militia reserve 19,916.[107] Cardwell, in short, inherited a totally inadequate army reserve.

In the post-Crimean years, several factors had determined the outcome of the reform campaigns. Wars or the threat of wars were of primary importance. The Crimean catastrophies had provided the initial spur; the wartime reporting had revealed dreadful shortcomings and had enabled reformers to find a receptive audience for their ideas during and immediately after the war. The invasion panic of 1859 and the dramatic rise of Prussia as a military power had a similar, though much less stunning, impact. By reviving press and Parliamentary interest in the state of the national defences, they had stimulated debate about the actual or supposed weaknesses of the armed forces, often provoking ministerial initiatives, if only to allay public anxieties. Imperial conflicts, on the other hand, aroused fewer fears and trepidations. These conflicts neither threatened the security of Britain, nor reproduced the Crimean scale of administrative blunders, nor resulted in humiliating defeats. The quelling of the Indian Mutiny, followed by martial triumphs in China (1860), the North-West Frontier (1863), New Zealand (1860-64), and Abyssinia (1868) only revived confidence in the overseas forces.

The tactical skills of the army reformers contributed considerably to the prospects of their respective campaigns. The abortive Parliamentary motions which De Lacy Evans repeatedly moved against the purchase system contrasted sharply with the pressure exerted through the press, Parliament, and private channels by the health reformers. The difference reflected more than mere presentation and debating flair. Unlike the purchase abolitionists, with the possible exception of Sir Charles Trevelyan, the health reformers had constructed a viable alternative to the existing system and had campaigned in an essentially positive manner. In one critical respect, of course, their campaign faced much less daunting opposition: in promoting the objectives of improved sanitary and health care, they were not likely to interfere with the Royal prerogative. Facing the opposition of the Crown and the Horse Guards, the purchase abolitionists required a sympathetic ear and active support from the War Office: they never received it.

Where the Horse Guards and the Crown, or more specifically Prince Albert, favoured reform, this was immensely helpful. Their endeavours, coupled with the support of the War Office, and the advocacy of Herbert, gave a powerful impetus to educational reform. But even this triumvirate was not invariably successful; officially sponsored reforms could and did founder. Ministers had to carry the House of Commons, and if the Members remained unconvinced, and sufficiently obdurate, schemes like the amalgamation of Sandhurst and Woolwich could sink into oblivion. Quite apart from any deeply held opinions about the merits or demerits of particular schemes, Members were concerned about the cost involved. They would approve relatively inexpensive measures, like constituting the Volunteers and establishing General Peel's reserve, but baulk at the expenditure required to abolish purchase.

Finally Members of Parliament, like the press, were susceptible to movements in the climate of opinion. The salience of army reform as a national issue diminished rapidly towards the end of the 1850s. As memories of the Crimea receded, the intensity of the wartime outrage burned less and less fiercely, save in the breasts of a few indomitable reformers. Although Florence Nightingale remained a resolute and formidable campaigner, her influence waned markedly in the 1860s: her shoals of letters and protests no longer worried a securely entrenched and blissfully complacement War Office. Nevertheless the movement of opinion had not been entirely fruitless. The House of Commons, after many years of debating amendments to the Annual Mutiny Bills, had voted by one vote in 1867, and then decisively, by twenty-five votes, in 1868, to abolish flogging. Ratification of Disraeli's Reform Bill in August 1867 had probably influenced the vote, and the readiness of the government to accept the vote. In moving the abolitionist motion, on 26 March 1868, Arthur J. Otway reminded the House that it had 'admitted the fathers and brothers of the nation's soldiers within the pale of the Constitution'; it should now, he continued, 'endeavour to elevate, instead of degrade the soldier, and make him feel he is the armed citizen of a free country'.[108]

Flogging was an exceptional issue, however. It had always aroused fierce passions. It would not cost anything to abolish. By 1868, it could have, or so the abolitionists claimed, a possible impact upon electoral politics. Other army reforms paled by comparison. Even the abolition of purchase, which George Otto Trevelyan revived as a Parliamentary issue in 1867-68,[109] never excited the same controversy. To abolish purchase, in any case, would prove horrendously expensive, and on that count alone was hardly an electoral asset. By the late 1860s, army reform was no longer perceived, other than by a dwindling body of reformers, as an issue of pressing national significance. So complete an erosion of interest left Edward Cardwell with enormous scope as well as some formidable problems.

Notes and references

1. J. W. Fortescue, *op. cit.*, Vol. XIII, p. 524.
2. See above, Chapter 4, pp. 155-6.
3. *Reynolds's Newspaper,* 9 Mar. 1856, p. 9.
4. *The Times,* 15 Nov. 1856, p. 9.
5. The Purchase Commission 1857, *op. cit.*, p. xxx.
6. *Ibid.*, pp. xxxii-xxxiv.
7. *Ibid.*, p. xxxvi.
8. *Report of the Right Hon. Edward Ellice M.P., Lieut.-General Edward Buckley Wynyard, C.B., and Major-General Sir Henry John Bentinck, K.C.B.*, C.2,292, 1857-58, XIX.
9. *Report of the Commissioners Appointed to Inquire Into the Present System of Recruiting In the Army,* C.2,762, 1861, XV, p. 328.

10. *The United Service Gazette,* 20 Jan. 1855, p. 4 and 17 Mar. 1855, p. 4, and *The Naval and Military Gazette,* 28 July 1855, p. 473.
11. *The Naval and Military Gazette,* 22 Aug. 1857, p. 536 and 10 Mar. 1860, p. 152.
12. *The United Service Gazette,* 17 May 1862, p. 4. See also 22 Aug. 1857, p. 4, and 10 Mar. 1860, p. 4.
13. *The Times,* 14 Nov. 1861, p. 6, and 2 June 1862, p. 5.
14. Sir W. Mansfield to Viscount Goderich, March 1855, Ripon Mss., B.M. Add. Mss. 43,619, f. 2 and *The United Service Gazette,* 7 June 1862, p. 4.
15. S. Herbert to the Duke of Cambridge, 7 Dec. 1859, Cambridge Mss., R.A., Add. Mss., E/1/2,454.
16. *Ibid.*
17. Duke of Cambridge to S. Herbert, 10 Dec. 1859, Cambridge Mss., R.A., Add. Mss., E/1/2,462.
18. **A. P. C. Bruce,** *The system of purchase and sale of commissions in the British army and the campaign for its abolition 1660-1871,* unpublished Ph.D. thesis, University of Manchester, 1973, p. 329.
19. Queen Victoria to Lord Palmerston, 4 Mar. 1860, Broadlands Mss., RC/F/941.
20. Prince Albert to S. Herbert, 3 Feb. 1860, Herbert Mss., Wilton House, Wilton. Quotations are by permission of Lord Pembroke and Dr James Provan, who is currently preparing a biography of Sidney Herbert.
21. Queen Victoria to Lord Palmerston, 4 and 5 Mar. 1860, Broadlands Mss., RC/F/941, 943.
22. S. Herbert to Lord Palmerston, 5 Mar. 1860, Broadlands Mss., GC/HE/62.
23. *Parl. Deb.*, Third Ser., Vol. 157, 6 Mar. 1860, col. 49.
24. *The Times,* 6 Mar. 1860, p. 9, and 8 Mar. 1860, pp. 8-9.
25. *Parl. Deb.*, Third Ser., Vol. 157, 6 Mar. 1860, col. 41.
26. *Parl. Deb.*, Third Ser., Vol. 157, 23 Mar. 1860, cols. 1,140-1.
27. *The Times,* 31 May 1862, p. 11.
28. S. Herbert to Viscount Hardinge, Jan. 1854, Appendix 5 to the *Report from the Select Committee on Sandhurst Royal Military College,* hereafter referred to as the Sandhurst Report, C.317, 1854-55, XII.
29. Evidence (Q.1,277) before the Sandhurst Committee.
30. Evidence (Qs.2,292-2,293) before the Sandhurst Committee.
31. Appendix 3, Sandhurst Report, p. 189.
32. *Report of the Commissioners appointed to consider the best mode of re-organizing the system for Training Officers and for the scientific corps.* C.57, 1857 Sess. 1, VI, pp. xix-xl.
33. *The Naval and Military Gazette,* 3 Jan. 1857, p. 10; 17 Jan. 1857, p. 42, and 28 Mar. 1857, p. 202.

34. **B. J. Bond,** *The Victorian Army and the Staff College, 1854-1914,* Eyre Methuen, London, 1972, pp. 58, 64, 75.
35. *Parl. Deb.*, Third Ser., Vol. 142, 5 June 1856, cols. 980-1,001.
36. J. H. Lefroy, 'On the Organization of a Department of Military Education', 8 Nov. 1856, Dalhousie Muniments, S.R.O., GD 45/8/388.
37. Lord Panmure to Lord Palmerston, 19 Jan. 1857, *The Panmure Papers,* Vol. 2, pp. 337-8.
38. Lord Panmure to Queen Victoria, 15 Feb. 1857, and Queen Victoria to Lord Panmure, 17 Feb. 1857, *The Panmure Papers,* Vol. 2, pp. 352-4, 355-6.
39. General Order no. 685 cited in **Brevet-Major A. R. Godwin-Austen,** *The Staff and the Staff College,* Constable, London, 1927, pp. 97-9.
40. *Parl. Deb.*, Third Ser., Vol. 147, 28 July 1857, cols. 569-608.
41. Report of the Purchase Commission 1857, *op. cit.*, p. xxxiv.
42. B. J. Bond, *op. cit.*, p. 73.
43. *Parl. Deb.*, Third Ser., Vol. 149, 26 Apr. 1858, col. 1,726.
44. Duke of Cambridge to Lord Panmure, 29 Apr. 1858, Dalhousie Muniments, S.R.O., GD 45/14/759.
45. *Parl. Deb.*, Third Ser., Vol. 142, 5 June 1856, cols. 992-3 and Lord Stanmore, *op. cit.*, Vol. II, p. 385.
46. *The United Service Gazette,* 25 May 1861, p. 4.
47. *The Press,* 15 Mar. 1862, p. 1.
48. *Parl. Deb.*, Third Ser., Vol. 142, 5 June 1856, cols. 1,021-2.
49. *The Naval and Military Gazette,* 2 Oct. 1858, pp. 633-4 and *The Saturday Review,* 7 May 1859, p. 557.
50. *Parl. Deb.*, Third Ser., Vol. 149, 26 Apr. 1858, cols. 1,726-7.
51. C. Woodham-Smith, *Florence Nightingale,* p. 289.
52. *Ibid.*, p. 309.
53. Evidence (Q.52) before the Army Sanitary Commission, *op. cit.*, and *The Times*, 21 May 1862, p. 5. See also Dr A. Smith to S. Herbert, 14 Sept. 1853, Herbert Mss., III A 62(a).
54. *The Times,* 9 May 1856, p. 6, and *Parl. Deb.*, Third Ser., Vol. 142, 19 June 1856, cols. 1,706-12.
55. Report of the Army Sanitary Commission, *op. cit.*, p. lxxvi.
56. S. Herbert to Lord Panmure, 7 Aug. 1857, quoted in Lord Stanmore, *op. cit.*, Vol. II, pp. 133-4.
57. S. Herbert to Lord Panmure, 11 Nov. 1857, quoted in Lord Stanmore, *op. cit.*, Vol. II, pp. 136-7.
58. C. Woodham-Smith, *Florence Nightingale,* pp. 310-11, and Florence Nightingale to S. Herbert, 12 Mar. 1858, Nightingale Mss., B.M. Add. Ms. 43,395, ff. 5-6.
59. *The Times,* 8 Feb. 1858, p. 8.
60. **J. T. Howell,** 'The Health of the Army', *The Edinburgh Review,* **108**, No. 219, July 1858, p. 154. See also **S. Herbert,** 'The Sanitary Condition of the Army', *The Westminster Review,*

71, Jan. 1859, pp. 52–98; **A. Wynter,** 'The Lodging, Food, and Dress of Soldiers', *The Quarterly Review,* **105**, No. 209, Jan. 1859, pp. 155–76; **J. H. Burton,** 'The Soldier And The Surgeon', *Blackwood's Edinburgh Magazine,* **84**, No. 513, July 1858, pp. 136–65.

61. *Parl. Deb.*, Third Ser., Vol. 149, 26 Mar. 1858, cols. 798, 802–3.
62. *Parl. Deb.*, Third Ser., Vol. 150, 12 May 1858, cols. 473–95.
63. *Statement by Members of the Board of Examiners of Candidates for the Army Medical Department, with reference to the Report of Committee upon that Department,* C.2,213, 1878–79, XLIV, p. 3.
64. **J. L. Brand**, *Doctors and the State*, Johns Hopkins Press, Baltimore, 1965, p. 139.
65. *General Report of the Commission appointed for Improving the Sanitary Condition of Barracks and Hospitals,* C.2,839, 1861, XVI, pp. 34, 155–7.
66. *P.P.*, C.22, 1861, XXXVI, p. 101 and C.50, 1864, XXXV, p. 49.
67. W. E. Gladstone to S. Herbert, 26 Jan. 1861, Gladstone Mss., B.M. Add. Mss. 44,211, f. 258 and Lord Stanmore, *op. cit.*, Vol. II, pp. 359–60.
68. *P.P.*, C.126, 1862, XXXII, p. 708; *The Times,* 15 Apr. 1862, pp. 8–9; *P.P.*, C.3,404, 1864, XXXVI, p. 6.
69. F. B. Smith, 'Ethics and disease in the later nineteenth century: the Contagious Diseases Acts', *Historical Studies,* **15**, No. 57, Oct. 1971, pp. 119–21.
70. Florence Nightingale to D. Galton, 25 June 1861, Nightingale Mss., B.M. Add. Mss. 45,759, f. 236.
71. Florence Nightingale to J. Sutherland, 22 Aug. 1870, Nightingale Mss., B.M. Add. Mss. 45,755, ff. 40–1. For accounts of the campaign, see **E. M. Sigsworth and T. J. Wyke,** 'A study of Victorian prostitution and venereal disease', *Suffer and Be Still: Women In the Victorian Age,* ed. M. Vicinus, Indiana University Press, Bloomington, 1973, pp. 94–9, and J. L'Esperance, 'The work of the Ladies' National Association For The Repeal Of The Contagious Diseases Acts', *Bulletin of the Society for the Study of Labour History,* **26**, Spring 1973, pp. 13–15.
72. *Parl. Deb.*, Third Ser., Vol. 138, 4 May 1855, cols. 127–8; Vol. 139, 6 July 1858, cols. 540–1; Vol. 141, 7 Apr. 1856, cols. 566–86.
73. *The Naval and Military Gazette,* 11 Aug. 1855, p. 507; *The United Service Gazette,* 1 Sept. 1855, p. 4, and *Parl. Deb.*, Third Ser., Vol. 140, 29 Feb. 1856, cols. 1,577–8.
74. *Reynolds's Newspaper,* 25 Oct. 1857, p. 8 and *The Daily News,* 15 Dec. 1859, p. 4.
75. *Report of the Commissioners appointed to enquire into the*

Establishment, Organization, government and direction of the militia, hereafter referred to as the Militia Commission, C.2,553, 1859 Sess. 2, IX.

76. **C. A. C. Keeson,** *The History and Records of Queen Victoria's Rifles 1792–1922,* Constable, London, 1923, p. 492.
77. **I. W. F. Beckett,** *The English Rifle Volunteer movement, 1859–1908,* unpublished Ph.D. dissertation, University of London, 1975, pp. 23–4, and C. A. C. Keeson, *op. cit.,* pp. 504–19.
78. **B. Rose,** 'The Volunteers of 1859', *J.S.A.H.R.,* **37**, 1959, p. 100, and **Captain J. Orr,** *History of the Seventh Lanarkshire Rifle Volunteers,* Anderson, Glasgow, 1884, p. 9.
79. I. W. F. Beckett, *op. cit.,* p. 24.
80. *The Times,* 22 Sept. 1857, p. 8.
81. The Duke of Cambridge to Lord Panmure, 25 Sept. and 2 Oct. 1857, *The Panmure Papers,* Vol. 2, pp. 435, 439.
82. Lord Panmure to the Duke of Cambridge, 6 Oct. 1857, *The Panmure Papers,* Vol. 2, p. 444.
83. Evidence (Qs.6,572, 6,574) before the Militia Commission, *op. cit.*
84. **T. Martin,** *The Life of His Royal Highness the Prince Consort,* 5 vols., Smith Elder, London, 1879, Vol. 4, p. 278.
85. **H. Cunningham,** *The Volunteer Force: a Social and Political History 1859–1908,* Croom Helm, London, 1975, p. 7.
86. *The Times,* 19 Apr. 1859, p. 9.
87. *Parl. Deb.,* Third Ser., Vol. 155, 5 July 1859, cols. 689–92.
88. T. Martin, *op. cit.,* Vol. 4, pp. 436–7; **R. P. Berry,** *A History of the Formation and Development of the Volunteer Infantry,* Simpkin Marshall, London, 1903, pp. 125–8.
89. S. Herbert to Lord Tweeddale, n.d., quoted in Lord Stanmore, *op. cit.,* Vol. II, p. 389.
90. *Parl. Deb.,* Third Ser., Vol. 156, 26 Jan. 1860, cols. 158–9.
91. *The Times,* 10 Apr. 1860, p. 10.
92. *The Nonconformist,* 7 Dec. 1859, p. 978.
93. In Lancashire in 1862 it was reckoned that an officer's annual expenses, excluding his uniform, would be £50. Evidence (Q.2,707) before *The Commissioners appointed to inquire into the condition of the volunteer force,* C.3,053, 1862, XXVII.
94. **N. Tailliefer,** *Rondeaux of the Auxiliary Forces, Militia and Volunteers,* Lucas, London, 1883, p. 94, and H. Cunningham, *op. cit.,* pp. 60–1.
95. H. Cunningham, *op. cit.,* pp. 18–50.
96. *The Morning Star and Dial,* 18 Oct. 1861, p. 4; *Parl. Deb.,* Third Ser., Vol. 163, 7 June 1861, col. 805.
97. **A. J. Semple,** 'The Fenian infiltration of the British army', *J.S.A.H.R.,* 52, 1974, pp. 133–60.
98. **Sir J. H. A. Macdonald,** *Fifty Years of It: the Experiences and*

Struggles of a Volunteer of 1859, Blackwood, Edinburgh, 1909, p. 149.

99. **J. Luvaas,** *The Military Legacy of the Civil War – The European Inheritance,* University of Chicago Press, Chicago, 1959, p. 115.
100. *The Times,* 16 Aug. 1866, p. 8.
101. *The Times,* 23 Aug. 1866, p. 6.
102. Evidence (Qs.1,523–1,525, 630, 1,312) before the *Commission appointed to inquire into the recruiting for the army,* hereafter referred to as the Panmure Recruiting Commission, C.3,752, 1867, XV.
103. Evidence (Qs. 2,398–2,399) before the Panmure Recruiting Commission, *op. cit.*
104. Report of the Panmure Recruiting Commission, *op. cit.*, pp. xv–xvi.
105. *Parl. Deb.*, Third Ser., Vol. 185, 7 Mar. 1867, cols. 1,463–9.
106. *The Daily News,* 9 Mar. 1867, p. 4.
107. **B. J. Bond,** 'Prelude to the Cardwell reforms 1856–1868', *Journal of the R.U.S.I.,* **106**, May 1961, p. 236; *Detailed Statement of the present strength of the Army of Reserve,* C.104,1870, XLII, p. 1.
108. *Parl. Deb.*, Third Ser., Vol. 191, 28 Mar. 1868, cols. 322–3.
109. *Parl. Deb.*, Third Ser., Vol. 186, 30 Apr. 1867, cols. 1,787–825, and Vol. 192, 19 May 1868, cols. 514–78.

7 The Cardwell Reforms

Edward Cardwell was Secretary of State for War from December 1868 to February 1874. During his term of office, the organization of the army was transformed completely. Short-service enlistment was introduced, enabling the formation and growth of a new army reserve. Purchase was abolished. The so-called 'dual government' of the army was ended; all duties of the War department were formally centralized under the Secretary of State. The home army was localized; regiments were accorded specific territorial areas and were affiliated to the local auxiliary forces. Regiments were supposed to establish permanent local connections and to find their recruits from within these areas. Although the Estimates were cut, the strength of the home army was increased by twenty-five battalions and by 156 field guns. In reviewing these achievements, the hagiographer of Cardwell has claimed 'that a system was introduced, where no system could be said to have existed before'.[1]

Army reform had not figured prominently in the general election campaign of 1868. The Liberal party, which was swept into office with a majority of 112 seats, had not assailed the government over the state of the armed forces. Neither Gladstone, the leader of the Liberal party, nor the Marquess of Hartington, the Liberal spokesman on military matters, nor Cardwell himself had stressed army reform in their campaign speeches. Gladstone, in his speaking tour of South-West Lancashire, rarely mentioned the armed services other than to condemn the profligate expenditure of the Conservative government. He even condemned the £500,000 spent in augmenting the rates of pay of the ordinary soldier.[2] The Marquess of Hartington, though willing to endorse the recent spending upon pay and arms; was no less critical of 'the spirit of laxity and extravagance' in the expenditure upon the army and navy.[3] Cardwell, the former Colonial Secretary (1864–66), barely mentioned the army in his campaign speeches. Only raising the topic on three occasions, and very briefly in each instance, he argued that the next government should withdraw troops from the colonies and should seek enhanced efficiency while reducing military expenditure.[4] Viewing the campaign from the Horse Guards, the Duke of Cambridge was understandably perturbed. As he informed Lord Dalhousie, he feared retrenchment and not reform: 'Gladstone & Bright', he wrote, 'seem determined to cut us down vigorously'.[5]

Although the Liberal emphasis upon retrenchment would be reflected in Cardwell's early Estimates, his administration would embark upon far-reaching and, in one instance, very expensive reforms. To resolve the apparent contradiction, some historians have argued that Cardwell had made 'a careful study' of army reform long before he took office.[6] They base their assertion upon a memorandum, entitled 'The Army', which Cardwell sent to Gladstone on the day the new premier was interviewed by the Queen. Admittedly the memorandum, dated 3 December 1868, confirms that Cardwell had thought recently about army problems. Two-thirds of the document is devoted to the administration of the War Office, particularly the evidence which was submitted eight years previously to a Select Committee of Enquiry. The remaining third, about 550 words in length, merely outlined subjects like the appointment and promotion of officers, recruiting, and retirement which could be raised in the House of Commons. The government, argued Cardwell, could not adopt 'a merely passive attitude' towards these issues, but had to be willing to investigate them with the aim of increasing efficiency while decreasing expenditure. Cardwell did not indicate in the memorandum how these objectives could be realized; a month in office elapsed before he submitted specific proposals to Gladstone.[7]

It would have been surprising had Cardwell entered office with preprepared proposals. He had never shown any previous interest in military matters. He had not participated in the purchase debates of the 1860s. He had even been appalled at the prospect of entering the War Office, when the appointment had been mooted by Lord Russell in October 1865. Henry Austin Bruce reported a conversation with Cardwell, in which he 'dwelt much upon his horror of the War Office: he will fight hard to escape it'.[8] Indeed he might have escaped the post in 1868, had not Lord Hartington been rejected by the constituents of North Lancashire. Once the vacancy appeared, Cardwell seems to have suppressed his former horror of the War Office; the memorandum of 3 December was almost certainly a bid for a senior cabinet post. For Gladstone, Cardwell had several advantages as a prospective Secretary of State for War. He was a man of proven administrative competence, who had handled financial problems with considerable expertise. He was an old Peelite ally. He held a seat in the House of Commons. He had never promoted contentious army reforms and had not, as a consequence, incurred the displeasure of the Queen and her cousin. Having feared the appointment of Bright as Secretary of State,[9] the Duke of Cambridge could only welcome the choice of Cardwell.

Appointed in December 1868, the new Secretary of State had to focus immediately upon the Army Estimates, due for presentation in the following March. Free from any external pressure to introduce reform, Cardwell concentrated upon reducing the size of the Estimates in accordance with the expectations of the premier and his cabinet colleagues. Promoting increased efficiency 'at a greatly reduced cost' was, in any case, his own priority. In the hope of realizing this objective, he sent a list of proposals to Gladstone in a letter dated 9 January 1869. He proposed to reduce the army abroad from 50,000 to 26,000 men. He recommended that the Militia should be reorganized by officering it with half-pay regular officers, placing it under the discipline of the War Office, and training it with the army. He hoped to weed out the inefficient Volunteer Corps, training the remainder, more frequently than hitherto, with the Militia and regulars. Cardwell anticipated little opposition to the most important of these changes, the withdrawal of troops from overseas. Encouraging colonial self-reliance had been the policy of successive governments; he was merely acting upon their precedent. He perceived, however, that the withdrawal of troops from distant stations, which would save a considerable sum of money, would also facilitate the reorganization of the home army. Protracted periods of overseas service, he believed, had discouraged enlistment from 'the more respectable portions of the population' and had thwarted any attempt to reduce the period of enlistment. Short service, he affirmed, was essential to improve the army and realize further economies. Reducing the period of Colours service to 'five or seven years' would ensure that the army contained only soldiers 'in the prime of life'. It would also facilitate the formation of a reserve of ex-regulars from the civil population, and slash the pension vote by nearly £1,500,000.[10] Gladstone was delighted with the letter: 'It is really like seeing a little daylight after all these years, and a return to reason from what has been anything except reason'.[11]

The Duke of Cambridge was not so enamoured. He deplored the removal of so many troops from colonial stations, the abandonment of some overseas garrisons, and the reduction in the size of the cadre establishments. Although he concurred with Cardwell that reducing the number of men in a cadre was preferable to reducing whole battalions, the Duke disliked the idea of infantry battalions which numbered 560 rank and file. Once raw recruits were deducted, he doubted that the ranks would contain more than 300 men - 'a very sorry account for a Regiment of Infantry which may be called upon for service in Ireland, or for any other special duty'.[12] He feared, too, for the effectiveness of the overseas battalions, even though they would be slightly larger in number and would not include any new recruits. These battalions, he suspected, might not remain effective units once disease and dissipation had taken their toll. Aware that the Reserve could not be mobilized for small colonial wars or localized emergencies, he wished to preserve as large a body of men in the ranks as possible.[13]

Cardwell was not dissuaded. For his fifteen months in office, he sought to implement his original proposals. On 11 March 1869 he introduced his first Estimates. He announced a saving of £1,196,650 over the previous year, the product of troop withdrawals from the colonies and the reduction of battalion establishments. He outlined the first stages of reform: his desire to introduce short-service enlistments, to abolish the Militia property qualification, to enhance the efficiency of the Volunteers. His speech was well received. Sir John Pakington, his Conservative predecessor, proffered congratulations. Colonel Lloyd-Lindsay and Lord Elcho, who would soon become trenchant critics, praised him warmly. Only George Anderson, a radical, embarrassed by the chorus of Conservative approval, deprecated the Estimates. He demanded larger reductions by the removal of military sinecures, especially those held by Royalty. As Anderson's philippic attracted little interest and less support, Cardwell was able to conclude the debate by thanking the Committee of Supply 'for the marked kindness with which it had received his statement'.[14]

Nevertheless Cardwell would encounter opposition from Parliament, some sections of the press, and the Horse Guards. Advocates of a national army, though favouring the trend of Cardwell's proposals, urged him to go much further. *The Pall Mall Gazette* insisted that the Reserves should be made effective (if necessary by introducing a Militia ballot), with all regiments localized, on the Prussian model.[15] Lords Monck and Elcho espoused similar views in the Lords and Commons respectively, but neither gained any significant support. Cardwell rejected the ideas as too drastic and unnecessary; Sir John Pakington echoed these sentiments from the Conservative benches.[16] Introducing compulsion through the Militia ballot had neither party nor mass support; indeed it had very little appeal in the relatively tranquil international atmosphere. Cardwell overcame this opposition without any difficulty.

More troublesome opposition came from the radical wing of the Liberal party and from its editorial supporters. They disliked the style of Cardwell's administration, the size of his financial savings, and the scope of his proposed reforms. Cardwell never inspired enthusiasm as a ministerial spokesman. Neither an impressive orator nor a partisan politician, he delivered his Parliamentary pronouncements in a calm, deliberate and unemotional manner. His arguments betrayed neither prejudice nor passion, and seemed merely the product of a careful, pragmatic approach to his administrative duties. When Cardwell confirmed the abolition of flogging in the peacetime army, he did so in a manner so dispassionate that *The Daily Telegraph* feared for his lack of 'backbone'.[17] Radical Members of Parliament like James White and George Anderson derided the size of Cardwell's financial savings.[18] Others, including George Otto Trevelyan, exhorted him to undermine the bastions of privilege and aristocratic influence within the army. They urged him to limit the tenure of the Duke of Cambridge as Commander-in-Chief.[19] Even more incensed at the Secretary of State were the radical and religious activists who campaigned throughout his term of office against the Contagious Diseases Acts.

Equally distressed by the policies of Cardwell were the Horse Guards and the military press. *The United Service Gazette* and *The Naval and Military Gazette* deplored the scale of the troop reductions and the passion for economy which had gripped the Government.[20] The Duke of Cambridge criticized not only the reductions but the whole trend of Cardwellian thinking, especially the belief in short-service enlistments and in an Army Reserve. The Duke doubted that the organization of the army could be improved upon. He never admitted that long-service recruiting had failed to meet the manpower needs of the army in the 1860s. Arguing from his premise that 'Changes are always bad, and . . . should not be made without a pressing necessity', he dismissed the Reserve as simply a 'popular' error, derived from the desire to amass large bodies of men in the Continental fashion. Continental armies, he noted, could raise vast numbers of men because they were based on conscription. Short-service men, raised by voluntary enlistment, would never compare, in his opinion; once they had left the Colours, they would be '*lost* to the State' and could not be relied upon to turn out at a moment of danger. He preferred to depend upon the Militia, if necessary to increase the size of the Militia Reserve, created by General Peel, by augmenting the numbers eligible for the increased bounty.[21]

When Cardwell, in November 1869, mooted the possibility of modifying the purchase system, the Duke was adamantly opposed to reform. In reply to Cardwell's query about whether he would prefer to commence selection from the rank of captain or of major, the Commander-in-Chief chose the senior rank, but reiterated at length, his opposition to any change of system. If it was the aim of Cardwell, in raising the issue, to ascertain whether the Duke had modified his well-known views, he was grievously disappointed. The Duke reaffirmed that purchase, 'however theoretically objectionable', had attracted gentlemen into the officer corps, and had kept the officers young in years. Abolishing purchase, he added, would prove extremely expensive. He doubted that selection would ever be feasible as a method of promotion; he did not believe that officers could be selected from an army scattered all over the world, performing a host of different duties. The only alternative, he concluded, would be promotion by 'strict seniority', which would have to be coupled with new retirement provisions to ensure that serving officers remained young and efficient.[22]

Cardwell was not perturbed by the early criticism of his proposals. He had the support of his cabinet colleagues and of an overwhelming bi-partisan majority in the Commons. *The Times,* too, was a fervent supporter. Of all the policy commitments of the Liberal government, it believed that 'none has given more satisfaction to the public than that which relates to the Military and Naval Services'.[23]

Cardwell would receive further accolades for the Estimates he introduced on 3 March 1870. He announced a saving of £1,136,900 and the withdrawal of another 10,561 men from the colonies. By reducing the colonial strength to 25,709 men, he had redeemed his pledges of the previous session. Although there was grumbling from the Conservative benches about the size of the reductions and the weakened state of the residual forces, the policy itself was widely endorsed.[24] *The Times* waxed lyrical: the saving of £2,230,800 since 1868–69 had 'an eloquence to which nothing need be added', the reorganization would ensure that the army was not 'frittered away in Colonial Garrisons, but massed at home, where it may learn the art of war, and not merely the details of drill and the routine of barrack life'.[25]

From his speech of 3 March 1870, however, Cardwell encountered his first serious rebuff. He proposed, as part of his reductions, to abolish the ranks of cornet and ensign and to appoint all new officers at the rank of lieutenant. The idea was not original. It had been devised by Sir John Pakington, approved by the Conservative cabinet, and endorsed by the Queen. Only the defeat of Disraeli's Government in the general election had prevented its presentation before Parliament. The idea suited Cardwell as he planned to reduce the number of subalterns per battalion from twenty to fourteen. He proposed that the ten senior lieutenants should remain with the ten companies, and that the four supernumeraries, required to cover any vacancies caused by sickness or leave, should hold the same rank, but, as junior officers, should receive an ensign's pay. As the proposal would abolish the first rank of the purchase ladder, he requested that officers, who had already purchased their commissions as an ensign or a cornet, should be compensated at the regulation rate. He estimated that the cost of the compensation would be £509,500. A byproduct of the plan, he argued, would be a modest reform of the purchase system, diminishing the ultimate cost of abolishing the system 'if ever it is wound up'.[26]

Although Cardwell deplored the purchase system, he did not propose, at this time, to abolish it, nor even to move towards the termination of a system 'so perplexing and so embarrassing'.[27] He had introduced the abolition of the ranks of cornet and ensign as a non-contentious measure. As it had originated with Sir John Pakington, a known defender of the purchase system, and as it derived from a policy of reducing cadre establishments already accepted by the House of Commons, Cardwell did not anticipate the opposition which erupted. Both in the House of Commons and among some officers,[28] protests were immediately aired. From the radical benches, Cardwell was criticized for failing to tackle the root of the problem, the purchase system itself. From the other side of the House, Lord Eustace Cecil protested that Cardwell had made no provision for the repayment of over-regulation sums. A week later, on 10 March, Colonel C. W. White requested a postponement of the issue until officers in the purchase regiments could have 'an opportunity of meeting and deliberating'.[29] Confronted by such unexpected opposition, and by a cabinet refusal to authorize any over-regulation payments,[30] Cardwell withdrew his proposal, and announced the establishment of a Royal Commission, headed by Sir George Grey, to investigate the subject.

In spite of this rebuff, Cardwell still retained considerable support for his declared policy objectives. During the same Parliamentary session, he realized his first major reform - the introduction of short-service enlistments. In his Estimates speech, he outlined the main innovations of the Army Enlistment Bill. He proposed that the first term of engagement should be twelve years, only part of which would be served in the Colours, the residue in the Reserve. For regiments about to go to India, he recommended that the period of service should be six years; for regiments at home, he reserved the right to reduce the service still further, to as little as three years. He stressed that the Bill had not been intended to replace the present mode of enlistment, merely to supplement it with the option of short service. In the first instance short service would only be applied to the infantry, not to the cavalry and artillery. Couching his statement in a cautious moderate manner, he would deny, throughout the course of the second reading debate, that he had any 'revolutionary' intentions. His aims were simply to form a Reserve, reduce the pension list, and induce, if possible, a different class of man to enter the army.[31]

The original reception of the short-service reform contrasted sharply with the controversy which would subsequently surround the topic. In 1870, the reform was immensely popular. By curtailing substantially the size of the pension vote, it was hailed as an important measure of retrenchment. The prospect of a much larger Reserve mollified the critics of Cardwellian policy: *The Pall Mall Gazette* welcomed the measure as a step towards a national army.[32] *The Times,* although doubtful that the army could attract sufficient recruits on a six years' enlistment, lauded the plan as it seemed likely to mitigate the distinction between a military and a civil career.[33] Some reservations were aired in the House of Commons. Major Dickson feared that the army would be fatally weakened if composed of men 'young in service and young in years'. And Major-General Sir Percy Herbert perceptively queried whether '1*s* 2*d* per day would obtain a better class of men for six years than 1*s* 2*d* per day did now'.[34] Such reservations were confidently swept aside; the Bill was passed after a short debate without a division.

The Army Enlistment Act of 1870 did not, as some commentators have alleged,[35] establish a standard period of six years' service in the Colours, followed by six years' in the Reserve. That was the original infantry requirement, but the terms were flexible and could be varied according to the policies of the War Office and the Treasury. Apart from the infantry, the original enlistment terms were eight years in the Colours and four years in the Reserve. During the 1870s, one quarter of the total enlistment, including non-commissioned officers, were still recruited for long service, that is for twelve years in the Colours; one half of the artillery recruits enlisted for long service.[36] Cardwell had hoped, nonetheless, that the appeal of the army as a career would be enhanced by the advent of the short-service soldier. Having enlisted at the age of eighteen or twenty, the soldier would return to civilian life at about twenty-five or twenty-seven, still able to work if he could find employment. For the duration of his Reserve service, he would be paid 4*d* a day, so remaining liable to recall and to a short period of training with the regulars and the Militia of his brigade district. Without the deterrent of protracted overseas service, it was claimed that the scheme would sustain a steady supply of recruits and, hopefully, a better quality as well.

Creating a Reserve of 60,000 men was the objective of introducing short service. Theoretically the Reserve would enable the Wa Office to maintain existing cadres at lower establishments, yet still retain the capacity to expand them quickly should a national emergency arise. The Reserve, in other words, would not be a reserve *per se,* merely a means by which the home-based units could be brought up to their war establishment. The weakness of the concept was clearly foreseen by the Duke of Cambridge. Writing to Cardwell, in January 1870, he stressed 'that, though we hope nominally to have a Reserve of men, the Reserve does not really belong to Regiments, & can only be incorporated with them in the breaking out of a war. Consequently, in times of emergency or anxiety short of war, we can do nothing but recruit up, & we may have difficulty in obtaining them'.[37] When emergencies or small wars arose, expeditionary forces had to be formed by 'raiding' different battalions for experienced men, a practice regularly adopted by Sir Garnet Wolseley throughout the 1870s and 1880s. As the practice contradicted the concept of regimental *esprit de corps,* it became a source of heated controversy within the army and a focal point of the army reform debates. Nevertheless a Reserve materialized over the next few decades; it emerged as a fit and reliable body of men, approximately 80,000 strong, by the end of the century.

The Army Enlistment Act was much less successful in securing a steady flow of recruits and attracting a better class of man into the army. To realize this objective, the Cardwell administration had bolstered the Act by several reforms of the recruiting service. It had abolished the payment of bounties and the provision of escorts for new recruits. Recruiting sergeants were told to eschew public houses and to refrain from enlisting men with bad characters. Soldiers were prohibited from re-engaging once they had left the service. Efforts were made, in other words, to modify the elements of fraud, deception and dissipation associated with the recruiting process. These measures, however, neither ensured a steadier supply of recruits nor raised the status and appeal of an army career. In the first place,

Parliament voted supply on an annual basis, hence the Estimates and the establishments varied from year to year. The recruiting intake varied accordingly, rising from 11,739 in 1869 to over 23,000 in 1870 and 1871 (the years of the Franco-Prussian War), before it dropped to 17,371 in 1872. In January 1874, Cardwell estimated that over 32,000 recruits would be required annually, to build up the Reserve and maintain the supply of drafts and reliefs to the overseas garrisons: he ruefully added that 'the number obtained in 1873 has been only half'.[38] Although recruiting improved numerically in the 1880s, there was little evidence of a new class of man being attracted to the Colours. Not only were the rates of pay unattractive, but the difficulties of ex-soldiers finding employment proved a real deterrent. Fortescue recalled that the first batch of Reservists was not well received; he remembered 'swarms of them begging in the streets of London'.[39]

The other piece of legislation completed in 1870 was the passage of the War Office Act. Since the hasty reorganization of the department during the Crimean War, the relationship between the Horse Guards and the War Office had never been precisely defined. A Select Committee, chaired by Sir James Graham, examined the relationship in 1860. It found that the patents appointing the Secretaries of State had 'uniformly been couched in general terms, simply nominating them to office, without limitation of powers'.[40] It recommended that the traditional division of authority between the War Office and the Horse Guards should be maintained. It accepted, in effect, that the Duke of Cambridge, formally Field Marshal Commanding-in-Chief, should retain his authority, derived from the Crown as the ultimate Commander-in-Chief, over the command and discipline in the army. The Secretary of State would remain responsible for matters of finance, troop dispositions, the auxiliary forces, and all political decisions concerning the use of the army. The Committee declared that this division of authority would ensure that the patronage of the army remained in the hands of 'an officer independent of political pressure'.[41]

Preserving a division of authority merely provided scope for the periodic conflicts over policy which bedevilled relations between the Horse Guards and the War Office. Although these conflicts re-emerged in 1869, over the policy of colonial troop withdrawals, they did not arouse the interest of Cardwell in the constitutional question. Even before he entered office, he had decried the lack of clarity in the existing arrangement. As a lawyer, he disliked the ambiguities and the variety of interpretations which could be drawn from the patent of the Secretary of State. He agreed with Earl Grey that it was 'radically impossible to divide the administration of the Army into two parts', that this merely blurred the supreme control of the civil authority. He was aware, too, that it might be difficult to defend the compromise of 1860 before the reformed Parliament.[42] Radical Members of Parliament, like Trevelyan and James White, had never concealed their dislike of the Duke of Cambridge; they would resume their attacks on the system of 'dual government' and on the Duke personally in the early months of 1869.[43]

Once in office, Cardwell appointed Lord Northbrook, his Under-Secretary of State, to chair a War Office Committee, charged with investigating the conduct of business within the department. That Committee uncovered the excessive centralization, ill-defined responsibility, duplicated labour, and unnecessary checking within the War Office and the Horse Guards. It proposed that the whole army administration should be placed under one roof, with all departments subordinate and responsible to the Secretary of State. It recommended that the Commander-in-Chief should be relegated to the status of a military department, equal to the chiefs of the financial and control departments. It suggested that the Commander-in-Chief's staff should be drastically reduced, that the Military Secretary should become no more than a private secretary, and that the offices of Adjutant-General and Quartermaster-General should be amalgamated.[44]

Far from settling the constitutional question, the report, which was delivered in the autumn of 1869, left several issues unresolved. Gladstone noted that the report did not confirm a readiness on the part of the Duke of Cambridge to suffer a loss of authority, a point admitted by Northbrook himself.[45] The Queen disliked the implications of the Commander-in-Chief occupying rooms in the War Office. As she informed Cardwell, this would be to 'place him in evident subordination to the Secy. of State for War, & thus to lower his position in the eyes of the Army'.[46] The Duke of Cambridge was equally concerned. He protested that he should be no mere chief of staff under the Secretary of State; he demanded the retention of a separate department called the Horse Guards, and an unlimited tenure of office.[47] Cardwell and Gladstone accepted these stipulations. Indeed Cardwell assured the Queen that he 'had no desire to interfere with the command and discipline of the Troops': his sole desire was to establish the civil supremacy of the Secretary of State.[48] Cardwell, in effect, was hoist on his own petard. As he did not wish to concentrate ever more duties and authority in the hands of the Secretary of State, he left the Duke with the source of his authority intact - his powers over discipline, appointments, and promotion.

Based largely upon the recommendations of the Northbrook report, though the offices of Adjutant-General and Quartermaster-General were not amalgamated, the War Office Bill was introduced in the Commons in February 1870. It aroused little controversy and was passed relatively easily. The Act did not remove the likelihood of tension between the Secretary of State and the Commander-in-Chief. It probably guaranteed that business was conducted more expeditiously than hitherto, that the duplication of labour was modified, and that the appearance of 'dual government' of the army was removed. But in reality the assertion of supreme control was pointless. As *The Times* observed, there had not been a 'principle of "duality" in the administration of the British Army. . . . The military element is distinctly subordinate; the civil element distinctly supreme'.[49] Cardwell had been tilting at windmills when he imagined that a clear statement of principles and a new 'superstructure' within the department would ensure a more effective administrative arrangement. The Duke of Cambridge remained an immensely powerful figure, bolstered by his royal connections, limitless tenure of office, and enormous departmental responsibilities. Paradoxically, the Act had enhanced these responsibilities, perhaps as a gesture to soothe the sensibilities ruffled by the movement of offices. The Commander-in-Chief became responsible not only for the command and discipline of the army, but also for the Reserve Forces, the Military Education department, the Chaplain's department, and the newly created Topographical department, which ultimately became the Intelligence department. Such centralization, under a man who would hold office for another generation, would compound the administrative problems of future years.

Bureaucratic difficulties, however, were not the main concern of Cardwell in 1870. His reforms had been thwarted by the opposition to abolishing the ranks of ensign and cornet. As a consequence, a Royal Commission had been formed to investigate the issue of over-regulation payments. It reported unanimously, in June 1870, that there had been 'a tacit acquiescence' by civil and military authorities in the illegal practice of making over-regulation payments. Officers, it concluded, were justified in inferring that although the practice was '. . . contrary to the letter of the law, it was not seriously disapproved, and they might continue it without the fear of incurring the penalties of the law or the displeasure of the military authorities'.[50] Once the report was shown to the law officers of the Crown, they accepted that the government could not prevent the practice under the provisions of the existing Statute Law. Having read the law officers' report, Cardwell concluded that 'the law must in some way be altered'.[51]

Cardwell decided to alter the law by abolishing the purchase system. He seized upon this initiative, by far the most daring of his administration, in the wake of the Commission's report, and sent his new proposal to Gladstone on 22 September 1870.[52] His motives are by no means clear. As he left little evidence, other than retrospective arguments, various interpretations have been proffered to explain his actions. His biographer has claimed that the oubreak of the Franco-Prussian War, inasmuch as it coincided with the report of the Royal Commission, had a catalytic effect on Cardwell's thinking. The War, he asserted, rendered it imperative that the regular and auxiliary forces should be welded together into a cohesive unit. It was now mooted that the British army could profitably adopt some aspects of the Prussian military system which had achieved such 'admirable results'. But reforms could not be accomplished without interfering with the pecuniary interests of the purchase officer. Above all, the amalgamation of the purchase officers of the army with the non-purchase officers of the reserve forces would be impossible without abolishing purchase. For administrative reasons, therefore, Cardwell had to abolish the purchase system, and in so doing, to honour the recommendations of the Purchase Commission and pay compensation for the over-regulation prices.[53] While accepting this view, Arvel B. Erickson adds that Cardwell was a 'middle-class' politician who disliked the class overtones of the purchase system. Cardwell, argues Erickson, was an advocate of promotion by merit and so wished to abolish a promotion system, which was unreliable, desultory, and inefficient in its procedures.[54]

More recent scholarship by Drs Moses, Bruce and Gallacher has revised these interpretations. All three scholars agree that the Franco-Prussian War could not have been an immediate causal factor in the decision-making of Cardwell. Although the Prussian success, especially her use of reserves and the professionalism of her officer corps, left a profound impression upon Britain, the decision to abolish purchase was taken before the decisive battles of the War.[55] The War may have made it politically easier for Cardwell to grasp the nettle of purchase. 'Since Parliament rose', he wrote in October, 'the great events on the Continent seem to have given rise to a great feeling in this country which may make the question of army organization a less hopeless one than it has been hitherto'.[56] On the other hand, he specifically rejected any imitation of the Prussian model. Conscription, the lack of colonial responsibilities, the proximity of a dangerous neighbour, and the smaller proportion of industrial workers were four cardinal reasons, in the opinion of Cardwell, why Prussia could not be taken as a model.[57]

Administrative considerations were undoubtedly central to Cardwell's decision. He was not a doctrinaire abolitionist; indeed he could never have reconciled such a commitment with his strong preference for economy. Had Cardwell wished to abolish purchase for class reasons, he would have had to insist upon higher pay for officers and severe restrictions upon extravagance. During the debates on the purchase bill, he specifically denied that his aim was to alter the class composition of the army. 'It is a libel upon the old aristocracy', he declared, 'to say that they are ever behindhand in any race which is run in an open arena, and in which ability and industry are the only qualities which can insure success'.[58] The main concern of Cardwell was not the class composition of the army, but the prevalence of over-regulation payments, and the inability of the government to reform the army without recognizing these illegal transactions. The government could only avoid connivance in an illegal practice by prohibiting the buying and selling at over-regulation prices. This prohibition, moreover, could only be effective if the whole purchase system was eliminated. As the Royal Commission had explained: 'In these transactions, when one man has something of value to sell, which can legally be sold, and another man is desirous of purchasing it, the opportunity being afforded them of coming to a mutual understanding, it has been found useless . . . to prescribe by law or regulation the precise terms on which the sale is to be effected'.[59]

Dr Gallacher has added an important caveat to this interpretation. He has claimed that much of the inspiration for the decision to abolish purchase came not from Cardwell himself, but from his staff at the War Office. He has based his assertion upon a memorandum, 'Arguments for and against the purchase system', prepared by Lieutenant Evelyn Baring of the Topographical and Statistical Department of the War Office. As the conclusions of this document cohere with several other minutes and memoranda by more senior officers, notably Major-General Sir George Balfour and Brigadier John Adye, Dr Gallacher believes that they can be taken as representative of the arguments against purchase, as propounded by members of the War Office staff.[60] Baring, a non-purchase officer himself, objected to purchase because it had inhibited the development of professional attitudes within the army. He focused his attack upon the buying of promotions rather than the buying of the first commission. He maintained that purchase had allowed men to remain in the service without studying their profession; it also enabled many to leave after a few years of self-indulgent amusement. Under the purchase system, incompetent officers could still rise to regimental command: only by a system of selection, argued Baring, could these officers be weeded out of the service. Abolishing purchase, too, would eliminate the custom of exchanges, by which richer officers exchanged places with their poorer colleagues for a monetary consideration, so ensuring that the most arduous duties of overseas service were undertaken by poorer officers. To remove these abuses and stimulate more professional attitudes, Baring insisted that purchase had to be abolished. He did not believe that abolition would remove the aristocracy from military life; on the contrary, he claimed that purchase had attracted a mixture of officers from the upper middle classes, including the offspring of the *nouveaux riches,* 'the sons of rich manufacturers, etc.', and that abolition would enable the 'poor members of very good families' to reconsider the army as a career. This was vital, Baring affirmed, because the scions of the aristocracy were the custodians of 'that feeling of honour which is so essential to the well-being of any military body . . .'.[61]

Although these views may have been aired in the departmental deliberations during the summer of 1870, there is no conclusive proof that they inspired the actual decision. All the documentary evidence dates from several months after the decision was taken to abolish purchase. Baring's memorandum appeared nearly six months after the decision, on 14 February 1871. It was essentially a briefing document, culled from and supported by extensive quotations from the testimony before various Royal Commissions, for the benefit of the cabinet, and especially for those Ministers who were about to face a protracted Parliamentary debate. Preparing the document was a fairly mundane task (though imaginatively undertaken by Baring); it was delegated to a junior staff officer, a well-connected lieutenant (he was a cousin of Lord Northbrook) but one who had only just joined the War Office in March 1870. From this document, prepared for the forthcoming debates, it cannot be inferred that either Baring or his senior officers converted Cardwell to abolition. Their objections to purchase were not new. Cardwell was almost certainly aware of them before the summer of 1870; in the previous March, he had decried the purchase system as indefensible, admitting that he 'would not be very sorry to see the system terminated'.[62] Yet he did not act upon these arguments until confronted with the report of the Royal Commission on over-regulation payments. The administrative impasse was decisive: he could either tolerate an illegality and abort his reforms or remove the source of the illegality. As a lawyer, and a Minister with a stern sense of public duty, he could not administer his department in open violation of the law. Ever mindful of the dictum of Lord Grey: 'If you touch the system of purchase at all, it would be wiser to abolish it altogether',[63] he acted accordingly.

Once Cardwell had taken the decision, in consultation with Lord Northbrook, he informed Gladstone and the Duke of Cambridge. Neither were enthusiastic. The Duke reiterated his well-known objections. He urged Cardwell not to take any risks: 'See what the Prussians have done with their officers – all gentlemen and *not one* from the ranks; the French all from the ranks. Let us keep our old class of officers only giving them a lot more opportunity of instruction and we shall do wisely and well . . .'.[64] The Prime Minister also expressed misgivings. He suggested that Cardwell should make 'a full and careful study' of the Prussian system of officering. He trusted that the decision to abolish purchase would not be pressed until an alternative method of promotion was clearly perceived. He feared that Cardwell was acting too quickly and that decisions should not be taken at a time when the public mind is 'excited and imbalanced in no small degree'.[65] Cardwell was not dissuaded. He insisted that his scheme was not too ambitious, and that the Government had to prepare a comprehensive scheme for the next session of Parliament. He proposed to couple the abolition of purchase with new requirements for the education of officers and the training of recruits, the removal of the discipline of the Militia from the Lords-Lieutenant, and the combination of the regular, reserve and auxiliary forces under one command. Only by such a scheme, he implied, could the Government keep pace with public expectations.[66]

Undoubtedly the excitement occasioned by the events of the Continent had influenced the Secretary of State. When queried about the possibility of sending an expeditionary force of 20,000 men to Antwerp to secure the neutrality of Belgium, he recognized that this was virtually impossible so long as the army remained on a peace footing. On 2 August 1870 he sought and received from Parliament a vote of 20,000 additional men for the army. Although only five Members opposed the supplemental vote, Conservatives dissociated themselves from the retrenchment policies of the Liberal Government, so puncturing the bipartisan support which Cardwell had previously enjoyed.[67] Newspapers across a broad political spectrum castigated the state of the army, blaming Cardwell for many of the weaknesses, real or imagined.[68] Initially, the Secretary of State had thought that the clamour might be useful and might enable him to find support for his wide-ranging reforms. He may even have viewed benignly the speaking tours of George Trevelyan in the autumn and winter of 1870, in which he harangued numerous audiences about the evils of the purchase system.[69] But he soon began to recoil from the barbs of criticism. By November, Cardwell was bemoaning his predicament and confessing a fear of being unable to defend his proposals in the House of Commons. He described the public as 'in a growling humour, & a little in the spirit they were towards Lord Aberdeen'. The critics were insatiable, he complained. In spite of a slashed expenditure and an increased army at home, they wanted to have everything and pay nothing. By 3 January 1871, he proffered his resignation in view of the 'altered state of the public mind on military questions'.[70]

Gladstone, who was never impressed by movements of opinion in military matters, reassured his Secretary of State. He had already chosen not to press his reservations about the abolition of purchase. After the despatch of a lengthy memorandum on 13 October, he had admitted, on the following day, that his knowledge of military administration was limited, and that his observations may have been crude and wide of the mark.[71] Apart from refusing to allow the financing of abolition to be paid by Treasury loans,[72] he assured Cardwell of his support. He even found an assistant for him in the House of Commons, by securing a Parliamentary seat for General Sir Henry Storks, the chief of the Control Department of the War Office. Fortified by the Prime Minister, Cardwell gained the endorsement of the cabinet and introduced his Army Regulation Bill in the Commons on the evening of 16 February 1871.

The Bill was limited in scope. Cardwell sought Parliamentary approval for several fundamental points - the termination of purchase, the compensation of officers' investments (at a cost of an estimated £7,500,000-£8,500,000), and the unification of the regular, auxiliary and reserve forces under one command. He did not intend to consult Parliament upon the details of reorganization. The Bill did not include the proposed rules for promotion and retirement. Nor did it contain information about the future size of the army and possible improvements in ordinance, training and logistics, the issues which had preoccupied leader-writers over the past six months. Outside the House of Commons, the Bill evoked little reaction and even less support. After the initial comment in the editorial columns and a few pamphlets by individuals, interest waned rapidly. Only one letter was printed in *The Times* during the three weeks which elapsed between Cardwell's speech and the first debate on the second reading.[73] There were few public meetings in support of abolition. The Liberal press in the provincial cities reported widespread indifference towards the Bill, especially after the cessation of Continental hostilities on 1 March. By 25 May 1871, not one petition of support had been sent to the House of Commons.[74] By early July, Cardwell conceded that 'the breeze of popular enthusiasm has died away during the contest . . .'.[75]

Within the House of Commons, the Bill experienced a difficult passage. As soon as the second reading debate began on 6 March, some serving and retired officers, headed by Colonel Lloyd-Lindsay, mounted a fervent defence of the purchase system. They feared for the financial position of individual officers. Several Liberals joined the chorus of criticism, protesting about the cost of abolition and the propriety of compensating officers for over-regulation payments. Although the Bill found some support, notably from Trevelyan, opponents were more conspicuous in the chamber and a division was only avoided by the intercession of Disraeli. Although he disliked the Bill in many respects, Disraeli was not a die-hard opponent of abolition. He mollified his more extreme back benchers, arguing that the Bill could be examined in detail and possibly amended in committee. At this time, he asserted, while the 'eyes of Europe are on England re-organizing her Army', it was imperative that Parliament should show, if possible, an unbroken front.[76] Though restrained on the night, the opponents of the Bill would redouble their efforts in committee.

Filibustering occurred throughout the committees on Supply and Ways and Means. During the committee stage, the debates dragged on from 8 May to 19 June. Discussed on thirteen separate occasions, the Bill was opposed on almost every clause. The government lost the support of the Conservative leadership and struggled to maintain its majority. Colonel A. H. Anson, a Liberal, aided by Lord Elcho, another Liberal, led the attack. Government majorities were whittled away, falling from 65 to 39, until 25 May, when Colonel Anson moved that all half-pay officers and officers below the rank of major should receive the regulation value of their commissions at once, without waiting until retirement. Aimed at those radicals who deplored the payment of over-regulation prices, the motion failed by a mere 19 votes. On the same day, Sir William Russell, another Liberal opponent, moved that officers should be offered a choice of regulation payment at once or regulation, along with over-regulation, payment at retirement. Attracting the support of 17 Liberals, the motion fell by only 16 votes.[77]

At this nadir in the government's fortunes, Gladstone wished to compromise with the opponents and possibly meet the substance of Russell's motion.[78] Cardwell refused to conciliate. He feared, not the genuine opposition of Russell, but the fickleness of some government supporters. He believed that

> There sits below the gangway on our side a plutocracy, - who have no real objection to Purchase, - and are in truth more interested in its maintenance than the aristocratic gentlemen opposite. They use popular arguments, like young Mr. Seeley, & they say in private that they want something *more* for the money involved; that something being the removal of the Duke of Cambridge: - while in truth they wish to purchase an aristocratic position for personal connections, who would never obtain it otherwise.[79]

Cardwell, in other words, believed that some of his critics in the Liberal party, who argued that the Bill should be improved, probably did not want it to pass at all. However perceptive, this insight did not mean that the Bill was doomed. G. G. Glynn, the Liberal chief whip, assured the Prime Minister that a majority could be sustained. Members, he conceded, were apathetic and discontented with the Bill, partly reflecting a lack of 'strong pressure from the constituencies'. Nevertheless, he felt that a large number had not stayed away deliberately on 25 May, and that better whipping would ensure success.[80]

Ultimately Glynn proved correct, although the premier insisted upon deleting several clauses from the Bill. Disraeli used the curtailment of the Bill as an excuse for withdrawing his co-operation. With party lines more clearly drawn on the third reading (3 July), Glynn's whipping turned out a healthy majority of 58 votes. Only 12 Liberals, five of them army officers, strayed into the Opposition lobby, while 10 Conservatives voted with the government.[81] Although officers had provided the bulk of the Parliamentary opposition, this does not mean that officers generally opposed the Bill. Spokesmen on both sides of the debate claimed to have military opinion with them. Soundings were taken by Lord Eustace Cecil and by Sir Frederick Ponsonby, the Queen's private secretary, which proved conclusively that the military were either overwhelmingly opposed to abolition or adamantly in favour of it![82] Whatever the division of opinion about the principle of abolition, it was probably true that purchase officers resented the inability to realize their capital until retirement. On the other hand, they could hardly complain that the terms offered by the government were other than just and liberal.

Once the Army Regulation Bill had passed the Commons, the government faced an even more daunting hurdle in the House of Lords. To sway or at least neutralize the huge Conservative majority in the Upper House, the government had sought the active support of the Duke of Cambridge. Cardwell reminded him that his tenure of office had not been limited to five years because the government expected his open and cordial assistance on matters of military policy.[83] The Duke protested that, constitutionally, he should have 'no politics' and should not take part in political discussion. He preferred to confine himself to the professional aspects of subjects discussed in the House of Lords.[84] Neither Cardwell nor Gladstone would accept this reply; they pressed the Queen to induce her cousin to speak, and eventually he agreed although he refused to vote. His speech which was inaudible in parts of the chamber had little impact. The Bill evoked strong party feelings and was defeated by 25 votes on 17 July.

Having anticipated defeat, the cabinet decided on 15 July to terminate purchase, if necessary, by issue of a Royal Warrant. Legislation was not required to abolish the system, as, under the Brokerage Act of 1809, it was only preserved as a regulation issued by the Crown. That regulation could be revoked by Royal Warrant, an act undertaken on 20 July, 1871. This initiative aroused a storm of opposition from Conservatives in Parliament and in the press. The government was assailed for exercising the Royal prerogative to overcome an adverse vote in Parliament.[85] Aware of this likely reaction, the majority of the cabinet had resolved that they could no longer tolerate the illegality of over-regulation payments. They feared, too, that the discipline of the army might be impaired should the issue be prolonged for another year. Promotion would almost certainly be halted, as officers would be reluctant to make over-regulation payments without the certainty of Parliamentary approval for compensation in 1872.[86] Unwilling to let matters drift or to risk the possibility of another defeat and wasted session in 1872, the cabinet braved the inevitable outcry and abolished purchase.

Effective from 1 November 1871, the abolition of purchase did not transform the social composition of the officer corps. Although this had been a principal aim of Trevelyan and the more zealous reformers, Cardwell had never sought this objective. He neither raised the rates of pay of the officer corps, nor imposed sumptuary controls upon mess expenditure. The army continued to seek officers from the upper class and from the wealthier ranks of the middle class. On the other hand, Cardwell had maintained that abolishing purchase would inaugurate a new era of professional reform, with promotion by merit providing an incentive for more study and professional application. The Duke of Cambridge would confound this expectation; an arch-opponent of selection, he relied upon seniority as a basis for promotion. Mediocre and incompetent officers could still attain regimental command. Promotion, too, became much slower than it had been in the purchase army, so contradicting the forecasts of Cardwell.[87] In November 1874 a Royal Commission under the chairmanship of Lord Penzance was appointed to consider how promotion could be made more rapid. Reporting nearly two years later, it recommended compulsory pensionable retirements for post-purchase captains who had not become majors after twenty years' service and for post-purchase majors who had not become lieutenant-colonels after twenty-seven years' service. It also proposed that officers should be allowed to retire voluntarily on a pension after eight years' service, and that special retirement provisions should be made for purchase officers who had not been promoted since abolition.[88] These recommendations, slightly modified, were implemented by Royal Warrant in August 1877. Only this scheme for retirement prevented promotion in the post-purchase army from grinding along at an agonizingly slow pace.

Abolition, nonetheless, enabled Cardwell to proceed with the fusion of the regular, auxiliary and reserve forces. On 22 February 1872 he introduced his Localization Bill in the House of Commons. He proposed the creation of sixty-six territorial districts in each of which would be based two line battalions, two Militia infantry battalions, and a certain quota of Volunteers. Each district would be formed into an administrative brigade, centred upon a brigade depot. This localization of forces, he claimed, would ease the burden of recruiting by the development of local connections. It would also induce men from the Militia to enter the army, would improve the morale and efficiency of the auxiliary forces (Volunteeer Corps, placed under the command of their district lieutenant-colonels, would be required to attend brigade instruction once a year, receive a small allowance for doing so, but become liable to forfeit their capitation grant if less than half the enrolled strength attended). The scheme, finally, would provide, in the permanent depot, a training centre for new recruits, as well as a centre for the payment, training, and discipline of Reservists. Cardwell requested that £3,500,000 should be authorized to construct twenty-six new stations and to convert the other forty, which were currently occupied by regular units. By investing money in this scheme, he concluded, the State would be maximizing its investment in the regular and auxiliary forces and would be enhancing the national defences.[89]

The Bill was in some respects an unsatisfactory compromise. Instead of amalgamating the two infantry battalions into double battalion regiments, as was already the case with the first twenty-five regiments of the Line, the battalions were left as independent units. The Duke of Cambridge had insisted upon this compromise. Originally he had agreed that the linked regiments should be fused into one corps. When he sounded the opinion of senior officers, he found them 'unanimously opposed to throwing two linked Regiments permanently together as one Corps'.[90] Fearing the loss of their traditional numbers and facings, senior officers opposed any change which might jeopardize battalion *esprit de corps.* The Duke of Cambridge required that the Localization Committee, chaired by Major-General Sir Patrick MacDougall, should accept this view: the linked regiments should continue as 'separate Corps for the Officers' but be 'made to act as much as possible in mutual support'.[91] The Committee prepared a scheme on this basis; its detailed recommendations formed the core of the Localization Bill.

After the acrimonious debates of the previous year, this Bill was accorded a much more favourable reception. As critics since the outbreak of the Franco-Prussian War had demanded localization, the linking of regular and reserve forces, and the imposition of more stringent training requirements upon the Volunteers, their complaints had largely been met. The Bill was welcomed by the Conservative press and endorsed by Sir John Pakington in the House of Commons.[92] Determined but somewhat desperate opposition was mounted from the radical benches. Appalled at the cost of the scheme, radicals reminded their front-bench spokesmen of their election promises. After the defeat of France, the invasion shadow had lifted: how could the Government, asked Sir Wilfred Lawson, reconcile this massive defence expenditure with its pacific foreign policy? Even more repugnant, argued Henry Richard, were the moral implications of covering the country with a 'web-work of military institutions'. These establishments, he declared, would sow the seeds of militarism in the community, and become centres of vice and immorality. Having campaigned against the Contagious Diseases Acts, he was convinced that wherever 'a body of soldiers was stationed, it became a corrupting and demoralizing agency'.[93] His exhortations had little effect; the expenses of the scheme were approved on 29 July 1872 by 170 votes to 24.

Improved recruitment was a primary objective of the Localization Act. Cardwell had hoped that regiments, by forming 'ties of kindred and of locality', could reverse the decline of enlistments from rural areas, attract a better class of men, and swell the recruiting numbers.[94] These expectations proved far too sanguine. Undoubtedly, localization enabled recruiting drives to reach areas which had hitherto been relatively neglected. Also, those regiments which established local connections claimed to have attracted much better men than if they had relied on general recruiting.[95] Many line battalions, however, rarely ever visited their nominal locality. The establishment of local depots had been extremely slow; only forty had been formed by 1874, and officers had not been freely transferred between affiliated battalions.[96] Successive governments had never maintained the essential parity between the battalions at home and abroad. By this parity, Cardwell had envisaged the home-based battalion supplying drafts and reliefs for its linked battalion abroad. In 1872, there had been seventy battalions at home and seventy-one abroad; by 1879, after a series of small colonial wars, there were eighty-two battalions abroad and fifty-nine at home. Forced to provide a larger proportion of overseas drafts, the home battalions shrank in size and recruiting standards had to be lowered.

In 1879, a Committee of officers chaired by Lord Airey reported upon the reorganization of the army. It found that the demand for men was so great that recruits were not being properly trained at the depots, which were, in any case, inadequate in size and facilities. It warned that the transfer of the best men from battalions at home to those overseas was damaging *esprit de corps*. It believed that the home battalions were being dangerously weakened; it noted that some battalions, when they came onto the roster for foreign service, could only leave the country at fighting strength by taking volunteers from other regiments.[97] The Airey Committee underlined that there was a considerable body of military opinion which disliked the consequences of short service, localization, and the two-battalion regiment. Neither the Conservative Government, which suppressed the Airey report, nor its Liberal successor would abandon the Cardwell reforms. Although willing to publish the report in 1881, the Liberal government would not endorse its findings. It had the support of several officers, like MacDougall and Wolseley, who believed that the Cardwellian machinery had never been fairly tested.[98] Hugh Childers, the Secretary of State for War (1880–82), responded to the controversy by reaffirming his commitment to short service and localization. In 1881, he marginally increased the length of the first term of Colour service to seven years, reducing the period of reserve service to five years. He also abandoned the compromise of 1872; he fused the linked battalions and added two Militia battalions to form a territorial regiment. He replaced the old regimental numbers by territorial titles and severed many historical traditions.

By reaffirming its faith in Cardwellian principles, the government crushed opposition within official circles. The debates had been fanned by criticism in the regimental messes, in the press, in evidence before Select Committees, and occasionally in Parliament. Reflected by the dissension was the anguish caused by the loss of the old regimental numbers and facings, and the supposed harm that had been done to *esprit de corps*. Also apparent was the failure of the reforms to fulfil the expectations raised by Cardwell and, latterly, by Childers. Localization, as a recruiting reform, had little prospect of redressing the effects of rural depopulation. The army could never find sufficient recruits by concentrating upon local districts or regimental headquarters. Whereas 83.8 per cent of recruits were found locally in 1874 (the remainder being raised from special recruiting districts centred upon large urban areas), only 63.3 per cent of the intake were recruited locally in 1898.[99] In other respects, localization was relatively successful. It enlarged the basic unit of army organization from the battalion to the regiment of two or more battalions. It benefited the auxiliary forces by enabling them to train periodically with the regulars, or to camp at the brigade depot. During his own term of office, Cardwell had determined to maximize these benefits by arranging joint manoeuvres in 1871, 1872, and 1873. The events proved immensely popular and enhanced relations between the regulars and the reserves. The Cannock Chase manoeuvres attracted 150,000 spectators. 'As if by magic,' claimed *The United Service Gazette,* 'a friendly behaviour sprang up between our Army and our civilian population'.[100] 'The Autumn campaign', added *The Naval and Military Gazette,* 'did more to ingratiate the Volunteers with the Army than anything that has taken place since the formation of the force'.[101] Economic constraints prevented large scale manoeuvres from becoming a regular occurrence; a generation would elapse before the next manoeuvres were held in 1898.

The Cardwell reforms acquired an almost legendary reputation during the last quarter of the nineteenth century. As recounted by Cardwell's biographer, the reforms enabled the country to maintain a voluntary system of enlistment and a tolerable volume of military expenditure, while meeting the strategic needs of a European and an imperial power. Written in 1904, the biography reflects a view of Cardwell's achievements which held sway in the War Office and in successive cabinets, both Conservative and Liberal. Endorsed by Printing House Square and by some officers like MacDougall, Adye and Wolseley, this view underlined the appeal of the reforms and the apparent lack of any viable alternative. Initially, the proposals of Cardwell were well received by Parliament and the press. Apart from the fierce passions aroused by the abolition of purchase, his reforms, which straddled the currents of mainstream opinion on army reform, earned a high measure of bipartisan support. Cardwell adopted ideas either launched by his predecessors (colonial withdrawal, forming a Reserve, abolishing the ranks of cornet and ensign), or concepts, like localization, which were currently in vogue on account of recent Prussian triumphs. He embodied these ideas in his legislative proposals. Unlike his predecessors, he moved beyond purely administrative measures and pressed for the abolition of purchase, a prerequisite for further reforms. This display of courage and leadership would not be forgotten by senior departmental officials. Sir Ralph Thompson, Sir Arthur (later Lord) Haliburton, and Sir Ralph Knox, the Permanent Under-Secretaries of State from 1878–1901, would become the foremost champions of the Cardwell reforms.

During his term of office Cardwell incurred criticism from the radical benches and, more importantly, from the Horse Guards. The Duke of Cambridge proved a persistent and hostile critic until his retirement in 1894. His ill-concealed antipathy ensured that the supporters of Cardwell would repeatedly rally to the defence of short service and localization. When juxtaposed with the reactionary views of the Duke, the reforms of Cardwell seemed ever more worthy of preservation. In fact, many of the criticisms of the Duke would be verified by subsequent events; but, as they were basically negative criticisms, their impact was minimal. Having favoured the purchase system, a long-service army, the Militia Reserve, and much larger Estimates, the Duke's opinions carried little credibility in ministerial circles. An alternative scheme of reform was not fashioned until the late 1880s and 1890s, but, by then, the admirers of Cardwell would claim that his reforms had been largely successful. The Estimates had been kept within tolerable limits. The army seemed to be efficient; it had been consistently successful in the small colonial wars. Short service and localization may have contributed marginally to the larger influx of recruits during the last two decades of the century. Above all, a Reserve had been formed, from which over 80,000 men would rejoin the Colours in 1899 to fight in South Africa.

This rationalization is not entirely convincing. The fundamental basis of Cardwell's reforms - an approximate parity between the battalions at home and abroad - barely survived his ministry. As future governments of both parties embarked upon a much more active colonial policy, they sent an increasing proportion of battalions abroad in a flood-tide of imperial expansion. Home-based battalions suffered as a consequence; some were unable to take the field themselves, and languished as little more than training units for raw recruits. Although recruiting numbers increased, a better class of man was not attracted by the call to arms. To meet the increased turnover of men caused by short-service enlistments, the army had to lower its physical standards and seek a larger proportion of recruits from the urban slums. Compounding this strain were the demands of small colonial warfare, especially the periodic need to form expeditionary forces from the battalions retained in the United Kingdom. The Army Reserve could not be raided continually to replenish under-strength units. Although called out on some occasions short of a national emergency, the Reserve was neither designed nor able to cope with a multitude of small colonial wars.

The reforms, moreover, failed to infuse the army with a new professional spirit. Cardwell had claimed that abolishing purchase would alter attitudes within the military profession, especially if replaced by promotion by merit. The Duke of Cambridge had never agreed. Only willing to supervise promotion on the principle of seniority tempered by selection, the Duke would blunt any competitive stimulus over the next twenty years. He would bow before political pressure and promote meritorious generals, like Wolseley and Buller, but generally he relied upon seniority as a criterion untainted by fears of favouritism or jobbery. Although aware that this approach was likely, Cardwell had refrained from either pressing his views upon the Commander-in-Chief or limiting his tenure of office. Preferring to avoid a constitutional clash with the Crown and to retain the services of the Duke during the delicate transition from a purchase to a post-purchase army, Cardwell almost certainly knew that his public pronoucements would never be realized. Abolishing purchase remained an administrative necessity, even if the prospects of professional reform remained largely rhetorical.

Cardwell, in devising his reforms, was too preoccupied with the recruiting difficulties which had bedevilled the post-Crimean army. His proposals did not overcome these difficulties. Short-service, localization, and some reforms of the recruiting process did not radically improve the image of a military career. Nevertheless, localization was geared to recruiting purposes; it fulfilled neither the requirements of strategic planning nor the need for training in large scale military formations. Localization accentuated the dispersal of battalions throughout the country; many units were located in small barracks with inadequate facilities for training and recreation. The dispersal increased the costs of holding military manoeuvres; it also ensured that the army corps which embarked on some expeditionary forces were principally administrative and not tactical formations. Cardwell, in short, had reformed the organizational structure of the army without envisaging how that structure might function in war, or even in a series of small colonial wars.

To recognize that Cardwell's reforms had shortcomings merely redresses the balance of argument. Like other Secretaries of State, Cardwell had to choose his order of priorities, work within a limited period of time, and accept the constraints of contemporary politics. He can hardly be faulted for failing to introduce measures which were beyond the realm of practical politics: he could neither introduce conscription nor vastly increase the rates of pay for officers and men. He recognized that reforms would not be accepted if they imposed an intolerable strain on the Army Estimates. By seeking the twin objectives of economy and efficiency, Cardwell was both prudent and realistic. But he can be faulted for raising expectations excessively. Though usually laconic and urbane in debate, he promised sweeping changes from reforms which were intrinsically limited. Had this optimism not permeated his devoted body of admirers, the debates of the next twenty-five years might have proved more fruitful and more constructive. Army reform stagnated, as successive governments permitted only minor changes in the structure he had fashioned.

Notes and references

1. Sir R. Biddulph, *op. cit.*, p. 229.
2. *The Manchester Guardian,* 13 Oct. 1868, p. 5, and 21 Oct. 1868, p. 5.
3. *Ibid.*, 18 Nov. 1868, p. 7.
4. *Oxford Chronicle & Berks. & Bucks. Gazette,* 27 June 1868, p. 6, and 5 Sept. 1868, p. 2.
5. Duke of Cambridge to Lord Dalhousie, 10 Nov. 1868, Dalhousie Muniments, S.R.O., GD 45/14/759.
6. Sir R. Biddulph, *op. cit.*, p.v, and **T. F. Gallacher,** '"Cardwellian Mysteries": The Fate of the British Army Regulation Bill, 1871', *Historical Journal,* **18**, No. 2, 1975, p. 329.

7. E. Cardwell, 'The Army', 3 Dec. 1868 reproduced in Sir R. Biddulph, *op. cit.*, pp. 249-54.
8. Letter, 18 Nov. 1865, quoted in *Letters of the Rt. Hon. Henry Austin Bruce, G.C.B., Lord Aberdeen of Duffryn,* 2 vols., private, Oxford, 1902, Vol. 1, p. 232.
9. Earl Granville to Gladstone, 2 Aug. 1868, Gladstone Mss., B.M. Add. Mss. 44,165, f. 170.
10. Cardwell to Gladstone, 9 Jan. 1869, Gladstone Mss., B.M. Add. Mss. 44,119, ff. 21-5.
11. Gladstone to Cardwell, 11 Jan. 1869, Cardwell Mss., P.R.O., 30/48/2/6, f. 32.
12. Duke of Cambridge to Cardwell, 2 Jan. 1870, Cardwell Mss., P.R.O., 30/48/3/13, ff. 3-4. See also the Duke of Cambridge to Cardwell, 3 Aug. 1869 and 14 Dec. 1869, quoted in **Col. W. Verner,** *The Military Life of H.R.H. George, Duke of Cambridge,* 2 vols., John Murray, London, 1905, Vol. 1, pp. 394-9.
13. Duke of Cambridge to Cardwell, 11 Jan. 1870, Cardwell Mss., P.R.O., 30/48/3/13, ff. 16-18.
14. *Parl. Deb.,* Third Ser., Vol 194, 11 Mar. 1869, cols. 1,111-73.
15. *The Pall Mall Gazette,* 4 Jan. 1869, p. 1.
16. *Parl. Deb.,* Third Ser., Vol. 195, 23 Apr. 1869, cols. 1,420-36, and Vol. 196, 10 June 1869, cols. 1,499-519.
17. *The Daily Telegraph,* 14 Apr. 1869, p. 5.
18. *Parl. Deb.,* Third Ser., Vol. 194, 11 Mar. 1869, cols. 1,112, 1,164.
19. *The Hawick Advertiser and Roxburghshire Gazette,* 9 Jan. 1869, p. 4.
20. *The United Service Gazette,* 5 Mar. 1870, p. 4, and *The Naval and Military Gazette,* 1 Jan. 1870, p. 6.
21. Duke of Cambridge to Cardwell, 6 Feb. 1869, Cambridge Mss., R.A., E/1/5,992.
22. Duke of Cambridge to Cardwell, 24 Nov. 1869, Cardwell Mss., P.R.O., 30/48/3/12, ff. 150-1.
23. *The Times,* 22 Feb. 1870, p. 7.
24. *Parl. Deb.,* Third Ser., Vol. 199, 3 Mar. 1870, cols. 1,158-234.
25. *The Times,* 4 Mar. 1870, p. 9.
26. *Parl. Deb.,* Third Ser., Vol. 199, 3 Mar. 1870, col. 1,174.
27. *Ibid.,* col. 1,172.
28. A. P. C. Bruce, *op. cit.,* p. 364 and *The Army and Navy Gazette,* 5 Mar. 1870, p. 153, and 12 Mar. 1870, p. 169.
29. *Parl. Deb.,* Third Ser., Vol. 199, 3 Mar. 1870, cols. 1,205-6, 1,231 and 10 Mar. 1870, col. 1,629.
30. Cabinet memorandum, 5 Mar. 1870, Gladstone Mss., B.M. Add. Mss. 44,638, f. 33.
31. *Parl. Deb.,* Third Ser., Vol. 199, 3 Mar. 1870, cols. 1,175-77, and Vol 203, 18 July 1870, cols. 444-7.

32. *The Pall Mall Gazette,* 4 Mar. 1870, p. 4, and 17 May 1870, pp. 1-2.
33. *The Times,* 4 Mar. 1870, p. 9.
34. *Parl. Deb.,* Third Ser., Vol. 203, 18 July 1870, cols. 436, 447-8.
35. H. S. Wilson, *op. cit.,* p. 209, and **A. V. Tucker**, 'Army and society in England 1870-1900: A reassessment of the Cardwell reforms', *Journal of British Studies,* 2, No. 2, May 1963, p. 130.
36. **B. J. Bond**, *The introduction and operation of short service and localization in the British army, 1868-1892,* unpublished M.A. thesis, University of London, 1962, pp. 92-3.
37. Duke of Cambridge to Cardwell, 11 Jan. 1870, Cardwell Mss., P.R.O., 30/48/3/13, f. 17.
38. Cardwell, memorandum, 3 Jan. 1874, Gladstone Mss., B.M. Add. Mss. 44,120, f. 197.
39. **J. W. Fortescue,** *The Empire and the Army,* Cassell, London, 1928, p. 275.
40. *Report of the Select Committee on Military Organization,* C.441, 1860, VII, p. vii.
41. *Ibid.,* p. xxi.
42. Cardwell, 'The Army', 3 Dec. 1868 quoted in Sir R. Biddulph, *op. cit.,* p. 250-1.
43. *The Hawick Advertiser and Roxburghshire Gazette,* 9 Jan. 1869, p. 4 and *Parl. Deb.,* Third Ser., Vol. 194, 11 Mar. 1869, cols. 1,094-99.
44. *Reports of a Committee appointed to inquire into the Arrangements in Force for the Conduct of Business in the Army Departments,* C.54, 1870, XII, pp. x-xv.
45. Gladstone to Cardwell, 21 Nov. 1869, Gladstone Mss., B.M. Add. Mss. 44,537, ff. 146-7 and Lord Northbrook to Cardwell, 30 Jan. 1870, Cardwell Mss., P.R.O., 30/48/4/19, ff. 30-3.
46. Queen Victoria to Cardwell, 22 Dec. 1869, Cardwell Mss., P.R.O., 30/48/1/1, f. 88.
47. Duke of Cambridge to Cardwell, 5 Dec. 1869, Cardwell Mss., P.R.O., 30/48/3/12, ff. 180-5.
48. Cardwell to Gladstone, 16 Jan. 1870, Cardwell Mss., P.R.O., 30/48/2/7, f. 14.
49. *The Times,* 2 Mar. 1869, p. 9.
50. *Report of the Commissioners appointed to Inquire into Over-regulation Payments on Promotion in the Army,* hereafter referred to as the Over-Regulation Commission, C.201, 1870, XII, p. xxiv.
51. Cardwell, memorandum on 'Military Organization', n.d. but probably Oct. 1870, Granville Mss., P.R.O., 30/29/28, f. 84. For the date of the memorandum see Cardwell to Gladstone, 5 Oct. 1870, Gladstone Mss., B.M. Add. Mss. 44,119, f. 155.
52. Cardwell to Gladstone, 22 Sept. 1870, Gladstone Mss., B.M. Add. Mss. 44,119, ff. 151-2.

53. Sir R. Biddulph, *op. cit.*, pp. 98-9.
54. **A. B. Erickson,** 'Abolition of purchase in the British army', *Military Affairs,* **23**, 1959, p. 69.
55. N. H. Moses, *op. cit.*, p. 113; A. P. C. Bruce, *op. cit.*, p. 369; **T. F. Gallacher**, 'British military thinking and the coming of the Franco-Prussian War', *Military Affairs,* **39**, 1975, p. 20.
56. Cardwell, 'Military Organization', *op. cit.,* f. 32.
57. Cardwell to Gladstone, 22 Sept. 1870, Gladstone Mss., B.M. Add. Mss. 44,119, ff. 151-2.
58. *Parl. Deb.*, Third Ser., Vol. 205, 16 Mar. 1871, col. 137. See also N. H. Moses, *op. cit.*, pp. 110-12.
59. Report of the Over-Regulation Commission, *op. cit.*, p. xi.
60. T. F. Gallacher, *Historical Journal,* p. 332 and *Military Affairs,* p. 20.
61. Lieutenant E. Baring, 'The Arguments for and against the Purchase System', 14 Feb. 1871, Granville Mss., P.R.O., 30/29/68, f. 235.
62. *Parl. Deb.*, Third Ser., Vol. 199, 3 Mar. 1870, col. 1,172.
63. Cardwell, 'The Army', 3 Dec. 1868, quoted in Sir R. Biddulph, *op. cit.*, p. 253.
64. The Duke of Cambridge to Cardwell, 30 Sept. 1870, Cardwell Mss., P.R.O., 30/48/3/14, ff. 190-1.
65. Gladstone to Cardwell, 14 Oct. 1870, Cardwell Mss., P.R.O., 30/48/2/7, ff. 155-6. See also Gladstone to Cardwell, 23 Sept. and 8 Oct. 1870, P.R.O., 30/48/2/7, ff. 136, 142.
66. Cardwell to Gladstone, 10 Oct. 1870, Cardwell Mss., P.R.O., 30/48/2/7, ff. 146-7.
67. *Parl. Deb.*, Third Ser., Vol. 203, 2 Aug. 1870, cols. 1,440-63.
68. *The Times,* 17 Oct. 1870, p. 9; *The Manchester Guardian,* 17 Oct. 1870, p. 3; *The Saturday Review,* 27 Aug. 1870, pp. 225-6 and 17 Oct. 1870, pp. 512-13; *The Leeds Mercury,* 22 Aug. 1870, p. 2.
69. A. P. C. Bruce, *op. cit.*, pp. 369-70.
70. Cardwell to Gladstone, 17 Nov. 1870 and 3 Jan. 1871, Gladstone Mss., B.M. Add. Ms. 44,119, ff. 173-4, 191-2; Cardwell to Gladstone, 26 Dec. 1870, Cardwell Mss., P.R.O., 30/48/2/7, f. 207; Cardwell to R. Lowe, 21 Dec. 1870, Cardwell Mss., P.R.O., 30/48/5/22, f. 126.
71. Gladstone, memorandum on 'Army Questions', 13 Oct. 1870, Gladstone Mss., B.M. Add. Mss. 44,759, ff. 169-80, and Gladstone to Cardwell, 14 Oct. 1870, Cardwell Mss., P.R.O., 30/48/2/7, f. 155.
72. Gladstone to Cardwell, 19 Jan. 1871, Gladstone Mss., B.M. Add. Mss. 44,539, f. 139.
73. *The Times*, 18 Feb. 1871, p. 8. See also N. H. Moses, *op. cit.*, pp. 186-7.
74. *The Manchester Guardian,* 24 May 1871, pp. 4-5; *North British*

Daily Mail, 19 July 1871, p. 4; *The Birmingham Daily Mail,* 20 June 1871, p. 4; *Parl. Deb.,* Third Ser., Vol. 206, 25 May 1871, col. 1,303; T. F. Gallacher, *Historical Journal,* p. 342.

75. Cardwell to Sir H. Ponsonby, 3 July 1871, Cardwell Mss., P.R.O., 30/48/1/2, f. 108.
76. *Parl. Deb.*, Fourth Ser., Vol. 205, 17 Mar. 1871, col. 244.
77. *Parl. Deb.,* Fourth Ser., Vol. 206, 25 May 1871, cols. 1,274-9, 1,279-308.
78. Gladstone to Cardwell, 27 May 1871, Gladstone Mss., B.M. Add. Mss. 44,540, ff. 40-4.
79. Cardwell to Gladstone, 28 May 1871, Gladstone Mss., B.M. Add. Mss. 44,119, f. 243.
80. G. G. Glyn to Gladstone, 27 May 1871, Gladstone Mss., B.M. Add. Mss. 44,348, ff. 100-7.
81. *Parl. Deb.,* Third Ser., Vol. 207, 3 July 1871, cols. 1,073-7. See also T. F. Gallacher, *Historical Journal,* p. 346.
82. *Parl. Deb.,* Third Ser., Vol. 204, 13 Mar. 1871, col. 1,957; Vol. 206, 22 May 1871, col. 1,134; Vol. 206, 5 June 1871, col. 1,567; Vol. 206, 5 June 1871, cols. 1,565-6; and Ponsonby to Cardwell, 28 Feb. 1871, Cardwell Mss., P.R.O., 30/48/1/3, f. 57.
83. Cardwell to the Duke of Cambridge, 3 June 1871, Cardwell Mss., P.R.O., 30/48/4/15, ff. 181-2.
84. Duke of Cambridge to Cardwell, 3 June 1871, Cardwell Mss., P.R.O., 30/48/4/15, ff. 186-8.
85. *The Pall Mall Gazette,* 22 July 1871, pp. 1, 3; *The Saturday Review,* 22 July 1871, pp. 97-8; *The Standard,* 22 July 1871, p. 4; *The Globe,* 24 July 1871, p. 4.
86. Cardwell, memoranda, 11 July [1871] and 18 July 1871, Cardwell Mss., P.R.O., 30/48/2/6, f. 83, and 30/48/2/8, ff. 103-8. See also N. H. Moses, *op. cit.,* pp. 343-7.
87. *Parl. Deb.,* Third Ser., Vol. 204, 3 Mar. 1871, col. 1,272 and Vol. 205, 16 Mar. 1871, col. 144.
88. *Report of Royal Commission on Army Promotion and Retirement,* C.1,569, 1876, XV, pp. xv-xvi, xviii-xxxix.
89. *Parl. Deb.,* Third Ser., Vol. 209, 22 Feb. 1872, cols. 893-906.
90. Duke of Cambridge to Cardwell, 17 May 1872, Cardwell Mss., P.R.O., 30/48/4/16, f. 52.
91. Duke of Cambridge, memorandum, n.d. quoted in Sir R. Biddulph, *op. cit.,* pp. 167-9.
92. *The Pall Mall Gazette,* 24 Feb. 1872, pp. 1-2, and *Parl. Deb.,* Third Ser., Vol. 212, 23 July 1872, col. 1,644.
93. *Parl. Deb.,* Third Ser., Vol. 212, 15 July 1872, col. 1,210, and 23 July 1872, col. 1,650.
94. *Parl. Deb.,* Third Ser., Vol 209, 22 Feb. 1872, col. 901, and Cardwell to Queen Victoria, 18 Dec. 1871, Cardwell Mss., P.R.O., 30/48/1/3, ff. 250-1.

95. *Reports of the Inspector-General of Recruiting,* C.5,953, 1890, XIX, p. 7, and C3,169, 1882, XVI, p. 1.
96. *Report of the Committee on Certain Questions Relative to the Militia and the Present Brigade Depot Systems,* C.1,654, 1877, XVIII, pp. iii–v.
97. *Report of a Committee of General and Other Officers of the Army on Army Re-Organization,* C.2,791, 1881, XXI, p. 10.
98. J. Luvaas, *The Education of an Army: British Military Thought, 1815–1940,* Cassell, London, 1964, p. 123.
99. *General Annual Returns of the British Army,* C.1,323, 1873, XLIII, p. 13, and C.9,426, 1899, LIII, p. 16.
100. *The United Service Gazette,* 4 Jan. 1873, p. 5.
101. *The Naval and Military Gazette,* 6 Jan. 1872, p. 2.

8 The late Victorian army

During the last quarter of the nineteenth century, the role of the army in preserving and expanding the Empire attracted unprecedented interest. War, though still 'a noise far away', was a noise which aroused a more intense and popular appeal than ever before over a comparable period of time. War correspondents followed the army around the globe. Vivid and lyrical despatches were telegraphed home. Minor reverses were described in apocalyptic terms; minor victories were hailed with paeans of praise. Campaign histories and military biographies appeared in vast numbers, while writers of military fiction found an apparently insatiable market for romantic and idealistic accounts of martial adventure in distant parts of the Empire. Yet this upsurge of interest concealed several paradoxes. The army was never seriously tested on the field of battle. Although involved in fighting or in colonial expeditions throughout the years from 1859 to 1899, with the exceptions of 1869 and 1883,[1] the army encountered neither a European foe nor a crisis as grave as the Indian Mutiny: it was only embroiled in a series of small colonial wars. Political leaders, too, did not recklessly exploit the jingoistic sentiment. Even those who promoted the Imperial ideal did not unleash the purse-strings and send the army forth, save on a few occasions, in search of fresh territorial conquests. Politicians and their constituents, with a few notable exceptions, did not press for the reform of the organization and training of the army; indeed this was a period of ossification in army reform. And the fascination with the adventure and pageantry of army life did not promote a rush to the Colours: the army, as a career, retained its lowly appeal. Theodore von Sosnosky, a foreign observer of the army, found this paradox utterly baffling. 'How this blind glorification and worship of the Army', he wrote, 'continues to coexist with the contemptuous dislike felt towards the members of it, must remain a problem in the national psychology'.[2]

All these paradoxes derived from the nature of the duties expected of the late Victorian army. Apart from aiding the civil power in the United Kingdom, these duties were primarily colonial. By 1870 the policy of withdrawing troops from the partially or wholly self-governing colonies had reduced the colonial contingent to nearly 24,000 troops, excluding the Indian garrison. Some battalions languished in small islands like Malta and Mauritius, Bermuda and St Helena, protecting bases from which the navy controlled vital trade routes. Other garrisons preserved more substantial territories from external aggression, and fulfilled the no less exacting duty of maintaining law and order. Internal policing varied enormously in the scope and scale of operational requirements. The army was involved in the suppression of race riots in Bermuda (1875-76), in protracted guerrilla campaigns against the dacoits of Burma (1885-91), and in the quelling of minor rebellions, as in Canada (1870 and 1885). Occasionally the army was required to assume the offensive and mount expeditions on foreign soil. The motive was often punitive, designed to avenge a wrong or to wipe out an insult. The Abyssinian expedition of 1867-68 was undertaken to compel the release of prisoners seized by King Theodore; it did not result in permanent occupation. But annexation followed some punitive wars (the Ashanti War of 1873-74 and the Burma War of 1885), and conquest was a motive in some campaigns (the first South African War of 1880-81 was provoked by Britain's annexation of the two Boer republics in 1877).

To fulfil these duties, the army relied upon troops stationed abroad, assisted by locally raised units and often by expeditionary forces despatched from the United Kingdom. In the absence of a General Staff, each expeditionary force had to be hastily improvised. The army relied upon the organizational expertise of their commanding officers. Whether operating from a home, colonial, or Indian base, commanders like Wolseley, Roberts and Kitchener had to be resourceful and adaptable They could not hope for success by adhering to the textbook rules of conventional warfare. As Colonel (later Major-General Sir) C. E. Callwell indicated in his work, *Small Wars: Their Principles and Practice* (London, 1896), wars against irregular forces were inherently diversified. The all-embracing term, 'small colonial wars', concealed the enormous variety of these military campaigns, and the demands which this variety made upon the late Victorian army.[3]

British forces encountered a host of different opponents and different tactical formations. Some armies like those of Arabi Pasha in Egypt (1882), by virtue of their European training, fought in the form and organization of a regular army. Others, like the Afghans (1878-80), had the organization but not the armaments of a regular army. The Zulu impis were totally different; they were well disciplined, organized in their own distinctive formations, capable of carrying out precise battlefield manoeuvres, but lacked any sophisticated weapons. The Boers, conversely, were a determined, well-armed, and skilfully led foe, but were largely unorganized in 1881. The British army had to adapt to the shock tactics of the tribes in East and West Africa, to the guerrilla campaigns of the Maoris, to the demands of hill fighting on the North-West Frontier, and to the use of irregular cavalry by the Moors, Arabs and Tartars. While some campaigns were waged against habitual foes on familiar terrain, others took place in partially explored territory against an enemy of unknown strength, weapons, and fighting qualities. In these circumstances, improvization and adaptability were imperatives. Any British misfortunes, argued Wolseley, have occurred from 'a close literal adhesion on the part of colonels and generals to the dry-as-dust rules taught in every work as military science'.[4]

In small colonial wars, nature could prove as formidable an adversary as the military opponent. Adverse climates, barren and infertile terrains, the absence of road and rail links posed formidable problems. In at least two campaigns, the Abyssinian War and the Ashanti War, British commanders had to complete their expeditions as quickly as possible lest torrential rains block their retreat. Lines of communication had to be constructed to provide supplies, reinforcements, and information, to protect escape routes, and to remove the sick and the wounded. Only in the marches of Sir Donald Stewart from Kandahar to Haider Kel and of Sir Frederick Roberts from Kabul to Kandahar (1884) did British commanders dispense with their lines of communication.[5] Officers, generally, paid minute attention to the details dictated by natural and climatic factors. Wolseley constantly campaigned for a loose-fitting khaki coloured uniform, for a more varied service diet, and for greater care of the sick and wounded.[6] He set a splendid example in medical arrangements, ensuring that his men on the Ashanti campaign were supported by a hundred-bed field hospital, four hospital ships, and the means by which patients could be trans-shipped, via the Cape Town lines, to Gibraltar or England. Kitchener, an Engineer, was even more punctilious in his handling of matters connected with transport and supply; he had 230 miles of railway constructed prior to his advance on Omdurman.[7] British officers became proficient in anticipating and securing their logistical requirements.

Small colonial wars also entailed the assumption of a strategic offensive. British forces had to launch vigorous assaults to dissuade waverers in the disaffected population from swelling the ranks of the enemy. Only by seizing the offensive could the army overcome its natural position of strategic inferiority. Burdened by an organization, lines of communication and cumbersome equipment, and faced by an enemy possessing powers of sudden dispersal and concentration, the army always sought open battle. In combat alone could superior armament, discipline, an acknowledged chain of command, and *esprit de corps* give a real advantage to a regular army. The aim, ultimately, was not merely to beat the enemy, but to beat him thoroughly. As positions in colonial warfare were relatively, though not invariably, unimportant, the size of the casualty list assumed a greater significance. By inflicting the largest possible number of casualties, the army could shorten the war and prevent a recrudescence of hostile activity. To achieve this objective, the army tended to eschew both conventional artillery bombardments and frontal assaults lest the opponent withdraw, without substantial loss, along an unthreatened line of retreat. Commanders preferred to combine frontal and flank attacks and to follow them up with a determined pursuit of the enemy. A passive defence was wholly inapposite: the attack or at least an active defence with prominent counter-attacks was the only strategic posture. The aim, as Colonel Callwell affirmed, was to undermine the enemy's will to resist (a wider concept than defeating an opponent in arms): the enemy had to recognize the dominance of the 'forces of civilization'.[8]

In colonial warfare, the army used some tactics which were anachronistic by the standards of conventional combat. Commanders regularly employed 'the square' in offensive and defensive situations. A less rigid concept than implied by its name, the square was merely a formation which showed a front to the flanks and rear as well as to the proper front. It sometimes had only three sides, was an elastic arrangement in jungle and hill warfare, but was usually rigid when confronted by a fanatical attack. The square enabled the army, burdened with impedimenta, to face a mobile and numerically superior opponent: it also ensured that the army could counter an opponent, in an unknown position, who could attack from any quarter. Within a square, the army could preserve its advantage in armaments; it conserved ammunition and maximized fire power by strict fire discipline and volley-firing. Should an enemy launch a determined attack, substituting shock action for fire action, the infantry would frequently reply in kind with bayonet charges: the cavalry, if available, would counter-attack with the *arme blanche*. Even the artillery, though usually unable to fire preparatory bombardments, could seek engagement at close quarters and so maximize its advantage over irregular warriors.[9] Tactics, like the square, volley-firing and charges with the *arme blanche*, which had become less and less useful in conventional warfare, were applicable and at times imperative in small colonial wars.

Generalship, staff work, and tactics were shaped fundamentally by the many years of small colonial warfare. Relatively few troops were used in each campaign. The largest force deployed was in the Egyptian war of 1882: it numbered about 35,000 men. Lord Chelmsford amassed a 'surfeit of strength' in assembling 16,000 European troops and 7,000 Natal Kaffirs for his second invasion of Zululand.[10] Sir Robert Napier commanded only 13,000 soldiers in the invasion of Abyssinia and lost a mere thirty-five men. Commanders and their staffs lacked experience in controlling and manipulating large-scale formations, a factor which may have contributed to the lack of interest in Staff College training. Only thirty-two graduates emerged from the College per annum, too few to fill even the peacetime appointments. As regimental officers without a p.s.c. (passed Staff College) had to supplement the staff, staff work suffered from a lack of uniformity. Lacking sufficient permanent staff, except at Aldershot, commanding officers continued to rely upon improvisation and their own past experience.[11] Prolonged involvement in small colonial wars had restricted the scope of the staff officer, a drawback exposed in the South African War where some 450,000 troops were employed.

Even worse, small colonial warfare did not prepare the army for wars dominated by modern armaments. Admittedly, several regiments had suffered from well-aimed rifle-fire during the first Boer War. After the military setbacks of Bronkhurst Spruit, Laing's Nek and the Ingogo, General Colley's forces were routed at Majuba Hill. Out-shot by the Boer marksmen, the 58th Foot resolved to improve its own musketry standards; the regiment entered the next South African campaign with a musketry standard averaging 'marksmen'.[12] Tactics had also been modified in some campaigns. The hill warfare of the North-West Frontier had placed a premium on individual skill with the rifle, open order formations, and the careful use of cover. Tactical innovation, however, had not penetrated the confines of Aldershot. Military authorities in the home army did not accept that tactics had to change radically to meet the threat posed by the emergence of the smokeless magazine rifle. Introduced in the 1890s, this small-calibre, long-range, flat trajectory weapon was able to fire between twenty and thirty shots per minute. Smokeless powder enabled riflemen to sustain rapid, aimed fire without black powder obscuring their field of vision. It increased the tactical power of the defensive, allowing entrenched marksmen to retain the advantage of cover and shoot without betraying their position. Conversely, offensive forces, who lost the covering cloud of smoke, confronted flat trajectory bullets with an increased range of penetration: at Omdurman the Guards claimed effective fire at 2,700 yards.[13]

Although prepared to endorse open order formations and the use of cover to conceal lines of attack,[14] senior officers refused to accept that the technology had circumscribed the offensive. After years of success in colonial warfare, they insisted that the moral effects of the offensive were immutable. They dismissed the breechloading experience of foreign wars and the tactical reforms advocated by some junior officers. Viscount Wolseley utterly deprecated the use of entrenchments as liable to depress the attacking zeal of the defending forces.[15] Major-General J. Keith Fraser, Inspector-General of Cavalry, maintained that the absence of smoke would increase the value of the *arme blanche* by enhancing the moral effect of cavalry charges upon shaken infantry.[16] Major-General G. H. Marshall, Commander of the Royal Artillery Aldershot, insisted that technology had not altered the principles of artillery employment. The quest for cover, he declared, was pernicious: 'the best protection from the enemy's fire, is to overwhelm him with your own'.[17] After thirty years of martial triumphs, marred by the occasional but rarely decisive reverse, senior officers had become blinkered by their own success. As Colonel G. F. R. Henderson wearily admitted, 'Men, especially in practical matters, are always inclined to remember what they have seen rather than what they hear, and to give more weight to their own stale experience, gained under obsolete conditions, than to the impressions of others'.[18]

The drawbacks of the prolonged immersion of the army in small colonial warfare were not readily perceived by contemporaries. The army had been conspicuously successful over the many years of colonial campaigning, notwithstanding the defeats of Isandhlwana (1879), Majuba Hill (1881), Maiwand (1880), and the failure to relieve Gordon in Khartoum (1884–85). Officers and other ranks had had their courage and physical endurance repeatedly tested on active service. The country possessed, by virtue of the garrisons east of Malta, a unique body of seasoned soldiers. Facing an ever-present menace, but blessed with complete establishments and unrivalled facilities for practical training, this part of the army remained on a permanent war footing. These were, as Henderson claimed, 'strong men, horse, foot and artillery, soldiers of whom no conscript army has seen the like . . .'.[19] Their military activities, and nearly all the major campaigns of the period, were extensively reported by an ever expanding galaxy of war correspondents.

Coverage of the army in the national press paralleled the massive expansion of the newspaper industry. In the wake of Forster's Education Act of 1870, and the enforcement of compulsory school attendance from 1880, a larger reading public emerged. Circulations increased, and the popular press mushroomed, as the number of newspapers doubled between 1880 and 1900. Editors and the proprietors of the popular press knew their market; they knew that wars could boost sales, especially if vividly described in the form of adventure narratives, and if speedily reported via the telegraph. *The Daily News* had trebled its circulation during the Franco-Prussian War. Reports of war in distant and exotic parts of the Empire, focusing upon the courage and carnage of battle, provided a vicarious outlet for those trapped in the drab monotony of office and factory life.

The craft of a war correspondent had altered radically since the heyday of Russell in the Crimea. By the 1870s Russell was still an active reporter, the doyen of his fraternity, but a man whose time had passed. He had never adjusted his reporting to the telegraphic age. Throughout the Franco-Prussian War, he had been scooped repeatedly by other reporters, especially by Archibald Forbes of *The Daily News*. Following time-honoured methods, Russell had sent comprehensive, eloquent, and reasonably accurate despatches by field-post or courier, via the slow and circuitous mail train. Forbes, conversely, made extensive use of the telegraph, so ensuring that details of forthcoming operations, elicited from the staff of the Saxon army, were set up in type even before an attack was launched. Ironically Forbes, who regarded Russell as his professional exemplar, had grasped the essence of war correspondence, namely the despatch of the 'earliest intelligence'. As he wrote in his memoirs, 'the man whose main gift is that he can paint pictures with his pen is beaten and pushed aside by the swift, alert man of action, who can get his budget of dry, concise, comprehensive facts into print twenty-four hours in advance of the most graphic description that ever stirred the blood. In modern war correspondence the race is emphatically to the swift, the battle to the strong'.[20]

With so much at stake, newspapers invested heavily in their war correspondents. During the Russo-Turkish War, Forbes was sending messages of more than 8,000 words apiece, at a cost of 18*d* a word. The reporters themselves took immense risks to reach the scene of battle and to relay their observations as quickly as possible. Several died in action. Frank le Poer Power perished with Gordon in the Sudan. Another *Times* correspondent, the Hon. Hubert Howard, died at Omdurman; Bennett Burleigh of *The Daily Telegraph* and Charles Williams of *The Daily Chronicle* were wounded in the same battle. Personal safety was placed at a discount as reporters pressed ever closer to the front line in battle. Winwood Reade, *The Times* correspondent during the Ashanti War, accompanied the advance column of the Black Watch as it drove back the enemy and took its camp. 'In this country', wrote Reade, 'a war correspondent can witness nothing unless he goes very near the enemy. In thick bush there are no bird's eye views to be had'.[21] Reporters were no less intrepid in other wars. At the battle of Ulundi (1879), Forbes paced back and forth inside the British square, jotting down impressions of the Zulu attack, while Melton Prior of *The Illustrated London News* sat nearby, sketching details of the battle itself. Thereafter Forbes, upon learning that Lord Chelmsford did not intend to send an official despatch immediately, rode through the Zulu lines to the nearest telegraph office of Landsmann's Drift, over 100 miles away. His account of the victory was the first intelligence received in the United Kingdom; it was read by Government ministers to both Houses of Parliament.

Readers identified with the daring exploits of each correspondent – Forbes's 'Ride to Death' was widely acclaimed. They savoured the racy narratives of battlefield action, the accounts of valour and heroism, the grisly descriptions of death and slaughter. Of the war correspondents, few matched the evocative writing of George Warrington Steevens, the young journalist of *The Daily Mail*, who reported Kitchener's reconquest of the Sudan. At the battle of Atbara (1898), he followed the Cameron Highlanders as they advanced through bullets, 'swishing and lashing now like rain on a pond. But the line of Khaki and purple tartan never bent nor swayed; it just went slowly forward like a ruler'. The officers, he recorded, were calm and phlegmatic – 'they might have been on the hill after red deer'. The men, 'unkempt, unshaven Tommies', were transformed in battle. 'The bullets', he wrote, 'had whispered to raw youngsters in one breath the secret of all the glories of the British Army'.[22] Accounts of sterling British fortitude, coupled with passing references to the admirable fighting of native auxiliaries, were magnified by reference to the fanatical zeal, courage, and even, occasionally, the tactical flair of their opponents. Of the Dervishes at Omdurman, wrote Steevens, 'no white troops would have faced that torrent of death for five minutes', but, eventually, that 'dusky line . . . bent, broke up, fell apart, and disappeared'.[23] Following the battles came gruesome descriptions of the body-strewn field, detailed casualty lists, and hasty post-mortems. Tactical blemishes were not ignored, whether the use of column formations in the West African bush or the costly, if courageous, charge of the 21st Lancers at Omdurman.[24] Criticisms, however, rarely marred the ecstatic reports of victory; martial triumphs were regularly attributed to the superior arms, leadership, organization, and moral purpose of the British forces.

In popularizing the army and its Imperial role, the importance of war correspondents cannot be gainsaid. Forbes likened his profession to a national 'necessity', an essential supplement to the meagre and not always candid communications from official sources. He saw neither himself nor his colleagues as dispassionate observers, concerned primarily about the moral or political consequences of war. War correspondents, he affirmed, should record 'how our countrymen, our dear ones, toil and thole, vindicate Britain's manhood, and joyously expend their lives for Queen and fatherland'.[25] Writing in this vein undoubtedly had an impact; but it did not, as was sometimes claimed, turn the war correspondent into 'the most successful recruiting officer of the Queen's army'.[26] Although newspaper reports may have attracted some recruits, the campaigns were too short to have provided a continuous stimulus over twenty-five or thirty years. Recruiting remained a problem throughout this period in spite of the profusion of small colonial wars.

On the other hand, the press boosted the careers and reputations of several senior officers. Some officers had realized that the press could promote their ideas and themselves. Wolseley was particularly skilful, though obvious, in his self-advertisement. On his own campaigns, he allowed correspondents enormous latitude in their reporting from the scene of battle. He also wrote about his own expeditions and proposals for reform, so earning a useful supplementary income while keeping his name in the periodical press. He became a folk hero in the 1870s and 1880s; he was caricatured as 'the modern major-general' by W. S. Gilbert: the phrase 'All Sir Garnet' became a synonym for efficiency. This penchant for publicity had its drawbacks; it earned the cordial loathing of the Queen and the Duke of Cambridge. But his public reputation, coupled with a fervent support of the Cardwell reforms, attracted some influential patrons in Government, without whom Wolseley would have had no career in the Horse Guards. By 6 November 1881 the Duke of Cambridge sadly informed the Queen that Wolseley might be 'forced upon' him as Adjutant-General. The appointment of Wolseley, wrote the Duke, could only 'produce bad results' for the army and prove deleterious to the public service: 'His communication with the Press is what I so greatly dread'.[27]

Even more dramatic was the role of the press in ensuring the despatch of General Gordon to Khartoum and in reporting his activities thereafter. On 4 January 1884 the Gladstone government had decided to withdraw Egyptian garrisons from the Sudan, in the wake of the Mahdi's revolt and the annihilation of General Hicks's army at El Obeid. Four days later General Gordon, who had just returned from Palestine, was interviewed by W. T. Stead, the editor of *The Pall Mall Gazette*. Gordon deplored the idea of evacuation, viewing it as both dishonourable and impracticable. Stead printed the interview on the following day and urged the government, in a front-page editorial, to reverse its policy. He advocated the despatch of Gordon, 'who on more than one occasion has proved himself more valuable than an entire army' to the Sudan.[28] Other papers reprinted the interview and endorsed Stead's demand. Within nine days the government bowed before the editorial clamour and requested Gordon to go to the Sudan.

Ministerial policy had not changed, however. The cabinet required Gordon to report on the military situation in the Sudan and to consider the best means of evacuating the interior and of securing the safety of the Red Sea ports. Almost as soon as he arrived in Khartoum, Gordon renounced this mission and resolved to challenge the Mahdi. Within a month he found himself besieged. From the beleaguered city, the sole source of information other than the despatches of Gordon were the telegrams of Frank le Poer Power, the young Irish correspondent of *The Times*. Gordon and Power liked each other,[29] dined together, and lived within the Governor's palace. All the despatches of Power were sent with the full knowledge and approval of Gordon. As the plight of the city became increasingly desperate, Power pleaded for a relief force: 'We are daily expecting British troops. We cannot bring ourselves to believe that we are to be abandoned by the Government. Our existence depends on England'.[30] Printing House Square endorsed these pleas. To the acute embarrassment of the government, another campaign was mounted to reverse its policy. On 13 May 1884, the government barely survived a motion of censure in the House of Commons, by 303 votes to 275. Pressure continued throughout the summer, mainly in the form of leading articles, until, eventually, Lord Hartington threatened to resign from the cabinet unless a relief expedition was sent. On 5 August, Gladstone capitulated and moved a vote of credit to facilitate the relief operation.

On 29 September 1884, *The Times* published the last despatches from Khartoum. After several months of silence, these two reports, dated 28 April and 30 and 31 July, described the daily engagements, the conditions within the city, and the abject state of morale: 'all hope of relief by our Government is at an end . . .'.[31] *The Times* roundly condemned the government for leaving Gordon to a martyr's fate, and became even more bitter when it learnt of the death of Power,

Colonel J. D. H. Stewart, and the French Consul, whom Gordon had sent by boat in search of help.[32] The recriminations reached a crescendo on 5 February 1885, when news arrived that Khartoum had been taken and Gordon slain on 26 January, only two days before the arrival of a relief column. A ferocious outcry erupted in Parliament and in the press. Gladstone was bitterly denounced for his failure to send relief in time. In the music-halls, his initials G.O.M. ('Grand Old Man') were changed to M.O.G. - 'Murderer of Gordon'. Gordon, on the other hand, was revered as a martyr, although he had disobeyed orders, remained in a highly vulnerable position, and had shown not the slightest desire to leave Khartoum even had a relief force arrived in time.[33] Over the thirteen months, newspapers had played a critical role; they had altered ministerial policy, urged the despatch of a relief force, and had contributed to the legacy of bitterness and recrimination. Even before his death, journalists had fashioned the legend of Gordon. 'No difficulties', wrote Archibald Forbes, 'will abate his loyal courage; no stress of adversity will daunt his gallant heart. For him life has no ambition, death no terror. He will do his duty'.[34]

The relationship between the army and the press was by no means wholly cordial. Those officers, headed by the Duke of Cambridge, who had deplored the reporting of Russell from the Crimea, were never enamoured of the journalistic profession. Wolseley and Gordon were relatively exceptional in their willingness to mix socially with men who rarely conformed to the standards and behaviour of Victorian gentlemen. Few officers accepted with equanimity the criticisms of war correspondents, many of whom had either aborted military careers at an early stage or had never entered the army. When Russell dared to criticize the choice of staff by Wolseley in South Africa, in 1879, Wolseley disparaged him as 'no gentleman', a fellow 'who has behaved like the scoundrel and low snob he always was'.[35] More fundamentally, the military had lost its control over the flow of news from the field of battle. Although some commanders were able to use and manipulate the press, others were reluctant or unable to do so. Official despatches, bearing the imprint of the commanding officer, had lost their impact. Ever present, in these circumstances, was the fear that correspondents might reveal secrets or intentions which could be of use to the enemy. Censorship became more regularly enforced, first in India during the advance on Kabul and latterly in the Sudan, where Kitchener limited the telegraphic facilities of the twenty-six war correspondents to 200 words a day and refused to give any interviews or briefings. Nevertheless, correspondents, though irked by the restrictions, were still effusive in their praise of Kitchener. Press comment only enhanced his image and stature. Steevens could not imagine Kitchener other 'than as seeing the right thing to do and doing it. His precision is so inhumanly unerring, he is more like a machine than a man'.[36]

War correspondents had not simply enhanced the stature of particular generals; they had also promoted the army as the instrument of Imperial mission. By the 1880s and 1890s that mission had attained an unprecedented degree of popularity. Writers were justifying recourse to war and the expansion of the Empire with reasons which ranged from crude Darwinism to the propagation of the Christian ethic.[37] The role of the army in fulfilling that mission attracted considerable interest and not merely in the realm of campaign reporting. Several war correspondents left journalism, finding more lucrative rewards from writing about military history, famous regiments, distinguished generals, or pure fiction based on a military theme. Among the writers who were formerly war correspondents were Forbes, Winwood Reade and, above all, George Alfred Henty, the prolific writer of schoolboy yarns. Admittedly, the interest in the Imperial role of the army was neither new nor even as intensely felt as during the early months of the Indian Mutiny. During the last two decades of the century, however, both the output of books and the market demand for writing upon military or quasi-military themes reached new heights. Never before had the army attracted so many authors and the production of so many books over a comparable period of time.

Of the various writers none was more influential than Rudyard Kipling, a man who never saw a shot fired in anger until 1900. Kipling had spent seven formative years in India from 1882 to 1889, a period of relative peace on the North-West Frontier. During the mid 1880s Imperial wars had erupted in Egypt (1884–85) and in Burma (1885–87), but Kipling lacked first-hand knowledge of either country. His sole experience of Egypt was a passage through the Suez Canal in 1882. For information on the Egyptian campaign, he seems to have relied upon an old schoolfriend 'Stalky', Major-General L. C. Duntersville, who had served at Suakin in the Red Sea and later came to Lahore. Kipling knew nothing of Burma until he briefly visited Rangoon and Moulmein as a steamship passenger in 1889. Consequently, his Burmese works, like 'The Ballad of Boh da Thone' (August 1898) and 'A Conference of the Powers' (May 1890), though vividly descriptive of wartime incidents, lack the local colour and insights of his Indian writing.[38]

Charles Carrington has indicated that Kipling relied heavily upon secondary sources for his stories about army life in India. Kipling found many of his yarns and anecdotes from the files and reference works of *The Civil and Military Gazette*, his father's library, and his father's immense knowledge of India. 'The Drums of the Fore and Aft' was a story recorded by Robert Orme in his history of British military transactions in India; 'The Lost Legion' was a legend of 1857 based upon John Nicholson's punishment of the mutinous 55th Native Infantry; 'Snarleyow' was an episode from Sergeant Bancroft's history of the Bengal horse artillery; and 'The Taking of Lungtungpen' was a fictionalized version of an achievement by the 2nd Queen's Regiment, which Kipling wrote only a few weeks after the event had been reported in *The Civil and Military Gazette.*[39] Yet Kipling formed many contacts with the army while based in Lahore, the capital of the Punjab, a frontier province still policed by the army. In this outpost of the Empire, the military ethos was more pronounced and pervasive than in the rest of British India. The majority of civil administrators were army officers. Various regiments were stationed in the cantonment of Mian Mir, just outside Lahore, notably the 5th Northumberland Fusiliers from 1886 to 1888. Kipling often dined in the mess. He formed contacts with officers and men, from which derived his fascination of the army life and his awe of the 'military virtues'.

Kipling, in his earliest writing about the army, dealt primarily with officers, particularly with the life-style and attitudes of young subalterns. Several of the stories reproduced in *Plain Tales from the Hills* (1887) centred upon the horseplay and practical jokes of life in the officers' mess, notably 'The Arrest of Lieutenant Golighty' and 'His Wedded Wife'. The rigours, hardships, and the possibility of an unheroic death were vividly depicted in the poem, 'Arithmetic on the Frontier':

> A scrimmage in a Border Station -
> A canter down some dark defile -
> Two thousand pounds of education
> Drops to a ten-rupee jezail -
> The Crammer's boast, the Squadron's pride,
> Shot like a rabbit in a ride![40]

Even more evocative, perhaps, was the characterization of 'Bobby Wicks', the hero of 'Only a Subaltern'. In his description of 'Bobby Wicks', Kipling encapsulates the virtues of honesty, loyalty, propriety, and unflinching moral and physical courage, so exalted in the code of an officer gentleman.

But it was the writing of Kipling about the private soldier which was strikingly original. It would broaden his own appeal as an author and as a poet. *Soldiers Three* (1890) and *Barrack-Room Ballads* (1892) were utterly new in subject matter and in style to the Victorian reading public. No-one had chosen to write so extensively about the serving private soldier (as distinct from the retired soldier who figures fairly prominently in English literature). No-one, in the period of Yeats, Wilde and Conard, had composed their work 'in the language of the people and with the rhythm of the music-hall'.[41] Kipling understood the importance of dialect and never used it merely for comic effect. He made his Irishman, Mulvaney, his Cockney, Ortheris, and his dalesman from the West Riding, Learoyd - the characters of 'The Three Musketeers' (March 1887) and *Soldiers Three* - use local words, grammatical forms, and speak in a language which is both convincing and appropriate. Kipling used the vernacular of the London working class for the majority of his speakers in the *Barrack-Room Ballads*; he was the first author to treat that speech as a dialect in its own right.[42]

Equally impressive was the stark realism of his depiction of army life in India. His 'Tommy Atkins' led a boring and tedious life, with few pleasures, little glamour, and less status:

> I went into a theatre as sober as could be,
> They gave a drunk civilian room, but 'adn't none for me;
> They sent me to the gallery or round the music-'alls,
> But when it comes to fightin', Lord! they'll shove me in the stalls![43]

Serving in India, as Kipling described it, was a life of grinding inactivity, dominated by the climate – 'the worst o' your foes is the sun over'ead' – and bedevilled by recurrent epidemics of cholera.[44] To escape from the heat and the fever, his soldiers turned to drink, whoring, and barrack-room brawling. His characters were never standardized, however. Speaking in soliloquies, or occasionally in dialogues, the characters reveal themselves as decent and deceitful, heroes and cowards, honest and wayward. Some are idiosyncratic – the 'Gentleman Rankers'; a few are female – women of the camp, 'ruined' and deserted by their roguish amours; all are different. Keenly aware of detail, Kipling recorded a profoundly realistic picture of the British Tommy:

> Wot makes the soldier's 'eart to penk, wot makes 'im to perspire?
> It isn't standin' up to charge nor lyin' down to fire;
> But it's everlastin' waitin' on a everlastin' road
> For the commissariat camel an' 'is commissariat load.[45]

Kipling's work earned criticism as well as applause. His writing failed to impress Oscar Wilde and aroused the everlasting antipathy of Max Beerbohm. His characterization of Tommy Atkins neither convinced nor pleased some retired soldiers. Robert Blatchford, a former NCO, found that the tales of the *Soldiers Three* were lacking in plausibility and in realism. No non-commissioned officer, he opined, would have permitted the excesses and latitude enjoyed by Kipling's heroes. Nor could Blatchford accept the dialect of the *Barrack-Room Ballads* as anything other than 'comic caricature'. He conceded that barrack-room slang was prevalent, and that many soldiers were recruited from the 'illiterate classes' of London. He believed, nonetheless, that '. . . soldiers speak more correctly than civilians of their own rank in life, the tendency of barrack life being to assimilate all dialects and slightly to amend the level of merit in grammar and pronunciation – the amendment being due partly to travel and experience and partly to the example of educated officers'.[46] This criticism seems plausible, but it should be juxtaposed with the subsequent reflection of Sir George Younghusband. Younghusband agrees that in his youth neither he nor his brother officers had ever heard the words or expressions that Kipling's soldiers used. But, several years later, 'the soldiers thought, and talked, and expressed themselves exactly like Rudyard Kipling had taught them in his stories! . . . Rudyard Kipling made the modern soldier'.[47] Although this assertion smacks of hyperbole, it indicates the immense popularity of Kipling's works within the ranks, a point corroborated by the hearty receptions he received wherever he met the troops in the South African War. He had shown interest in them. He had sympathized with the underdog. He had stripped away the pretence, and, within the realms of poetic licence, had described the soldier's life with his own 'bitter honesty'.[48]

Notwithstanding the popularity of the war literature, enlistment was still shunned by the vast majority of the populace. Distance, possibly, lent enchantment. While many were fascinated by the romantic and idealistic aspects of army life, and were amused by the escapades of soldiers in remote and exotic places, few altered their opinion of the army as a career. Indeed the writing of Kipling may have reinforced the traditional attitudes about the military life – that it was poorly paid, lacked status, and was bereft of prospects; that it attracted recruits from the least respectable sections of the population; and that it was characterized, in many instances, by dissolute and licentious behaviour. Soldiers in uniform were still objects of discrimination. They were frequently prevented by the rules of some steamship companies from using second-class saloons. They were debarred by some theatres and music-halls from occupying particular places in their auditoriums. Occasionally soldiers were even prevented from riding on omnibuses because they were wearing the Queen's uniform.[49]

Within the United Kingdom, moreover, the army was still required to aid the civil power in the maintenance of public order. Troops were called out on twenty-four occasions between 1869 and 1910.[50] They acquitted themselves with varying degrees of success. A timely intervention by the Guards enabled the police to restrain a riotous mob in Trafalgar Square on 13 November 1887. A detachment from the 1st battalion, South Staffordshire Regiment, performed less creditably during the lock-out at the Ackton Hall Colliery, Featherstone, on 7 September 1893. Outflanked, outnumbered, and sorely provoked, Captain Barker ordered his twenty-eight soldiers to open fire: two innocent bystanders were killed and between eleven and fourteen persons were injured. Although aiding the civil power was a recognized military duty, this role hardly enhanced the image and appeal of the army among sections of the working class.

If attitudes towards the army as a career were not transformed, ministerial policy was equally steadfast. Economy remained an ever-present concern; a generation would elapse before the imbalance between the battalions at home and abroad would be corrected. Governments were not impervious to war scares and invasion literature, but after each crisis the navy and not the army benefited. Not only did the navy enjoy a longer tradition of public sentiment, but it also kept the lanes of commerce open, an absolute priority in the eyes of most politicians. Preserving or expanding the Empire, though sometimes a source of economic gain, was more often considered a burden or a duty which was invariably expensive. The navy benefited, too, from a powerful Blue Water lobby, backed by influential naval officers, *The Times*, and by respected Parliamentarians like Lord George Hamilton and Sir John Colomb. As W. S. Hamer has argued, 'The naval acts of 1885, 1889, 1894, and 1896 are all evidence of which branch of the armed services profited from the spirit of the age'.[51]

During one invasion scare in April 1888, Lord Wolseley, the Adjutant-General, and the Duke of Cambridge joined the alarmists in protesting about the state of the national defences. In an after-dinner speech Wolseley condemned the system of party government as the 'curse of modern England'. Every incoming minister, he averred, had tried to build a 'claptrap reputation' by reducing the service Estimates.[52] The Duke of Cambridge was equally outspoken. As the Secretary of State had refused his request for an additional 11,000 men, he could not be responsible for the under-strength and inefficient army.[53] Though rebuked by the Prime Minister, Lord Wolseley reiterated his complaints in the House of Lords on 14 May. 'Our defences at home and abroad', he declared, were in such an 'unsatisfactory condition' that even the safety of the capital could not be guaranteed.[54] On the following day, the government announced the appointment of a Royal Commission under the Marquess of Hartington to investigate the state of the army and navy departments, and to examine their relations with the Treasury.

After a year's deliberations, the Commission issued two reports, the first on 10 July 1889 and the second on 11 February 1890. Having found that there was practically no communication between the War Office and the Admiralty, the Commission proposed that a defence committee, composed of cabinet ministers, soldiers, and sailors, should be established. That committee, it stated, should be empowered to examine the Estimates of the two services before they were submitted to the cabinet, to examine questions of defence policy, and to determine the requirements of the services from an overall plan of Imperial defence The Commission also recommended that the post of Commander-in-Chief should be abolished, and a War Office Council created. The Commission felt that consultative, executive, and administrative duties were grossly over-centralized in the office of the Commander-in-Chief. It believed, too, that the Commander-in-Chief, by standing between the Secretary of State and the subordinate heads of military departments, effectively prevented the Secretary of State from receiving adequate professional advice. Hence the Commission proposed that a Council should be created, consisting of the Secretary of State, the Parliamentary and Permanent Under-Secretaries, the Financial Secretary, and the five senior military officers, a Chief of Staff, the Adjutant-General, Quartermaster-General, Director of Artillery, and Inspector-General of Fortifications. Finally, the Commission recommended that a General Staff should be created with a remit to study the military requirements of the Empire. The new Chief of Staff would head the department; he would be required to advise the Secretary of State, liaise with the First Lord of the Admiralty on inter-service questions, and submit an annual report to the Secretary of State upon the military requirements of the Empire.[55]

Two members of the Commission dissented from the majority report. Lord Randolph Churchill, the former Chancellor of the Exchequer, took his cue from Lord Wolseley and argued in favour of a radical change to free the conduct of military affairs from the evils of party interference. He recommended a unification of the army and navy in a Ministry of Defence, presided over by a single Minister. This Minister of Defence should be both a Member of Parliament and a high-ranking soldier or sailor; he would be responsible to Parliament for the efficiency of both services.[56] Sir Henry Campbell-Bannerman, a former Liberal Secretary of State for War, opposed the concept of a General Staff. He viewed the idea as unnecessary and as a potential evil. Britain, he argued, did not need to imitate continental practice because she did not have ambitious designs on her neighbours: she could respond to colonial disputes by adapting to the demands and circumstances of each situation. Campbell-Bannerman feared that a department, without a specific field of activity, might be tempted 'to create such a field for itself'.[57] His fears of the military, as revealed in private correspondence, were even more profound. Securing the best professional advice was not his sole concern; preserving 'civilian control on the neck of it' was more important. The military, he stressed, 'may be made good servants, but they would be bad masters'. To guard against this 'terrible danger', he wrote, 'I scotched on the Hartington Commission, the fine project of a "Chief of the Staff" who was to invent "military policies" for us. Military plans yes, for each occasion. But "Military Policy", we do not want'.[58]

As evidence of deeply-rooted liberal suspicions of the military, this letter is instructive; as a testimony to the influence of Campbell-Bannerman, it is positively misleading. Much more important opposition swayed the Conservative government and 'scotched' the Hartington Report. The Queen berated Lord Salisbury, claiming that her constitutional position would be undermined by abolishing the office of Commander-in-Chief.[59] Delighted to hear of this protest, the Duke of Cambridge confirmed that he would not accept a reduction in the 'status or dignity' of his position and would not accept any altered title.[60] Equally adamant in their opposition were Wolseley and Roberts, who both had hopes of succeeding the Duke as Commander-in-Chief. Wolseley thought that the idea of a General Staff had been promoted within the Commission by Sir Henry Brackenbury, the Director of Military Intelligence. As Brackenbury was the man best fitted to assume the post of Chief of the Staff, Wolseley viewed the scheme as merely naked self-promotion by the ambitious 'Brack'.[61] Confronted with the barrage of protests, the government compromised. Unwilling to press for the resignation of the Duke, it abandoned the concept of a General Staff and established a War Office Council with the Commander-in-Chief as the first military member.

The Council enhanced civilian control. The four heads of the military departments became responsible to, and could be directly consulted by, the Secretary of State. As Wolseley discovered when he became Commander-in-Chief in 1894, he had overall responsibility for military matters without any real control. The Commander-in-Chief, he declared, had become 'a fifth wheel' on the coach.[62] Britain, on the other hand, remained the only major power in Europe which had not emulated Prussia in the formation of a General Staff. An Intelligence Department had been created from the Topographical and Statistical Department in 1873. But the new Department was simply involved in the collection of facts and information. It benefited from the additional funding secured from the Treasury by Wolseley in 1886, and from the enlightened directorship of Brackenbury during his term of office (1886–91). Henceforth a series of intelligence reports were issued for the use of War Office officials and other departments of government. Without a General Staff, there was no agency required to use these reports in policy-making, operational planning, and in co-ordination with the naval authorities. A gap remained, in short, between the collecting of information and operational planning, which, insofar as it existed, was the responsibility of the Commander-in-Chief.

The General Staff was by no means the only reform which foundered in this period. Civilians and serving officers campaigned in favour of army reforms throughout the 1880s and 1890s, but with little success. The leading civilian reformers were Henry Spencer Wilkinson, a journalist and military historian, Sir Charles Dilke, a radical MP, specialist in Imperial defence and the author of *Problems of Greater Britain* (1890), and H. O. Arnold-Forster, a Liberal Unionist MP, who became an amateur expert on the technical details of naval and military organization. These pundits kept abreast of military developments in Britain and Europe. They attended manoeuvres, military exercises, and gunnery displays. They provided literary and intellectual leadership for the campaign in favour of reform. Military endorsement and information came from the officer corps in India – the faction which supported Lord Roberts in his rivalry with Viscount Wolseley and in his opposition to the Cardwell proposals. To advance their ideas in Parliament and to influence the cabinet, the reformers sought the backing of the service Members. As a large proportion of these Members had always disliked the Cardwell system, they usually proffered vocal support for any proposal to mitigate its effects.

In books, articles, and letters to the press, the reformers outlined their criticisms of the Cardwell system and their alternative proposals. They denounced the terms of enlistment. By 'the so-called Short-Service System', argued Arnold-Forster, 'men are enlisted for a longer term of service than in any other Army in the world'.[63] He believed that the terms of service had contributed to the recruiting malaise, and to the increasing reliance upon 'specials' (i.e. recruits who failed to measure 5 ft. 3½ in. in height and/or 33 in. round the chest). Like Dilke and Wilkinson, he favoured a radical reform of the terms of enlistment. Taking their cue from the writing of Roberts,[64] the reformers advocated two separate terms of enlistment: three years in the Colours followed by nine years in the Reserve for home service, or a twelve-year enlistment for overseas service, with the option of either three years of the enlistment in the Reserve or another nine years service with pension rights. The reformers believed that these terms, along with improvements in pay and in the conditions of service, would attract more recruits. Even more importantly, two separate terms of enlistment would provide seasoned soldiers for overseas duties. As Roberts had explained to the Duke of Cambridge, these measures would suit 'the military requirements of our empire, viz., a short service for home defence with its consequent reserve, and a long service for our Indian and colonial garrisons'.[65]

The reformers were equally critical of the double battalion system, territorial localization, and the Army Reserve. Double battalions, in their view, had led to the emasculation of the home battalion as a fighting unit. Without parity between battalions at home and abroad, some home battalions had incurred increasing strain; they had become little more than depots for the reception and training of new recruits. Territorial localization had also failed, in the opinion of Dilke, Wilkinson and Arnold-Forster. As many battalions moved so frequently from barracks to barracks, they had established few local attachments. The Reserve, finally, had never become a supplement for the peacetime army; it was merely a substitute for the ineffectives (soldiers who were too young or too sick for overseas service) and the shortages in the home battalions. The reformers feared that the Reserve would remain an unknown quantity, liable to be rapidly exhausted in a major war, while of little use for the multitude of small colonial wars. To overcome these deficiencies, they recommended the unlinking of battalions, the restoration of the old regimental numbers, and the feeding of overseas battalions from large depots at home. They insisted that the government should replenish the peacetime units in men, guns, and horses. They advocated a devolution of administrative responsibility from the War Office and a quartering of the home army in divisions or corps so that the men could be trained in large formations.[66]

To influence the Government, the reformers used Parliamentary debates, direct appeals to the cabinet, and campaigns in the press. The debates and appeals, which relied upon the support of the service Members, were the least successful approach. The service Members had a high opinion of their own influence. Along with other back-bench Conservatives, they had, by a cunning ruse, defeated the Liberal government over the cordite vote on 21 June 1895, after which that government had resigned. Their influence in the subsequent Parliament was more apparent than real, however. Many of them enjoyed the caustic criticisms which Dilke and Arnold-Forster hurled at both front benches. They sent a letter of protest to the Secretary of State, stating that the army had suffered from the malfunctioning of the Cardwell system, the erosion of regimental spirit, and the malevolent influence of War Office 'clerks'.[67] On the other hand, these Members had little to offer by way of positive support. Some, like Lieutenant-General Sir H. Havelock-Allen and Captain J. Sinclair, believed that the Cardwell system could be made to work,[68] while others supported the proposals of Dilke and Arnold-Forster. But the overwhelming majority had neither studied the finer points of army organization nor had an interest in the army beyond their own regiment or military arm. As Campbell-Bannerman shrewdly observed, 'It is the barrack-yard alone that is represented among the militaires in the House of Commons . . .'.[69] Within Parliament, in short, there was little scope for a positive or coherent campaign in favour of army reform. Even when Dilke and Arnold-Forster simply criticized the malaise in the home army, the service Members provided vocal rather than voting support. They were reluctant to vote against the Conservative whip, and shuddered at the prospect of sharing a lobby with the radicals and Irish Members, who gladly supported any division against the Army Estimates. When Dilke divided the House over the terms of enlistment, the service Members voted 33 to 10 against the motion which was lost by 197 to 63 votes.[70]

A press campaign begun by Arnold-Forster in November 1897 achieved more success. It was a well-timed campaign following the highly publicized admission of the Commander-in-Chief that 'Our Army machinery is overstrained and is out of gear . . . no longer able to meet effectively the demands now made upon it'.[71] In six letters to *The Times*, Arnold-Forster did not add anything to his previous pronouncements on army reform but, at a time when the cabinet was discussing the Army Estimates, made a greater impact. For a rare and passing moment the reformers aroused press and ministerial interest. The questions raised in the cabinet, coupled with the answers provided by the Secretary of State and his proffered resignation, testified to the unease which the campaign had evoked.[72]

Sir Arthur Haliburton, a recently retired Permanent Under-Secretary of State at the War Office, entered the lists in defence of the Cardwell system. In four letters to *The Times*, later reprinted in *A Short Reply to Long Service* (1898), he only acknowledged the need for minor changes in the organization of the army – a limited liability upon Reservists to serve in small wars, parity between battalions at home and abroad, and an increased proportion of guns to sabres. He ascribed all improvements in the army since 1870 to the Cardwell system. Any contemporary shortcomings he attributed to the failure to implement fully the original proposals. The War Office, he insisted, was the true custodian of army reform. The advocates of change were, in his opinion, little different from the opponents of change in 1870. Hence any revision of the terms of service would be a retrograde victory for those who had opposed the present system from its inception.[73]

Lord Lansdowne, the Secretary of State for War (1895–1900), presented a less rigid defence of the Cardwell system. As a newcomer to the War Office, he had not manned the barricades for over a generation in defence of Cardwellian principles. Also his relations with Viscount Wolseley, the Commander-in-Chief and the foremost military advocate of the present system, were far less cordial than those which he had already established, while Governor-General in India (1888–93), with Lord Roberts, an ardent reformer. He cited Lord Roberts and Sir Charles Dilke as 'high military authorities' in the 'Army Proposals' which he submitted to the cabinet at the height of the press campaign.[74] He did not believe that the present difficulties merely derived from a failure to give the system a fair trial; he recognized that imperfections existed within the system. Addressing the Primrose League, in Edinburgh, on 9 December 1897, Lord Lansdowne admitted that the system 'seems to be wanting in elasticity and to be too easily disorganized whenever the exigencies of the service require the simultaneous absence of both battalions'.[75]

Acting upon this premise, he moved beyond the wishes of Haliburton and Wolseley. He pressed the cabinet to increase the size and number of battalions, augment the proportion of guns to sabres, and introduce a limited liability upon some Reservists for service in small colonial wars. He intimated that the additional battalions would be raised in groups of four to offset the lack of elasticity. This innovation would enable the War Office to experiment in three-year enlistments and to ameliorate the conditions of service for efficient soldiers. Lord Lansdowne also proposed several minor improvements – the abolition of grocery stoppages, differential payments between boys and efficient soldiers, the promise of preferential treatment for ex-soldiers in governmental employment, opportunities to learn a trade in the Colours, and a reduction in deferred pay (i.e. the proportion of a soldier's pay set aside and deferred until he entered the Reserve). On the other hand, he refused to compromise upon the essential features of the Cardwell system. The army of 1897, he argued, was a substantial improvement upon the army of 1870: the Establishment was stronger by 30,000 men, the battalions were larger, and a Reserve of 78,000 men existed. Reintroducing large depots and long-service enlistments would, in his view, depress morale, deprive short-service men of the advantage of short tours of duty in India, and, above all, vastly increase the pension vote.[76] Unwilling to introduce radical and costly reforms, Lord Lansdowne offered concessions in detail and substantial increases in men and material. He resolved, in short, to preserve the basic structure of the Cardwell system.

By this approach, Lord Lansdowne used and controlled the

debate. After the presentation of uncompromising positions by Arnold-Forster and Haliburton, the Secretary of State appeared as the conciliatory figure, untrammelled by departmental dogma and yet reluctant to cast aside a functioning system for an unpredictable alternative. At the same time, he used the reform agitation and 'public' expectations as a bargaining lever within the cabinet. 'Public opinion', he wrote, 'is, apparently, unanimous in demanding a large augmentation of the Force'.[77] He secured, as a consequence, the largest Establishment and the greatest increase of the army in peacetime, an achievement which mellowed the service Members and prompted Dilke to withdraw his ritual amendment to the Army Estimates. What this success had indicated was the inherent strength of the War Office when assumptions were shared in common by the department and its critics. A consensus had emerged on this occasion about the existence of a crisis, its source in the Cardwell system, and its repercussions among the home battalions. Lord Lansdowne had focused upon increased numbers and better conditions of service as a means of correcting the malfunctioning system. He had, thereby, not only placated the transitory enthusiasm for army reform, but he had also crowned its gradual debasement as a concept. Debates about army reform had become preoccupied with the functioning of the Cardwell system; they had lost sight of the purposes of that system. More important than the correction of manpower shortages was the manner in which the army was being prepared for war. The failure to perceive this did not reveal the sophistry of the debates so much as their inherent complacency. As Lord Lansdowne reassured his audience in Edinburgh, 'I am tempted to add one small argument which is perhaps worth your consideration, namely, that since 1870 this country has engaged in a number of military operations in different parts of the world, and that we have succeeded in getting through not only without disgrace, but with considerable credit to the forces concerned'.[78]

Senior officers fully shared this complacency. After the wave of reforms launched by Cardwell, the Duke of Cambridge remained profoundly suspicious of army reform. Believing that the army owed a personal fealty to the Crown, a view undiminished by Parliamentary control of finance, he disliked the 'interference' of civilian politicians. He felt that reform had damaged the prestige and status of the army, inasmuch as it implied that the army had been unable to fulfil onerous and prized responsibilities. He doubted that the army needed reform; he viewed its efficiency as demonstrated by wartime successes and by the turnouts at the endless round of field days and parades which he personally inspected. Reform, in his opinion, could only damage the army. After the abolition of purchase, the introduction of short service and the territorial localization of regiments, the Duke recoiled in horror from the prospect of double battalions. He feared that reform would impair 'the old Regimental system of our glorious Army. It has stood many shocks, and has done its duty nobly by the Crown and by the Country. It is worth saving'.[79] In fact, regimental *esprit de corps* would prove remarkably pliable and resilient. Although friction erupted at first, especially over the loss of historic facings and numbers, this was less persistent and the changes were less deleterious than the Duke had imagined.

Using the terminology of Alfred Vagts, it might appear that the Horse Guards was more concerned with preserving militarist rather than military values. In other words, it was preoccupied with the customs, status, and prestige of the army as distinct from its fighting efficiency.[80] But the Duke of Cambridge and the majority of officers did not perceive any contradiction between the traditions and interests which they defended and the maintenance of military efficiency. As the heirs of the Wellingtonian army, they viewed these traditions and interests as an integral part of the army's effectiveness. War was an uncertain business: what had succeeded in the past was the only touchstone for success in the future. Officers who championed reform, like Wolseley and his 'ring', remained a small and isolated group. The majority of officers placed a premium not only on obedience and loyalty to the Duke, but also on conformity, on a solid wall against the enemy. Any deviant was suspect. When the critics labelled Wolseley as a 'radical through and through',[81] it revealed more about the critics than about the criticized. As Wolseley assured his wife, 'I detest Radicals: men of Mr Gladstone's stamp are abhorrent to every instinct within me, because they are church wardens & parish vestry men more than Englishmen'. He yearned for the day when

> the licence of democracy & socialism will be conquered by the sword, and succeeded by cruel military despotism. Then it will be that the man of talk will give way to the man of action, and the Gladstones, Harcourts, Morleys & all that most contemptible of God's creatures will black the boots of some successful Cavalry Colonel. A new Cromwell will clear the country of these frothing talkers, & the soldiers will rule. Would that my lot could have been cast in such an era.[82]

To regard Wolseley as a radical was a ludicrous distortion; it could only have emanated from a Horse Guards riven by doubts and apprehension – the products of a citadel mentality.

So long as the Duke remained in command, he had little to fear from Wolseley and his phalanx of reformers. 'The young school with advanced ideas' were both young and promotion conscious. They depended upon the Duke for career advancement, and at times this muted their reforming zeal. Even Wolseley, who was thrust upon the Duke by his political patrons, achieved relatively little; he languished in office without scope for initiative.[83] As a group, the reformers were distinguished by their experience in small colonial wars: Wolseley had first gathered his 'ring' of specially chosen officers to fight in the Ashanti War. Wartime service gained the reformers public acclaim and provided opportunities for faster promotion. On the other hand, the demands of the wars and of post-war colonial administration served as a powerful distraction from writing about army reform. No less important was the divorce of the home-based reform movement from its counterpart in India. Two schools of reform emerged with different ideas, reflecting different 'war experiences' and different strategic priorities. Army reform, in short, had scant opportunity to flourish within the army commanded by the Duke of Cambridge.

Even the appointment of Lord Wolseley as Commander-in-Chief on 19 August 1894 failed to inaugurate a period of army reform. Wolseley proffered two explanations for his failure in office. Privately, he blamed the control of the army by ignorant and parsimonious politicians, especially Lord Lansdowne, the incumbent Secretary of State. 'It is difficult', he wrote to his wife, 'to lead my little man of small mind and undecided views. He does so look like a cross between a French dancing master and a Jewess'.[84] Publicly, he was more discreet, preferring to disparage the restrictions which had been placed upon his office, rendering him a 'fifth wheel on the coach'. Contemporaries were not entirely convinced. Some attributed his failure in office to the decline of his mental faculties. Having assumed office in his middle sixties, Wolseley contracted an acute illness in 1897 and suffered thereafter from periodic lapses of memory. The deterioration of his health, coupled with his increasingly infrequent visits to the War Office, enabled his critics to argue that the man and not the office had failed the army.[85]

Undoubtedly there was friction between the Commander-in-Chief and the Secretary of State, and the ill-health of Wolseley may have impaired his performance in office. Yet it is arguable whether the ideas of Wolseley, if implemented fully, would have obviated the early disasters of the South African War. The main concern of Wolseley was the inability of the existing system, as fashioned by Cardwell and Childers, to fulfil the strategic requirements of the army. Outlined by Edward Stanhope in his memorandum of 1891, these requirements included support of the civil power, the maintenance of overseas garrisons, the ability to despatch an expeditionary force of two army corps, and the organization of auxiliary forces for home defence.[86] Wolseley believed that the army could fulfil these requirements, if the original criteria of Cardwell were met. In his early memoranda as Commander-in-Chief, he had insisted that an additional eleven battalions of infantry and fifteen companies of garrison artillery were the basic needs of the home army. Restoring the balance between the battalions at home and abroad would, in his view, re-establish the home battalions as viable military cadres, capable of expansion by Reservists 'into an efficient fighting machine'. He never doubted that the necessary recruits could be found, if the rates of pay were substantially increased. Indeed he wished to upgrade the Stanhope recommendations; he proposed that three army corps, wholly composed of regular troops, should be retained at home, instead of two army corps, one of which was partially composed of Militia.[87] Lord Wolseley, in effect, largely equated army increase with army reform. He believed that the army had already been reformed, that the structure was basically sound, and that the home battalions would become efficient if only the necessary increases were sanctioned.

The South African War would confirm that the proposals of Wolseley and the increases approved by Lord Lansdowne lacked scale and perspective. The manpower demands of the war would exceed anything contemplated by either civilian or military spokesmen in the War Office. Even more serious was the exclusive focus upon the organization or structure of the army to the neglect of reforms in training and tactics. Admittedly, under *The Order in Council of 21st November 1895*, Wolseley only had powers of general supervision over military training. He had correctly argued that the training of the home battalions had been impaired by the malfunctioning of the army structure. Nevertheless he had presumed that if the malfunctioning could be rectified, then the efficiency of the army was virtually assured.

Underpinning this complacency, which pervaded the senior echelons of the army, was the belief in several immutable characteristics of war. In the first place, the human factor was considered to be the ultimate arbiter of military success. This was a product of the heroic, chivalrous concept of warfare and successive victories against numerically superior foes. It provided the source of the popular fallacy that if both sides were armed with modern weapons then the attacker, if he had the better men, was bound to triumph.[88] Secondly, previous wartime experience was regarded as the soundest guide for future combat. When critics argued that modern technology had rendered obsolete the lessons of past campaigns, Sir Redvers Buller, the Adjutant-General, replied 'But the thing that strikes me most in this lecture is the fact that there is nothing new under the sun, and when improvements are made in military arms and tactics they almost always follow along the same lines'.[89] Deriving from these assumptions was a third belief that war was essentially a moral, physical, and practical activity, one which allowed little scope for theoretical speculation. After years of improvisation in colonial warfare senior officers could not accept that a mere theory or 'fad' of the moment could undermine the priorities which had served them so well in the past. In explaining the early disasters of the South African War, Leo Amery recognized that since the late Victorian army had neglected

> all study of military history and military theory, the only operations it took cognizance of were the primitive expeditions

> against troublesome savages, or the marches to relieve garrisons cut off by some sudden outbreak of rebellion, which it dignified by the name of wars. As tests of energy, endurance and physical courage, these expeditions were undoubtedly useful. Of the principles and methods of serious warfare between tactically equal forces they taught nothing.[90]

The 1890s were not entirely bereft of innovation. After the passage of the Manoeuvres Act of 1898 and the purchase of 41,000 acres at Salisbury Plain, the army was able to assemble two army corps for peacetime training. This tardy recognition of the need for large-scale manoeuvres hardly compensated for the lack of training in the rest of the year. Barely two months per annum could be spared for military training. During the rest of the year the soldier drilled, paraded, and mounted guard; he cleaned his equipment, maintained his barracks, and undertook a multifarious range of fatigue duties. A score of days were devoted to route marching, and another three weeks to field training in which entrenchments were avoided. Musketry was practised by each man firing 200 rounds of ammunition at a fixed target. Volley-firing remained the core of musketry training. Equally anachronistic was the preference of the artillery for fighting by battery sections. Battery majors resented incursions upon their traditional prerogatives, a view which earned the sympathy of their brigade commanders. Brigade practice was neglected; indeed the training of the field artillery in large formations was decidedly weak.[91] The cavalry devoted itself to drill and to the practice of mounted formations, especially knee-to-knee charges with the *arme blanche*. More mundane tasks like scouting, reconnaissance, and dismounted action were rarely practised; the cavalry never doubted its capacity to make a decisive breakthrough on the modern battlefield.

The army, in sum, failed to appreciate that changes in technology might require changes in tactics and training. Senior officers clung to values which related to their experience in small colonial warfare. They valued improvisation, previous military experience, the moral effect of the offensive, and the dominant role of the human element. Using success in small colonial wars to buttress a heroic, chivalrous concept of war, the army regarded technology as merely a tool. Senior officers could not accept that this tool, even in the hands of capable marksmen, might radically alter the character of modern war. The consequences would be revealed in South Africa, where the army was defeated at Stormberg, Magersfontein, and Colenso, in the 'Black Week' of December 1899. As Sir Neville Lyttelton recalled, 'Few people have seen two battles in succession in such startling contrast as Omdurman and Colenso. In the first, 50,000 fanatics streamed across the open regardless of cover to certain death, while at Colenso I never saw a Boer all day till the battle was over and it was our men who were the victims'.[92]

Notes and references

1. **B. J. Bond** (ed.), *Victorian Military Campaigns,* Hutchinson, London, 1967, Appendix 1, pp. 309-11.
2. **T. von Sosnosky,** *England's Danger: The Future of British Army Reform,* Chapman & Hall, London, 1901, p. 80.
3. **Colonel C. E. Callwell,** *Small Wars: Their Principles and Practice,* H.M.S.O., London, 1896, pp. 22-3.
4. **General Viscount Wolseley,** 'The Army', *The Reign of Queen Victoria,* ed. T. H. Ward, 2 vols., Smith and Elder, London, 1887, Vol. 1, p. 189.
5. **B. J. Bond**, 'Colonial wars and primitive expeditions 1856-99', *History of the British Army,* eds. Brigadier P. Young and Lieutenant-Colonel J. P. Lawford, A. Barker, London, 1970, p. 179.
6. Gen. Viscount Wolseley, 'The Army', *op. cit.,* p. 189 and 'The Standing Army of Great Britain', *Harper's New Monthly Magazine,* European edition, **80**, Feb. 1890, p. 346.
7. **Earl of Cromer,** *Modern Egypt,* 2 vols., Macmillan, London, 1908, Vol. II, p. 107.
8. Col. C. E. Callwell, *op. cit.,* pp. 75-6, 85, 91, 151-71.
9. *Ibid.,* pp. 256-8, 389-98, 401, 429-30.
10. **D. R. Morris,** *The Washing of the Spears: The Rise & Fall of the Zulu Nation,* Jonathan Cape, London, 1966, p. 498.
11. **Colonel G. F. R. Henderson,** *The Science of War,* Longman, London, 1905, pp. 397-400, and **B. J. Bond,** *The Victorian Army and the Staff College, 1854-1914,* p. 177.
12. **Colonel J. R. Dunlop,** *The Development of the British Army 1899-1914,* Methuen, London, 1938, p. 37.
13. **Brevet Lieutenant-Colonel Elmslie,** 'The Possible Effect on Tactics of Recent Improvements in Weapons', *Aldershot Military Society,* Paper 72, 6 Feb. 1899, p. 14.
14. **Field Marshal Viscount Wolseley,** *Report on Manoeuvres, August and September 1898,* 27 Oct. 1898, W.O. Library, pp. vii, ix.
15. **Viscount Wolseley,** 'An English View of the American Civil War', *North American Review,* No. 394, Article 4, Sept. 1889, p. 283.
16. Comments upon the lectures of Captain G. E. Benson, 'Smokeless Powder and its Probable effect upon the Tactics of the Future', *Aldershot Military Society,* Paper 45, 23 Mar. 1893, p. 3, and of Captain W. H. James, 'Magazine Rifles, their latest Developments and Effects', *Journal of the Royal United Service Institution,* **306**, No. 175, Sept. 1892, p. 936.
17. Comments on the lecture of Lt.-Col. Elmslie, in Elmslie, *op. cit.,* p. 16.
18. Col. G. F. R. Henderson, *op. cit.,* p. 418.

19. *Ibid.*, p. 405.
20. **A. Forbes,** *Memories and Studies of War and Peace,* Cassell, London, 1895, p. 225.
21. *The Times,* 17 Mar. 1874, p. 11.
22. **G. W. Steevens,** *With Kitchener to Khartum,* Blackwood, London, 1898, pp. 146-7.
23. *Ibid.*, pp. 264, 282. For praise of native auxiliaries see *ibid.*, pp. 150-1, 292 and *The Times,* 17 Mar. 1874, p. 11.
24. *The Times,* 17 Mar. 1874, p. 11 and G. W. Steevens, *op. cit.*, pp. 292-3.
25. **A. Forbes,** 'War Correspondents and the Authorities', *The Nineteenth Century,* **7**, 1880, pp. 190-1. See also **P. Knightley,** *The First Casualty,* A. Deutsch, London, 1975, pp. 44-5.
26. 'The War Correspondents and the Sirdar', *The Academy,* **54**, 1898, p. 331.
27. Duke of Cambridge to Queen Victoria, 6 Nov. 1881, Cambridge Mss., R.A., E/1/9,819.
28. *The Pall Mall Gazette,* 9 Jan. 1884, p. 1.
29. General C. G. Gordon to his sister, 3 Mar. 1884, *Letters of General C. G. Gordon to his sister,* ed. M. A. Gordon, Macmillan, London, 1888, p. 380, and F. Power to his mother, 22 Feb. 1884, quoted in F. Power, *Letters from Khartoum,* Sampson Low, London, 1885, p. 96.
30. *The Times,* 1 Apr. 1884, p. 5.
31. *Ibid.*, 29 Sept. 1884, p. 5.
32. *Ibid.*, 3 Oct. 1884, p. 7, and 17 Nov. 1884, p. 9.
33. **A. Nutting,** *Gordon: martyr and misfit,* Constable, London, 1966, pp. 277-8.
34. **A. Forbes,** *Chinese Gordon: a succinct record of his life,* Routledge, London, 1884, p. 252.
35. Lord Wolseley to Lady Wolseley, 2 Jan. 1880, Wolseley Mss., W/P, 9/I.
36. G. W. Steevens, *op. cit.*, p. 46.
37. **C. O. Ovington,** 'War and Evolution', *Westminster Review,* **153**, 1900, p. 411-20; **Lord Wolseley,** 'Is a Soldier's Life Worth Living?', *Fortnightly Review,* **45**, 1889, pp. 597-609; **H. F. Wyatt,** 'The Ethics of Empire', and 'War as the Supreme Test of National Value', *Nineteenth Century,* **41**, 1897, pp. 516-30 and **45**, 1899, pp. 216-25.
38. **C. Carrington,** *Rudyard Kipling: His Life and Work,* Penguin edition, London, 1970, pp. 142-3, and *The Complete Barrack-Room Ballads of Rudyard Kipling,* hereafter referred to as *Barrack-Room Ballads,* ed. C. Carrington, Methuen, London, 1973, p. 24.
39. C. Carrington, *Rudyard Kipling,* pp. 143-4.
40. 'Arithmetic on the Frontier', *Rudyard Kipling's Verse. Definitive Edition,* Hodder and Stoughton, London, 1946, p. 45.

41. **P. Mason,** *Kipling: The Glass, The Shadow and The Fire,* Jonathan Cape, London, 1975, p. 73.
42. **P. Keating,** *The working classes in Victorian fiction,* Routledge & Kegan Paul, London, 1971, pp. 139-66.
43. 'Tommy', *Rudyard Kipling's Verse Definitive Edition,* p. 398.
44. 'The Young British Soldier', *ibid.,* pp. 416-17.
45. 'Oonts', *ibid.,* p. 408.
46. **R. Blatchford,** *My Life in the Army,* Daily Mail novels, London, 1910, p. 160.
47. **Sir G. T. Younghusband,** *Soldier's Memories in War and Peace,* H. Jenkins, London, 1917, p. 187.
48. M. Edwardes, 'Oh to meet an army man', *Rudyard Kipling; the man, his work and his world,* ed. J. Gross, Weidenfeld and Nicolson, London, 1972, p. 41.
49. *Report of the Airey Committee,* p. 30 and *Parl. Deb.,* Third Ser., Vol. 350, 19 Feb. 1891, col. 1,143.
50. **R. Clutterbuck,** *Protest and the Urban Guerilla,* Cassell, London, 1973, p. 18.
51. **W. S. Hamer,** *The British Army: Civil-Military Relations, 1885-1905,* Clarendon, Oxford, 1970, p. 218.
52. **Sir F. Maurice** and **Sir G. Arthur,** *The Life of Lord Wolseley,* Heinemann, London, 1924, pp. 238-9.
53. *The Spectator,* 28 Apr. 1888, p. 569.
54. *Parl. Deb.,* Third Ser., Vol. 326, 11 May 1888, cols. 1-7, and 14 May 1888, cols. 100-1.
55. *Preliminary and Further Reports (with Appendices) of the Royal Commissioners appointed to inquire into the Civil and Professional Administration of the Naval and Military Departments, and the relation of those Departments to each other, and to the Treasury,* hereafter referred to as the Hartington Report, C.5,979, 1890, XIX, pp. vi-viii, xix-xxvii.
56. *Ibid.,* pp. xv-xvii.
57. *Ibid.,* pp. xxix-xxxi.
58. Sir H. Campbell-Bannerman to V. Nash, 14 Sept. 1903, Campbell-Bannerman Mss., B.M. Add. Mss. 41,236, ff. 164-5.
59. Sir H. Ponsonby to the Duke of Cambridge, 25 Mar. 1890, *The Letters of Queen Victoria,* ed. G. Buckle, 3rd Ser., Vol. I, p. 589.
60. Duke of Cambridge to Sir H. Ponsonby, 9 Apr. 1890, *The Letters of Queen Victoria,* 3rd Ser., Vol. I, p. 594.
61. Lord Wolseley to Lady Wolseley, 6 Aug. 1895, Wolseley Mss., W/P, 24/83.
62. Lord Wolseley to Lord Salisbury, November 1900, P.R.O., CAB 37/53/78.
63. **H. O. Arnold-Forster,** 'Memorandum with regard to the condition of the Army and the existing military system', 16 June 1897, Balfour Mss., B.M. Add. Mss. 49,722, f. 20.

64. **Lieutenant-General Sir F. S. Roberts,** 'Free Trade in the Army', *Nineteenth Century,* **XV**, No. lxxxviii, June 1884, pp. 1,055–74.
65. Sir F. S. Roberts to the Duke of Cambridge, 19 Dec. 1884, Roberts Mss., N.A.M., R/163. See also **Sir C. W. Dilke** and **H. S. Wilkinson,** *Imperial Defence,* Constable, London, 1892, p. 156.
66. **Sir C. W. Dilke,** *Army Reform,* Service & Paton, London, 1898, pp. 56–7, 61–4, 67; **H. O. Arnold-Forster,** *Army Letters, 1897–98,* Arnold, London, 1898, pp. 86–98, 100, 106–8; Sir C. W. Dilke and H. S. Wilkinson, *op. cit.,* pp. 149, 155–60.
67. Service Members Committee to Lord Lansdowne, 20 Jan. 1898, quoted in H. O. Arnold-Forster, *Army Letters,* pp. 187–91.
68. *Parl. Deb.,* Fourth Ser., Vol. 51, 23 July 1897, cols. 943–4, and Vol. 54, 25 Feb. 1898, cols. 91–2.
69. Sir H. Campbell-Bannerman to Sir A. Haliburton, 6 Jan. 1898, quoted in **J. B. Atlay,** *Lord Haliburton,* Smith, Elder & Co., London, 1909, p. 212.
70. *Parl. Deb.,* Fourth Ser., Vol. 45, 8 Dec. 1897, cols. 1,625–8.
71. *The Times,* 24 Sept. 1897, p. 4.
72. **Lord Lansdowne,** 'Mr. Arnold-Forster's Letters to The Times, December 1897 and January 1898', 13 Jan. 1898, and 'Linked Battalions versus depots', 25 Jan. 1898, P.R.O., CAB 37/46/4, 11. See also Lord Lansdowne to Lord Salisbury and the reply on the same date, 2 Feb. 1898, in **Lord Newton,** *Lord Lansdowne: A Biography,* Macmillan, London, 1929, pp. 149–51.
73. **Sir A. Haliburton,** *A Short Reply to Long Service,* Stanford, London, 1898, pp. 57–61, 63–4, 90.
74. **Lord Lansdowne,** 'Outline of Army Proposals', 2 Dec. 1897, P.R.O., CAB 37/45/42, pp. 13–17.
75. *The Scotsman,* 10 Dec. 1897, p. 8.
76. *Ibid.* and Lord Lansdowne, 'Outline of Army Proposals', pp. 1–17.
77. **Lord Lansdowne,** 'Note on Proposals made by the Chancellor of the Exchequer', 26 Jan. 1898, P.R.O., CAB 37/46/13.
78. *The Scotsman,* 10 Dec. 1897, p. 8.
79. Duke of Cambridge to Queen Victoria, 27 Dec. 1880, quoted in W. Verner, *op. cit.,* Vol. 2, p. 217.
80. **A Vagts,** *The History of Militarism,* Norton, New York, 1937, p. 13.
81. G. R. St Aubyn, *op. cit.,* p. 206.
82. Lord Wolseley to Lady Wolseley, 20 Mar. 1880, Wolseley Mss., W/P, 9/15, and 1 Nov. 1890, W/P, 19/51.
83. Lord Wolseley to H. E. Childers, 23 Aug. 1881, Wolseley Mss., W/P, 10/6.
84. Lord Wolseley to Lady Wolseley, 4 July 1899, Wolseley Mss., W/P, 28/35.

85. Sir R. Buller to Sir H. Campbell-Bannerman, 5 Jan. 1899, Campbell-Bannerman Mss., B.M. Add. Mss. 41,212, f. 230; **Lord G. Hamilton,** *Parliamentary Reminiscences and Reflections,* 2 vols., John Murray, London, 1902, Vol. 2, pp. 293–4.
86. Col. J. K. Dunlop, *op. cit.,* Appendix A, p. 307.
87. Lord Wolseley to Permanent Under-Secretary of State for War, 30 Oct. 1896, P.R.O., W.O. 33/56.
88. Comments of Major-General Sir H. Brackenbury, Lieutenant-Colonel E. Hunter and Major A. Pollock upon the lecture of Captain W. H. James, 'Modern Weapons and their influence on Tactics and Organization', *Journal of the Royal United Service Institution,* 43, No. 262, Dec. 1899, pp. 1,300, 1,302, 1,307.
89. Comment on lecture of Lt.-Col. Elmslie, in Elmslie, *op. cit.,* pp. 18–19.
90. **L. S. Amery,** *The Times History of the War in South Africa 1899-1902,* 7 vols., Sampson Low, London, 1900-09, Vol. 3, p. 550.
91. **Major-General Sir C. E. Callwell** and **Major-General Sir J. Headlam,** *The History of the Royal Artillery,* 2 vols., Hugh Rees, London, 1931–37, Vol. 1, pp. 254–5.
92. **General Sir N. G. Lyttelton,** *Eighty Years: soldiering, politics and games,* Hodder & Stoughton, London, 1927, p. 212.

9 The South African War

Leo Amery served as a war correspondent for *The Times* during the South African War (1899–1902). He believed that the war had revealed 'how slight and uncertain was the reserve of military power of the British Empire . . .'.[1] He was appalled by the early reverses at Stormberg, Magersfontein and Colenso, the Black Week of 10–15 December 1899, followed by the humiliating defeat at Spion Kop on 24 January 1900. Like many contemporaries, he exhorted the government to learn from the lessons of the war and to embark upon army reform. Neither the government nor its military advisers could ignore these criticisms. During the course of the war and its immediate aftermath, they struggled to perceive the appropriate lessons and to implement remedial measures. Reforming an army over the years from 1900–05 would prove to be a difficult and demanding task.

The Boer War had erupted after several years of acrimonious relations between Britain and the Boer republics. Britain retained suzerainty over the foreign relations of the Transvaal, but the Boers remained fiercely independent, determined to brook no interference in their domestic affairs. Boer domestic policy became a source of increasing concern as the English-speaking Uitlanders, who had entered the republics in search for gold, complained to Britain about their lack of civil rights. By 1899, the Uitlanders comprised a majority of the white settlers in the Transvaal and paid five-sixths of its taxes. Furious about their denial of the franchise, they sent a petition to Queen Victoria which arrived in April 1899. Before the cabinet could frame a reply, Sir Alfred Milner, the British Commissioner in South Africa, sent a telegram for publication to Joseph Chamberlain, the Colonial Secretary. Milner argued that Britain now had an overwhelming case for intervention: 'The spectacle of thousands of British subjects kept permanently in the position of helots . . . does steadily undermine the influence and reputation of Great Britain . . .'.[2] Thereafter the cabinet endorsed Chamberlain's draft despatch, intimating that Britain could no longer ignore the grievances of the Uitlanders. War fever intensified in both countries. On 8 September, the cabinet decided to reinforce its army of 12,000 men in South Africa by the despatch of 10,000 soldiers, mainly from India. The Boers replied with an ultimatum, drafted by Jan Smuts and issued by Paul Kruger, President of the South African Republic, calling upon the British government to withdraw its troops from the frontiers and to send away all reinforcements. The cabinet rejected these demands; it sent an Army Corps of 47,000 men to the Cape.

Within Britain the war aroused intense emotion. Imperialist passions were at their height. Barely a year had passed since Omdurman and the Fashoda incident in which French forces had recoiled from a confrontation with Kitchener's army. The Boer ultimatum shocked many editors in Fleet Street. *The Times* published 'The Old Issue' by Kipling, in which the poet denounced Kruger – 'cruel in the shadow, crafty in the sun' – and reminded England of her traditional opposition to tyranny.[3] The majority of the press, Conservative-inclined, were firmly in favour of the war. The Liberal press, like the Liberal party, was deeply divided. The main organs of Liberalism in London, *The Westminster Gazette, The Daily Chronicle,* and *The Daily News,* until it changed hands in January 1901, followed Lord Rosebery and the Liberal Imperialists in support of the war. *The Morning Leader, The Star,* and above all *The Manchester Guardian* endorsed the views of Harcourt, Morley, and Lloyd George, the leaders of the pro-Boer faction of the party. Anti-war opinion was voiced, both vigorously and passionately, but with little impact amid the jingoistic clamour. Enormous crowds gathered at the pro-war meetings and thronged the troops on their departure. A massive wave of fund-raising followed the publication of Kipling's 'The Absent-Minded Beggar' in *The Daily Mail* on 31 October 1899. Kipling urged his readers to save the soldiers' families from the workhouse:

> When you've shouted 'Rule, Britannia', when you've sung
> 'God save the Queen',
> When you've finished killing Kruger with your mouth,
> Will you kindly drop a shilling in my little tambourine
> For a gentleman in khaki ordered South?[4]

The poem appeared on ashtrays, tobacco jars, pillow-cases, plates and in many other forms. It was recited on the stage. Set to music by Sir Arthur Sullivan, it was sung in music-halls, smoking-concerts and drawing-room recitals. It raised at least a quarter of a million pounds.[5]

Viscount Wolseley had fuelled the confidence of the Government and the nation. As early as August 1899, he had pressed the cabinet to reinforce the troops in Natal, believing that an early show of force would have overawed the Boers.[6] He exuded confidence in the expeditionary force, commanded by Sir Redvers Buller. That force, wrote Wolseley, included 'the very ablest soldiers', was 'thoroughly equipped for war', and would present 'a very different condition of things from that which existed in the Army sent to the Crimea in 1854'.[7] Speaking at the Guildhall, on the occasion of the Lord Mayor's banquet, on 10 November 1899, he disclaimed any surprise at the success of the mobilization and the turnout of the Reserve. The success, he affirmed, was entirely predictable in view of the preparatory planning: 'We all anticipated what has taken place'.[8]

Equally optimistic were the ministerial spokesmen and their civil servant advisers. George Wyndham, the Parliamentary Under-Secretary of State at the War Office, believed that 'the Army is more efficient than at any time since Waterloo'.[9] Sir Ralph Knox, the Permanent Under-Secretary, was even more impressed by the efficacy of the mobilization arrangements and the return of 98 per cent of the Reservists to the Colours. The return of the Reservists, in his opinion, had vindicated the Cardwell system and had routed the arguments of the War Office critics. 'I peg along cheerily', he wrote, 'much elated with the success of short service and all our machinery, and the diminution of Forster & Co.'.[10] From the Opposition front bench came further words of encouragement. Campbell-Bannerman, though a critic of the government's diplomacy, commended the government for the organization of Britain's largest ever expeditionary force. Having been Financial Secretary to Cardwell and Childers, and twice Secretary of State for War (1885 and 1892–94), he had become the foremost spokesman of the Liberal party on military matters. As he explained in the Commons on 20 October 1899, the organization of the army 'for which hardly anybody sometimes had a good word to say . . . has completely fulfilled the purpose for which it was created'.[11]

Editors spent freely to ensure the maximum coverage of the war. Expecting a decisive triumph by Christmas, they despatched war correspondents in unprecedented numbers: at one stage *The Times* used twenty special correspondents and carried excerpts from official despatches as well.[12] Veteran correspondents like Bennet Burleigh of *The Daily Telegraph,* Melton Prior of *The Illustrated London News* and H. H. S. Peace of *The Daily News* worked alongside the rising stars of the profession, G. W. Steevens of *The Daily Mail* and Angus Hamilton of *The Times*. Dr Conan Doyle sallied forth as a correspondent and wrote an immensely popular account of the war. Edgar Wallace, who had gone to South Africa as a medical orderly, joined the staff of *The Daily Mail* and made his name by writing vivid, though largely fictitious, accounts of atrocity stories. Winston Churchill, at the age of twenty-four, secured an appointment as the principal war correspondent of *The Morning Post*. Hired at £250 a month, with a four months' minimum guarantee of employment, all expenses paid, and entire discretion as to movements and opinions, he enjoyed terms which were higher than any previously paid to war correspondents from Britain.[13]

The vast number of journalists ensured neither reliable nor accurate reporting. The 'war news' became peppered with hyperboles, contradictions, and chauvinistic bias. With so many rivals in the field, some reporters sacrificed accuracy for speed. Aware of the expectations of their editors and readers, they described the 'dauntless bravery of

English officers' and the daring deeds of the 'sweating, swearing, grimy, dirty, fearless and generous Tommy'.[14] While their accounts were often sensational and dramatic, their sources of information were generally second-hand. Battles, dominated by long-range rifles and smokeless powder, were no longer easily observed. 'A battle', wrote J. B. Atkins, had become 'vague, scattered, sometimes even insufferably tedious'. Accurate reporting, he argued, had suffered as a consequence: 'After Colenso I spoke to an onlooker who had not the least idea that the British arms had suffered a reverse'.[15] War correspondents also suffered from extremely strict censorship and from their reliance, in many instances, upon the military for a line of communications. The main scandals of the war, as a consequence, were revealed not by journalists but by visitors from Britain. Conditions in the concentration camps were exposed by Emily Hobhouse, a Quaker, who visited the front as leader of the South African Conciliation Committee. The appalling state of the military hospitals, in which a large proportion of the 16,168 deaths from wounds or disease occurred (74 per cent of all fatalities), was revealed by William Burdett-Coutts, an MP who toured the hospitals. Similarly, the most perceptive and critical accounts of the military operations came, not from the front-line reporters, but from the home-based correspondents, like Captain William Elliot Cairnes of *The Westminster Gazette*. Though stationed at Wakefield, he joined the staff of the paper in November 1899 and wrote a daily article on the war until April 1901. He also wrote several books on the army, *An Asbent-Minded War* (1900), *Social Life in the British Army* (1900) and *The Army from Within* (1901), which were pungent, critical, and spiced with sarcasm. These works became widely acclaimed, as the early popularity of the war rapidly waned.

Black Week, though an immense shock, did not immediately provoke an outburst of indignation and criticism. Editorials exhorted the country to stand firm and encouraged a new rush to the Colours. The War Office called out the whole of the First Class Army Reserve and invited the Militia to come forward. It also waived the bar upon non-regular troops, but insisted that any Volunteers had to present themselves already organized and equipped. Volunteers responded enthusiastically; some 30,000 saw active service in South Africa. They either enrolled in Active Service Companies or joined the Imperial Yeomanry or enlised directly into the army. They included the City Imperial Volunteers (C.I.V.) - 1,726 infantry marksmen from forty-seven different Volunteer Corps, commanded by the Earl of Albemarle. Funded by public subscription of £100,000, two-thirds of which was raised within four days, the C.I.V. were presented with the freedom of the City of London. Steamship companies rallied round with offers of free transport, and the first 2,000 Volunteers were at sea within the month. The paucity of numbers reflected not any want of patriotism (many who volunteered their services were not accepted), but the lack of military training in all save a fraction of the Volunteer Force, and the passive obstruction and disdain of the military authorities. The auxiliary forces, in short, were not organized to provide the means of support and expansion for the regular army in a large-scale war.

More distressed by the tidings of Black Week were senior military officers. Lord Roberts did not require newspaper criticism to pinpoint the blame. Writing to Lord Lansdowne on 15 December 1899, he claimed that 'Buller's reverse makes it clear that both our strategy and tactics are at fault. We have had terrible losses without one single success, and unless some radical change is made at once, our Army will be frittered away and we shall have to make an ignominious peace'.[16] The sheer completeness of the British defeats at Stormberg, Magersfontein and Colenso had prompted this outburst of criticism. The Government responded by appointing Lord Roberts as the new Commander-in-Chief in the field, aided by Kitchener as his chief of staff. For once the factionalism within the army - the division of officers into supporters of Wolseley and Roberts respectively - had an advantage: it enabled changes to be undertaken without any regard for offended sensibilities.

Initially Lord Roberts received full support from the Conservative government. Bitterly disappointed by Wolseley and Buller, ministers looked to Roberts for success in the field and for reforms of tactics and training. They resented criticism, already aired in private conversation and correspondence, that the war had revealed shortcomings in the Cardwell system. Writing to St John Brodrick, a former junior minister at the War Office, Viscount Curzon declared: 'Our disasters are so unbroken, our generals so uniformly incompetent, our inability to make any headway so consistent as to engender suspicions that our system must be rotten at the core'.[17] Brodrick testily replied, 'Surely Buller's defeats do not prove our system rotten. We have put half as many again of men and horses into the field as we ever proposed to keep for foreign service and could have done it weeks earlier if the soldiers had asked'.[18] Ministers believed that the generals and not the War Office had failed, but felt unable to say so in public. Arthur Balfour, First Lord of the Treasury, summarized their dilemma: 'I do not think these blunders were due to War Office maladministration, and until I see reason to think so, nothing will induce me to say so. The chief blunders have been made in my private opinion, by our Generals in the field - but I do not of course, think it desirable to make such a statement in public'.[19]

When Balfour disclaimed War Office responsibility in his speeches at Manchester on 8, 9 and 10 January 1900, he merely aroused editorial scepticism. Once news arrived of another defeat at Spion Kop, an outburst of angry condemnation followed. The war had been a series of calamitous mistakes, thundered *The Times*; a disgraceful muddle, relieved only by the courage of the soldiers.[20] Conservative and Liberal writers fulminated upon the military incompetence and the failings of 'the system'. This criticism, though strident and persistent, would be partially defused by the news in February of the victory at Paardeberg, followed by the relief of Kimberley, Ladysmith and Mafeking, and the capture of Pretoria on 5 June 1900. Confident of victory in South Africa, the Government rushed to the polls in the following autumn. Able to exploit the division in Liberal ranks, the Conservatives scored a resounding success in the 'Khaki Election'. Equally confident of an imminent military triumph, Lord Roberts returned home in November 1900; he received a hero's welcome, the Garter, an Earldom, and a grant of £100,000.

The war, however, lasted for another eighteen months. Once their cities had fallen, the Boers retreated to the veld, from which they waged a resourceful guerilla campaign. Unable to 'mop up' the Boer commandos, Kitchener settled for a war of attrition. He continued an official internment policy, using concentration camps to corral the women and children of Boer commandos. He evolved a blockhouse system by which the blockhouses, originally erected to protect the railways, were used to divide the land mass into manageable units, so that his forces could attack the Boers in systematic and piecemeal fashion. His weekly 'bag' of captives and confiscations had little popular appeal. Casualties mounted. The war became increasingly expensive, costing £1½ million per week. And the Boers persisted with their lightning attacks upon British detachments. The press, with a few exceptions, fumed at the succession of ambuscades and the small, but humiliating, number of surrenders. After news of the Koorn-Spruit ambush, *The Times* berated officers for the systematic 'neglect of the most elementary principles of their profession . . .'.[21] The use of concentration camps and farm burning aroused a furious controversy: Campbell-Bannerman denounced the army for using 'methods of barbarism' in South Africa.[22]

Critics demanded the reform of the army upon 'business principles'. Dilke, Wilkinson, and Arnold-Forster resumed their pre-war attacks upon the Cardwell system. Conservative and Liberal politicians exhorted the government to profit from the 'lessons of the war' and to reorganize the army accordingly. Liberal Imperialists, in particular, were fiercely critical of the failings and shortcomings which the war had exposed. Following the example of Lord Rosebery, Asquith and Haldane, they used army reform as a tactical issue, a means by which they could criticize the government while still favouring the prosecution of the war to a successful conclusion. Unlike the pre-war reformers, the Liberal Imperialists did not endorse any specific scheme of army reform. Aware of their own lack of military expertise, they all too readily accepted 'the great man' solution so often voiced in the newspaper columns. Lord Rosebery advocated Lord Kitchener as a 'man of genius' who could reorganize the War Office. Haldane endorsed this view; he argued that the reform of the War Office should be entrusted to Lord Kitchener because he 'was accustomed to have his own way without very much regard to other people's emotions'.[23]

Other critics poured forth more positive, though not necessarily more constructive, proposals in articles for the daily press and quarterly journals, and in the plethora of books and pamphlets about army reform. They assailed almost every facet of the campaign in South Africa, apart from the personal bravery of officers and men. They condemned faulty intelligence, officer incompetence, inadequate training, indifferent staff work, out-dated weaponry, deplorable hospital conditions, erroneous tactics, poor marksmanship, and maladministration of the stores and remounts. Reformers unfolded these criticisms in a piecemeal and desultory fashion. They neither agreed on their lists of shortcomings nor on the proposed reforms. Captain Cairnes, though a champion of improved staff work, more demanding musketry standards, and more emphasis upon mounted infantry, defended the artillery gun as 'well up to date at the outbreak of the war'.[24] Reformers became almost as heated in their debates over particular proposals as they did in their attacks upon the War Office and the officer corps. In the columns of *Nineteenth Century,* Colonel Lonsdale Hale derided the suggestion of Conan Doyle that henceforth 600,000 riflemen should be enrolled for home defence. He rightly considered that the scheme, which had been widely acclaimed, was 'crude, impracticable and dangerous . . .'.[25]

The quality of the writing varied considerably. Only a few writers had visited the front; the remainder relied upon correspondence from the front. They gleaned their lessons of the war from official despatches, reports from war correspondents, letters from officers in South Africa, and articles in the foreign press. Some, like Arnold-Forster, found lessons from the war which merely substantiated their own preconceived opinions. Others, like Conan Doyle, derived lessons for 'the modern battle' from South Africa, but made little allowance for the unusual terrain and the peculiarities of a guerilla campaign. Others merely condemned the War Office and castigated the Secretary of State. Lord Lansdowne was lampooned mercilessly by H. H. Munro ('Saki') and F. Carruthers Gould in their cartoons for *The Westminster Gazette.* So diverse and variable were the articles, books, and pamphlets that they hardly constituted a guide for legislation. Yet the profusion of criticism was important; it represented, as Sir Edward Hamilton, a Treasury official, observed, 'the half conscious, half unconscious shriek of a nation in its agony'.[26] However discordant, this shriek could not be ignored.

The cabinet was aware not only of the failings exposed by the war, but also of the strain which the war had imposed upon the military system. By March 1900, only a single battalion of regular troops remained in the country, and stocks of modern artillery were virtually exhausted.[27] Reforms were essential to pacify critics and to prevent a recurrence of the dislocation. Lord Lansdowne realized that he could not introduce reforms; as Secretary of State, he no longer commanded the confidence of many Members of Parliament and many editors in Fleet Street. He proffered his resignation on the eve of the general election, and was duly appointed Foreign Secretary by Lord Salisbury. The Prime Minister installed St John Brodrick as the new Secretary of State for War.

Expected to produce reforms at the opening of the new Parliamentary session, Brodrick resolved to capitalize upon the transitory wave of interest in the army. As he assured Lord Roberts, 'I can carry a big scheme now', but it would be difficult in two years hence when the 'public will be sick of expenditure'.[28] He believed that the army had suffered from a lack of manpower and organization in its regular and auxiliary forces. He recommended that six districts should be created in the United Kingdom, in each of which an army corps could muster, train, and manoeuvre in its entirety. The first three corps would be wholly regular in composition and would form the new expeditionary force of 120,000 men. The other three corps would be composed of regular and auxiliary troops and would form the core of the home defence force. To establish these corps, he proposed the enrolment of an additional 126,500 men, including an extra eighteen battalions of regular troops. To equip these corps and improve the monetary inducements for the auxiliary forces, he requested an additional £2,000,000 bringing the Estimates to £30,030,000, an increase of 50 per cent above their pre-war total. When he presented this scheme before the House of Commons on 8 March 1901, Brodrick stressed that he would not sacrifice any part of it for the want of voluntary recruits. Should recruits, once the war was over, fail to appear in sufficient numbers, Brodrick indicated that 'my adhesion to the voluntary system is strictly limited by our ability to obtain under it a force with which our military authorities can satisfy the government that they have sufficient force to resist invasion'.[29]

The scheme encountered a mixed reception. While cabinet colleagues and the majority of Conservative Members rallied to the Secretary of State, others doubted that he would obtain the recruits. The scepticism expressed on the back benches, and in the editorials of *The Times*,[30] was compounded by the unabashed hostility of the Liberal party. The Opposition united in common cause. Campbell-Bannerman denounced the scale and cost of the proposals and the implicit threat of conscription. He disparaged reforms based upon the lessons of a war 'exceptional in the demands made upon us, exceptional in the nature of the war'. He denounced conscription as an infringement of political rights, a social inconvenience, and a strain upon industrial resources. He believed that it was totally unnecessary for an army whose primary duty in peacetime was to garrison tropical stations. He deplored, too, the massive increase of forces assigned to home defence. He reaffirmed the traditional Liberal view that home defence was primarily the responsibility of the navy: if it failed, no defensive army could save the country. In repudiating the scheme, Campbell-Bannerman found support from all quarters of his party. The reforms, he declared, had raised the spectre of militarism which ran counter 'to the whole genius and tradition of our people. Our position in the world has been made and is held by commerce and peace and amity; it must be maintained in the same manner, and not by the stirring up of the military spirit'.[31]

Liberal opposition posed less of a problem for Brodrick than the imminent return of peacetime recruiting. The threat of conscription was essentially hollow. Brodrick failed to overcome the fears of his cabinet colleagues about the political and economic consequences of compulsory service. Should recruiting return to its pre-war level, his scheme would founder through a lack of men. He sought new recruiting incentives. Supported by Lord Roberts, who had replaced Wolseley as Commander-in-Chief, Brodrick pressed the cabinet to approve new terms of enlistment and improved rates of pay. He recommended that soldiers should be enlisted for three years in the Colours, and should thereafter have the option of entering the Reserve or of extending their Colours service for an extra 6*d* a day (subject to character suitability and a second-class standard of shooting). By these measures, argued Brodrick, India could be garrisoned with long-service soldiers, the Reserve could be expanded quickly, and the army could attract more and better recruits, thereby relying less upon 'specials' and immature boys.[32] Lord Salisbury and the Chancellor of the Exchequer, Sir Michael Hicks-Beach, deplored a further increase of the military budget and counselled delay. But the cabinet majority were reluctant to begrudge the army in its moment of trial; the new measures were carried, as Brodrick recalled, 'agst. Lord S[alisbury] - by a majority - after an appeal such (as) he never made to the Cabinet in his life, and we all thought he would go . . .'.[33]

Lord Roberts welcomed the proposals of the Secretary of State. An old campaigner for flexible terms of service, he believed that the new proposals would enhance the appeal of a military career. Nevertheless, he was much less confident than Brodrick that the department could satisfy the clamour for army reform. On his return from South Africa, he had informed Brodrick of his own qualms and forebodings: 'I hope we shall be able to satisfy the public in their desire for "Army Reform". It will not be an easy matter, and I doubt much if any of those who cry out the loudest would be able to define what they really think should be done'.[34] He determined to pursue his own concept of army reform - the revision of the drill books, training and instructional courses to embody the tactical reforms which he had already introduced in South Africa.

On 26 January 1900, within days of his arrival in Cape Town, Lord Roberts had issued his confidential 'Circular Memorandum No. 5', authorizing changes in infantry tactics, artillery bombardments, horsemastership, and the organization of transport. He stressed that careful reconnaissance should precede an attack, that direct attacks in column formation should be avoided, and that infantry should adopt extended formations with troops, if necessary, six to eight paces apart. He emphasized that the changes involved a delegation of responsibility to battalion and company commanders as orders in the field had to be communicated precisely. Cover, he insisted, had to be utilized wherever available. These precautionary tactics, though based on the author's Indian experience, were applicable to battle zones swept by smokeless magazine rifles. To increase the effectiveness of artillery fire, Lord Roberts ordered batteries to eschew positions within range of enemy infantry, and urged continuous rather than sporadic bombardments. He exhorted cavalrymen to march where possible, and reorganized transport by removing it from regimental command and placing it entirely under the Army Service Corps.[35] In sum, Lord Roberts had introduced a series of tactical reforms which were the harbingers of future changes in peacetime training almost as soon as he arrived in South Africa. He had done so without any reliance upon civilian advice.

His ten months in South Africa merely confirmed his preconceived opinions. He had always been a critic of traditional cavalry tactics. He believed that the cavalryman would have to learn to fight dismounted, to rely on his rifle, and to carry it on his person. He derived these views not from events in the Transvaal but from a chaotic day's campaigning in the Chardeh Valley, near Kabul, on 11 December 1879. He constantly recalled the spectacle of 200 troopers from the 9th Lancers struggling to fight mounted and dismounted, while clutching their lances, and losing forty carbines in the process.[36] The performance of the cavalry in South Africa merely confirmed his worst fears. During his brief period of field command, he dismissed eleven of the seventeen cavalry commanders and berated the arm for a lack of initiative, failures in reconnaissance, and inadequate care of its horses. He believed that charges with the *arme blanche* would be a rare occurrence in future battles, and that the cavalry should acknowledge the dominance of fire power, by preparing to act generally as dismounted riflemen. 'For this reason', remarked Lord Roberts, 'I would do all in my power to encourage musketry and to make Cavalrymen understand that they must not think it in any way *infra dig* being trained to fight on foot'.[37]

Lord Roberts, an old artillery officer, favoured the complete rearmament of the artillery arm. Once again he had formed his views before ever setting foot in South Africa; he had advocated the introduction of quick-firing artillery as early as 1893.[38] The advantages of rapid, aimed artillery fire were another derivative of smokeless powder. Once the recoil of the gun was absorbed by means of brakes or buffers, without impairing the mobility of the weapon, effective artillery fire could be increased from four to five rounds per minute to twenty to thirty rounds per minute. Quick-firing artillery was not used in South Africa, but its virtues were displayed by the French at their manoeuvres in 1900. Early reports from the war, however, had stressed the long range of Boer artillery fire, an advantage readily accepted by the government in its search for explanations of the early failures. The government committed itself to the rearmament of the artillery; it formed equipment committees of senior artillery officers and purchased 108 quick-firing field guns from the Ehrhardt factories in Germany. Lord Roberts believed that this purchase had advanced the artillery 'by five, if not by ten years in our knowledge of what Field Guns might do'.[39]

Over the infantry, the arm which had been the primary victim of Boer fire-power, Lord Roberts discounted the advice of civilian pundits. W. A. Baillie-Grohman, a big game hunter and winner of over seventy awards for rifle shooting, had disparaged both the rifle and the marksmanship of the British soldier. He condemned the .303 service rifle for its excessive weight, lower muzzle velocity, worse trajectory, inferior trigger pull, weaker bolt, and slower rate of fire than the clip loading, continental rifles used by the Boers. He also believed that musketry training should be radically transformed; he advocated individual, long-range, shooting practice at unknown distances.[40] Lord Roberts and his advisers were less critical of the Lee Enfield rifle. Uninterested in a carefully adjusted and delicate piece of mechanism, they required that the rifle should be usable under extreme climatic conditions, sufficiently durable to withstand rough treatment and scanty cleaning, and yet always reliable for a soldier more or less skilled in the arts of musketry. Lord Roberts confirmed that the rifle had met these criteria in South Africa. Only minor modifications were necessary – an adjustment in the sighting, the addition of a clip loading system, and a reduction in the length of the barrel for cavalry use. Similarly, he did not believe that the introduction of long-range firing practice at unknown distances was either a practical or a necessary proposition. He insisted that effective fire at short ranges was the main requirement in contemporary battles. Hence he recommended an increase in the ammunition allotted to annual musketry practice, a diminution of collective practice and volley-firing, and more individual firing at fixed and mobile targets over short to medium ranges.[41]

The primary focus of army reform, in the view of Lord Roberts, was the improved professional training of officers and men. He accepted that this focus should reflect the altered circumstance of the modern battlefield. With closed formations at an end, he maintained that future training should promote the ability of the private soldier to think and act for himself. It should also require that junior officers accept an ever-increasing amount of responsibility. These ideas were not based upon lessons from the Boer War; indeed, contrary to popular opinion, there were not any self-evident lessons in the War –

only a range of experience which would be interpreted in a highly personal manner. Lord Roberts never forgot his forty years of soldiering in India; he had derived assumptions about training and tactics from these years which he used to interpret the military experiences of the South African War. On musketry training and artillery practice, he informed the editor of the *United Service Magazine* 'that my experiences in South Africa have not caused me to modify but have rather confirmed the opinions I have expressed for the last seventeen years on this most important part of a soldier's training'.[42]

New drill books were issued, modifying tactics and training in the light of particular interpretations of the South African experience. *Field Artillery Training 1902* doubled the distances of the pre-war range tables, recognized dispersed batteries as a viable tactical formation, urged the use of cover, and accepted that the artillery could not clear enemy trenches by itself. *Cavalry Training 1904* underlined the importance of dismounted duties, and stressed that the rifle had replaced the sword as the main cavalry weapon. Neither of these works nor the infantry manuals published in 1905 would be accepted as final definitive judgements. *Musketry Regulations 1905* emphasized the shift from collective medium-range firing to the development of individual musketry skills at short range. *Combining Training 1905,* though still wedded to the infantry offensive, at least acknowledged that smokeless powder, entrenchments, and the flat trajectory of modern weapons had increased the effectiveness of defensive fire. Within each arm of the service, debates continued about tactics and training. The Russo-Japanese War (1904–05) would be scrutinized for any lessons of relevance. The impact of the new technology, particularly of quick-firing artillery, would be examined throughout the Edwardian period.

Lord Roberts accepted that army reform would be a gradual and evolutionary process. Having taken the initiative in wartime, he recognized that the development of each aspect of reform would be dictated by the availability of specialist advice. He feared, however, that this gradual and piecemeal approach would not placate 'the public'.[43] He was abundantly correct. In the first place, the war lasted until 31 May 1902, approximately eighteen months after the press and war-weary public had expected it to finish. The cost and controversy of Kitchener's campaign, coupled with scandalous revelations, especially over the blunders of the remounts department, plagued the War Office. Disillusion with the duration and character of the war left a deeper impression than the reforms initiated by the Commander-in-Chief. Secondly, the reforms which Lord Roberts had launched were highly technical and specialized; they excited only limited interest outside the army. Writing to G. W. Forrest on 19 January 1902, Lord Roberts catalogued the reforms initiated during his first year in office. They included experiments on rifles, artillery guns, lighter ambulance and store wagons, barrack cubicles and traction engines;

changes in military uniforms, artillery and infantry drills, and in the organization of the mounted infantry; and the formation of committees to inquire into Sandhurst and Woolwich, canteen arrangements, and the curtailment of unnecessary regimental expenses.[44] Though potentially significant, these measures had failed to appease the critics. 'In the War Office', wrote Captain Cairnes, 'there is nothing but chaos. B[rodrick] is in despair and Lord R[oberts] is quite happy, hatching little jobs and beaming on everyone'.[45]

Even more frustrating for the Commander-in-Chief was his inability to assuage fears about the professional competence of the officer corps. These fears had persisted throughout the war: 'We need an army', wrote Captain Cairnes, 'which is an up to date fighting machine not a mere organization for the purpose of providing an elegant employment for the leisure hours of the wealthy classes'.[46] Both the expensive life-style of an army officer and his lack of professional incentive had attracted adverse comment. A Select Committee chaired by Lord Stanley, confirmed that junior officers could not live on their pay. It reckoned that the annual expenses of army life presumed a private income of £100 to £150 for an infantry officer, and of £600 to £700 for a cavalry officer.[47] Similarly a Select Committee, chaired by Akers-Douglas, took evidence from senior officers and found

> that the majority of young officers will not work unless compelled; that 'keenness is out of fashion'; that 'it is not the correct form'; the spirit and fashion is 'rather not to show keenness'; and that the idea is . . . to do as little as they possibly can.[48]

The solutions of both Committees aroused opposition from within the army. A ban on polo, stricter supervision of mess and uniform expenditure, and more subventions by the government were advocated by the Stanley Committee. By implementing these proposals, the Committee maintained that dependence upon private income could be reduced to £60 per annum for an infantry officer and to £120 per annum for a cavalry officer.[49] Lord Roberts and the cavalry commanders, though willing to endorse the objectives of the report, modified the proposals substantially. They rejected a ban on polo and opposed economies in uniform expenditure. They recommended that cavalry officers should live within a private income of £300 per annum.[50] Brodrick approved these modifications, and agreed that the State would provide officers with chargers, saddlery, field kit, and furniture (at a small rent). As the Government would neither increase pay nor enforce sumptuary laws, Brodrick could only rely upon the voluntary co-operation of serving officers. 'You must carry the spirit of the regiment and the colonels with you', he advised the House of Commons on 10 March 1903.[51] The majority of Members on both sides of the House concurred; they were unwilling to spend the money which would establish proper salary rates for the officer corps. Reform was thwarted. Private means remained as the principal requirement for a commission in the home army.

Promotion by merit, the measure proposed by the Akers-Douglas Committee,[52] met an even swifter demise. It encountered traditional objections that jobbery and favouritism would attend selection and that the process would damage regimental *esprit de corps.* Ever since the end of promotion by seniority in 1885, the Selection Board had relied upon confidential reports compiled by commanding officers. These reports tended to be either unduly favourable or wholly vague in their professional comments; some laid exclusive emphasis upon skills in polo and field sports and attributes like 'success in society'. Unable to evaluate professional merit, the Selection Board could only promote by seniority and reject the blatantly incompetent (usually those who had committed a specific act, involving neglect of duty or even worse). So long as promotion remained within the confines of the regiment, the sole source of information was the regimental commanding officer. Lord Roberts was unwilling to abandon the regimental system of promotion, and hence remained dependent upon the co-operation of the commanding officer. In these circumstances, he felt unable to recommend a change of the promotion system. As he perceptively asked: 'What reason have we to suppose that a change of system would in itself lead to a change in the procedure of those who would have to carry it into effect?'[53]

Unable to placate critics over the officer corps, Lord Roberts suffered from the spillover of criticism about other army problems. Apart from the disillusion occasioned by the war, a wave of scepticism mounted over the reforms of Brodrick. Though evident in March 1901, this scepticism became ever more pronounced over the next two years and tended to obscure the substance of the reforms accomplished by the Commander-in-Chief. When the army first displayed its new tactical skills in the autumn manoeuvres of 1903, they received but one page of comment from Leo Amery in a 200-page onslaught upon the Brodrick reforms.[54]

A modified scepticism had greeted the original announcement of the six army corps scheme. It became more and more pronounced as support for the war waned. A Unionist back-bench group, known as the Hughligans (after Lord Hugh Cecil, one of their leading members), began to challenge the level of military spending. The campaign emanated from the early opposition of Winston Churchill to the Brodrick proposals: an opposition founded upon retrenchment - the cause of his father's fall from office in 1886.[55] The group of Members who joined Churchill were not specialists in military matters. They were unable to agree, let alone formulate, any measures of reform. They relied upon the articles of Leo Amery in *The Times* for positive proposals. As Amery recalled, 'I naturally found myself colloquing with them, though with somewhat diminishing respect for their general outlook . . .'.[56] Their main concern remained the bloated state of the Army Estimates. Their focus upon retrenchment ensured the isolation of the Hughligans from the pre-war army reformers, like Dilke, and the majority of the service Members.

The effects of the Hughligan campaign were cumulative rather than immediate. Press and Parliamentary interest in army reform had diminished steadily as controversies arose over Balfour's Education Act (1902) and over tariff reform. The Hughligans hounded Brodrick at question time; they poured scorn and derision upon his 'phantom army' in the army debates of 1902 and 1903. Ernest Beckett and Major Seely even moved an amendment to the King's speech on 23 February 1903. As Brodrick had failed to form three of his corps on account of faulty estimates in recruiting and in the post-war deployment of battalions, the Hughligans gained a sympathetic hearing. Beckett condemned 'extravagant expenditure with inadequate results . . .'. Major Seely added that spending as much on the army as on the navy was fundamentally wrong, since a navy could not be improvised 'while an army, to a large extent could be . . .'. Even worse, he believed that an expeditionary force of three army corps was too small for continental wars, but too large for colonial wars. Winston Churchill rounded off the attack, arguing that the issue turned upon the command of the sea: 'If we had it, we required fewer soldiers, if we had it not we wanted more ships'.[57] Although Government whips ensured a ministerial majority, more than a score of Unionists voted with the Opposition. Disillusion with the War Office had deepened considerably.

The final straw was the report of the Royal Commission on the South African War, which was delivered on 9 July 1903. The government judiciously refrained from publishing the findings until after the prorogation of Parliament at the end of August. Chaired by Lord Elgin, the Commission had received its patent on 9 September 1902. It spent fifty-five days examining 114 witnesses and asking 22,200 questions. It accumulated a wealth of information about the war, and recorded the opinions of soldiers and administrators in two bulky volumes of evidence. The report drew attention to specific shortcomings, including the lack of any plan of campaign, the shortage of stores for a war on this scale, the strain imposed upon the regular forces at home from February to June 1900, the deficiencies of some weapons, the need to improve staff work, and the training of new recruits.[58] But the majority of Commissioners neither passed judgement upon the causes of the early defeats, nor offered any guidance upon army reform. Their report was simply a guide to the facts and opinions stored in the appendices and minutes of evidence.

Lord Esher dissented from the majority report. A former Liberal Member of Parliament (1880–85), Esher had been private secretary to the Marquess of Hartington and joint secretary with Sir George Clarke to Hartington's Royal Commission. Having abandoned party politics, he had served as secretary to HM Office of Works (1895–1902) becoming responsible for the organization of the Jubilee celebrations and the Royal Funeral. He had gained the confidence of King Edward VII and had established a reputation as an Imperial strategist. He believed that the War Office had suffered from a lack of co-ordination between the different branches of the department, and from the absence of a proper system of inspection. He recommended, in his minority report, that a Council or Board should be established in the War Office along 'the lines of the Admiralty'. He maintained that the War Office, by discussing matters in Council, followed by a collective appeal to the cabinet, could deal more effectively with the Treasury and with Parliament. Establishing an Admiralty system of administration, he added, would render the post of Commander-in-Chief anomalous. Were that post abolished, 'as recommended by the Hartington Commission', then a general officer commanding the army could be appointed to inspect the military organization: he would be directly responsible to the Secretary of State for War.[59]

Controversy erupted in the wake of the Elgin Report. Liberals paused, briefly, from the assault upon Chamberlain's tariff proposals to assail the Government for its conduct of the war. The Liberal (Imperalist) League poured forth pamphlets entitled *An Improvised Army, The War Scandals: The Ignorance of the Tory Government,* and *Lord Rosebery and the War Office Blunders.* W. T. Stead, the moving force behind the Stop the War Committee, produced a digest of the evidence in the report entitled *How Britain Went to War* (1903). He used the evidence to denounce the policies of Lansdowne and Chamberlain. The press, though grateful for the evidence compiled by the Commission, had mixed feelings about the report. While some journals accepted that reforms could only be proposed by specialists,[60] others asserted that the Commission had been too timid and inconclusive. 'The Report', declared *The Illustrated London News,* 'is the mildest-mannered document that ever rebuked incapacity'.[61] A reviewer in *The Edinburgh Review,* echoed these sentiments; he believed that the minority report merited consideration because the War Office system no longer commanded public confidence. The system proposed by Esher, he added, had been a success at the Admiralty and had been recommended by the Hartington Commission some twelve years previously.[62]

Balfour hesitated before responding to the uproar occasioned by the report. 'The public', he assured Brodrick, 'do not find it easy to think of more than one thing at a time, fiscal reform will prove a formidable rival to army reform'. He was indignant, too, 'at the injustice which has been done to the War Office administration since '96'.[63] Belfour had taken a keen interest in strategic questions ever since he had become Prime Minister in the summer of 1902. In the following December he had reorganized the defence Committee of the cabinet into the Committee of Imperial Defence. Under his guidance, the Committee met regularly to discuss issues of concern to both services, like the defence of the homeland and the problems involved in reinforcing the North-West Frontier. Balfour believed that clarifying Imperial policy would serve as a prerequisite for further reform.

But a cabinet crisis in mid-September compelled him to act. The divisions within the government over tariff reform reached a climax on 16 September 1903, when Joseph Chamberlain tendered his resignation. Ritchie, the Chancellor of the Exchequer, Lord George Hamilton, the Secretary of State for India, Lord Balfour of Burleigh and Arthur Elliot also resigned from the cabinet. A cabinet reshuffle became essential at a time when Brodrick was thoroughly discredited as Secretary of State for War. Equally pressing were the demands for War Office reform, not least from the King himself.[64] Balfour resolved to act upon both fronts; he transferred Brodrick to the India Office and spent nearly a fortnight in search of his successor. Five candidates refused the post, including Esher, who preferred an influential role behind the scenes to the burdens of public office. Eventually Balfour offered the post to Arnold-Forster, making his acceptance subject to the assistance of a small independent committee, under the chairmanship of Esher, charged with the task of reorganizing the War Office.

The Esher Committee was constituted in early November 1903. Serving alongside Esher were Sir John Fisher, then Commander-in-Chief of the Portsmouth Dockyard, and Sir George Clarke, the former Governor of Victoria, with Lieutenant-Colonel Gerald Ellison as secretary. Although Clarke did not arrive in England until 28 December, the Committee issued its first report on 11 January 1904 and its third and final report on 9 March 1904. Contemporaries were astonished by the rapid production of reports which were so radical in their implications. The first proposed that the Committee of Imperial Defence should be strengthened by the addition of a permanent secretariat, and that an Army Council should be established in the War Office. It also urged that an Inspector-General of Forces should replace the Commander-in-Chief. The second report recommended the creation of a General Staff and the decentralization of executive duties from the War Office to the officers commanding military districts. The third report expounded upon the methods of financial control, the responsibilities of the Inspector-General of Forces, and the duties of the General Staff in the field. The Committee advised that the General Staff should be headed by a Chief of the General Staff who should also have a seat on the Army Council. The Chief of the General Staff would be responsible for three Directorates, of Military Operations, of Staff Duties and of Military Training. General Staff officers, argued the Committee, should be recruited mainly from the Staff College for a maximum of four years' service. After serving on the General Staff, officers 'in all cases' would be eligible for accelerated promotion.[65]

The Esher Committee had insisted that their reforms should be preceded by a 'clean sweep' of the War Office - the removal of Lord Roberts and the heads of the four military departments. Balfour accepted this requirement; he used Letters Patent and Orders in Council to constitute the Army Council and authorize new appointments. Having acceded to the demands of the Esher Committee, Balfour left the details of forming a General Staff to the new officials. The Prime Minister focused upon questions of Imperial strategy, and Arnold-Forster submitted new proposals for army reform: both virtually ignored the development of the General Staff. To the chagrin of Esher, the new officials could not resolve their differences over the qualifications desired, the status of a 'passed Staff College' certificate, and the propriety of rewarding General Staff work with accelerated promotion. Some favoured a *corps d'élite,* others abhorred the idea. The Chief of the General Staff, Sir Neville Lyttelton, proved to be weak and ineffectual; he neither composed the internal quarrel in the Army Council nor pressed for a political initiative. By mid-June 1905, Esher re-formed his Committee on an unofficial basis to produce a more specific memorandum. The Committee recommended the division of the General Staff into two categories: a special War Office department required to prepare the army for war, and specially trained officers seconded to the Command staffs able to perform specific duties in war and peace. Again Esher pressed for changes in personnel, particularly the replacement of Lyttelton, but he was not successful. Arnold-Forster, baulked over his own proposals, took up the issue in the following autumn. He pressed the cabinet to support the formation of a General Staff; but Balfour, in the last throes of his government, refused to act.[66]

During its last two years of office, the Balfour government was preoccupied, in military matters, with the army reform proposals of Arnold-Forster. Prior to his appointment in October 1903, the Secretary of State for War had written extensively about army reform. Determined to implement his ideas on entering office, he proved a tactless and self-opinionated Minister. Senior officers, wrote Amery, 'complained, not altogether without reason, that he was too apt to lecture them and too little inclined to listen . . .'.[67] He was a man in a hurry. Having suffered a severe heart strain while riding in 1903, Arnold-Forster was frequently ill thereafter. The disability only stiffened his resolve to act as quickly as possible. He had, moreover, inherited the profligate policies and the abortive reforms of his predecessor. Substantial savings were expected by both the House of Commons and the Treasury. New proposals were also required to rectify the enlistment crisis bequeathed by Brodrick. When three-year enlistments were introduced, Brodrick had calculated that nearly three-quarters of the men would voluntarily extend their service and serve as drafts for overseas garrisons. Rankers were much more shrewd; they either flocked into the Reserve or awaited the offer of additional bounties to extend their service. The crisis, already evident in the autumn of 1903, progressively worsened. By 1 May 1904, only 12 per cent of the eligible infantry had extended their service.[68]

Arnold-Forster proposed to abandon the army corps scheme and the Cardwell system of linked battalions. He advocated the formation of large depots from which drafts could be supplied to groups of battalions. He wished to create an army with concomitant long and short terms of service - the long-service men, enlisted for nine years in the Colours, would garrison foreign stations and provide a striking force, while the short-service men, retained at home, would feed the Reserve. As a firm believer in the ability of the navy to defend the country against invasion, he saw no need to preserve large auxiliary forces for home defence. He sought economies in the military budget by the reduction of the Militia and Volunteers. He wished to absorb about half of the Militia battalions into the home army, while disbanding the remainder. He proposed to reduce the Volunteers' Establishment from 346,000 to 200,000 and to limit its field strength to 180,000 men. These proposals were sensible in many respects. The force was deficient in training and in equipment. It was more than 105,000 men short of its present establishment. Some Corps were so short of funds that they had enrolled non-efficients to earn their grant. Arnold-Forster was merely seeking to rationalize a declining body. Of the 180,000 men, he recommended that 60,000 should be retained on higher efficiency conditions and receive higher allowances, so distinguishing between those who could give their time and those who could not.[69]

These proposals encountered tenacious opposition from within the cabinet. Neither Brodrick nor Lansdowne welcomed the reversal of their own policies and reforms. Two Militia officers, Lord Selborne, the First Lord of the Admiralty, and Lord Cranborne, the Lord Privy Seal, deplored the reduction of the Militia and blocked this part of the scheme. Without savings on the auxiliary forces, the scheme would add another £913,100 onto the Estimates, which totalled £28,895,624 in 1904-05. The cost appalled both the Chancellor of the Exchequer, Austen Chamberlain, and the Prime Minister. Balfour informed the King that Arnold-Forster had left the cost of his scheme 'at a level which will bitterly disappoint public opinion, and which in the present state of public finance the country will scarcely tolerate'.[70] As Arnold-Forster refused to modify his proposals, Balfour instructed him to make a general statement of his own views in the House of Commons, but on no account to commit the government. He made his statement on 14 July 1904, and met a sceptical deputation of Militia officers six days later. On the following day, 21 July, he learnt that Lord Lansdowne had stated in the House of Lords that 'popular sentiment' against the Militia changes had proved 'too strong' to justify their recommendation. Appalled by this 'slap in the face', Arnold-Forster proffered his resignation, which Balfour prudently declined to accept.[71]

Though retained in office, Arnold-Forster was only permitted to present his Volunteer plans before Parliament. With full cabinet support, he set aside the proposals of a Royal Commission on the Militia and Volunteers, which had reported on 20 May 1904. The Commission, chaired by the Duke of Norfolk, had recommended the raising of a home defence army on the basis of compulsory service, an option quickly rejected. Arnold-Forster met Members of both Houses of Parliament interested in the Volunteers on 25 July 1904. As a result of this meeting, he amended his scheme slightly: he offered to keep the two classes of efficient Volunteers in entirely separate units. Members were not mollified, however. Churchill, now a Liberal, condemned the proposals for reflecting 'all the prejudices and jealousies of the professional and Regular soldiers'.[72] When Arnold-Forster formally outlined his scheme in January 1905, the opposition became more organized and more obstructive. As soon as Parliament reassembled, Captain Norton, seconded by Major Seely, tabled an amendment to the King's speech, opposing any reduction of the Volunteers. Faced with the animosity of over forty Volunteer MPs, and a motley group of allies, including Churchill, Arnold-Forster endured the first of many gruelling debates. Lacking the support of his cabinet colleagues, or even of the majority of the Army Council, Arnold-Forster became increasingly isolated and vulnerable. During protracted debates on the Army Estimates in April 1905, Balfour intervened to undermine the case of his Secretary of State. Seeking to reassure the House, Balfour promised that any savings made by a reduction of Volunteer numbers would be spent on improving the efficiency of the force.[73] In short, the saving of £300,000 per annum, a vital element in the scheme, was completely eliminated.

Arnold-Forster still endeavoured to reduce the Volunteers. On 13 April 1905 the Army Council agreed that the force could not be reduced in the current vears, but that its fitness could be ascertained as a basis for future policy. General Officers Commanding-in-Chief were asked to report any Volunteer units which might be disbanded or amalgamated on the grounds of inefficiency of lack of numbers. In the same circular, dated 20 June 1905, the medical officers of each corps were asked to state what proportion of men were not fit for active service in the field. From the ambiguous wording, many Volunteers feared that the government was trying to reduce the force by insinuating that the men were unfit and by enforcing compulsory medical examinations. Volunteer MPs and some, but not all, newspapers protested so vigorously that Arnold-Forster withdrew the circular and reissued it on 11 July in a less offensive form. The Secretary of State had always maintained that his circulars aroused less opposition in the country than in the Commons. In this assumption he was proved correct; by November 1905, some 187,880 men out of 239,543 had agreed to be examined, of whom 84 per cent were declared to be fit. Nevertheless, Volunteer MPs continued to obstruct proceedings in the House of Commons. Government whips became increasingly dismayed; they feared the possibility of substantial defections should the policy of reductions be put to the vote. The majority of the Army Council became less and less resolute. They eventually proposed, and Arnold-Forster grimly accepted, that Parliament should be asked for more, not less, money for the Volunteers. In the memorandum to the cabinet of 11 November 1905, Arnold-Forster formally aborted his previous policy: he requested that the Estimates should be increased by about £170,000 to improve the existing Volunteer force.[74]

While the Volunteer proposals were openly defeated in Parliament, the rest of the 'New Army Scheme' was challenged in a more furtive fashion. The proposals were scrutinized by members of the Committee of Imperial Defence and by the Army Council. Lord Esher and Sir George Clarke, permanent secretary of the C.I.D., disliked many aspects of the Scheme. They deplored the dislocation of the army during the period of innovation, the destruction of the Militia, and the sacrifice of the home army as a force 'encamped and ready for war'.[75] They intrigued behind the scenes, making the maximum use of Esher's contacts with Balfour, the King, and their private secretaries (Sandars and Knollys). From their machinations emerged a Sub-Committee of the C.I.D. with a remit to investigate Arnold-Forster's proposals in January and February 1905. That Sub-Committee endorsed an entirely different plan, proposed by Balfour, which was based upon the retention of the Militia.[76] More criticisms emanated from the Army Council, where three of the four military members feared that the aims of the Scheme were utterly impractical. With the exception of Major-General Plummer, the Quartermaster-General, they doubted that infantry recruiting could be increased by 35 per cent in peacetime. They questioned the feasibility of greatly increased officer targets; claimed that the additional barracks and training facilities for the short-service battalions would prove prohibitively expensive; and feared for the wartime efficiency of battalions in which Reservists comprised 80 per cent of the strength. On 10 June 1905 they protested to the cabinet that the Scheme was unrealistic, based more upon conjecture than upon avaiable resources.[77]

These protests did not immediately prevail. Esher and Clarke could only bombard the Prime Minister with critical correspondence; they could not influence ministerial policy. Balfour shared their doubts about the practicality of the 'New Army Scheme'. Having taken a keen interest in strategic questions, he had regularly chaired meetings of the C.I.D. and had arbitrated between the naval and military views on home defence. Having concluded that invasion was unlikely in view of Britain's naval strength, he accepted that the main role of the army was to reinforce the Indian garrison in time of war. He believed that these reinforcements should not exceed 100,000 men in the first twelve months of war, and that the army should maintain a striking force of two divisions constantly available for overseas service.

To fulfil these requirements, he recommended the formation of a long-service army, in which soldiers served for seven years in the Colours followed by five years in the Reserve, backed by an enlarged and improved Militia.[78]

Balfour never forced these views upon Arnold-Forster. The Prime Minister neither wished to seek another Secretary of State for War nor to trespass upon the ministerial responsibility of his chosen minister. Indeed the cabinet permitted Arnold-Forster, in October 1904, to replace three-year enlistments by nine-year enlistments to ensure the flow of drafts to India and the colonies. And, on 22 June 1905, the cabinet conceded a Pyrrhic victory to the resolute and uncompromising Secretary of State. He was authorized to undertake a limited experiment in short-service recruiting, an experiment attenuated in its impact by the fall of the government in the following December.

Thereafter the failure of Arnold-Forster to convince 'informed' opinion reaped a predictable reward. His criticism on the Army Council and the Committee of Imperial Defence continued to proffer advice and to reiterate their fears to the incoming Liberal administration. They were only preaching to the converted. Liberals had not overlooked the Unionist paralysis over army reform. Nor were they likely to sustain reforms which were antithetical to the Cardwell system. As Campbell-Bannerman happily remarked, 'A. F. is done . . .. It is quite understood that his scheme is dead . . .. The odd thing is that the young bloods whose one cry for some years has been away with horrid Linked Batt^ns^ System, are now ardent Cardwellians, all for double batt^ns^ and 7 & 5 years service'.[79] The disarray in the War Office and the volume of hostile criticism evoked by Arnold-Forster ensured that the Liberals would adopt a fresh approach over army reform.

While in opposition, the Liberal party had never fashioned an alternative policy on army reform. During the early months of the war, Liberals, apart from their Imperialist wing, had been more concerned about the origins of the conflict than about the efficiency of the army. As the war drew to its close, Liberal interest had focused increasingly upon social reform, the implications of Balfour's Education Act, and the threat to free trade posed by Chamberlain's advocacy of tariff reform. Liberals believed that the Unionist Government had become too preoccupied with army reform. 'It is part of the Imperialist heresy', wrote Campbell-Bannerman, 'to try to make war, defence, military policy etc., take precedence of all other questions'.[80] Even Haldane, a leading Liberal Imperialist, agreed that the Government had lost sight of social objectives in its quest for army reform. Like other Liberals, he rated retrenchment above reform in military matters; he claimed that nearly £5 million could be saved in the Army Estimates by transferring the defence of home ports and naval bases from the army to the navy.[81]

Fiscal economy was not the sole objective of those Liberals who demanded retrenchment in military spending. The party leadership had always been somewhat ambivalent in its attitude towards army reform. Lacking specialist military advice, it had refrained from proposing the adoption of new equipment and transport, and the reorganization of training manuals, tactical doctrine, and methods of mobilization. Yet it had not ignored entirely the interest in army reform, especially the fears about the professional competence of the officer corps. As a remedy, Campbell-Bannerman had recommended an increase of the promotions from the ranks. More promotions from the ranks would placate those radicals who yearned for a democratized officer corps. It would also, in the opinion of Campbell-Bannerman, increase the proportion of career-orientated officers and stimulate recruiting for the rank and file.[82]

Although less expensive than the pay rise secured by Brodrick, this proposal was bound to be expensive. It could not be effective on a large scale without a readjustment of the rates of pay for officers which had not been raised since 1806. Should the policy prove too successful, it might attract a better quality of recruit, so impinging upon the skilled labour resources of the country. Campbell-Bannerman recognized the dilemma. He accepted that the army attracted many of its recruits from the least able of the urban poor, and rehabilitated many of them by the provision of regular food, exercise, and discipline. He feared that if the army attracted a higher quality of recruit 'the loss to the community would be greatly heavier than that of the loafers and idlers whom we at present get and make men of'.[83] Practical difficulties bedevilled the policy of seeking additional promotions from the ranks. Promoted non-commissioned officers would be much older than their colleagues and might encounter social prejudice within the mess. They might not come forth at all unless mess expenditure was rigidly controlled. Liberals neither resolved these difficulties nor pressed the proposal as a policy option.

Unlike the government, the Liberals became less and less interested in army reform. They were preoccupied with other issues and their defence policy suffered from the indolence of Campbell-Bannerman. Militarism remained a deep-rooted fear, especially after the bloated Estimates and threat of compulsion from St John Brodrick. Liberals did not fear that a reformed army would threaten the State, as it would still be largely employed in Imperial defence. But they did suspect that improving the efficiency of the army might detract from the productive power of the country, and, more seriously, might cause an eruption of unruly passions within the civil population. Increasing armaments, Campbell-Bannerman had asserted, 'may be provocative to your neighbours: and worse still it may stimulate an ambitious and aggressive spirit among your people'.[84] Many Liberals were appalled by the jingoism and passions evoked by the war, which found their crescendo on Mafeking night. Sir William Harcourt hoped that peace would 'inspire a soberer sentiment in the people of this country, and that the time will come when the melodies of the music halls and the Mafeking mobs will not be regarded as the true exponents of English statesmanship'.[85] Haldane had shared the delight of the 'patriotic crowds' who thronged the streets after the relief of Mafeking, but he distinguished between those crowds and the jingoistic mobs. He deplored the latter as dangerous phenomena; indeed he feared that an aggressive foreign policy and bloated armaments would encourage jingoism and would undermine the nation's prosperity.[86] Liberals united in deploring the expense and the failure of the government's reforms. They never committed themselves to any scheme of reform. They merely expected from the next Liberal Secretary of State for War a massive reduction in military spending.

Army reform, in sum, had flourished briefly as an issue during and immediately after the South African War. The pressure from the press in favour of reform reflected neither a coherent campaign nor a precise commitment to particular measures. On the contrary, it reflected dismay after the early defeats, disillusion with the course of the war, and anger over the findings of various Select Committees and Royal Commissions. To allay these feelings, the government embarked upon reform in wartime. Brodrick, in trying to exploit the current mood, gambled upon the outcome of the war, the post-war level of recruiting, the likely deployment of battalions in peacetime, and the value of formulating reforms while some advisers were 6,000 miles away. Above all, he risked making erroneous deductions from the immediate problems encountered in South Africa.

Brodrick barely recognized these difficulties. He believed that risks of a different but still damaging nature would attend delay. As the war had aroused an unprecedented clamour for reform, he sensed that the time was ripe to seek a massive increase in military spending, the basic prerequisite for his own proposals. Any delay would hazard post-war apathy and fiscal retrenchment. Even before peace returned, however, this strategy began to unravel. The army could not be reformed to meet wartime requirements alone. The army had to fulfil peacetime duties, particularly the supply of drafts for overseas garrisons; it had to remain, over an indefinite period of peace, as a tolerable burden upon the Exchequer. As neither of these objectives were met, the Brodrick reforms were soon discredited and quickly abandoned.

Arnold-Forster, a more radical and ambitious reformer, found even less support for his proposed reforms. He had come to office in the wake of the Elgin report and the renewed demands for army reform. He had offered the prospect of financial savings and a military system which would meet the peacetime requirements of an Imperial army. But he failed to carry the support of his political colleagues and military advisers. He encountered fervent opposition from the civilian pundits in the Committee of Imperial Defence. Personal shortcomings, tactical mistakes, over-ambitious proposals, and the influence of vested interests within the Conservative party largely accounted for his failure in office.

Notwithstanding the failures of Brodrick and Arnold-Forster, several reforms were accomplished by the Balfour government. New institutions were created, notably the Committee of Imperial Defence and the Army Council. A belated commitment was given to the embryonic General Staff. The maritime view of home defence was endorsed. New items of equipment were sanctioned for each arm of the service. The short Lee Enfield rifle, loaded on a clip system, was adopted for the cavalry and infantry. Quick-firing guns were approved – a 12½-pounder for the horse artillery and a 18½-pounder for the field artillery. The lance was withdrawn as an active service weapon. New drill books were issued, modifying training and tactics in light of the South African War. Yet these measures had failed to placate the critics of the War Office. The abortive reforms of Brodrick and Arnold-Forster had left a host of issues unresolved. On the eve of the government's demise, Haldane, who had hopes of becoming the next Lord Chancellor, had forecast that 'a good deal of the time of the next ministry will be taken up with the reform of the army. I don't envy the man who has got that job'.[87]

Notes and references

1. L. S. Amery, *op. cit.*, Vol. 3, p. 3.
2. Sir A. Milner to J. Chamberlain, 4 May 1899, *The Milner Papers (South Africa 1897–1899)*, ed. C. Headlam, Cassell, London, 1931, pp. 352–3.
3. *The Times*, 2 Oct. 1899, p. 7.
4. 'The Absent-Minded Beggar', *Rudyard Kipling's Verse. Definitive Edition*, p. 459.
5. **G. Shepperson**, 'Kipling and the Boer War', *Rudyard Kipling: the man, his work and his world,* p. 84.
6. Lord Wolseley to Lord Lansdowne, 18 and 24 Aug. 1899, P.R.O., CAB 37/50, ff. 52, 56 and Lord Wolseley to Lady Wolseley, 19 Sept. 1899, Wolseley Mss. W/P, 28/33.
7. Lord Wolseley to Lady Wolseley, 29 Sept. 1899, Wolseley Mss., W/P, 28/61.
8. *The Times*, 10 Nov. 1899, p. 7.
9. G. Wyndham to his mother, 6 Oct. 1899 quoted in **J. W. McKail and G. Wyndham**, *Life and Letters of George Wyndham*, 2 vols., Hutchinson, London, 1925, Vol 1, p. 361.
10. Sir R. H. Knox to Sir H. Campbell-Bannerman, 2 Dec. 1899, Campbell-Bannerman Mss., B.M. Add. Mss. 41,221, f. 266.
11. *Parl. Deb.*, Fourth Ser., Vol. 77, 20 Oct. 1899, cols. 421–2.
12. P. Knightley, *op. cit.*, p. 66.

13. **W. S. Churchill**, *My Early Life*, Odhams, London, 1930, p. 227.
14. **M. Prior**, *Campaigns of a War Correspondent*, E. Arnold, London, 1912, p. 287.
15. **J. B. Atkins**, 'The Work and Future of War Correspondents', *The Monthly Review,* 4, No. 3, September 1901, pp. 84-5.
16. Lord Roberts to Lord Lansdowne, 15 Dec. 1899, Roberts Mss., N.A.M., R/117/1.
17. Lord Curzon to W. St J. Brodrick, 8 Jan. 1900, Midleton Mss., B.M. Add. Mss. 50,073, f. 274.
18. W. St J. Brodrick to Lord Curzon, 9 Feb. 1900, Curzon Mss., India Office, Eur.F. 111/10A, f. 131.
19. A. J. Balfour to a friend, 24 Jan. 1900, Balfour Mss., B.M. Add. Mss. 49,853, f. 189.
20. *The Times*, 27 Jan. 1900, p. 11.
21. *Ibid.*, 25 July 1900, p. 11.
22. *Ibid.*, 15 June 1901, p. 12. On the tactics used by Lord Kitchener, see **R. Kruger**, *Goodbye Dolly Gray: The story of the Boer War*, Cassell, London, 1959, pp. 391-2, 428-30, 443.
23. *Lord Rosebery at Edinburgh*, 1 Nov. 1902, Liberal League pamphlets, Houghton Library, London School of Economics and *The Scotsman*, 3 Oct. 1902, p. 6.
24. *The Westminster Gazette*, 7 Apr. 1900, p. 6.
25. **Colonel Londsdale Hale**, 'Sham versus Real Home Defence', *Nineteenth Century,* **49**, No. 287, Jan. 1901, pp. 248-66.
26. **Nemo,** 'Lord Wolseley as Commander-in-Chief', *Contemporary Review,* **79**, Feb. 1901, p. 161.
27. **H. R. Moon**, *The invasion of the United Kingdom: public controversy and official planning 1888-1918*, unpublished Ph.D. thesis, University of London, 1968, p. 148.
28. W. St J. Brodrick to Lord Roberts, 21 Dec. 1900, Roberts Mss., N.A.M., R/13/15.
29. *Parl. Deb.*, Fourth Ser., Vol. 90, 8 Mar. 1901, col. 1,060.
30. *Ibid.*, Vol. 90, 11 Mar. 1901, cols. 1,241-3, and 14 Mar. 1901, cols. 1,624-31; *The Times*, 11 Mar. 1901, p. 9.
31. *Parl. Deb.*, Fourth Ser., Vol. 90, 14 Mar. 1901, cols. 1,608, 1,612.
32. W. St J. Brodrick, 'Pay and Terms of Service in the Army', 4 Jan. 1902, P.R.O., CAB 37/60/2.
33. W. St J. Brodrick to Lord Curzon, 15 Mar. 1903, Midleton Mss., B.M. Add. Mss. 50,074, f. 124.
34. Lord Roberts to W. St J. Brodrick, 9 Nov. 1900, Roberts Mss., N.A.M., R/117/3/72.
35. **Lord Roberts,** 'Circular Memorandum No. 5, Notes for Guidance in South African Warfare', 26 Jan. 1900, Roberts Mss., N.A.M., R/111/1/36. See also Lord Roberts to Lord Lansdowne, 15-17 Jan. 1900, Roberts Mss., N.A.M., R/117/1/11.

36. Lord Roberts to Lieutenant-Colonel Godley, 13 Jan. 1902, Roberts Mss., N.A.M., R/112/3/218.
37. Lord Roberts to Sir E. Wood, 29 Sept. 1901, Roberts Mss., N.A.M., R/112/2/140.
38. Lord Roberts to Lord Kitchener, 10 Jan. 1902, Roberts Mss., N.A.M., R/112/3/120.
39. Lord Roberts to Lord Lansdowne, 16 Aug. 1901, Roberts Mss., N.A.M., R/122/2/126.
40. **W. A. Baillie-Grohman**, 'One Cause of our Defeats: The Service Rifle', *The Fortnightly Review,* New Series, **67**, Mar. 1900, pp. 376-9, and 'Marksmanship Old and New', *Nineteenth Century*, **47**, No. 279, May 1900, pp. 756-7.
41. Lord Roberts to Lord Lansdowne, 29 Aug. 1900, Roberts Mss., N.A.M., R/117/2/71, 72, and 'Army Order', 1 Sept. 1902, Roberts Mss., N.A.M., R/122/4/325.
42. Lord Roberts to the editor of the *United Service Magazine*, 13 Jan. 1902, Roberts Mss., N.A.M., R/122/3/217
43. Lord Roberts to W. St J. Brodrick, 9 Nov. 1900, Roberts Mss., N.A.M., R/117/3/72.
44. Lord Roberts to G. W. Forrest, 19 Jan. 1902, Roberts Mss., N.A.M., R/122/3/225.
45. Captain W. E. Cairnes to Lord Rosebery, 4 Oct. 1901, Rosebery Mss., N.L.S., Box 76.
46. **Capt. W. E. Cairnes**, *The Absent-Minded War*, Milne, London, 1900, p. 146.
47. The Stanley Report, pp. 7-8.
48. *Report of the Committee appointed to consider the Education and Training of Officers of the Army,* hereafter referred to as the Akers-Douglas Report, Cd. 982, 1902, X, p. 29.
49. The Stanley Report, pp. 22-3.
50. 'Minute by Commander-in-Chief on conditions for Competition for Cavalry Commissions' sent to W. St J. Brodrick, 21 Feb. 1903, Roberts Mss., N.A.M., R/124/3/726.
51. *Parl. Deb.*, Fourth Ser., Vol. 119, 10 Mar. 1903, col. 311.
52. The Akers-Douglas Report, p. 31.
53. Lord Roberts to the Secretary of State for War, 21 Jan. 1901, P.R.O., W.O. 32/8637.
54. **L. S. Amery**, *The Problem of the Army*, E. Arnold, London, 1903, p. 46.
55. *Parl. Deb.,* Fourth Ser., Vol. 93, 13 May 1901, col. 1,566.
56. **L. S. Amery,** *My Political Life,* 3 vols., Hutchinson, London, 1953, Vol 1, p. 195.
57. *Parl. Deb.*, Fourth Ser., Vol. 118, 23 Feb. 1903, cols. 517, 532 and 24 Feb. 1903, col. 697.
58. *Report of His Majesty's Commissioners appointed to inquire into the Military preparations and other matters connected with the War in South Africa*, hereafter referred to as the

Elgin Report, Cd. 1,789, 1904, XL, pp. 23, 26, 41, 44, 53, 95.
59. *Ibid.*, pp. 144–5.
60. 'The Cabinet and the War Office', *The Quarterly Review*, **198**, No. 394, Oct. 1903, p. 584.
61. *The Illustrated London News*. 5 Sept. 1903, p. 330.
62. 'The Truth about the Army', *The Edinburgh Review*, **198**, Oct. 1903, p. 456.
63. A. J. Balfour to W. St J. Brodrick, 8 Sept. 1903, Balfour Mss., B.M. Add. Mss. 49,720, ff. 217–18.
64. *Ibid.*, f. 218.
65. *Report of the War Office (Reconstitution) Committee*, Part II, Cd. 2,002, 1904, VIII, pp. 21–4.
66. **J. Gooch**, *The Plans of War: The General Staff and British Military Strategy c.1900–1916*, Routledge & Kegan Paul, London, 1974, pp. 62–97.
67. L. S. Amery, *My Political Life*, Vol. 1, p. 209.
68. *Parl. Deb.*, Fourth Ser., Vol. 135, 18 May 1904, cols. 160–1.
69. H. O. Arnold-Forster to the Army Board, 24 Nov. 1903, Arnold-Forster Mss., B.M. Add. Mss., 50,303, ff. 139-46.
70. A. J. Balfour to King Edward VII, 14 June 1904, P.R.O., CAB 41/28/19. See also **A. V. Tucker**, 'The issue of army reform in the Unionist government 1903–5', *Historical Journal,* **9**, 1966, pp. 96–7.
71. H. O. Arnold-Forster, diary, 20, 21 and 22 July 1904, Arnold-Forster Mss., B.M. Add. Mss. 50,339, ff. 59–60, 62–3, 69–70, and *Parl. Deb.*, Fourth Ser., Vol. 138, 21 July 1904, col. 736.
72. *Parl. Deb.*, Fourth Ser., Vol. 139, 8 Aug. 1904, cols. 1,416–19.
73. *Ibid.*, Vol. 144, 5 April 1905, cols. 513–20.
74. H. O. Arnold-Forster, diary, 7 Nov. 1905, Arnold-Forster Mss., B.M. Add. Mss. 50,352, ff. 44–8; Memorandum of the Adjutant-General, 14 Nov. 1905, P.R.O., W.O. 163/10; I. W. F. Beckett, *op. cit.*, pp. 355–62; H. Cunningham, *op. cit.*, pp. 137–8.
75. Viscount Esher to J. S. Sandars, 21 Nov. 1904, and Viscount Esher to A. J. Balfour, 13 Dec. 1904, Balfour Mss., B.M. Add. Mss. 49,718, ff. 135, 147–9; Sir G. S. Clarke to A. J. Balfour, 18 June 1904, and Sir G. S. Clarke to A. J. Balfour, 27 June 1904, Balfour Mss., B.M. Add. Mss. 49,700, ff. 31–4, 53.
76. **P. Fraser**, *Lord Esher: A Political Biography*, Hart-Davis, MacGibbon, London, 1973, pp. 108–48.
77. 'Objections of the three military members of the Army Council to the proposals of the Secretary of State', 10 June 1905, P.R.O., CAB 37/78/107.
78. **A. J. Balfour**, 'A Note on Army Reform and the Militia Needs of the Empire', 22 June 1904, P.R.O., CAB 4/1/26B, and 'Memorandum by the Prime Minister on Army Reorganisation', 30 Mar. 1905, P.R.O., CAB 37/75/54.

79. Sir H. Campbell-Bannerman to Lord Haliburton, 7 Apr. 1905, Campbell-Bannerman Mss., B.M. Add. Mss. 41,218, f. 354.
80. Sir H. Campbell-Bannerman to V. Nash, 14 Sept. 1903, Campbell-Bannerman Mss., B.M. Add. Mss. 41,237, f. 163.
81. *The Glasgow Herald*, 15 Oct. 1904, p. 8.
82. *Parl. Deb.*, Fourth Ser., Vol. 93, 13 May 1901, col. 1,502.
83. Sir H. Campbell-Bannerman to Sir R. Knox, 2 Jan. 1899, Campbell-Bannerman Mss. B.M. Add. Mss. 41,221, f. 258.
84. *Parl. Deb.*, Fourth Ser., Vol. 93, 13 May 1901, col. 1,492.
85. *Ibid.*, Vol. 90, 14 Mar 1901, col. 1,640.
86. R. B. Haldane to his mother, 19 May 1900, Haldane Mss., N.L.S., Ms. 5,963, f. 156. See also *The Scotsman*, 5 Oct. 1901, p. 10, and **R. Price**, *An Imperial War and the British Working Class*, Routledge & Kegan Paul, London, 1972, ch. IV.
87. *The Chester Chronicle,* 2 Dec. 1905, p. 7.

10 The Haldane Reforms

Unlike his immediate predecessors, Richard Burdon Haldane did not enter the War Office with pre-prepared proposals for army reform. He had never coveted the post of Secretary of State for War. He had no military expertise. A philosopher by training and a lawyer by profession, he had hoped to become Lord Chancellor in a cabinet headed by Asquith. Having tried through an abortive cabal, known as the Relugas compact, to replace Campbell-Bannerman as leader of the Liberals in the Commons, Haldane could expect few favours from the new Prime Minister. Campbell-Bannerman appointed Sir Robert Reid as Lord Chancellor and offered the War Office to Haldane, a post which held little attraction for Liberals of ministerial rank. Haldane had spoken occasionally about the army, though usually outside the House of Commons. A close associate of Admiral Sir John Fisher, he had embraced Blue Water ideas, believing that the army should abandon its commitment to home defence. As a Liberal Imperialist, he had expressed concern about the state of the army during the South African War. Once the war was over, he had deplored the levels of military spending; he had urged removal of costly coastal defences. Nevertheless, he had accepted the seals of office, aware of the failures of Brodrick and Arnold-Forster and the immense task yet to be accomplished in army reform.

Haldane entered a War Office riven with dissension and disagreement over the proposals of Arnold-Forster. Determined to unify 'the Generals', he assured them at the first meeting of the Army Council that he had not any preconceived ideas about reform. He secured their agreement to arrest the schemes of his predecessor, pending a fresh review. He replaced General Plummer, who had supported Arnold-Forster, by General Sir William Nicholson. He also reassured his advisers by the tone of his public statements during the general election campaign of January 1906. Addressing party rallies in the City of London and in Dunbar, he acknowledged responsibilities other than mere retrenchment. Reductions, he claimed, had to be consistent with military efficiency: if necessary, the government would find 'more men and more money for the promotion of efficiency'.[1] These strident comments puzzled Fleet Street editors, as Campbell-

Bannerman had promised, in his Albert Hall speech of 21 December 1905, that his government would not rely upon huge armaments and would never embark upon a policy of aggression and overseas adventure. Haldane wrote quickly to his leader, insisting that his speech was not intended to contradict 'any word of yours at the Albert Hall'. Haldane explained that he had risked 'even a little misunderstanding by some of our own people. There will be quite enough heard of economy when we present our cut-down estimates, & I am anxious that we should have the generals at our backs then'.[2]

Measures of economy were a priority for Haldane. Having been appointed in December, he had to prepare Estimates for presentation to Parliament in the following March. He had inherited draft Estimates from Arnold-Forster which proposed an increase of £1,630,000 over the existing Estimates of £29,813,000. As these were completely unacceptable, Haldane began a reappraisal of army finances. He was assisted by two new appointments - Charles Harris, the permanent head of the Financial Department, and Colonel Gerald Ellison, a military private secretary, who had been recommended by Lord Esher and Sir George Clarke. During their retreat to Haddington and then to Cloan in December and January, Haldane and Ellison, though seeking 'fresh ideas' and 'general principles' of army reorganization, were also in search of economies in the military budget. As Haldane informed Asquith, the Chancellor of the Exchequer, in a letter from Cloan on 28 December 1905, 'I have Col. Ellison here & we have drawn up a memorandum on Economy in Army Administration. If the ideas work out - I think I see my way to a substantial saving'.[3]

Completed on 1 January 1906, the memorandum proposed that expenditure on a reorganized army should not exceed £28 million. In the same document, Haldane outlined the objectives of reorganization. He maintained that the army had to be unique to meet the long distance, overseas commitments of the British Empire. 'A highly-organized and well-equipped striking force' was a prerequisite, one which could be 'transported with the least possible delay, to any part of the world . . .'.[4] To sustain that force in war required a large reserve, which could only be raised, in the opinion of Haldane, from the ranks of the Militia. In a second memorandum, written one month later, he was even more specific. During a war, he argued, the Militia and Yeomanry would have to furnish not merely drafts, but also ancillary services for the striking force. He claimed that a striking force of three army corps could be fashioned within a financial ceiling of £28 million. He also recommended that a Territorial Army should be created from the Volunteers and from the residual elements of the Militia and Yeomanry. The Territorial Army, he envisaged, would support and expand the striking force in the later stages of a protracted war.[5]

In these two memoranda, drafted within two months of his entering office, Haldane had proposed a radical reform of the regular and auxiliary forces. He had advocated a rationalization of existing forces into a two-line army, able to undertake and sustain an overseas campaign. After many hours of reading and of discussion with Ellison, he had grasped the basic principles of his future reform of the regular and auxiliary forces. He had not deliberated under pressure of war, or from a campaign in favour of army reform, or from colleagues in the cabinet and the Parliamentary party. Army reform had never dominated the general election of January 1906. Few Liberal candidates had professed any interest in the army, apart from the burden of military expenditure. In these circumstances, Haldane had seized the initiative; by drafting the memoranda, he had ensured that his ideas would dominate the subsequent debates and would focus the thinking of his advisers.

Described as 'rough notes' by Haldane, these memoranda were circulated to sound opinion in the Army Council and in the Committee of Imperial Defence. Another four memoranda were distributed in similar fashion during the first half of 1906: they were used as a basis for departmental study within the War Office and for conferences with Lord Esher and Sir George Clarke at the Committee of Imperial Defence. Although the original details and phraseology were amended, the concepts of an Expeditionary Force and a Territorial Army remained. Speculation centred upon the source of these new proposals. Haldane insisted that he, personally, had devised the scheme. Writing to his mother at the end of January, he claimed that 'I have drawn the draft of a great Army Scheme with the aid of Col. Ellison who is an enthusiastic convert to it, & has worked out the technical details of it'.[6] Contemporary sceptics were not convinced. Sir George Clarke and Spencer Wilkinson, aggrieved at the lack of attention paid to their own ideas, feared that Ellison had simply foisted his own views upon the Secretary of State. 'So far as I can see', wrote Clarke, 'the whole scheme is from Ellison's book, with much of which I absolutely disagree'.[7]

Ellison had written a book entitled *Home Defence* in 1898. An opponent of conscription, he had argued that an army earmarked for overseas service should be composed of regulars and should be raised on a voluntary basis. Such an army, in his view, could not fulfil its duties effectively if burdened simultaneously with responsibility for home defence. The Militia, he added, could not defend the homeland; it had become little more than an army of reserve for the regular forces. He had concluded, therefore, that the country required a separate 'Army of Home Defence', modelled possibly upon the Swiss organization. In private notes, compiled during the Boer War, Ellison added that securing the numbers and organization of a home defence army should take priority over the quality of the training. Its administration, he maintained, should be decentralized and localized.[8] As many of these ideas reappeared in the six memoranda, Ellison had undoubtedly influenced the thinking of Haldane. Nevertheless, Haldane had not entered office bereft of ideas. Imbued with 'Blue Water' principles, Haldane had wished to remove 'home defence' thinking from all branches of the army (save for a residual requirement to guard against coastal raids). By insisting upon an overseas commitment, Haldane's scheme differed significantly from Ellison's home defence army organized on the Swiss model. Haldane required, too, that any scheme should keep within a strict financial ceiling. Above all, he believed that the reforms should embrace the army as a whole, and should aim to realize a peculiarly British version of a 'nation in arms'. As he explained in the 'Second Memorandum',

> The main objects to be kept steadily in view in dealing with the military forces of the State must be the education and organization of the Nation for the purposes of Imperial defence.
>
> Consequently the basis of our whole military fabric must be the development of the idea of a real national army, formed by the people and managed by specially organized local Associations. The Army must be capable of evolution with the least possible delay into an effective force of all arms should serious danger threaten the Empire. It might be styled the Territorial Army.[9]

In his memoirs, Haldane would claim that this reorganized army was designed to meet a specific strategic purpose. On 8 January 1906, Sir Edward Grey, the Foreign Secretary, had written to Haldane forewarning him of a possible German attack upon France in the following spring. Although Britain was only linked to France by the Entente Cordiale, a limited agreement over colonial issues, Grey anticipated that popular feeling might compel the government to assist France. Whereupon, he thought, Haldane might be asked what assistance he could proffer.[10] Haldane met Grey at Berwick on 12 January. They agreed that talks should be arranged between the French and British General Staffs. Two days later Haldane instructed Lyttelton to authorize communications between the Director of Military Operations and Colonel Huguet, the French military attaché in London. Haldane also ordered a review of the mobilization arrangements, which revealed that a maximum of 80,000 men could be placed in the field after an interval of two months. In *Before the War*, Haldane argued that this revelation acted as a catalyst in the process of army reform. The 'new army problem', he stated, was to ensure that Britain could mobilize and concentrate 'a force calculated as adequate . . . to make up for the inadequacy of the French armies'.[11]

Formerly, the claim of Haldane that a continental strategy determined the size, structure, and readiness of the Expeditionary Force was readily accepted. Cyril Falls, the military historian, wrote that Haldane had resolved upon an Expeditionary Force of six divisions, in the hope of making 'the difference between initial victory and initial defeat'.[12] Other commentators have applauded his reforms, claiming that Haldane had an intellect so developed by his philosophical training that he could 'think clearly about the actual function of the army in war'.[13] More recently, scholars have cast doubt on the traditional view. They have questioned the feasibility of a Secretary of State being able to reform an army in peace, with its wartime purpose as a clear objective. Believing that a host of other considerations impaired the scope of Haldane's reforms, they have concluded that his reorganization was 'highly nebulous', that the Expeditionary Force 'bore little correspondence to actual British needs or obligations', and that Haldane was hampered by economic constraints.[14] The significance of a continental strategy, therefore, warrants analysis.

Adopting a continental strategy was a radical departure in military planning. It consummated a trend away from home defence, begun by Balfour and Arnold-Forster and endorsed by Haldane in his first memorandum. Haldane would endorse the views of Balfour and Arnold-Forster in Parliament, using them to justify his own reforms. He would claim a 'continuous policy' in military strategy, merely reiterating that the Expeditionary Force was committed to an overseas role, implicitly to an Imperial role.[15] Inasmuch as a continental strategy jettisoned the preoccupation with home defence, it was indeed continuous. Haldane, however, exaggerated this element of continuity to conceal from the majority of his party colleagues the new departure in military planning. Although Imperial requirements hardly warranted an Expeditionary Force of 160,000 men, this purpose was more acceptable from a Liberal perspective than preparation for a war with Germany.

To meet the demands of a continental war required the formation of a fully equipped and readily transported Expeditionary Force. The mobilization timetable was too precise and too short to allow the improvisation of essential services. Providing all ancillary services in advance of mobilization became an imperative in the reform of the regular army. As economic restrictions precluded complete reliance upon regular troops, Haldane earmarked part of the Militia and other non-regular forces, trained on a Militia basis, for the ancillary duties. Approximately one-fifth of the Force, or about 30,000 men, would be engaged on this basis. To reassure critics, especially those who derided the prospect of 10,337 partially-trained artillerymen manning the ammunition columns and parks of the regular artillery, Haldane insisted that these civilians should be obliged to serve abroad with their regular instructors in time of war.[16]

But the demands of a continental strategy never dominated the reforms of Haldane. He could not reform the army purely to meet the demands of a European war. He accepted that peacetime constraints were all important; he had to maintain a voluntary system of recruiting, provide drafts and reliefs for overseas garrisons, and keep his spending within tolerable limits. To provide overseas drafts in sufficient numbers, he abandoned the reforms of his predecessors. He restored the old terms of service (seven or eight years' Colours service for the infantry of the line followed by five or four years' Reserve service). The Cardwellian system, he believed, had proved its simplicity, economy, and viability as a draft-producing arrangement. Its basic problem - a lack of balance between the battalions at home and abroad - remained: in 1905, 71 battalions at home fed 85 battalions abroad. In realizing economies within the military budget, Haldane sought to rectify this disparity. He reduced eight overseas battalions in 1906 and, two years later, withdrew three more battalions from South Africa to realize a parity of 74 battalions at home and abroad.

Haldane recognized that the size of the Expeditionary Force would be determined by the number of battalions retained at home for draft-finding purposes. The force of six large divisions (66 line battalions and 6 Guards battalions) and one cavalry division was the largest force which could be raised from the peacetime army. Haldane advised the cabinet that 'two considerations' dominated the problem of army organization. In their 'order of urgency', these considerations were '(a) the necessity for finding drafts in peace for units in India and in colonial garrisons, (b) the mobilization as an organized field force of the units which are maintained at home in view of (a)'.[17] Continental strategy did not determine the size of the Expeditionary Force; it merely served as a purpose for a force whose battalion strength was determined by its peacetime duties.

The reforms of Haldane had to conform to a financial ceiling of £28 millions. Formerly the reduction of the Estimates by Haldane was interpreted as merely a tactical ploy, a precautionary move to carry back-bench opinion.[18] But Haldane had been a critic of profligate military spending. He believed that the army should be reformed on the basis of existing forces and that units should be reduced wherever surplus to immediate requirements. His ceiling, too, was high by contemporary standards. Many Liberal Members of Parliament had campaigned in the election of 1906 in favour of a return to pre-war Estimates, to Estimates of £20 million or less. Sir George Clarke had argued that the army could operate within a financial ceiling of £25 million. Sir Austen Chamberlain, the last Conservative Chancellor, had sought Estimates of £27 million or less from Arnold-Forster. By imposing a ceiling less onerous than his generals might have feared, Haldane secured their consent and endorsement for his proposed reform of the regular army.

Haldane had to carry the support of his colleagues in the Liberal party. The Liberals had gained a massive victory in the election of 1906. In the newly elected Parliament, 377 Liberals sat on the Government benches; they were backed periodically by 83 Irish Nationalists and 53 Labour Members, and faced the opposition of only 157 Unionists. Haldane recognized the importance of Parliamentary opinion. He had already seen the proposals of his predecessors thwarted, at least partially, by campaigns mounted from the Government back benches. At the same time he could neither offend nor ignore his Conservative opponents. Balfour had attributed his electoral defeat to an upsurge of radicalism and socialism, a reflection of a similar movement which had swept through eastern Europe. Until that movement subsided in Britain, he had determined to block the more radical of the government's proposals by use of the Conservative majority in the House of Lords.[19] Haldane had to accommodate Liberal and Labour members in the Commons, without alienating the Conservative leadership and its supporters in the House of Lords.

Unlike Arnold-Forster, Haldane made certain of cabinet support before he faced the House of Commons. He carefully briefed friends who occupied key posts in the Government prior to cabinet meetings. In December 1905, he had written to Asquith assuring him of a 'substantial saving' in the Estimates, if not in 1906–07, then in subsequent years.[20] He had written to Grey, only five days after their meeting at Berwick, to inform him that the rearmament of the home batteries would be completed ahead of schedule. As India no longer required an immediate delivery of new artillery equipment, the rearmament of home batteries would take priority so increasing the force available for immediate despatch 'to about 105,000 men & 336 guns'.[21] Above all, Haldane sought to reassure Campbell-Bannerman. Aware that his leader loathed Arnold-Forster, Haldane stressed that he had undone the 'reckless schemes' of his predecessor, had removed the additional £1,630,000 proposed by him, and had secured the support of the Army Council for his reductions.[22] Clearly impressed, Campbell-Bannerman endorsed the proposals of his Secretary of State.

On 8 March 1906, Haldane presented his Estimates before the House of Commons. He was effusive in compliments. He praised the work of his Conservative predecessors; he endorsed the Blue Water principles which Balfour had enunciated one year earlier. He commended the 'new school of young officers', the military who had advised him since he had entered office. He accepted, too, that his department had a responsibility to reduce unnecessary expenditure. The economies already accomplished were, he insisted, the harbingers of further savings. He begged party colleagues to let him 'proceed circumspectly' in order to ensure 'more efficiency for less money'. This task, he added, could not be the sole responsibility of the War Office. The size and deployment of the army was the responsibility of the Government as a whole, acting upon the advice of the Foreign Secretary, the Secretary of the Colonies, the Secretary of State for India, and the First Lord of the Admiralty. Military expenditure, he conceded, had increased, but it had done so to support a much larger colonial establishment. Reductions, he implied, were possible, but only through changes in overseas policy.[23]

Haldane had triumphed completely. By discussing generalities, and by adopting a conciliatory and optimistic tone, he earned fulsome tributes from all sides of the House. Editors echoed these comments in the daily press. Even editors in the radical press, though disappointed by the absence of immediate reductions, applauded the prospect of economies for 1907-08. Radical editors, however, could not agree on proposals by which the economies might be realized. While *The Daily News* endorsed Haldane's proposal to create a small mobile army, backed by a partially trained reserve, *The Manchester Guardian* derided this approach, favouring the complete reduction of all battalions raised in the past ten years. Unimpressed by either of these options, *Concord* advocated a revival of international solidarity and arbitration as offering the only prospect of genuine disarmament.[24] The lack of an agreed alternative policy undermined the radical position. When Major Seely and Sir Charles Dilke moved an amendment to the Estimates on 15 March 1906, Haldane rounded on his critics. He defended the Cardwell system; he cited Sir Evelyn Wood and Lord Roberts as expert military opinion in favour of battalion and not depot training. He stressed that his critics had only united in proposing the reduction of 10,000 men. They had failed, he noted, to agree upon any alternative to the Cardwell system. Casting himself as the minister responsible for realizing economies within a functioning army system, Haldane earned the support of both front benches and 296 Members. Supporters of the amendment mustered a derisory 56 votes.[25]

Having routed his Parliamentary critics, Haldane could proceed with his reforms and his reductions of surplus personnel. A mere five days after his Parliamentary triumph, he sought the approval of the cabinet for 'work towards a reduction next year of 20,000 men'.[26] Within the month, the news had leaked out that Haldane was considering large cuts in the artillery, the reduction of some colonial garrisons, and the disbandment of ten battalions of infantry, including two battalions of Guards. Edward VII was appalled. He was furious over the possible loss of two battalions of Guards; he also deplored any reduction of the garrisons in South Africa and Egypt.[27] Protests poured into the Conservative press. The agitation was fanned by the letters and speeches of Brodrick and Arnold-Forster. Haldane was unperturbed. He had coupled his reforms of the regular army with the reduction of surplus units. Backed by the Army Council and the cabinet, he felt reasonably confident about defending his scheme in Parliament. As he explained to his mother, 'The London Society opposition & that of the Conservative papers is very strong. But every link in the plan has been worked out & tested by experts'.[28]

On 12 July 1906, Haldane revealed his proposals for the reorganization and reduction of the regular army. He forecast an increase of 50 per cent in the fighting efficiency of the home army. Henceforth, the home army would be prepared for an overseas role, ostensibly to reinforce 'the outposts of the Empire'. The Expeditionary

Force would represent the largest coherent force which could be fashioned from the battalions retained at home to furnish drafts for the overseas garrisons. The main bulk of the reductions would come from overseas battalions no longer required by the Colonial Office and the Admiralty. But Haldane confirmed that he proposed to dispense with 3,850 artillerymen and two of the four Guards battalions not earmarked for the Expeditionary Force. To ensure the necessary flow of peacetime drafts, he announced the restoration of the former terms of service. To sustain the Expeditionary Force in war, he insisted that the Militia must accept an obligation to serve abroad in war, albeit in units not smaller than companies. Unable to reveal his Volunteer proposals, as they were not completely ready, Haldane merely indicated that the Force would serve three functions. Should the regulars go overseas, the Volunteers would be required to man coastal fortresses, repel small coastal raids, and provide a second reserve for the regular army. The reorganized army, claimed Haldane would furnish the necessary drafts in peacetime, form an Expeditionary Force, and sustain that Force in war with a flow of highly trained reserves.[29]

Haldane now reaped an important political harvest in the vehement opposition of the Unionist party. From the Conservative benches, ex-Guards officers bemoaned the loss of the Coldstream Guards battalion. Balfour condemned the reduction of regular artillerymen. Arnold-Forster deplored the return of the Cardwell system. But the more Haldane was attacked by Conservatives, and by discredited reformers like Dilke, the more support he gathered on the Liberal benches. The reduction of 20,000 men and the prospect of a decrease in military expenditure ensured overwhelming support from the Liberal party and the Liberal press. 'The net result', as Haldane reflected, 'is that my own party is at my back, & this is the great thing'.[30] An unexpected windfall in funding enabled him to capitalize upon this success. Because artillery rearmament had proceeded more quickly than anticipated, Haldane could present much larger savings than the press had predicted. He was also able to relent upon the reduction of the 3rd Coldstream Guards battalion, which remained on garrison duty in Egypt. By recording savings of £2,600,000, he had brought the Estimates within the ceiling of £28 million. Haldane, in short, had gained support for his reforms in Parliament by coupling them with a tolerable level of public expenditure. Admittedly, his Estimates would come under renewed attack from Parliamentary radicals in the winter of 1907, and, more seriously, from a faction in the cabinet, headed by Lloyd George and Churchill, in the summer of 1908. But Haldane weathered both onslaughts. Aided by the briefing of Harris, and by the assistance of influential cabinet colleagues, he preserved his Estimates and the reforms which were based upon them.

In the autumn recess of 1906, Haldane was able to complete the formation of the General Staff. On entering office, he had been extensively briefed about the virtues of the General Staff by Esher and Clarke. He had also taken Esher's advice that new men would be required to implement the new system: he had authorized the appointment of Haig as Director of Military Training. After the Estimates speech on 8 March 1906, in which he publicly committed himself to the formation of a General Staff, Haldane provided the leadership and impetus on the issue which had previously been lacking. In the following April he circulated a draft Army Order for consideration inside and outside the War Office. He encountered vehement opposition on several points, especially the proposal that the sole power of patronage should be accorded to the Chief of the General Staff. The thought of Lyttelton drawing up and adding to the General Staff list appalled Esher and Clarke; it also split the military members of the Army Council.

Esher resumed his machinations. He intrigued behind the scenes, using his influence at Court to modify Haldane's proposal. He wrote to Lord Knollys, claiming that Lyttelton could not draft the list alone and that jobbery would be suspected unless he acted on the advice of the Selection Board.[31] Acting upon this advice, the King wrote to Haldane on 9 August. He protested that the Chief of the General Staff could not 'know enough of the officers, scattered through the Commands, to frame such a list, or add to it, without assistance, from the Selection Board'. He also feared that the royal prerogative over military appointments would not be safeguarded unless the appointments were made by the Secretary of State for War on the advice of the Chief of the General Staff.[32] Haldane reacted promptly. His relations with the King had deteriorated sharply since the battalion reductions were first mooted. He could not afford another row lest it delay the formation of the General Staff, and impair his relations with Esher. By the end of the month Haldane had drafted an amended Order and had secured its approval by the Army Council. He was fortunate inasmuch as the War Stores Commission had delivered its report in August, which severely criticized the military administration in South Africa under Lyttelton. Lyttelton offered his resignation, which Haldane declined to accept. Preferring to retain the services of a pliant and ineffectual Chief of the General Staff, Haldane gained the support of the latter for an Order which weakened his position considerably. As Haldane assured Esher, 'The *List* is to be settled with the Selection Board - i.e. the list of eligible officers. The individual *appointments* will be made by the S[ecretary] of S[tate] - not by the C[hief of the] G[eneral] S[taff]'.[33]

By the autumn of 1906, Haldane had completed two major reforms of the regular army. He had taken the initiative in both instances. He had acted without the stimulus of external pressure; indeed he had carried these measures in spite of the relative indifference of the press and Parliament. Reforming the auxiliary forces, however, was a different proposition. Grandiose schemes, outlined in memoranda or announced in Parliament would come to nought without the co-operation of the forces themselves. Haldane had to ensure that his proposals were as comprehensive as possible (hence the elaborate sounding of 'expert' opinion - both the civilian pundits in the Committee of Imperial Defence and the more able officers, Nicholson, Ellison, and latterly Haig). He then had to liaise with the representatives of the auxiliary forces, using the diplomatic talents of Esher wherever possible. He then had to promote his scheme publicly by speaking tours and by the extensive use of the press. Haldane took selected journalists into his confidence, particularly Charles a Court Repington, who had been the military correspondent of *The Times* since 1904. Like Esher, Repington believed in compulsion, but agreed that compulsory service would not be accepted until a final experiment of the voluntary system had been tried and found wanting. Thoroughly briefed by Haldane, Repington was commending the value of the Territorial Army in *The Times* as early as 26 March 1906.[34]

After lengthy deliberations in the War Office and in the Committee of Imperial Defence, Haldane issued his 'Fourth Memorandum' on 25 April 1906. Explaining his ideas in more detail, he indicated that there would be two distinct armies, the Striking Force (later dubbed the Expeditionary Force) and the Territorial Army (later called the Territorial Force). He emphasized that the Territorial Army, raised and administered by locally based and partly elected associations, would differ markedly from the old Volunteer Force. It would not be raised on the basis of home defence; it would be viewed primarily as a reserve for the Expeditionary Force. Unlike previous reformers, who had sought more efficiency and fewer numbers so that the Volunteers could meet an invasion, Haldane emphasized more numbers and, if necessary, less training. He believed that the Territorial Army could be trained after the outbreak of war under the protection of the Royal Navy. He vested his hopes in the next generation. He outlined a scheme whereby the local associations would be expected to encourage physical training and military drill in schools, cadet corps, and miniature rifle clubs. He acknowledged that the scheme would evolve slowly and gradually over many years, but hoped that the military structure would take root in the nation itself. The new two line army, he envisaged, would 'bear the distinctive character of being a natural development from a nation truly in arms'.[35]

Having prepared his scheme, Haldane began the delicate task of negotiating with the commanding officers of the auxiliary forces. He appointed an advisory committee, under Lord Esher, composed of representatives from the Militia, Yeomanry, and Volunteers, and other interested parties. Nicknamed the Duma, the committee consisted of thirty members and met on eleven occasions between 17 May and 15 June 1906. The Militia colonels, headed by the Duke of Bedford, blocked any progress. Fearing encroachments on their control over local units, they refused to join the Territorial Force and to come under the supervision of local or, as they were subsequently known, county associations. The Volunteers were equally reluctant to surrender some of their powers to the local associations. Unable to resolve these differences, the Duma adjourned on 15 June; it was never summoned again.[36]

Haldane tried separate negotiations with the Militia, Yeomanry, and Volunteers. Meetings with the Militia were convened at the War Office in June and at Knowsley, the home of Lord Derby, in the following autumn. On neither occasion would the Militia colonels compromise. They refused to join the Territorial Force and deplored the idea of furnishing drafts for the regular line in war. The Yeomanry commanders and Volunteer colonels were equally adamant in their meetings with War Office spokesmen: they would not accept the administration of county associations. Haldane had not anticipated such intransigence. But his idea of separating command from administration was new; it threatened the absolute control which auxiliary officers had exercised over all matters connected with their units. 'This proprietary notion', as Ellison recalled, 'was one of the very things Haldane was determined to get rid of'.[37] Paradoxically, Haldane's will began to weaken while his advisers, Ellison, Haig, and Lord Lucas, Parliamentary Under-Secretary in the Lords, became ever more resolute. Haldane was thought to be wobbling over the county associations in August; he even took seriously a memorandum from General Douglas, the Adjutant-General, which proposed looking to the Territorial Force for drafts while relying upon the Militia for units of expansion in war.[38] After the autumn recess, Haldane returned from Cloan ready to emasculate the county associations and to remove the elective element.

His advisers were appalled. Ellison, Haig, and Lucas dined with Haldane on 15 October and delivered a combined onslaught. They were partially successful. Haldane accepted that the Militia could only perform the functions of enabling 'the Exped. Force to mobilize & keep the Field for six months, and also to set free garrisons of regulars'.[39] The Militia as a separate force was finished. Haldane would assign the task of furnishing drafts to the Special Reserve, a new semi-professional force of seventy-four battalions, whose terms of service were designed to attract former Militiamen. Over the county associations, however, Haldane remained obdurate. Lucas asked Esher to intervene and he did so. He pressed Haldane to preserve the powers of the associations, even without the elective element. He could do so, argued Esher, because he had committed himself publicly to the purpose of the associations but not to their constitutions.[40] The appeal was completely successful. Haldane changed his mind again; he announced a restoration of financial responsibility to the associations but left their composition elastic, depending partially upon War Office nominations.[41] By abandoning the elective element, Haldane had fatally weakened the nation in arms concept, but he could now work with renewed enthusiasm upon the Parliamentary Bill required to constitute the Territorial Force. He kept closely in touch with Esher; he submitted the proofs of his Bill to him for private scrutiny. He also scythed the draft proposals put forward by Haig, preferring to seek a Territorial Force of fourteen divisions with an establishment of approximately 300,000 men.

On 4 March 1907 Haldane presented the Territorial and Reserve Forces Bill before a thinly attended House of Commons. Despite a generous allowance of Parliamentary time (three days for the second reading debate and eight days in committee), the Bill attracted little interest. Government supporters were apathetic; they found the contents of the Bill immensely dull and boring, a diversion from the true concerns of Liberalism. Only twenty-seven Liberals attended the first reading. The House was virtually empty during the second reading debate; it had to be counted on one of the Committee days. Discussion was rendered even more pointless by the efficiency of the Liberal whips (majorities of 279 and 223 votes were recorded on the second and third readings). Those who participated in the debates were largely concerned with the defence of particular interests. Militia spokesmen deplored the emasculation of their units. Yeomanry spokesmen criticized the new terms of service, especially the lower rates of pay. The Volunteers, a mere rump of the old pressure group, attacked the county associations and the imposition of stricter regulations. These critics could neither defeat nor frustrate the government. Any filibustering was doomed to failure, as Balfour had accepted that a guillotine procedure should operate throughout the committee stages of the Bill. The Bill passed its third reading on 19 June 1907.

Haldane had not anticipated an opposition so feeble and ineffective. On the contrary, he had feared that it would be 'very difficult to carry a measure of this kind in England. Almost all the experts and the Army are with me, but stupidity and prejudice are pretty powerful'.[42] To ensure the passage of the Bill, and to mollify those Volunteers who would form the core of the new Force, Haldane made several concessions. At the behest of the Volunteer Members, he extended the powers of control of the Army Council over the county associations. To appease the Unionist leadership in the Lords, he excluded the Militia cadres from the Territorial Force, so diminishing the likelihood of the Force ever reaching its target of 312,300 men. He also reassured radical and Labour sentiment by switching the purpose of the Force from an overseas mission to home defence, and by modifying the cadet corps clauses of the Bill. By re-emphasizing home defence, Haldane may have placated radical fears and coaxed a few more Volunteers into the Territorial ranks. But the shift in rhetoric would also diminish any prospect, already remote, of many Territorials committing themselves in peacetime to serve abroad in war. By amending the cadet corps clauses, which had enraged Ramsay

MacDonald, Haldane left the county associations with the power to encourage cadet corps for boys under sixteen, but not, in the words of Lord Esher, 'out of money voted by Parliament'. The amendment, as Sir Charles Harris recalled, had 'killed the general cadet scheme', a lynch-pin of the nation in arms concept.[43] Nevertheless, the Bill received the Royal Assent on 2 August 1907, the first Bill passed by the Liberal Government.

Once the Act was passed, Haldane had to establish the county associations, preferably by 1 April 1908 when the Volunteer units would cease to exist. Seeking to involve the traditional sources of county influence, Haldane wrote to the Lords-Lieutenant on 7 August asking them to preside over their county associations. He appointed a small committee, under the indispensable Lord Esher, to advise any county on its proposals. To overcome any lingering suspicions or hostility, Haldane set forth to meet the Lords-Lieutenant in the various parts of the country. After the first meeting at Blair Castle, the residence of the Duke of Atholl, Haldane believed that he had 'astonished' the conference by revealing 'everything thought and prepared even to minute details'.[44] Three other conferences, organized under the auspices of Lord Rosebery, the Duke of Westminster, and Lord Derby, were equally successful. Haldane clinched the support of the Lords-Lieutenant by securing royal assistance for the launching of the Territorial Force. Having summoned the Lords-Lieutenant of all the counties of England, Wales and Scotland to Buckingham Palace on 26 October, the King exhorted them to throw their local influence behind the county associations.

Royal intervention was vital. In the first place, a formal ceremonial endorsement in the Presence Chamber of the Palace legitimized the new Force in a more public and demonstrative fashion than a mere Act of Parliament. Secondly, it disarmed some critics, at least temporarily, especially the advocates of compulsory service in the National Service League. As the League was fiercely patriotic and loyal, it resolved initially to assist and support the county associations (thirteen of the Lords-Lieutenant were members of the League).[45] Thirdly, Royal intervention ensured that the county *élite* would become involved in the activities of the associations. The organizational structure depended upon the Lords-Lieutenant, as presidents of their associations, seeking assistance from the Deputy-Lieutenants, from the local nobility, and from the representatives of county and borough councils. By November 1909, 115 Members of the House of Lords were serving in the county associations (15 Dukes, 9 Marquesses, 44 Earls, 9 Viscounts, 1 Bishop and 37 Barons).[46]

Having launched the Territorial scheme, Haldane embarked upon a hectic round of public speaking engagements. He toured the country, preaching the virtues of the Territorial Force and opening branches of the Officers' Training Corps at various schools and universities. The OTC was a scheme designed by a War Office Committee to mitigate the shortage of 4,000 regular officers and 6,000 auxiliary officers. The Committee wished to enrol the existing school and university corps in the OTC, which would be officially sponsored and would impose a more rigorous period of training. Cadets who completed a prescribed period of training would qualify for certificates which would reduce their training should they subsequently join the Special Reserve. Haldane had endorsed the idea enthusiastically. He discounted Liberal fears that the OTC would spread militarism within the public schools, 'because the spirit of militarism already runs fairly high both there and at the universities. What we propose to do in our necessity is to turn to them and to ask them to help us by putting their militarism to some good purpose'.[47] Haldane hoped that the schools could provide 12,500 cadets, and that the universities could supply between 2,000 and 3,000 cadets. From these numbers, he expected over 800 officers per annum for the Special Reserve.[48]

Initially Haldane revelled in his evangelizing efforts. He received warm and heartening receptions from Volunteer units. He was cordially welcomed in most universities. The early recruiting returns were favourable. The Special Reserve was formed in January 1908; it attracted nearly 60 per cent of the Militia in the first month of its existence. After ten months' recruiting, the Territorial Force numbered in excess of 240,000 men. The numbers had mushroomed in the early months of 1909 in response to another invasion scare. A play by Guy du Maurier, entitled *An Englishman's Home*, had dramatized invasion fears and had proved immensely popular in London. Both the London Territorial Force, headed by Lord Esher, and the War Office had exploited the success of the play. Esher referred to the play in an interview with *The Daily Mail,* received a cheque for £10,000 from Lord Northcliffe and the backing of *The Daily Mail* for his recruiting campaign in London.[49] The War Office installed a recruiting booth in the theatre foyer and the Lord Chancellor prohibited any skits of *An Englishman's Home* in London. Haldane defended these 'modern methods of recruiting' as they had produced a net gain of over 30,000 recruits in the first seven weeks of 1909.[50]

Invasion fears soon receded once a new Dreadnought building programme was announced in July 1909. The recruiting momentum was not sustained. The Special Reserve never reached its establishment of 74,166 men. Although offered a bounty of £2 per man, a substantial minority of the 94,000 Militiamen would not transfer. By March 1914 the Reserve was still 13,699 men short of its establishment; some 29 per cent of its strength was under twenty years of age.[51] The glaring shortage of subalterns remained. Haldane was forced to admit, by May 1912, that the Officers' Training Corps had furnished a mere 283 officers for the Special Reserve from the 18,000 cadets who had completed some form of military instruction.[52] Even more depressing, the Territorials failed to reach the target of 312,300 men. The rate of recruiting slackened considerably over the winter of 1909-10. Serving

Territorials sought discharges in ever increasing numbers. Complaints were voiced about the long delays incurred in obtaining headquarters and drill halls for Territorial units. Over 107,000 Territorials failed to attend annual camp for a full fifteen days in 1911. From 270,000 men in February 1910, the Force slumped below a quarter of a million, falling to a mere 236,389 men by 30 September 1913.[53]

Haldane never accepted that he had set unrealistic targets. He preferred to believe the view of General Sir John French, Inspector-General of the Forces, that the activities of the National Service League had, at least partially, impaired recruiting for the Territorial Force. Officials of the League resented allegations that they had sabotaged the Territorials. Individual members of the League, like many newspaper columnists, had disparaged both the numbers and the training of the Force. The League, nonetheless, retained a substantial membership within the Force; it could not afford to pillory the Territorials for fear of alienating and possibly losing this section of its membership. Only in 1913-14, when disillusionment became more pronounced within the Territorial ranks, did the League become more actively hostile.[54] Haldane never appreciated the predicament of the League. Attacked over the shortfall in Territorial numbers by the press, by Conservatives in Parliament, and even by Lord Esher,[55] he responded in combative fashion. He authorized the publication of *Compulsory Service*, a vigorous defence of the voluntary system, written by Sir Ian Hamilton, the former Adjutant-General. The work merely exacerbated relations between the War Office and the League, who replied with an equally polemical tract, *Fallacies and Facts* (1911). *Compulsory Service* caused a short-lived but intense political controversy. By authorizing the book, Haldane had publicized the views of a serving officer on the active list; he had also added an initialled memorandum from the First Sea Lord to a second edition. He was severely criticized in the Commons as a consequence. *Compulsory Service*, however, did little to arrest the decline of the Territorials. During his last winter in office, 1911-12, Haldane resumed his speaking tours on behalf of the Territorials, speaking in towns as remote as Aberdeen and Barnstaple and covering almost every region of England and Scotland. As the Territorial image became increasingly tarnished, Haldane laboured to sustain the enthusiasm of the committed and to prevent the further erosion of support.

Attitudes towards military service had not radically changed in Edwardian Britain. Patriotism, fears of invasion, an interest in the military life, a desire to join friends, neighbours and workmates in social and recreational activities had moved a small proportion of citizens to join the Territorials. But part-time soldiering, like the military life itself, had a distinctly limited appeal. Even the Special Reserve, which offered pay, food, and accommodation during the six months of autumn and winter, failed to attract sufficient numbers from the unemployed. The vast majority of the populace were not interested in military service. Many senior officers, journalists, and politicians doubted the military value of the Territorial Force. Even those who joined the Force held a limited view of its likely purpose and role. Their outlook was restricted by notions of home defence. Though eager to serve abroad when the need arose, they were reluctant to commit themselves in advance. By September 1913, only 1,090 officers and 17,788 non-commissioned officers and men had volunteered to serve abroad on mobilization.[56]

The Territorials were not, as Spencer Wilkinson claimed, merely rechristened Volunteers.[57] The Territorial Force, though wedded to home defence, was more organized and more complete in its arms and equipment than the old Volunteers. It had field artillery, companies of engineers, medical, veterinary and supply services; it could have taken the field after the requisite training as a mobile force. Haldane had provided the machinery or framework of a reserve which could have been used in war. Ironically this reform, the most original of Haldane's term of office, was never tested under stress of battle. When war erupted in August 1914, Lord Kitchener was appointed Secretary of State for War. Knowing little of the home army, he refused to rely upon the Territorial organization. He preferred to raise additional soldiers by appealing directly to the people.

While Haldane concentrated upon raising and preserving his Territorial Force, the army completed its reform of training and tactics. Haig, as Director of Staff Duties (1907–09), supervised the preparation and testing of *Field Service Regulations Part II* (1909), a manual covering the organization of the army in the field. Sir John French, another senior cavalry officer, inspected the training of the six divisions during his four years as Inspector-General of the Forces (1907–11). In their pronouncements upon doctrine and training, neither French nor Haig felt the need to placate 'the public' as Lord Roberts had done. Although military activities were extensively reported, especially the large divisional manoeuvres which became a regular feature of the Edwardian years, army reform was no longer championed by the press and Parliament.

Occasionally issues were taken up by the press or by civilian reformers. The rapid rates of fire attained by the French four-gun batteries in their manoeuvres at Picardy (1910) startled British observers. Many correspondents, including Repington, urged the Royal Artillery to imitate French tactics and so maximize the advantages of quick-firing guns. But the artillery commanders were wary about imitating French practice. They were prepared to follow the French in adopting a more subordinate and supportive role in battle, aiming to ensure the tactical success of the infantry. Their guns, on the other hand, lacked an automatic fuse setter and could never emulate French standards of firing. They were fearful, too, of simplifying the battery organization. In a letter to Repington, Sir Ian Hamilton explained their forebodings. The Liberal government, he wrote, might accept a four-gun battery standard, so that it could 'refuse to create any more new four-gun batteries, and thereby reduce expense and guns by one-third. So whatever you do, my dear Repington, for God's sake keep quiet about this idea of four-gun batteries'.[58]

Similarly, senior officers were not moved when civilians entered the fray over cavalry tactics. French and Haig had bitterly resented the criticisms of the cavalry performance during the South African War. They had disliked the reforms imposed on the arm by Lord Roberts. Once able to influence doctrine and training, they secured the supremacy of shock tactics and saw the lance restored as an active service weapon. Erskine Childers, the author of the fifth volume of *The Times History of the South African War*, was an ardent critic of shock action based on the sword and the lance. In collaboration with Lord Roberts, he wrote a powerful critique of traditional cavalry tactics, entitled *War and the Arme Blanche* (1910). Advocating reliance upon mounted infantry armed with the rifle, Childers deprecated any compromise between fire-arms and steel weapons. 'The steel', he claimed, 'involves shock, and shock involves a whole structure of drill, training and equipment, which are not only antithetical to fire-action, but prejudicial to general mobility'.[59] These views had little impact, however. Minor modifications appeared in later manuals, but these were largely a reflection of changes in personnel. After Haig had left the War Office, *Cavalry Training* was re-issued in 1912 modifying the emphasis on the *arme blanche*. When General C. W. Douglas replaced General French as Inspector-General of the Forces, his annual reports again criticized the priority accorded to shock tactics in cavalry training. Nevertheless the cavalry, though better armed and trained in 1914, still entered the First World War as committed to shock tactics as it had been in 1899.

Military training had improved considerably in the Edwardian years. By frequent practice on the rifle range, rates of fire were developed (15 rounds per minute at 300 yards) which markedly exceeded the equivalent rates in conscript armies. By combining rapid shooting with reasonable accuracy, the army compensated for cuts in the ammunition allowance and for the refusal to concede more than two machine guns per battalion.[60] Using squads or sections attacking each other in company training, the principles of fire and movement in attack and of regulated fire from defensive positions were repeatedly practised. Often the exercises were conducted without any orders from officers or non-commissioned officers to ensure that the ranks acted increasingly on their own initiative. Seizing the offensive remained the essence of peacetime training. Fire support remained subsidiary to the movement of troops. The aim was to maximize the moral advantages of the assailant - his initiative, freedom of action, and power of manoeuvre - so overcoming the fire effect of contemporary weapons in defensive positions. Mobilization was regularly practised. Every winter selected units were brought up to war establishment. In

1910 one of the two Aldershot divisions was mobilized at the expense of the other, not only in front-line troops but also in ancillary services. Manoeuvres, in short, were conducted on as realistic a basis as possible.

The professional skills of the Edwardian army were not tested until August 1914. During the last few years of peace, the army was deployed in its traditional policing role within the United Kingdom. In the handling of industrial disturbances, appropriate lessons had been drawn from the Featherstone incident. Troops were usually deployed in strength, with the minimum of friction, and without recourse to fire-arms. After the Tonypandy disturbances of November 1910, the bitterest memories of the strikers concerned the mine owners, the Glamorganshire police, and Winston Churchill, the Home Secretary. Although military involvement was deeply resented, the troops under Major-General Nevil Macready were generally reckoned to have behaved with firmness and tact. As one member of the Cambrian Lodge Committee recalled, 'Not one word against the military was ever uttered by the Combine Committee'.[61]

Military discretion was possibly less evident during the constitutional crisis over Ireland. By March 1914, the opposition to the Irish Home Rule Bill in Ulster had become fiercely intransigent. At least 100,000 Ulster Volunteers were held under rigid discipline, and many of them were armed. The government had wished to move troops into Ulster to protect ammunition stores and outlying barracks. It had no intention of using troops to coerce Ulster; but that was exactly the fear which moved Brigadier-General Hubert Gough and fifty-seven officers of the 3rd cavalry brigade, stationed at the Curragh, to inform the Commander-in-Chief that they would 'prefer to accept dismissal if ordered north'. Gough was given a written assurance from the cabinet amended in more precise language by French, the Chief of the Imperial General Staff, that his troops would not be used to enforce Home Rule on Ulster. When news of the amended document reached the press, a furious row erupted in Parliament. The government repudiated any notion of a private bargain with a few rebellious officers. The three signatories of the document - French, Ewart, the Adjutant-General, and Seely, the Secretary of State for War (1912-14) - proffered their resignations. Although the source of intense controversy in the spring of 1914, the affair was more of an 'incident' than a mutiny. While fifty-eight cavalry officers chose dismissal from the army, 280 officers from the infantry, artillery and other units at the Curragh resolved to do their duty. The army was neither rent apart internally nor the object of profound distrust by the rest of society. Senior officers hardly suffered. French assumed command of the British Expeditionary Force, Gough took his brigade to France, and Ewart received the Scottish command. Arguably, the worst result of the incident was a legacy of suspicion between military and political leaders.[62]

Internal policing duties, though irksome, did not impair the training of the home army. The Expeditionary Force was well prepared for war in August 1914. Its social composition had not significantly changed since the South African War, but its professionalism undoubtedly had. Former critics, both civilian and military, had mistaken the essence of military professionalism: they had failed to perceive that professionalism required the development of skills in peacetime which were of relevance in time of war. An officer could gain these skills irrespective of his social background and career motivation. The source of military professionalism lay in the prescription of tactical and training skills appropriate to the new conditions of warfare. It presumed the provision of opportunities for their frequent practice at section, company, and divisional level. It required, above all, the organizational framework and sense of purpose provided by the Haldane reforms. It was abundantly true that 'In every respect the Expeditionary Force in 1914 was incomparably the best trained, best organized, and best equipped British Army which ever went forth to war'.[63]

Notes and references

1. *The Times*, 5 Jan. 1906, p. 13. See also *The Scotsman*, 11 Jan. 1906, p. 8.
2. R. B. Haldane to Sir H. Campbell-Bannerman, 5 Jan. 1906, Campbell-Bannerman Mss., B.M. Add. Ms. 41,218, f. 167.
3. R. B. Haldane to H. H. Asquith, 28 Dec. 1905, Asquith Mss., Bodleian Library, Oxford, Ms. 10, ff. 194–5.
4. **R. B. Haldane**, 'A Preliminary Memorandum on the present Situation. Being a rough note for consideration by the Members of the Army Council', 1 Jan. 1906, para. 4, Haldane Mss., N.L.S., Ms. 5,918, ff. 44–5.
5. **R. B. Haldane**, 'Second Memorandum', 1 Feb. 1906, Haig Mss., N.L.S., Vol. 32a.
6. R. B. Haldane to his mother, 29 Jan. 1906, Haldane Mss., N.L.S., Ms. 5,975, f. 37.
7. Sir G. S. Clarke to Lord Esher, 21 Mar. 1906, Esher Mss., 10/38. See also **H. S. Wilkinson**, *Thirty-Five Years: 1874–1909*, Constable, London, 1933, pp. 305–7.
8. **Captain G. F. Ellison**, *Home Defence*, E. Stanford, London, 1898, pp. 2, 5, 38, 49–55, 114, 126, and 'Some administrative lessons of the War: Part IV', n.d., Ellison Mss.
9. R. B. Haldane, 'Second Memorandum', *op. cit.*, para. 2.
10. Sir E. Grey to R. B. Haldane, 8 Jan. 1906, Haldane Mss., N.L.S., Ms. 5,907, f. 10. For the diplomatic background to this crisis, see **S. R. Williamson**, *The Politics of Grand Strategy:*

Britain and France Prepare for War, 1904-1914, Harvard U.P., Cambridge, 1969, pp. 59-88.

11. **Lord Haldane**, *Before the War*, Cassell, London, 1920, pp. 30-2.
12. **C. Falls**, 'Haldane and defence', *Public Administration*, **35**, 1957, p. 248.
13. **R. Blake**, *The Private Papers of Douglas Haig, 1914-1919*, Eyre and Spottiswoode, London, 1952, p. 21.
14. J. Gooch, *op. cit.*, p. 166; S. R. Williamson, *op. cit.*, p. 100; **K. Robbins**, *Sir Edward Grey: a biography of Lord Grey of Falloden*, Cassell, London, 1974, pp. 178-9.
15. *Parl. Deb.*, Fourth Ser., Vol. 153, 8 Mar. 1906, cols. 664-70 and Vol. 160, 12 July 1906, cols. 1,080-81. See also **A. J. Anthony Morris,** 'Haldane's army reforms 1906-8: the deception of the radicals', *History,* **156**, No. 186, Feb. 1971, pp. 17-34.
16. *Parl. Deb.*, Fourth Ser., Vol. 160, 12 July 1906, cols. 1,088-98.
17. **R. B. Haldane**, 'Considerations governing Peace Strength of the Regular Army', 1 Feb. 1907, P.R.O., CAB 37/86/11.
18. C. Falls, *op. cit.*, p. 248.
19. **S. H. Zebel**, *Balfour: a political biography*, Cambridge University Press, Cambridge, 1973, pp. 143-53.
20. R. B. Haldane to H. H. Asquith, 25 and 28 Dec. 1905, Asquith Mss., Ms. 10, ff. 237-9, 194-5.
21. R. B. Haldane to Sir E. Grey, 17 and 19 January 1906, Grey Mss., P.R.O., F[oreign] O[ffice] 800/102, nos. 12-13, 14-15.
22. R. B. Haldane to Sir H. Campbell-Bannerman, 5 and 27 Jan. 1906, Campbell-Bannerman Mss., B.M. Add. Ms. 41,218, ff. 163-8, 173-4.
23. *Parl. Deb.*, Fourth Ser., Vol. 153, 8 Mar. 1906, cols. 655-86.
24. *The Daily News*, 9 Mar. 1906, p. 6; *The Manchester Guardian*, 9 Mar. 1906, p 6; *Concord*, Vol. 22, No. 3, Mar. 1906, p. 37.
25. *Parl. Deb.*, Fourth Ser., Vol. 153, 15 Mar. 1906, cols. 1,441-93, 1,507-28.
26. Sir H. Campbell-Bannerman to King Edward VII, 21 Mar. 1906, P.R.O., CAB 41/30/50.
27. **S. Lee**, *King Edward VII*, 2 vols., Macmillan, London, 1927, Vol. 2, pp. 484-5.
28. R. B. Haldane to his mother, 12 July 1906, Haldane Mss., N.L.S., Ms. 5,976, f. 37.
29. *Parl. Deb.*, Fourth Ser., Vol. 160, 12 July 1906, cols. 1,077-114.
30. R. B. Haldane to his mother, 17 July 1906, Haldane Mss., N.L.S., Ms. 5,976, f. 47.
31. Lord Esher to Lord Knollys, 6 Aug. 1906, R.A. W 40/43.
32. Lord Knollys to R. B. Haldane, 9 Aug. 1906, Haldane Mss., N.L.S., Ms. 5,907, ff. 77-8.
33. R. B. Haldane to Lord Esher, 29 Aug. 1906, Esher Mss., 10/27.
34. *The Times*, 26 Mar. 1906, p. 7. See also **C. à C. Repington**,

Foundations of Reform, Simpkin Marshall, London, 1908, pp. 261–9.

35. **R. B. Haldane**, 'The Fourth Memorandum', 25 Apr. 1906, Haig Mss., N.L.S., Vol. 32a, and H. Cunningham, *op. cit.*, pp. 140–1.
36. Reports of the Territorial Army Committee, Esher Mss., 16/8. See also *Journals and Letters of Reginald Viscount Esher*, ed. M. V. Brett, 4 vols., Nicholson & Watson, London, 1934–38, Vol. II, pp. 163–4, 167–9.
37. **Lieutenant-General G. F. Ellison**, 'Reminiscences', *Lancashire Lad*, November 1935, p. 9.
38. M. V. Brett (ed.), *op. cit.*, Vol. II, p. 174. 'Memorandum by the Adjutant-General on the future of the Militia Infantry', 21 Sept. 1906, Precis No. 294, P.R.O., W.O. 163/11.
39. Sir D. Haig to Lord Esher, 17 Oct. 1906, Esher Mss., 10/27.
40. Lord Esher to R. B. Haldane, 19 Oct. 1906, Esher Mss., 4/1.
41. R. B. Haldane to Lord Esher, 23 Oct. 1906, Esher Mss., 10/27.
42. R. B. Haldane to his mother, 1 Apr. 1907, Haldane Mss., N.L.S., Ms. 5,977, f. 63.
43. **Sir C. Harris**, 'Lord Haldane at the War Office' in *Viscount Haldane of Cloan: The Man and His Work*, O.U.P., London, 1928, p. 15.
44. R. B. Haldane to Lord Esher, 15 Sept. 1907, Esher Mss., 5/23.
45. **M. J. Allison**, *The National Service issue, 1899–1914*, unpublished Ph.D. thesis, King's College, University of London, 1975, p. 110.
46. *House of Lords*, Vol. IV, 24 Nov. 1909, col. 925; H. Cunningham, *op. cit.*, p. 146.
47. *Parl. Deb.*, Fourth Ser., Vol. 169, 25 Feb. 1907, col. 1,321.
48. *Ibid.*, Vol. 185, 4 Mar. 1908, col. 718.
49. M. V. Brett (ed.), *op. cit.*, Vol. II, pp. 369, 371.
50. *Parl. Deb.*, Fifth Ser., Vol. 1, 4 Mar. 1909, cols. 1,596–7.
51. *Ibid.*, Vol. 59, 11 Mar. 1914, cols. 1,245, 1,256.
52. *Ibid.*, Vol. 11, 13 May 1912, cols. 984–6.
53. *The Annual Return of the Territorial Force for the year 1913*, Cd. 7,254, 1914, LII, p. 125.
54. M. J. Allison, *op. cit.*, p. 172.
55. **Lord Esher**, 'The Voluntary Principle', *National Review*, Vol. 156, No. 331, September 1910, p. 46.
56. *P.P.*, Cd. 7,254, LII, p. 5.
57. H. S. Wilkinson, *op. cit.*, p. 308.
58. Sir I. S. M. Hamilton to C. à C. Repington, 27 Oct. 1910, Hamilton Mss., Centre for Military Archives, King's College, London, 7/3/14/3.
59. **E. Childers**, *War and the Arme Blanche*, E. Arnold, London, 1910, pp. 358–9.
60. **Brigadier-General J. E. Edmonds**, *Military Operations, France*

and Belgium 1914, 2 vols., Macmillan, London, 1925, Vol. 2, p. 463, and **General Sir G. Barrow**, *The Life of General Sir Charles Carmichael Monro*, Hutchinson, London, 1931, p. 29.

61. **R. Page Arnot**, *South Wales Miners: A History of the South Wales Miners' Federation (1898-1914)*, Allen & Unwin, London, 1967, p. 204.
62. **Sir J. Fergusson**, *The Curragh Incident*, Faber & Faber, London, 1964, pp. 187-202.
63. Brig.-Gen. J. E. Edmonds, *op. cit.*, Vol 1, pp. 10-11.

Epilogue: Flanders

Ireland and not Europe had been the focus of British attention during the summer of 1914. The murder of Archduke Franz Ferdinand in Sarajevo on 28 June had evoked little interest in the press and Parliament. A civil war in Ulster still seemed more imminent than a major war in Europe. There was no war hysteria in Britain during the month of July. On the 27 July, as the European crisis worsened, the Foreign Office pressed the cabinet to declare its support for France and Russia. But the cabinet was divided and refused to take a decision. The Liberal press, with the exception of *The Westminster Gazette*, rallied in support of the anti-war faction. *The Daily News*, *The Nation*, *The Economist*, and above all *The Manchester Guardian* denounced the possibility of Britain entering a war. Indeed *The Manchester Guardian* feared 'an organized conspiracy to drag us into the war'.[1] Only the German violation of Belgian neutrality enabled Asquith and Grey to mobilize a pro-war majority in the cabinet. Britain sent an ultimatum to Germany demanding her evacuation of Belgium. Once the ultimatum had expired, Britain entered the war on the 4 August.

The country rapidly united behind the war effort. Only Burns and Morley resigned from the cabinet; neither provided any leadership for the anti-war movement. Ramsay MacDonald denounced the war, but he failed to carry the Labour Party and resigned from its leadership. The Independent Labour Party and the radical intellectuals who joined E. D. Morel's Union for Democratic Control opposed the war, but they had little popular following. C. P. Scott reversed the editorial policy of *The Manchester Guardian*. The leaders of the Trades Union Congress pledged their full cooperation. The Unionists and the vast majority of the Liberal party proffered whole-hearted support for the war, which many supposed would be a relatively short and decisive affair with victory secured by Christmas. Army officers, with some exceptions,[2] endorsed this view. Sir Archibald Murray, Chief of the Staff to Sir John French, believed that the war, if successful, would last for three months with the troops returning home by the end of the year. Eight months, he suggested, was the maximum possible duration: beyond that point financial disruption and the strain of maintaining mass armies in the field would ensure an end to hostilities.[3]

The British Expeditionary Force (BEF) was transported to France and concentrated in Belgium within fifteen days. The mobilization arrangements, perfected by the General Staff, were sufficiently flexible to overcome a delay in sending the Force and a reduction of two divisions in the Force despatched. By 20 August 1914 four divisions, one cavalry division, one additional cavalry and one additional infantry brigade were concentrated on the left of the French army between Mauberge and Le Cateau. The four divisions were arranged in two army corps under the command of Sir Douglas Haig and Sir Horace Smith-Dorrien. Overall command was entrusted to Sir John French. Officially, the BEF was entirely independent; it was so small, however, that it could only act in support of General Lanrezac's army. On this front the French, British, and Belgian forces comprised some twenty divisions; they faced three German armies, or thirty-four divisions, totalling 760,000 men.

Structurally, there were important differences between the BEF and its predecessor in 1899. Whereas each corps of the BEF contained two large divisions and numbered 37,406 men, an army corps, in 1899, was formed whenever three divisions were joined together, each division totalling 11,006 men. The larger divisions of 1914 included a smaller proportion of front-line troops (75 per cent as distinct from 88 per cent) and had some provision, though wholly inadequate, for field ambulances, signals, and a divisional train. On the other hand, the large divisions included a greater proportion of reservists (an average of 60 per cent in the infantry as compared with 48 per cent in 1899).[4] The difference was crucial inasmuch as the troops encountered the rigours of warfare almost as soon as they arrived in Flanders. British forces were engaged in the battle of Mons on 23 August (the II Corps bore the brunt of the action suffering 1,600 casualties from a force of 40,000 men). The BEF retreated thereafter over 200 miles of French countryside in a sweltering heat. At Le Cateau on 26 August the II Corps, reinforced by the newly arrived 4th Division, made another stand. It suffered over 7,000 casualties and lost thirty-eight guns, but still managed to beat off all attacks and to withdraw in an orderly manner in broad daylight. The retreat took thirteen days to complete, with the soldiers surviving upon three to four hours sleep per night. For the reservists, who were neither fully fit nor completely readjusted to army life, the retreat was an exhausting and demanding experience.[5]

At home, few citizens had any impression of the course and conduct of the military operations. Lord Kitchener, the Secretary of State for War, treated the press with near contempt. He refused to accredit war correspondents. He supplied the minimum of information to his cabinet colleagues. Ever fearful of leaks or disclosures which might aid the enemy, he tried to control the flow of news from the front. He appointed Colonel Ernest Swinton to the staff of the Commander-in-Chief to write official reports about the progress of the war. The reports of Swinton would be vetted by several generals and by Kitchener himself, before being released to the press under the by-line 'Eye-Witness'. After reading the first despatch, one editor reportedly quipped that 'Eye-wash would have been a better pseudonym'.[6] From September 1914 until July 1915, Colonel (later Major-General) Swinton sent a regular flow of reports, about twice a week, from the front. He never saw his role as a war correspondent. As he recalled in his memoirs,

> The principle which guided me in my work was above all to avoid helping the enemy. This appeared to me even more important than the purveyance of news to our own people. . . . For home consumption – that is for those who were carrying the burden and footing the bill – I essayed to tell as much of the truth as was compatible with safety, to guard against depression and pessimism, and to check unjustified optimism which might lead to a relaxation of effort.[7]

Attempts had been made to gather news in the normal manner. Arthur Moore of *The Times* and Hamilton Fyfe of *The Daily Mail* (both papers belonged to the Northcliffe 'stable') arrived in the area of the 4th Division on 28 August. Convinced that the BEF had suffered a crushing defeat, they filed colourful stories about the rapidity of the German advance. Moore, in his 'Amiens Dispatch', described broken British regiments, men weak with hunger and exhaustion, and the 'great losses' which the BEF had sustained. To the surprise of his editors, the report not only passed through the official censors, the Press Bureau, but was actually embellished by the chief of the Bureau, F. E. Smith, a distinguished King's Counsel and Unionist MP. In a crude attempt to boost recruiting, Smith added that the BEF 'has suffered terrible losses and requires immediate and immense reinforcement . . .'. *The Times* duly published Moore's report under the headline BROKEN BRITISH REGIMENTS BATTLING AGAINST ODDS. It also reprinted Fyfe's article from *The Weekly Dispatch*, Northcliffe's Sunday paper, under the headline GERMAN TIDAL WAVE – OUR SOLDIERS OVERWHELMED BY NUMBERS.[8]

Though sincerely written, the reports were a travesty of the truth. Every division was not in action, as Moore had claimed. Nor had any division 'lost nearly all of their officers'. Nor had the BEF sustained 'great losses'; indeed the 1st and 2nd Divisions had hardly seen any action and had incurred only negligible losses. The British forces had not retreated from Mons with any consciousness of defeat, although all were tired, some men had lost their nerve, and many units were temporarily disorganized.[9] The 'Amiens Dispatch' caused an immense controversy. The War Office promptly issued an official statement. It gave the army's total casualties as between 5,000 and 6,000 men, and stated that reinforcements of more than double this number had been sent to France. Other papers deplored the alarmist reporting of *The Times*; *The Morning Post* and *The Sketch* even advocated censorship of the press.[10] Within the House of Commons, a stormy debate ensued. Facing demands for more censorship from Conservative benches, and for less censorship from Liberal benches, the Prime Minister simply deplored the 'very regrettable' action of *The Times*. Applauding the 'patriotic reticence of the Press as a whole', he refused to send out official war correspondents 'under the altered conditions of modern warfare'. He promised, however, that the public would receive 'prompt and authentic information of what is happening at the front'.[11] One week later Colonel Swinton was appointed as the 'Eye-witness' correspondent.

Starving the public of news, or at least of news which was intelligible and accurate, had several consequences. In the first place, it ensured a revival of the former complacency which had been briefly shattered by the 'Amiens Dispatch'. Secondly some papers, lacking hard news from the front, focused upon other wartime issues - spy stories, atrocity allegations, and the nefarious activities of enemy aliens. Xenophobic propaganda served as a surrogate for battlefield reporting: Germans were portrayed as bestial and barbaric, the Kaiser as a monster and a madman, his army as a collection of rapists and sadists.[12] Malicious and vindictive campaigns were mounted against anyone suspected of pro-German sympathies: Prince Louis of Battenberg and Lord Haldane were driven from public office. Demagogues like Horatio Bottomley exploited the mass hysteria; Bottomley made a fortune from his recruiting and propaganda tours. Finally, the lack of news ensured that there was little or no understanding of the conditions endured at the front. While Swinton was reporting that the troops 'are well fed, and in spite of the wet weather of the past week are cheerful and confident', Captain Jack of the Cameronians was writing at the same time: 'The public at Home can never realise the repeated high trials sustained by regimental officers and men, nor the terrible conditions under which they carry out most of their duties . . .'[13].

With the press shackled by official censors, the generalship of Sir John French escaped close and critical scrutiny. He proved to be an excessively cautious, even a diffident commander. Shocked by the early losses, he had wired Lord Kitchener on 4 September: 'I do not seem to be able to bring home to the cabinet the shattered condition of 2 divisions of my small force and the necessity of rest and refitment for the remainder and the impossibility of making things right as long as we are in close contact with the enemy'.[14] When the opportunity came to advance, he moved the BEF forward at an agonizingly slow pace. The Force took three days to cross the Marne by 9 September, and another three to cover the thirty miles to the River Aisne. Had the BEF seized the bridgeheads and reached the high ground north of the river, it could have severed the three corps of General von Kluck from the rest of the German army. But General French neither issued any tactical guidance about the ground to be gained nor impressed upon his junior commanders the need for speed to exploit the fleeting opportunity.[15] Once the Seventh Army had reached the River Aisne on 13 September, it secured the position of von Kluck and thwarted the last possibility for a decisive encounter battle in the early fighting.

Unlike the high command, the various arms of the Expeditionary Force proved remarkably successful. Prior to the battle of Mons and during the subsequent retreat, the cavalry effectively screened the movements of the BEF. It provided accurate information about the strength and movements of the German army, and, where necessary, joined the firing-line as mounted infantry. In the walking and care of their mounts, the British cavalry excelled their allied counterparts; they also, on a minor scale, took effective mounted action against German patrols.[16] Nevertheless, in spite of suitable terrain, the lack of entrenchments, and the preference of all three cavalries for traditional mounted tactics, shock action was conspicuous by its absence. The only significant charge was attempted by the 9th Lancers near Elouges. Although it impeded the German assault momentarily, the charge was extremely costly in men and horses; it was not repeated in either the retreat from Mons or the battle of the Marne.[17] The early encounter battles merely underlined that shock action with the *arme blanche* had become redundant in contemporary warfare.

Operating in the industrial and coal-mining areas of Flanders proved more difficult for the horse and field artillery. The numerous buildings, deep ditches, and high slag heaps hampered the long-range observation favoured by British gunners. These features exacerbated the difficulty of finding suitable positions for batteries or even for single guns. Artillery commanders tried to overcome this problem by pushing their batteries forward; they even aligned them with infantry positions and provided close support for the defensive fire. When this tactic was adopted in open positions however, it proved disastrous. At Le Cateau, the artillery on the right flank of the 2nd Corps eschewed cover and exposed their guns for direct fire. By ignoring the experience of Colenso, the batteries lost twenty-six of their forty-two guns and only extricated the remainder by daring exhibitions of gallantry. Thereafter the arm avoided unnecessary exposure, preferring to adopt concealed positions behind the firing-line. Concealment not only protected the guns, but it also increased the effectiveness of the artillery fire. The gunners were able to fire on a wider arc without having to move, and could concentrate their fire on the same target by the use of several batteries.[18]

For the infantry, the early battles confirmed both the relevance of the pre-war training and its absorption by the rank and file. From concealed positions the infantry sustained remarkably accurate and rapid rates of fire. In standards of marksmanship, the BEF exceeded all other armies on the Western Front.[19] The infantry, too, proved extremely adept in the use of cover and concealed positions. Initially, they were more proficient than the Germans in the use of ground, although the latter quickly deployed in dispersed formations after several abortive assaults *en masse*. Occasionally, British battalions required heavy losses to remind them of the need for cautious deployments. At Le Cateau, the King's Own Royal Regiment (1st Battalion) adopted a quarter-column formation which proved an ideal target for enemy fire, resulting in over 400 casualties.[20] Nevertheless, mistakes of this kind were rare. The infantry displayed a high degree of professional competence in the opening encounters.

The main difficulty for the Expeditionary Force, reared in the doctrine of fire and movement, was the beginning of static defensive warfare. Starting at the River Aisne (13–27 September) and continuing near Ypres in the following months, the belligerents stumbled onto large-scale position warfare for which none of them had prepared. Only the Germans, who had contemplated swift assaults on the fortresses of Belgium and eastern France, possessed the appropriate apparatus for trench warfare (heavy guns, trench mortars, grenades, searchlights etc.). The British discovered shortages in entrenching tools, barbed wire, and sandbags: their troops, at first, had to seek cover in shallow shelter pits or behind natural obstacles.[21] The BEF, moreover, lacked heavy artillery. Possessing only four 60-pounders attached to each division and four batteries of the old pattern 6-inch howitzer, the British could hardly compete with the German fire in the early engagements.[22]

Equally serious was the shortage of machine-guns and their tactical neglect by the pre-war army. As a peacetime economy, the Liberal Government had refused to allow more than two machine-guns per battalion. In the Edwardian army, however, few senior officers had advocated the extensive use of the Maxim gun. With the notable exception of Sir Horace Smith-Dorrien,[23] they were unimpressed by a weapon which had not proved very effective in South Africa. Relatively uninterested in modern technology, they had viewed the machine-gun as a useful tool in savage warfare but not a weapon which could virtually dominate the conventional battle.[24] The army, too, had not anticipated the impact of modern firepower upon the demand for shells and ammunition. The reserves of ammunition, which were prescribed in light of the South African War, were not altered with the introduction of quick-firing artillery. They were barely sufficient for long periods of continuous fighting.[25] Bereft of the equipment for trench warfare, the BEF had to improvise where possible and simply await replenishment from the United Kingdom.

Though zealous and professionally competent, the British Expeditionary Force was doomed. It was simply too small to survive the carnage on the Western Front. '*Armées d'élite*', wrote Cyril Falls, 'would be invincible if wars were fought without casualties. Things being what they are, *armées d'élite* are unlikely to remain so long'.[26] In 1906, the Army Council had accepted projections about war wastage which were optimistic even by the recent standards of the Russo-Japanese War. The Department of Military Training would not accept as a criterion for 'civilised' warfare the scale of casualties tolerated by Asiatic opponents. Hence it calculated the wastage rate as the average between the losses suffered in the South African and in the Manchurian campaigns. For the first six months of war, it had projected a wastage of 44 per cent in the infantry (34,740 men), 36 per cent in the artillery (10,160 men), and 40 per cent for the whole six divisions (56,285 men).[27] By 30 November 1914, after approximately three months fighting, the British army had lost 3,627 officers and 86,237 other ranks. The majority of these men had fallen in the infantry of the first seven divisions, which had originally numbered 84,000 men. As the Official History records, 'In the British battalions which fought at the Marne and Ypres, there scarcely remained in the colours an average of one officer and thirty men of those who landed in August 1914'.[28]

In sum, the British Expeditionary Force performed with considerable professional competence on the fields of Flanders. Trained to fight in mobile encounter battles, it was well-armed, highly skilled on an individual level, and able to fight on the defensive when required. Unlike the army corps which embarked for South Africa in October 1899, the BEF faced a larger, more organized and more disciplined enemy within days of mobilization. Under immediate pressure and with a large proportion of reservists still adjusting to army life, the BEF vindicated the efforts of the pre-war reformers. Decimated after three months fighting, it formed the nucleus of the British force which endured the process of adapting to a prolonged and static war in the trenches on the Western Front.

Notes and references

1. *The Manchester Guardian*, 1 Aug. 1914, p. 8. See also **G. M. Thomson**, *The Twelve Days: 24 July to 4 August 1914*, Hutchinson, London, 1964, pp. 157–8.
2. **Sir D. Haig** to Lord Haldane, 4 Aug. 1914, Haldane Mss., N.L.S., Ms. 5,910, f. 251.
3. M. V. Brett (ed.) *op. cit.*, Vol. III, p. 177.
4. The Elgin Report, *op. cit.*, pp. 32–7 and Brig.-Gen. J. E. Edmonds, *op. cit.*, Vol. 1, pp. 88–9 and Appendix 2, p. 428.
5. **Lieutenant-Colonel H. Green**, *The British Army in the First World War*, Trehern, London, 1968, pp. 10–18.
6. P. Knightly, *op. cit.*, p. 86.
7. **Major-General Sir E. Swinton**, *Eye-Witness*, Hodder & Stoughton, London, 1932, p. 53.
8. *The Times*, 30 Aug. 1914, special edition.
9. **J. Terraine**, *Impacts of War 1914 & 1918*, Hutchinson, London, 1974, p. 58.
10. *Ibid.*, p. 60.

11. *Parl. Deb.*, Fifth Ser., Vol. 66, 31 Aug. 1914, col. 373.
12. P. Knightley, *op. cit.*, pp. 82–3.
13. **Sir E. Swinton**, *Eye-Witness's Narrative of the War*, E. Arnold, London, 1915, p. 14; *General Jack's Dairy*, ed. J. Terraine, Eyre & Spottiswoode, London, 1964, p. 55; J. Terraine, *Impacts of War 1914 & 1918*, p. 97.
14. Sir J. D. P. French to Lord Kitchener, 4 Sept. 1914, Kitchener Mss., P.R.O., 30/57/49.
15. **C. Falls**, *The First World War*, Longman, London, 1967, pp. 49–50 and **J. Terraine**, *Mons: The Retreat to Victory*, Batsford, London, 1960, pp. 216–17.
16. **J. Terraine**, *Douglas Haig, the educated soldier*, Hutchinson, London, 1963, pp. 92–4, 109–10.
17. Brig.-Gen. J. E. Edmonds, *op. cit.*, Vol. 1, pp. 100–2 and J. Terraine, *Mons*, pp. 116–17.
18. **S. Bidwell**, *Gunners at War*, Arms and Armour, London, 1970, pp. 23, 29.
19. Brig.-Gen. J. E. Edmonds, *op. cit.*, Vol. 1, p. 71, and Vol. 2, pp. 462–3.
20. *Ibid.*, Vol. 1, p. 155.
21. *Ibid.*, Vol. 1, pp. 375–8, and Vol. 2, pp. 460–1.
22. J. Terraine, *Douglas Haig, the educated soldier*, pp. 94–5.
23. **A. J. Smithers**, *The Man Who Disobeyed, Sir Horace Smith-Dorrien and His Enemies*, Leo Cooper, London, 1970, pp. 145–6.
24. **J. Ellis**, *The Social History of the Machine Gun*, Croom Helm, London, 1975, pp. 102–7.
25. Brig.-Gen. J. E. Edmonds, *op. cit.*, Vol. 2, pp. 12–13.
26. C. Falls, *The First World War*, p. 16.
27. These calculations assumed that the six divisions would number 140,000 men, excluding lines of communication. 'Memorandum drawn up in M.T. 1 on Wastage in War', 27 Apr. 1906, P.R.O., W.O./8813.
28. Brig.-Gen. J. E. Edmonds, *op. cit.*, Vol. 2, pp. 465–6.

Appendix 1

Methodological note

Once tables of officers were obtained from the relevant Army Lists, background information was acquired from the service records of some officers in the P.R.O., W.O. 25 and W.O. 76. For officers who were born before 1837, the registers in County Record Offices had to be consulted. The registers of Woolwich and Sandhurst cadets supplied useful information on the officers in 1899 and 1914. More details were gleaned from the standard reference works – *Burke's Peerage, History of the Commoners, Landed Gentry*, etc., J. Bateman, *Great Landowners of England*, E. Walford, *County Families of the United Kingdom*, F. Boase, *Modern English Biography, The Dictionary of National Biography, Who's Who, Men of the Time, Who was Who*, and *Who's Who at the War* (1900). For less famous officers, regimental records and museums were consulted with varying degrees of success, the obituaries of various officers in *The Times*, and the registers of twenty-five public schools. Information on non-English officers was sought from J. S. Crone, *A Concise Dictionary of Irish Biography*, A. Webb, *A Compendium of Irish Biography, The Dictionary of Welsh Biography down to 1940*, and J. Irving, *The Book of Scotsmen*.

Classifying the landed gentry was peculiarly difficult for Crimean officers, many of whom were born in the eighteenth century before the publication of official returns of landowners in the United Kingdom. Inclusion as gentry in local directories or in *Burke's Landed Gentry* had to suffice in some instances. For purposes of comparison in the later years, the minimum qualification was set at 1,000 acres where no other source of income was apparent.[1] The data was checked in the official returns of landowners (*P.P.*, C.11,097, 1874, LXXII, Parts 1 and 2, C.899, 1874, LXXII, and C.1,492, 1876, LXXX).

Reference

1. See J. P. Cornford, 'Hotel Cecil', *Ideas and Institutions of Victorian Britain*, ed. by R. Robson, G. Bell, London, 1967, p. 274.

Appendix 2

Regional background of senior officers in 1854, 1899 and 1914 expressed in percentage terms

Region	Colonels			Generals		
	1854	1899	1914	1854	1899	1914
Wales	2	5	1	2	2	4
Scotland	12	12	8	20	12	17
Ireland	13	21	7	16	16	13
North of England	15	6	13	7	4	7
West Midlands	8	6	4	7	6	1
East Midlands	6	5	1	5	2	2
South Midlands	5	3	8	6	6	4
London	8	9	9	10	12	7
East Anglia	2 } 41%	1 } 37%	6 } 57%	3 } 37%	8 } 50%	8 } 48%
Home Counties	10	7	18	3	9	9
South and South-West	16	17	16	15	15	20
Abroad	3	8	9	6	8	8
Total number	95	107	87	121	91	91

Note on population table

The regions were grouped in the following manner:

North of England	Cumberland, Westmorland, Lancashire, Yorkshire, Durham, Northumberland;
East Anglia	Norfolk, Suffolk, Essex;
Home Counties	Kent, Sussex, Middlesex, Surrey;
South and South-West	Cornwall, Devon, Somerset, Dorset, Hampshire, Berkshire, Wiltshire, Gloucestershire;
East Midlands	Lincolnshire, Nottinghamshire, Leicestershire, Rutland, Huntingdonshire, Northamptonshire;
West Midlands	Cheshire, Derbyshire, Warwickshire, Staffordshire, Worcestershire, Herefordshire, Monmouthshire, Shropshire;
South Midlands	Bedfordshire, Hertfordshire, Buckinghamshire, Oxfordshire, Cambridgeshire.

Appendix 3

The religious denominations of the officer corps

Although the religious affiliations of the officer corps were not recorded in the *General Annual Returns of the Army*, it would appear that the army was largely Anglican in composition. An official return for the Brigade of Guards was compiled for the years from 1855 to 1867. During those years, there were never more than five Roman Catholic officers in the eight battalions, and never any in the two battalions of Coldstream Guards (*P.P.* No. 59, 1867, XLI). From the cadet registers of the Royal Military Academy, Woolwich, over the years from 1870 to 1899, it would appear that some 3,380 cadets entered the Academy of whom 94 per cent professed to be Church of England. Of the 5,669 ex-public schoolboys who served in the South African War, only 1 per cent came from Roman Catholic schools (A. H. H. MacLean, *op. cit.*, pp. 12, 16-17). More important than mere statistics was the impression of Anglicanism. Some Irishmen, like Richard O'Dogherty, would even change their name before seeking a commission to avoid religious identification (Sir W. Butler, *op. cit.*, p. 10).

Bibliography

Abbreviations

JSAHR	*Journal of the Society of Army Historical Research*
N.A.M.	National Army Museum
N.L.S.	National Library of Scotland
Parl. Deb.	*Parliamentary Debates*
P.P.	*Parliamentary Papers*
P.R.O.	Public Record Office
R.A.	Royal Archives
S.R.O.	Scottish Record Office

The following list of books and articles merely represents a short guide to further reading. The list excludes the manuscript collections, Parliamentary Papers, Parliamentary Debates, dissertations, memoirs, and many of the biographical studies cited in the references and notes.

General and bibliographical works

Barnett, C. *Britain and Her Army 1509–1970, A Military, Political and Social Survey*, Allen Lane, London, 1970.
A concise but reasonably comprehensive survey.

Bruce, A. P. C. *An Annotated Bibliography of the British Army 1660–1914*, Garland Publishing, New York & London, 1975.
An invaluable bibliographical guide.

Fortescue, J. W. *A History of the British Army*, 13 vols, Macmillan, London, 1899–1930.
The standard history of the British army. Although somewhat dated, partisan, and limited in its remit (finishing with the passage of the Cardwell reforms), it is still a mine of useful information.

Higham, R. (ed.). *A Guide to the Sources of British Military History*, Routledge & Kegan Paul, London, 1972.

Contains some helpful essays but also some factual and typographical errors. The work has been superseded by Bruce.

Luvaas, J. *The Education of an Army. British Military Thought, 1815–1940*, Cassell, London, 1964.
An invaluable study of British military thought.

Omond, Lieutenant-Colonel J. S. *Parliament and the Army 1642–1904*, Cambridge University Press, Cambridge, 1933.
A general survey of civil-military relations.

The officer corps

Anderson, O. 'The growth of Christian militarism', *The English Historical Review*, LXXXVI, 1971.
An interesting essay on a much neglected topic.

Barnett, C. 'The education of military élites', *Journal of Contemporary History*, 2, No. 3. July 1967.

Cairnes, W. E. *Social Life in the British Army. By a British Officer*, John Long, London, 1900.
An invaluable account of the life-style of the British officer at the end of the nineteenth century.

Harries-Jenkins, G. *The Army in Victorian Society*, Routledge & Kegan Paul, London, 1977.
An erudite and perceptive study of the nineteenth-century army officer. A lucid and incisive book, based upon historical research and sociological analysis.

Otley, C. B. 'Militarism and the social affiliations of the British army élite', *Armed Forces and Society: sociological essays*, ed. J. van Doorn, Mouton, The Hague, 1968.

Otley, C. B. 'The social origins of British army officers', *Sociological Review*, 18, No. 2, July 1970.

Otley, C. B. 'The educational background of British army officers', *Sociology*, 7, No. 2, May 1973.

Razzell, P. E. 'Social origins of officers in the Indian and British Home Army', *British Journal of Sociology*, 14, No. 3. Sept. 1963.

Smyth, Brigadier Sir J. G. *Sandhurst. The history of the Royal Military Academy, Woolwich, the Royal Military College, Sandhurst, and the Royal Military Academy Sandhurst, 1741–1961*, Weidenfeld & Nicolson, London, 1961.
The best study of Sandhurst.

Turner, E. S. *Gallant Gentlemen: A portrait of the British officer 1660–1956*, Michael Joseph, London, 1956.
A popular account which contains some interesting material but little analysis.

The rank and file

Blanco, R. L. 'Army recruiting reforms 1861-1867', *JSAHR*, XLVI, 1968.

Blanco, R. L. 'Attempts to abolish branding and flogging in the army of Victorian England before 1881', *JSAHR*, XLVI, 1968.

Blanco, R. L. 'The attempted control of venereal disease in the army of mid-Victorian England', *JSAHR*, XLV, 1967.

Bond, B. J. 'Recruiting the Victorian army 1870-92', *Victorian Studies*, V, No. 1, Sept. 1961.
A scholarly study of the problems and difficulties involved in recruiting the late Victorian army.

De Watteville, Colonel H. *The British Soldier: His Life From Tudor To Modern Times*, J. M. Dent & Sons, London, 1954.

Hanham, H. J. 'Religion and nationality in the mid-Victorian army', *War and Society*, ed. M. R. D. Foot, Paul Elek, London, 1973.
An important analysis of the changes in the religious and national composition of the Victorian rank and file.

McGuffie, T. H. *Rank and file: the common soldier in peace and war 1642-1914*, Hutchinson, London, 1964.
A collection of extracts from the reminiscences of ordinary soldiers.

McGuffie, T. H. 'Recruiting the British army in modern times', *Memoirs and Proceedings of the Manchester Literary and Philosophical Society*, 96, 1954-55.

Skelley, A. R. *The Victorian Army at Home*, Croom Helm, London, 1977.
This work supersedes all previous studies of the rank and file. An extremely detailed and thoroughly researched work, it presents a comprehensive account of the social composition, life-style, and living conditions of the ranks from 1856 to 1899.

Wellington's army

Blanco, R. L. 'Reform and Wellington's post-Waterloo army', *Military Affairs*, 45, Fall 1965.

Bruce, A. P. C. 'The military services of Field-Marshal Lord Hardinge', *The Army Quarterly and Defence Journal*, CVI, 1976.

Howard, M. E. (ed.). *Wellington Studies. Essays on the first Duke of Wellington by five Old Wellingtonian historians*, Wellington College, 1959.
Contains a very useful article on the influence of Wellington over the peacetime army by M. E. Howard entitled 'Wellington and the British army'.

Longford, Lady Elizabeth. *Wellington: the pillar of the state*, Weidenfeld & Nicolson, London, 1972.

The best modern biography of the Iron Duke. It concentrates upon his post-Waterloo career.

Mather, F. C. *Public Order in the Age of the Chartists*, Manchester University Press, Manchester, 1959.
An invaluable analysis of the problems involved in the maintenance of public order in early Victorian Britain.

Moyse-Bartlett, Lieutenant-Colonel H. 'British army in 1850', *JSAHR*, LII, No. 212, 1974.

Read, D. *Peterloo: The 'Massacre' and its Background*, Manchester University Press, Manchester, 1958.
The standard account of the Peterloo Massacre.

Thomas, D. *Charge! Hurrah! Hurrah! A Life of Cardigan of Balaclava*, Omega, London, 1976.
A perceptive study of life within an early Victorian cavalry regiment.

Thomas, M. I. and Holt, P. *Threats of Revolution in Britain 1789–1848*, Macmillan, London, 1977.

Walmsley, R. *Peterloo: The Case Reopened*, Manchester University Press, Manchester, 1969.

Wellington, Duke of (ed.). *Despatches, Correspondence and Memoranda of Field Marshal Arthur Duke of Wellington K.G.*, 8 vols, Parker & Co., London, 1867–80.
An invaluable printed source for the opinions of the Duke of Wellington. This collection, edited by his son, is more reliable than the collection edited by Lieutenant-Colonel Gurwood.

The Crimean War

Atkins, J. B. *The Life of Sir W. H. Russell,* 2 vols, John Murray, London, 1911.

Bart, Sir G. D. and Ramsay, Sir G. D. (eds.). *The Panmure Papers*, 2 vols, Hodder & Stoughton, London, 1908.

Fitzherbert, C. *Henry Clifford V.C. his letters and sketches from the Crimea*, Michael Joseph, London, 1956.
An interesting collection of letters from the Crimea.

Hibbert, C. *The Destruction of Lord Raglan: A Tragedy of the Crimean War*, Pelican, London, 1963.
An excellent account of the war which is more objective than either Kinglake or Woodham-Smith.

Kinglake, A. W. *The Invasion of the Crimea: its origins and an account of its progress down to the death of Lord Raglan*, 8 vols, Blackwood, Edinburgh & London, 1863–67.
A monumental work which caused immense controversy at the time of its publication. It is neither objective nor complete. It ends with the death of Lord Raglan.

Russell, W. H. *The War: from the landing at Gallipoli to the death of Lord Raglan. (From the death of Lord Raglan to the evacuation of the Crimea)*, 2 vols, Routledge, London, 1855-56.
The despatches of Russell should be read in *The Times* or in their edited form by Russell. A single volume edition, entitled *Despatches from the Crimea 1854-1856*, has been edited by N. Bentley, Deutsch, London, 1966.
The History of the Times: The Tradition Established 1841-1884, London, 1939.

Woodham-Smith, C. *The Reason Why*, Constable, London, 1956.
A fiercely critical account of the senior officers in the Crimea, but somewhat selective in the use of sources.

The Indian mutiny

Bryne, J. 'British opinion and the Indian revolt', *Rebellion 1857 a symposium*, ed. by P. C. Joshi, People's Publishing House, New Delhi, 1957.
A useful account of British attitudes, especially those aired in the radical press.

Edwardes, M. *Battles of the Indian Mutiny*, Batsford, London, 1963.

Edwardes, M. *Red Year: the Indian rebellion of 1857*, Cardinal, London, 1975.
A good survey of the Mutiny, which includes a perceptive re-assessment of British attitudes.

Hibbert, C. *The Great Mutiny. India 1857*, Allen Lane, London, 1978.

Kaye, J. W. *A History of the Sepoy War in India 1857-58*, 3 vols, Allen, London, 1864-76.
A standard history, which remains an indispensable source of reference.

Mason, P. *A Matter of Honour: an account of the Indian Army, its officers and men*, Jonathan Cape, London, 1974.
A comprehensive study of the Indian army.

Metcalf, T. R. *Aftermath of Revolt: India, 1857-1870*, Princeton University Press, Princeton, 1964.

Russell, W. H. *My Diary in India, in the year 1858-59*, 2 vols, Routledge, London, 1860.
The diary is worth reading in the original form, but there is a new single volume edition, entitled *My Indian Mutiny Diary by William Russell*, edited by M. Edwardes, Cassell, London, 1957.

Sen, S. N. *Eighteen Fifty-seven*, Government of India, Ministry of Information and Broadcasting, Calcutta, 1957.

The post-Crimean period

Bond, B. J. 'Prelude to the Cardwell reforms 1856-1868', *Journal of the Royal United Services Institution*, 106, May 1961.

Bond, B. J. *The Victorian Army and the Staff College, 1854-1914*, Eyre Methuen, London, 1972.
An invaluable account of the origins of the Staff College which uses a wide range of primary sources.

Cook, E. T. *The Life of Florence Nightingale*, 2 vols, Macmillan, London, 1913.
The standard account of her life.

Cunningham, H. *The Volunteer Force: a Social and Political History 1859-1908*, Croom Helm, London, 1975.
The best published account of the Volunteer Force.

Denholm, A. 'Lord De Grey and army reform, 1859-1866', *The Army Quarterly and Defence Journal*, CII, 1971.

Luvaas, J. *The Military Legacy of the Civil War - The European Inheritance*, University of Chicago Press, Chicago, 1959.

Rose, B. 'The Volunteers of 1859', *JSAHR*, XXXVII, 1959.

Semple, A. J. 'The Fenian infiltration of the British army', *JSAHR*, CII, 1974.

Stanmore, Lord. *Sidney Herbert: Lord Herbert of Lea: A Memoir*, 2 vols, John Murray, London, 1906.
Pending the biography by Dr James Provan, this remains the standard work on Sidney Herbert.

Woodham-Smith, C. *Florence Nightingale, 1820-1910*, Constable, London, 1950.
A good biography but it does not supersede Cook.

The Cardwell Reforms

Biddulph, Sir R. *Lord Cardwell at the War Office*, John Murray, London, 1904.
The main account of Cardwell's term as Secretary of State for War. It lapses into hagiography, and is not reliable as an analysis of the reforms.

Bond, B. J. 'The effect of the Cardwell reforms on army organization, 1874-1904', *Journal of the Royal United Services Institution*, CV, 1960.

Bond, B. J. 'Edward Cardwell's army reforms 1868-1874', *The Army Quarterly and Defence Journal*, LXXXIV, 1962.
Two of the early revisionist articles on the Cardwell reforms.

Erickson, A. B. 'Abolition of purchase in the British army', *Military Affairs*, XXIII, 1959.

Gallacher, T. F. 'British Military Thinking and the Coming of the Franco Prussian War', *Military Affairs*, XXXIX, 1975.

Gallacher, T. F. '"Cardwellian Mysteries": the fate of the British Army Regulation Bill, 1871', *Historical Journal*, 18, No. 2, 1975.
An important contribution to the debate about the abolition of purchase.

St. Aubyn, G. R. *The Royal George, The Life of H.R.H. Prince George Duke of Cambridge, 1819-1904*, Constable, London, 1963.

Tucker, A. V. 'Army and society in England, 1870-1900: a reassessment of the Cardwell reforms', *Journal of British Studies*, 2, No. 2, May, 1963.
An interesting article which casts doubt on the view that the Cardwell reforms represent a turning point in the history of the army.

Verner, Colonel W. *The Military Life of H.R.H. George Duke of Cambridge*, 2 vols, John Murray, London, 1905.
This work is not entirely superseded by St Aubyn. It still contains some useful material.

The late Victorian army

Bond, B. J. (ed.). *Victorian Military Campaigns*, Hutchinson, London, 1967.
A useful collection of essays on various military campaigns.

Bond, B. J. 'Colonial wars and primitive expeditions 1856-99', *History of the British Army*, ed. Brigadier P. Young and Lieutenant-Colonel J. P. Lawford, A. Barker, London, 1970.

Bond, B. J. 'The late Victorian army', *History Today*, XI, 1961.

Callwell, Colonel C. E. *Small Wars: Their Principles and Practice*, H.M.S.O., London, 1896.
An invaluable study of the theory of small colonial warfare, which has been reprinted by E. P. Publishing, Wakefield, 1976.

Carrington, C. *Rudyard Kipling: His Life and Work*, Penguin, London, 1970.
The standard biography of Kipling.

Edwardes, M. 'Oh to meet an army man', *Rudyard Kipling: the man, his work and his world*, ed. J. Gross, Weidenfeld & Nicolson, London, 1972.

Farwell, B. *Queen Victoria's Little Wars*, Allen Lane, London, 1973.

Forbes, A. *Memories and Studies of War and Peace*, Cassell, London, 1895.
An excellent first-hand account of the techniques and problems of a war correspondent.

Green, R. L. (ed.). *Kipling: the Cultural Inheritance*, Routledge & Kegan Paul, London, 1971.

Hamer, W. S. *The British Army: Civil-Military Relations, 1885-1905*, Clarendon, Oxford, 1970.

One of the few good accounts of civil-military relations in Britain, but limited to 1885-1905.

Knightley, P. *The First Casualty*, A. Deutsch, London, 1975.

A wide-ranging and critical analysis of the role of the war correspondent.

Mason, P. *Kipling: The Glass, The Shadow and The Fire*, Jonathan Cape, London, 1975.

Another excellent study of Kipling.

The South African War

Amery, L. S. *The Times History of the War in South Africa 1899-1902*, 7 vols, Sampson Low, London, 1900-1909.

An invaluable source of information on the war and a powerful critique of many aspects of the pre-war army.

Arnold-Forster, H. O. *The Army in 1906: a policy and a vindication*, John Murray, London, 1906.

Cairnes, Captain W. E. *The Absent-Minded War*, Milne, London, 1900.

Possibly the most famous critique of the state of the army and the conduct of the war by the War Office.

Dunlop, Colonel J. K. *The Development of the British Army, 1899-1914*. Methuen, London, 1938.

A dated but still useful survey of reform in the wake of the South African War.

Farwell, B. *The Great Boer War*, Allen Lane, London, 1976.

The best modern account of the war.

Fraser, P. *Lord Esher: A Political Biography*, Hart-Davis MacGibbon, London, 1973.

Pending the official biography of Lord Esher by Professor Michael Howard, this is the most instructive account of Esher's political activities.

Gooch, J. *The Plans of War: The General Staff and British Military Strategy c. 1900-1916*, Routledge & Kegan Paul, London, 1974.

The definitive work on the origins of the General Staff.

Kruger, R. *Goodbye Dolly Gray. The Story of the Boer War*, Cassell, London, 1959.

An excellent account of the war with some useful insights on British attitudes towards it.

Price, R. *An Imperial War and the British Working Class*, Routledge & Kegan Paul, London, 1972.

Shepperson, G. 'Kipling and the Boer War', *Rudyard Kipling: the man, his work and his world*, ed. J. Gross, Weidenfeld & Nicolson, London, 1972.

Tucker, A. V. 'The issue of army reform in the Unionist government 1903-5', *Historical Journal*, 9, 1966.

The Haldane Reforms

Anthony Morris, A. J. 'Haldane's army reforms 1906-8: the deception of the radicals', *History*, 156, No. 186, 1971.
A good study of Haldane's Parliamentary tactics.

Bond, B. J. 'Richard Burdon Haldane at the War Office', *The Army Quarterly and Defence Journal*, LXXXVI, 1963.

d'Ombrain, N. *War machinery and high policy. Defence administration in peacetime Britain 1902-1914*, O.U.P., London, 1973.
A comprehensive analysis of the evolution of the Committee of Imperial Defence.

Falls, C. 'The army', *Edwardian England 1901-1914*, ed. S. Nowell Smith, O.U.P., London, 1964.

Fergusson, Sir J. *The Curragh Incident*, Faber & Faber, London, 1964.

Fox, Captain K. O. 'The Tonypandy riots', *The Army Quarterly and Defence Journal*, CVI, 1976.

Gooch, J. 'Sir George Clarke's career at the Committee of Imperial Defence, 1904-1907', *Historical Journal*, 18, No. 3, 1975.

Harris, Sir C. 'Lord Haldane at the War Office', *Viscount Haldane of Cloan: The Man and His Work,* O.U.P., London, 1928.

Howard, M. E. *Studies in War and Peace*, Maurice Temple Smith, London, 1970.
Contains a reprint of the author's lecture entitled 'Lord Haldane and the Territorial Army'.

Koss, S. E. *Lord Haldane, scapegoat for liberalism*, Columbia University Press, New York, 1969.

Maurice, Sir F. *Haldane 1856-1915 (1915-1928). The Life of Viscount Haldane of Cloan*, 2 vols, Faber & Faber, London, 1937.
The best account of Haldane's term of office as Secretary of State for War.

Teagarden, E. M. 'Lord Haldane and the origins of the officer training corps'. *JSAHR*, XLV, 1967.

Williamson, S. R. *The Politics of Grand Strategy: Britain and France Prepare for War, 1904-1914*, Harvard U.P., Cambridge, 1969.

The impact of war

Baynes, Major J. C. M. *Morale: a study of men and courage; the Second Scottish Rifles at the Battle of Neuve Chapelle, 1915*, Cassell, London, 1967.

Edmonds, Brigadier-General J. E. *Military Operations, France and Belgium 1914*, 2 vols, Macmillan, London, 1925.
The remarkably detailed official history of the war. Though circumspect in analysis, this work is still an invaluable work of reference.

Falls, C. *The First World War*, Longman, London, 1967.
A good introductory survey.

Hazelhurst, C. *Politicians at War July 1914 to May 1915. A prologue to the triumph of Lloyd George*, Jonathan Cape, London, 1971.

Liddell Hart, B. H. *A History of the World War, 1914–1918*, Faber & Faber, London, 1934.
Still the most scholarly study of the war as a whole.

Robbins, K. *The Abolition of War. The 'Peace Movement' in Britain, 1914–1919*, University of Wales Press, Cardiff, 1976.

Sixsmith, Major-General E. K. G. *British generaliship in the twentieth century*, Arms and Armour Press, London, 1970.

Smithers, A. J. *The Man Who Disobeyed. Sir Horace Smith-Dorrien and His Enemies*, Leo Cooper, London, 1970.

Spears, Sir E. L. *Liaison 1914*, Heinemann, London, 1930.

Swinton, Major-General Sir E. *Eye-Witness*, Hodder & Stoughton, London, 1932.

Terraine, J. E. *Mons: The Retreat to Victory*, Batsford, London, 1960.

Terraine, J. E. *Douglas Haig, the educated soldier*, Hutchinson, London, 1963.

Terraine, J. E. (ed.). *General Jack's Diary*, Eyre & Spottiswoode, London, 1963.

Terraine, J. E. *The Western Front, 1914–1918*, Arrow Books, London, 1970.

Terraine, J. E. *Impacts of War. 1914 & 1918*, Hutchinson, London, 1974.

Wavell, Sir A. *Allenby. Soldier and Statesman*, Harrap, London, 1946.

Index

Abbreviations

Gen	General	Maj	Major
Lt-Gen	Lieutenant-General	Capt	Captain
Maj-Gen	Major-General	Lt	Lieutenant
Col	Colonel	Sgt	Sergeant
Lt-Col	Lieutenant-Colonel	Pte	Private